VIRGIL

THE ECLOGUES
& GEORGICS

VIRGIL
THE ECLOGUES
& GEORGICS

Edited with Introduction
and Notes by
R. DERYCK WILLIAMS
(formerly Professor of Classics, University of Reading)

Bristol Classical Press

Cover illustration: Pastoral scene from *The Works of Virgil*
by John Dryden (1748).

First published by Macmillan Education Ltd in 1979

This edition published in 1996 by
Bristol Classical Press
an imprint of
Gerald Duckworth & Co. Ltd
61 Frith Street
London W1D 3JL
e-mail: inquiries@duckworth-publishers.co.uk
Website: www.ducknet.co.uk

Reprinted 1997, 2001

A catalogue record for this book is available
from the British Library

ISBN 1-85399-508-8

Contents

Preface

This edition of the *Eclogues* and the *Georgics* has the same aims as my
commentary on the *Aeneid* in the same series (*Aeneid* 1-6, 1972; *Aeneid*
7-12, 1973). It is intended to be suitable for the upper forms of schools and
for universities, and I hope that it will also be useful for more advanced
scholars. Within a relatively concise format I have tried to interpret the
poetic intentions and impact of the *Eclogues* and the *Georgics* without
neglecting grammatical explanations of the diction, an aid more than ever
necessary in modern times.

I have established a new text and in the introduction I have listed its
points of difference from Sir Roger Mynors' Oxford Text (second edition,
1972) and from its predecessor (Hirtzel, 1900). Section 1 of the introduction
(Life and Works of Virgil) has been reprinted from my edition of the *Aeneid*:
sections 2 and 3 are new: sections 4 and 5 have been adapted from my *Aeneid*
edition, slightly revised to make them relevant to the *Eclogues* and *Georgics*;
sections 6 and 7 are new. I have not overloaded the commentary with reference
to scholars whose work has helped me (many of these are listed in the
bibliography), but special mention must be made here of the debt I owe
to Page's Macmillan edition (1898) and to Conington, Saint-Denis and
Wilkinson. Coleman's full-scale edition (CUP 1977) reached me too late
for me to make full use of it.

I am most grateful once again to Dr E. L. Harrison who has read the first
draft of the whole work, and assisted me greatly by his comments; and
finally I should like to thank the printer and the publishers for the technical
skill and expertise which have helped to produce *quidquid hoc libelli.*

Reading, February 1978

Introduction

Virgil's poetry has for two thousand years been the most widely read and studied and imitated of all the poetry of antiquity.[1] In Roman times the *Eclogues* and *Georgics* had a great influence on subsequent poetry, while the *Aeneid* was regarded as the unique exposition of national glory and ideals. During the Middle Ages Virgil was admired as an allegorical teacher and a precursor of Christianity (mainly because of the fourth *Eclogue* and the moral values of the *Aeneid*). In the Renaissance and later he was venerated for his ethical teaching and as the classical examplar of perfect artistic form: his *Eclogues* were widely imitated (by Spenser, Milton, Pope and many others), and the *Georgics* gave the impetus for a special poetic genre in the eighteenth century (the English Georgic, as practised e.g. by Philips, Thomson, Smart and countless others). He was beloved by the nineteenth century for hi. pathos and sympathy, as the poet of the 'tears in things'. In the twentieth we respond especially to his exploration of contrasting attitudes and ideals, his juxtaposition of public and private aspiration, of divine and human causation in men's affairs — and of course, as every reader with enough Latin always has responded, to his mastery of diction and word-music, the 'sweetness of the sound' of his hexameters.

1 LIFE AND WORKS OF VIRGIL[2]

PUBLIUS VERGILIUS[3] Maro was born on 15 October 70 BC, of peasant stock, at a village called Andes near Mantua, in northern Italy in the area of the River Po. Here he spent his childhood on his father's farm, living a countryman's life and learning to love the beauties of the north Italian

1 For Virgil's influence generally see especially D. Comparetti *Vergil in the Middle Ages* (trans. Benecke, 1895); R. D. Williams *Changing Attitudes to Virgil (Dryden to Tennyson)* in *Virgil (Studies in Latin Literature and its influence)*, ed. D. R. Dudley (London, 1969), pp. 119-38, with bibliography given there). For the *Eclogues* see T. G. Rosenmeyer *The Green Cabinet* (Berkeley, 1969); for the *Georgics* see L. P. Wilkinson *The Georgics of Virgil* (Cambridge, 1969), ch. 10, and D. R. Dudley *Proc. Virg. Soc.* 1964-5, pp. 41f.
2 The main ancient sources (apart from the poems themselves) are to be found in the lives by Servius and by Aelius Donatus (the latter sometimes attributed to Suetonius); these are published in the *OCT Vitae Vergilianae Antiquae* (ed. C. Hardie, 1954). See also Mackail's *Aeneid*, Intro. pp. xxiiif., W. F. Jackson Knight *Roman Vergil*[2] ch. ii, and the introduction to E. de Saint-Denis' Budé *Eclogues* (1942).
3 Strictly, perhaps, his name in English should have been spelled Vergil, but the spelling Virgil has been traditional for so long that it seems inappropriate to abandon it.

landscape. He was educated at Cremona, Milan and then at Rome; we know
that for a time he studied with the Epicurean Siro. During his youth he
had met some of the men who were destined to play prominent parts in public
life, and through his poetry he met more (Pollio, Gallus, Varus, Octavian
himself); he became an important member of the literary court circle under
Maecenas, and though he himself took no part in military or political life,
he was on close terms with those who did, and was thus in constant touch
with national problems and aspirations.

His earliest poems[1] were the *Eclogues*, a collection of ten pastoral poems
written during the period 42-37 BC, and published in 37 BC. From the first
and ninth of these it seems that he was involved in the confiscation of property
in the Mantua area during the resettlement of the veterans of the civil wars;
at all events he did not return to live in the north, but spent the rest of his
life in Campania, at Nola or Naples. Here from 37-30 BC he composed the
Georgics, a poetic account (dedicated to Maecenas) of Italian farming which
bears full witness to his personal knowledge of the countryside, its crops,
its animals, its farmers, and of his deep love for rural Italy, as well as of his
mastery of the Latin hexameter.

During all this time Virgil had been preparing[2] himself to undertake an
epic poem, the peak of literary aspiration, and in 30 BC he began to compose
the *Aeneid*, a poem to express Rome's national greatness and destiny by
means of the story of her legendary origins. By 19 BC the *Aeneid* was
virtually complete,[3] but Virgil decided to give it a further three years'
revision, and set out on a voyage to Greece to give himself local colour for
the parts he meant to modify. Early in his travels he fell ill of a fever, and
was forced to return to Italy; he died at Brundisium within a few days of
landing. He left instructions that the *Aeneid* should be burnt, but Augustus
countermanded them and had the poem published posthumously.

2 THE ECLOGUES

The *Eclogues* are discussed individually in the introductory note to the
commentary on each one; here a few broad generalisations may be made. These
poems are Virgil's first experiments in poetry; some of them, generally the
earliest, are very dependent on his model Theocritus (2, 3, 5, 7, 8) but in
varying degrees aim to produce a different impact; others are unlike
Theocritus in their subject-matter (1, 4, 6, 9, 10), though there are still echoes
of Theocritus' phrases (especially in 9 and 10). Above everything Virgil aims
to translate the pastoral world of Theocritus into the delicate cadences of
the Latin hexameter, of which at this early stage in his career he was already
a master. The movement of the verses in the *Eclogues* lacks the variety and

1 There exists a number of minor poems attributed to Virgil, collected under the title
of the *Appendix Vergiliana*. Very few of these are likely to be genuine works of Virgil.
2 See *Ecl.* 6.3-5, *Geo.* 3.16f.; Servius tells us of a project to write on the Alban kings,
and Donatus that Virgil began a Roman theme but finding his material uncongenial
resumed pastoral poetry.
3 It has some fifty incomplete lines and some stop-gap passages, and clearly was
undergoing continuous revision and rewriting, but it is in no real sense unfinished.

power which Virgil was to achieve later, but it has a quiet beauty and charm which perfectly fits the pastoral landscape. Coleridge called the *Eclogues* 'most graceful and tender'; Horace defined their quality as *molle atque facetum* ('gentle and bright'): they are essentially delicate and fragile poems, set in a minor key.

In the earlier eclogues Virgil seeks to modify the immediate and vigorous impact of Theocritus' shepherds in the direction of added literary elegance; sometimes the structure is altered so as to add to the pathos (as in 2) or to set up a new tension in the poem (as in 5 and 8). Later he experimented with a quite new idea, the presentation of an idyllic Arcadia, stylised and far removed from the real world of shepherds so as to become a setting for an idyllic world. At the same time as he removed his pastoral world further from reality, he introduced into it aspects of reality in a way that Theocritus had never done. There was a precedent in Theocritus (a brief passage in *Idyll* 7) for the mention by the shepherds of real contemporary poets, and Virgil developed this further (Pollio in 3, 4, 8; Gallus in 6 and 10; Varius and Cinna in 9), but what was new was the idea of making real people enter the pastoral world in a pastoral guise (especially Gallus in 10), and of relating the Arcadian world with Roman political actuality (as in 1 and 9, and in a different way in 4). This was a new contribution to the pastoral genre which had a long history after Virgil (see the introduction to *Ecl.* 10).

This intrusion of real people and events into the imaginary pastoral setting has led many students of the *Eclogues* to search for allegorical equations (in addition to the real figures actually named), so that Daphnis in 5 becomes Julius Caesar, Menalcas in 9 becomes Virgil, and so on. But this type of interpretation runs into such difficulties as to suggest that it is not Virgil's method to indulge in masquerade, and it is better to speak of the impact of the poet's personal experience upon his poems rather than to see hidden allegories (see the introduction to *Ecl.* 1 and *Ecl.* 5).

Another marked difference between Virgil and Theocritus is the greater element of personal involvement in Virgil, especially in situations of pathos concerned with unhappy love or exile or death. Such subjects are portrayed in the *Eclogues* with a poignancy of muted sorrow which was the precursor of that sympathy with suffering that is so characteristic of some of the most memorable passages in the *Georgics* and the *Aeneid*. For all the added power and vigour of his later works, an element of continuity with the *Eclogues* is clearly to be seen.

But the essence of the *Eclogues* throughout is that they are concerned with song — both with the songs of the shepherds in their Arcadian world, and with the song of Virgil in his poetic apprenticeship — Saint-Denis expresses this exactly: *'un jeune poète cherche sa voie'*. We see Virgil moving from the music of his unambitious imitations of Theocritus in amoebaean contests towards a kind of song which is more specially Roman, the tributes to his fellow poet Gallus, the poems about expulsion from one's farm, finally to the great prophetic vision of the Golden Age to be reintroduced by the birth of a child, which the poet himself hopes to be permitted, when it occurs in the near future, to celebrate in song (see the introduction to *Ecl.* 4.)

Lastly something should be said about the arrangement of the collection of the ten eclogues. This has been much discussed in recent years, and symmetries of all kinds have been put forward — numerical, Theocritean, thematic. For an excellent discussion of this topic see Niall Rudd, *Lines of Enquiry*, Cambridge, 1976, pp. 119f. It is clear that Roman poets did arrange their individual poems for publication in a way other than haphazardly (for example, Horace's *Odes*), but it is easy to over-emphasise the significance of the arrangement. Some have seen a variation between monologues and dialogues; others have seen a balance between Theocritean poems (2, 3, 7, 8), partly Theocritean (5, 10) and non-Theocritean; others a symmetry (leaving 10 aside) between 1 and 9, 2 and 8, 3 and 7, 4 and 6 (with a balance in the number of lines in these pairs — 150, 181, 181, 149); Otis sees 'a forward-looking patriotic' note in the first five and 'a neoteric, ambiguous or polemic' tone in the second five. It is probable that some of these suggestions have truth in them — certainly a grouping of 7 and 8 to balance 2 and 3 is very evident — but the pure architecture of arrangement matters much less than the intrinsic merits of the individual poems; and it is on the poems themselves, with their strange ambiguity of setting, their poignant pathos and their lilting music that we should concentrate our attention.

3 THE GEORGICS

After the publication of the *Eclogues* Virgil spent the next seven years or so (37 BC to 30 or 29 BC) in composing his didactic poem on agriculture, the *Georgics*. The rate of composition averages out at about one line a day, and Donatus (22) uses the image of licking the poem into shape as a she-bear does her cubs. It stands with Horace's *Odes* as the most perfectly finished work in Latin poetry (the *Aeneid* of course was unrevised at Virgil's death) and gained from Dryden extravagant praise: 'the best poem of the best poet'.[1] Its external qualities of rhythm and word-music are of a beauty unsurpassed anywhere in the Latin hexameter, which Tennyson called 'the stateliest measure ever moulded by the lips of man'. Its inner qualities are less easy to define: Seneca (*Ep. Mor.* 86.15) wisely said that the poem was written 'not to instruct farmers but to delight readers'. The intellectual didactic material is, at a surface level, the subject of the poem; but the real subject is emotional or indeed spiritual, the appreciation of the beauty and divinity of the countryside with its farmworkers, its rural gods, its animals and birds and insects and plants.

The poem is dedicated at the beginning of each of its four books to Maecenas, a prominent statesman and patron of letters during the period of the end of the Republic and the beginning of the Empire. It contains passages in praise of Octavian (the future Emperor Augustus) which indicate poignantly the longing of the Romans for an end to the civil wars and the return of peace (see note on 1. 1-42). For Virgil this longing was focused on the desecration of the countryside during periods of war (note on 1. 498-514),

1 For the influence of the *Georgics* on subsequent literature see Wilkinson, ch. 10 and D. R. Dudley *Proc. Virg. Soc.* 1964-5, pp. 41f.

and the poem is therefore related to the political and social needs of the time, to the urgent desirability of restoring Italian agriculture.

Virgil had two distinct types of source material for his poem: one the factual material to be found in Greek poets like Hesiod, Aratus, Nicander and in Greek and Latin prose writers on agriculture such as Aristotle, Theophrastus, Cato, Varro and many more; and the other the poetic inspiration to be derived from previous writers of Latin hexameters, most notably Lucretius, who like Virgil had used this metre to convey both intellectual didactic material (in his case the philosophy of Epicurus) and emotional conviction. But the essence of the *Georgics* is that the source-material is used only as a basis for Virgil's expression of his own practical knowledge of the countryside, and his intense love for it.

The structure of the poem is most carefully organised: comments on the arrangement within each book will be found in the introductory notes to each book, but here something may be briefly said about the total structure. Books 1 and 2 are about aspects of plant life, the first book about soil and crops and the second about trees; books 3 and 4 are about living creatures, the third book about horses, cattle, sheep and goats and the fourth about bees. This is an obvious pattern: another, equally important, is that the first and third books both emphasise toil and sorrow (note particularly their pessimistic endings) while the second and fourth books are more optimistic, presenting the happier side of the countryman's life. The second book contains the famous 'praises of Italy' (see note on 136-76) and ends with an idyllic picture of the rewards of the farmer's life (notes on 2.458-74, 475-542), and in the fourth the description of the selfless devotion of the bees to their common tasks is bright and cheerful. The mythological story of Aristaeus, with which the book ends (see notes on 4.315-424 and 425-558), sets triumph and disaster in equipoise; it contains the tragic story of Orpheus and Eurydice, but it concludes with the successful expiation by Aristaeus of his crime and the rebirth of his bees, thus reinforcing the theme of immortality through rebirth which is a dominant feature of Virgil's presentation of nature and nature's creatures.

The reasons for the extraordinary poetic success of what might have been a versified manual (in the Alexandrian style) are many: a few suggestions may be offered here. Metre and diction come first: we see the poet of the gentle movement of the *Eclogues* using the same skills in a wider variety of material, and at the same time commanding other sorts of movement, more robust, more experimental, looking forward to the enormously varied cadences of the *Aeneid*. This technical skill with language becomes an instrument to convey deeply-felt emotions and personal involvement with the subject-matter. Love of the Italian countryside shines through all the time: it is especially seen in the frequent use of personification, not only of animals, but (especially) of bees and also of trees and plants, and in the metaphors from human activity applied to the life of Nature. Constant use of the first and second person (*saepe ego vidi . . ., quare agite . . .*) reflects the urgency of the poet's involvement, and the full-scale description of moments of triumph and disaster (the rustling corn in summer, the harvest gathered in, the onset of storm or fire or plague) invites the reader inside the framework of the poem.

Two special themes recur throughout the work: the first is the dignity of labour — *scilicet omnibus est labor impendendus* (2.61) . . . *omnia quae multo ante memor provisa repones si te digna manet divini gloria ruris* (1.167-8). This is explicitly elaborated in Virgil's mythological account of the abolition of the Golden Age (1. 118f., where see note): it was Jupiter's decision that the way of the farmer should not be easy, because of the satisfaction to be gained in tasks achieved. The second is the pantheistic philosophy which lies behind all the descriptions of Nature: each place has its local gods, its special rural worship of its deities, and in all the elements of the whole cosmos of Nature there is a spark of divinity; all are part of God's purposes. Man can and must work together with all the elements of his natural environment so that though individual people, animals and plants must die, yet the totality continues: rebirth follows death — *at genus immortale manet.*

4 VIRGIL'S HEXAMETER

The metrical movement [1] of Virgil's hexameter, the sheer word-music, has always been acclaimed even by those who would deny him much else, [2] and Virgil's achievement is very justly summarised in Tennyson's famous line 'Wielder of the stateliest measure ever moulded by the lips of man'. Here attention may be drawn to three aspects of Virgil's mastery.

First of all, Virgil more than any other Latin poet was able to exploit the possibility of interplay between sentence endings and line endings. In his predecessors generally speaking the line was the sentence unit; it had been relatively rare for a sentence to end elsewhere than at a line ending. Virgil in the Latin hexameter, like Milton in English blank verse, made new use of the kinds of emphasis available through run-on words, mid-line pauses, staccato short sentences. This aspect is much less evident in the *Eclogues* (where the nature of the poetry does not call for it); it begins to develop more fully in the *Georgics,* and reaches its final mastery in the infinite variety of the epic narrative of the *Aeneid.* [3]

Secondly Virgil achieved the variety he needed by the continued use, but within strict control, of metrical abnormalities and licences used by his predecessors. He occupies a middle place between the freedom or mannerisms of Ennius, Lucretius, Catullus and the disappearance of almost all irregularities in Ovid and afterwards. Earlier poetry is recalled by lengthening in arsis, hiatus, spondaic fifth feet, unusual caesurae, and (in the *Georgics* and *Aeneid*) monosyllabic endings, hypermetric elisions; but these features are employed rarely, and often with deliberate effect. Examples may be studied by use of the index under the heading 'metre'.

1 For methods of scansion see Huxley's edition of *Georgics* I and 4 (London, 1963) and Maguinness' edition of *Aeneid* 12 (London, 1953). For aesthetic appreciation see also L. P. Wilkinson *Golden Latin Artistry* (Cambridge, 1963).

2 Cf. Coleridge's famous question: 'If you take from Virgil his diction and metre, what do you leave him?'

3 For illustrations see indexes to my Oxford editions of *Aeneid* 3 and 5 under 'metre'.

Thirdly Virgil understood and exploited more than any other Latin poet
the two rhythms which were inherent in his metre ever since Ennius had
employed the quantitative hexameter (taken from the Greeks) for the more
strongly stressed Latin language. The result of this was to impose on the normal
stress pronunciation of Latin an artificial scheme of scansion according to
long and short syllables; and the effect was to make possible at every point
coincidence or conflict of these two rhythms.[1] The quantitative pattern called
for a metrical ictus, or beat, at the beginning of each foot of the hexameter;
the natural stress accent[2] on each word could occur in the same place as the
ictus or not, according to choice. Clearly the interplay of these rhythms can
be used for aesthetic effects of various kinds: in Virgil's

fáta vo/cánt, cŏn/dítquĕ ná/tántia/lúmina/sómnŭs (*Geo.* 4.496)

the coincidence of the two rhythms in the last four feet gives a drowsy lilt,
while in

ēt tó/tum īnvŏl/vīt flắm/mīs nĕmŭs/ēt rŭĭt/ắtrăm (*Geo.* 2.308)

the conflict in the first five feet causes a feeling of violence appropriate for
the description of fire. These are extreme examples; Virgil's mastery is to
be seen in the controlled use of these two rhythms throughout his poetry,
and it is this interplay of ictus and accent (or, as it equally is, of word pattern
within the metrical structure) which perhaps more than any other single
feature makes 'the stateliest measure'.

Using these technical devices, and many others (like the interplay of
spondees and dactyls, the subtle music of alliteration and assonance, the
variation of the Catullan patterned line for description with vigorous and
fast-moving rhythms for narrative or exposition) Virgil was able to an
extraordinary degree to make the sound suit the sense. In the last analysis
it is the range of metrical movement, corresponding with the range of mood
and emotion, which makes Virgil's poetry so unique.

5 THE MANUSCRIPTS OF VIRGIL'S POEMS
AND THE ANCIENT COMMENTATORS

The text of Virgil has been preserved far·better than that of any other Latin
poet. We possess manuscripts in capital letters from the fourth and fifth
century, as well as many citations in ancient authors such as Seneca, Quintilian,
Aulus Gellius, and the invaluable commentary of Servius (c. AD 400).
Ninth-century MSS (the date of our earliest testimony for very many authors)
abound for Virgil, and the recent collation of a dozen of these by Mynors
for his Oxford Text (1969) has served to confirm the enormous
reliability of our capital MSS. In most cases of doubt about the text in Virgil
the choice is between variants already existing by the fifth century; the

1 On this see especially W. F. Jackson Knight *Accentual Symmetry in Vergil* (Oxford,
1939), and *Roman Vergil,*[2] pp. 292f., as well as Wilkinson (cited above).
2 The rules for the Latin stress accent are very easy, being almost exactly the same as
English: thus if the last syllable but one is long it takes the stress (*amóris, condúntur*),
otherwise the stress is on the last syllable but two (*cármina, carmínibus*).

number of places in which our fifth-century testimony has to be rejected is very small indeed.

The following are the chief MSS:

M (*Mediceus*), fifth century, complete except for *Ecl.* 1.1-6.47.

P (*Palatinus*), fourth or fifth century, containing about nine-tenths of the poems, with sporadic gaps.

R (*Romanus*), fifth century, containing about four-fifths of the poems, with sporadic gaps; less reliable than M and P.

The missing portions of P and R can be restored with fair confidence by ninth-century MSS which are closely related to them: γ (*Gudianus*) for P, and *a* (*Bernensis*) for R.

In addition there are four other much more fragmentary capital MSS:

F (*Vaticanus*), fourth century, with illustrations, containing about a sixth of the poems.

V (*Veronensis*), fifth century, containing about a tenth of the poems.

G (*Sangallensis*), fifth century, small fragments only.

A (*Augusteus*), fragments of the *Georgics,* and four lines of the *Aeneid* (now lost, but known from a transcription).

The commentary of Servius (edited Thilo and Hagen, 1878-1902) is of the utmost importance in establishing the text as well as in explaining it. The commentary exists in two versions, a shorter and a longer (called Servius *auct.* or Servius *Dan.*); the relationship between these two has not yet been established, and I have not differentiated between them in this edition.

One of the outstanding merits of the commentary from the point of view of Virgil's text is the preservation of the views and readings of earlier grammarians like Probus, Asper, Aelius Donatus.

The *Saturnalia* of Macrobius (c. AD 400) contains very large numbers of citations from Virgil, and is of value (though less so than Servius) for the text as well as for its explanation.

6 DIFFERENCES IN TEXT

List of differences of text between this edition and those of Hirtzel (OCT 1900) and Mynors (OCT, 1969) (omitting minor points of orthography and punctuation).

Ecl.	*Williams*	*Hirtzel*	*Mynors*
2. 12	me cum	mecum	mecum
3.102	his	hi	his
3.105	caeli	Caeli	caeli
3.110	aut . . . aut	haud . . . haud	aut . . . aut
4. 55	vincat	vincet	vincet

Ecl.	Williams	Hirtzel	Mynors
5.27	ingemuisse	gemuisse	ingemuisse
6. 33	exordia	exordia	ex omnia
8. 11	desinet	desinam	desinam
9. 64	laedet	laedit	laedet
10.19	upilio	opilio	upilio

Geo.			
1.135	et	ut	ut
1.?08	dies	die	die
1.260	mox	post	mox
1.332	Athon	Athon	Atho
1.360	a curvis	curvis	a curvis
1.418	vias	vices	vias
1.418	umidus	uvidus	umidus
1.439	sequuntur	sequuntur	sequentur
1.454	incipiunt	incipient	incipiunt
1.513	in spatia	in spatio	in spatia
2. 52	voces	voles	voles
2.65	edurae	et durae	edurae
2.71	castaneas fagus	castaneae fagos	castaneae fagos
2. 82	mirata estque	miraturque	miratastque
2.106	dicere	discere	dicere
2.174	artis	artis	artem
2.187	despicere	dispicere	despicere
2.247	amaro	amaror	amaro
2.317	tunc	tunc	tum
2.330	tepentibus	trementibus	tepentibus
2.332	germina	gramina	gramina
2.379	admorso	admorsu	admorsu
2.413	rusci	rusci	rusti
2.456	Rhoetumque	Rhoetumque	Rhoecumque
2.469	at	et	at
2.487	Spercheosque	Spercheusque	Spercheosque
2.514	hinc	hinc	hic
3.194	provocet	tum vocet	tum vocet
3.202	hic	hinc	hinc
3.230	pernox	pernix	pernox
3.456	omina	omnia	omina
3.519	relinquit	relinquit	reliquit
4. 87	quiescunt	quiescent	quiescent
4.141	tinus	pinus	tinus
4.169	fragrantia	fragrantia	fraglantia

Geo.	Williams	Hirtzel	Mynors
4.202	refingunt	refigunt	refingunt
4.229	thesauris	thesauri	thesauris
4.291	post 293	post 292	post 293
4.327	pecudum	pecorum	pecudum
4.339	Cydippe	Cydippeque	Cydippe
4.415	diffundit	diffundit	defundit
4.455	ob	ad	ob
4.461	implevit	implerunt	implevit
4.493	Avernis	Averni	Avernis
4.505	qua	quae	quae
4.509	astris	astris	antris

7 BIBLIOGRAPHY

The entries are listed in chronological order. For fuller information see *Greece and Rome, New Surveys in the Classics No. 1: Virgil* by R. D. Williams, 1967, with the supplement in *Proc. Virg. Soc.* 1976-7. Additional bibliographical references are given in the appropriate places in the commentary.

(a) *Texts*
Ribbeck (1859-68); Hirtzel (OCT, 1900); Sabbadini (Rome, 1930); de Saint-Denis' Budé (*Eclogues*, second ed. 1949, *Georgics*, 1956); Mynors (OCT, second ed. 1972); Geymonat (Corp. Parav. 1973).

(b) *Commentaries*
Servius (ed. Thilo and Hagen, 1878-1902); Heyne-Wagner (fourth ed. 1830-41); Conington-Nettleship-Haverfield (1858-98); Page (1898); Plessis-Lejay (1919); Richter (*Georgics*, 1957); Holtorf (*Eclogues*, 1959); Perret (*Eclogues*, 1961); Huxley (*Georgics* 1 and 4, 1963); Coleman (*Eclogues*, 1977).

(c) *Translations*
Dryden (1697), Mackail (1889), Fairclough (Loeb, second ed. 1934-5), Jermyn (*Georgics*, 1947), Rieu (*Eclogues* 1949), Day Lewis (*Eclogues*, 1963, *Georgics*, 1940).

(d) *Literary criticism, etc.*: *Eclogues* and *Georgics* (see also (e) and (f))
W. Y. Sellar *The Roman Poets of the Augustan Age: Virgil* (Oxford, 1877; third ed. 1897)
T. R. Glover *Virgil* (London, 1904; seventh ed. 1942)
W. F. Jackson Knight *Roman Vergil* (London, 1944; second ed. 1966)
J. Perret *Virgile, l'homme et l'oeuvre* (Paris, 1952; second ed. 1965)
K. Büchner *Vergilius* (Pauly-Wissowa, *RE*, 1955)
Brooks Otis *Virgil: a Study in Civilised Poetry* (Oxford, 1963)
L. P. Wilkinson *Golden Latin Artistry* (Cambridge, 1963)
Steele Commager (ed.) *Twentieth Century Views: Virgil* (New Jersey, 1966)
F. Klingner *Virgil: Bucolica, Georgica, Aeneis* (Zürich, 1967)

R. D. Williams *Virgil (Greece and Rome, New Surveys in the Classics No. 1*, Oxford, 1967)

Gordon Williams *Tradition and Originality in Roman Poetry* (Oxford, 1968)

(e) *Eclogues — Literary criticism*

H. J. Rose *The Eclogues of Vergil* (Berkeley, 1942)

Bruno Snell *The Discovery of the Mind* (trans. Rosenmeyer, Oxford, 1953) ch. 13

T. G. Rosenmeyer *The Green Cabinet*, Berkeley, 1969

D. E. W. Wormell *The Originality of the Eclogues*, in *Virgil* (ed. D. R. Dudley, London, 1969)

M. C. J. Putnam *Virgil's Pastoral Art* (Princeton, 1970)

A. J. Boyle (ed.) *Ancient Pastoral* (Melbourne, 1975)

(f) *Georgics — literary criticism and technical studies*

T. F. Royds *The Beasts, Birds and Bees of Virgil* (Oxford, 1918)

J. Sargeaunt *The Trees, Shrubs and Plants of Virgil* (Oxford, 1920)

R. Billiard *L'Agriculture dans l'antiquité d'après les Géorgiques de Virgile* (Paris, 1928)

H. M. Fraser *Beekeeping in Antiquity* (London, 1931)

C. R. Ribbands *The Behaviour and Social Life of Honeybees* (London, 1954)

K. D. White *Agricultural Implements of the Roman World* (Cambridge, 1967)

L. P. Wilkinson *The Georgics of Virgil* (Cambridge, 1969; with a full bibliography)

K. D. White *Roman Farming* (London, 1970)

Brooks Otis *A new study of the Georgics (Phoenix*, 1972) pp. 40f.

The Eclogues

ECLOGUE 1

Meliboeus   Tityrus

M. Tityre, tu patulae recubans sub tegmine fagi
   silvestrem tenui Musam meditaris avena:
   nos patriae finis et dulcia linquimus arva.
   nos patriam fugimus: tu, Tityre, lentus in umbra
   formosam resonare doces Amaryllida silvas.   5

T. O Meliboee, deus nobis haec otia fecit.
   namque erit ille mihi semper deus, illius aram
   saepe tener nostris ab ovilibus imbuet agnus.
   ille meas errare boves, ut cernis, et ipsum
   ludere quae vellem calamo permisit agresti.   .   10

M. Non equidem invideo, miror magis; undique totis
   usque adeo turbatur agris. en, ipse capellas
   protinus aeger ago; hanc etiam vix, Tityre, duco.
   hic inter densas corylos modo namque gemellos,
   spem gregis, a! silice in nuda conixa reliquit.   15
   saepe malum hoc nobis, si mens non laeva fuisset,
   de caelo tactas memini praedicere quercus.
   sed tamen iste deus qui sit, da, Tityre, nobis.

T. Vrbem quam dicunt Romam, Meliboee, putavi
   stultus ego huic nostrae similem, quo saepe solemus   20
   pastores ovium teneros depellere fetus.
   sic canibus catulos similis, sic matribus haedos
   noram, sic parvis componere magna solebam.
   verum haec tantum alias inter caput extulit urbes
   quantum lenta solent inter viburna cupressi.   25

M. Et quae tanta fuit Romam tibi causa videndi?

T. Libertas, quae sera tamen respexit inertem,
   candidior postquam tondenti barba cadebat,
   respexit tamen et longo post tempore venit,
   postquam nos Amaryllis habet, Galatea reliquit.   30
   namque, fatebor enim, dum me Galatea tenebat,
   nec spes libertatis erat nec cura peculi.

quamvis multa meis exiret victima saeptis,
pinguis et ingratae premeretur caseus urbi,
non umquam gravis aere domum mihi dextra redibat.   35
M. Mirabar quid maesta deos, Amarylli, vocares,
cui pendere sua patereris in arbore poma;
Tityrus hinc aberat. ipsae te, Tityre, pinus,
ipsi te fontes, ipsa haec arbusta vocabant.
T. Quid facerem? neque servitio me exire licebat   40
nec tam praesentis alibi cognoscere divos.
hic illum vidi iuvenem, Meliboee, quotannis
bis senos cui nostra dies altaria fumant.
hic mihi responsum primus dedit ille petenti:
'pascite ut ante boves, pueri; summittite tauros.'   45
M. Fortunate senex, ergo tua rura manebunt,
et tibi magna satis, quamvis lapis omnia nudus
limosoque palus obducat pascua iunco:
non insueta gravis temptabunt pabula fetas,
nec mala vicini pecoris contagia laedent.   50
fortunate senex, hic inter flumina nota
et fontis sacros frigus captabis opacum.
hinc tibi quae semper vicino ab limite saepes
Hyblaeis apibus florem depasta salicti
saepe levi somnum suadebit inire susurro: 55
hinc alta sub rupe canet frondator ad auras;
nec tamen interea raucae, tua cura, palumbes
nec gemere aeria cessabit turtur ab ulmo.
T. Ante leves ergo pascentur in aethere cervi,
et freta destituent nudos in litore piscis,   60
ante pererratis amborum finibus exsul
aut Ararim Parthus bibet aut Germania Tigrim,
quam nostro illius labatur pectore vultus.
M. At nos hinc alii sitientis ibimus Afros,
pars Scythiam et rapidum cretae veniemus Oaxen   65
et penitus toto divisos orbe Britannos.
en umquam patrios longo post tempore finis,
pauperis et tuguri congestum caespite culmen,
post aliquot, mea regna, videns mirabor aristas?
impius haec tam culta novalia miles habebit,   70
barbarus has segetes? en quo discordia civis
produxit miseros: his nos consevimus agros!

insere nunc, Meliboee, piros, pone ordine vitis.
ite meae, quondam felix pecus, ite capellae.
non ego vos posthac viridi proiectus in antro   75
dumosa pendere procul de rupe videbo;
carmina nulla canam; non me pascente, capellae,
florentem cytisum et salices carpetis amaras.
T. Hic tamen hanc mecum poteras requiescere noctem
fronde super viridi: sunt nobis mitia poma,   80
castaneae molles et pressi copia lactis,
et iam summa procul villarum culmina fumant,
maioresque cadunt altis de montibus umbrae.

ECLOGUE 2

Formosum pastor Corydon ardebat Alexin,
delicias domini; nec quid speraret habebat.
tantum inter densas, umbrosa cacumina, fagos
adsidue veniebat. ibi haec incondita solus
montibus et silvis studio iactabat inani: 5
   'O crudelis Alexi, nihil mea carmina curas?
nil nostri miserere? mori me denique cogis?
nunc etiam pecudes umbras et frigora captant;
nunc viridis etiam occultant spineta lacertos,
Thestylis et rapido fessis messoribus aestu   10
alia serpyllumque herbas contundit olentis.
at me cum raucis, tua dum vestigia lustro
sole sub ardenti, resonant arbusta cicadis.
nonne fuit satius tristis Amaryllidis iras
atque superba pati fastidia? nonne Menalcan,   15
quamvis ille niger, quamvis tu candidus esses?
o formose puer, nimium ne crede colori!
alba ligustra cadunt, vaccinia nigra leguntur.
despectus tibi sum, nec qui sim quaeris, Alexi,
quam dives pecoris, nivei quam lactis abundans.   20
mille meae Siculis errant in montibus agnae,
lac mihi non aestate novum, non frigore defit.
canto quae solitus, si quando armenta vocabat,
Amphion Dircaeus in Actaeo Aracyntho.
nec sum adeo informis: nuper me in litore vidi,   25

cum placidum ventis staret mare. non ego Daphnin
iudice te metuam, si numquam fallit imago.
o tantum libeat mecum tibi sordida rura
atque humilis habitare casas et figere cervos,
haedorumque gregem viridi compellere hibisco!   30
mecum una in silvis imitabere Pana canendo
(Pan primum calamos cera coniungere pluris
instituit, Pan curat ovis oviumque magistros),
nec te paeniteat calamo trivisse labellum:
haec eadem ut sciret, quid non faciebat Amyntas?   35
est mihi disparibus septem compacta cicutis
fistula, Damoetas dono mihi quam dedit olim,
et dixit moriens: 'te nunc habet ista secundum';
dixit Damoetas, invidit stultus Amyntas.
praeterea duo nec tuta mihi valle reperti   40
capreoli, sparsis etiam nunc pellibus albo;
bina die siccant ovis ubera; quos tibi servo.
iam pridem a me illos abducere Thestylis orat;
et faciet, quoniam sordent tibi munera nostra.
huc ades, o formose puer: tibi lilia plenis   45
ecce ferunt Nymphae calathis; tibi candida Nais,
pallentis violás et summa papavera carpens,
narcissum et florem iungit bene olentis anethi;
tum casia atque aliis intexens suavibus herbis
mollia luteola pingit vaccinia calta.   50
ipse ego cana legam tenera lanugine mala
castaneasque nuces, mea quas Amaryllis amabat.
addam cerea pruna (honos erit huic quoque pomo),
et vos, o lauri, carpam, et te, proxima myrte,
sic positae quoniam suavis miscetis odores.   55
rusticus es, Corydon; nec munera curat Alexis,
nec, si muneribus certes, concedat Iollas.
heu heu, quid volui misero mihi? floribus Austrum
perditus et liquidis immisi fontibus apros.
quem fugis, a! demens? habitarunt di quoque silvas   60
Dardaniusque Paris. Pallas quas condidit arces
ipsa colat; nobis placeant ante omnia silvae.
torva leaena lupum sequitur, lupus ipse capellam,
florentem cytisum sequitur lasciva capella,
te Corydon, o Alexi: trahit sua quemque voluptas.   65

aspice, aratra iugo referunt suspensa iuvenci,
et sol crescentis decedens duplicat umbras;
me tamen urit amor: quis enim modus adsit amori?
a, Corydon, Corydon, quae te dementia cepit?
semiputata tibi frondosa vitis in ulmo est:　　　70
quin tu aliquid saltem potius, quorum indiget usus,
viminibus mollique paras detexere iunco?
invenies alium, si te hic fastidit, Alexin.'

ECLOGUE 3

Menalcas　　　*Damoetas*　　　*Palaemon*

M. Dic mihi, Damoeta, cuium pecus? an Meliboei?
D. Non, verum Aegonis; nuper mihi tradidit Aegon.
M. Infelix o semper, oves, pecus! ipse Neaeram
　　dum fovet ac ne me sibi praeferat illa veretur,
　　hic alienus ovis custos bis mulget in hora,　　　5
　　et sucus pecori et lac subducitur agnis.
D. Parcius ista viris tamen obicienda memento.
　　novimus et qui te transversa tuentibus hircis
　　et quo—sed faciles Nymphae risere—sacello.
M. Tum, credo, cum me arbustum videre Miconis　　　10
　　atque mala vitis incidere falce novellas.
D. Aut hic ad veteres fagos cum Daphnidis arcum
　　fregisti et calamos: quae tu, perverse Menalca,
　　et cum vidisti puero donata, dolebas,
　　et si non aliqua nocuisses, mortuus esses.　　　15
M. Quid domini faciant, audent cum talia fures?
　　non ego te vidi Damonis, pessime, caprum
　　excipere insidiis multum latrante Lycisca?
　　et cum clamarem 'quo nunc se proripit ille?
　　Tityre, coge pecus,' tu post carecta latebas.　　　20
D. An mihi cantando victus non redderet ille,
　　quem mea carminibus meruisset fistula caprum?
　　si nescis, meus ille caper fuit; et mihi Damon
　　ipse fatebatur, sed reddere posse negabat.
M. Cantando tu illum? aut umquam tibi fistula cera　　　25
　　iuncta fuit? non tu in triviis, indocte, solebas

stridenti miserum stipula disperdere carmen?
D. Vis ergo inter nos quid possit uterque vicissim
experiamur? ego hanc vitulam (ne forte recuses,
bis venit ad mulctram, binos alit ubere fetus)   30
depono: tu dic mecum quo pignore certes.
M. De grege non ausim quicquam deponere tecum:
est mihi namque domi pater, est iniusta noverca,
bisque die numerant ambo pecus, alter et haedos.
verum, id quod multo tute ipse fatebere maius   35
(insanire libet quoniam tibi), pocula ponam
fagina, caelatum divini opus Alcimedontis,
lenta quibus torno facili superaddita vitis
diffusos hedera vestit pallente corymbos.
in medio duo signa, Conon, et—quis fuit alter,   40
descripsit radio totum qui gentibus orbem,
tempora quae messor, quae curvus arator haberet?
necdum illis labra admovi, sed condita servo.
D. Et nobis idem Alcimedon duo pocula fecit,
et molli circum est ansas amplexus acantho,   45
Orpheaque in medio posuit silvasque sequentis.
necdum illis labra admovi, sed condita servo.
si ad vitulam spectas, nihil est quod pocula laudes.
M. Numquam hodie effugies; veniam quocumque vocaris.
audiat haec tantum—vel qui venit ecce Palaemon.   50
efficiam posthac ne quemquam voce lacessas.
D. Quin age, si quid habes; in me mora non erit ulla,
nec quemquam fugio: tantum, vicine Palaemon,
sensibus haec imis (res est non parva) reponas.
P. Dicite, quandoquidem in molli consedimus herba.   55
et nunc omnis ager, nunc omnis parturit arbos,
nunc frondent silvae, nunc formosissimus annus.
incipe, Damoeta; tu deinde sequere, Menalca.
alternis dicetis; amant alterna Camenae.
D.   Ab Iove principium, Musae: Iovis omnia plena;   60
ille colit terras, illi mea carmina curae.
M. Et me Phoebus amat; Phoebo sua semper apud me
munera sunt, lauri et suave rubens hyacinthus.
D. Malo me Galatea petit, lasciva puella,
et fugit ad salices et se cupit ante videri.   65
M. At mihi sese offert ultro, meus ignis, Amyntas,

notior ut iam sit canibus non Delia nostris.
D. Parta meae Veneri sunt munera: namque notavi
ipse locum, aeriae quo congressere palumbes.
M. Quod potui, puero silvestri ex arbore lecta   70
aurea mala decem misi; cras altera mittam.
D. O quotiens et quae nobis Galatea locuta est!
partem aliquam, venti, divum referatis ad auris!
M. Quid prodest quod me ipse animo non spernis, Amynta,
si, dum tu sectaris apros, ego retia servo?   75
D. Phyllida mitte mihi: meus est natalis, Iolla:
cum faciam vitula pro frugibus, ipse venito.
M. Phyllida amo ante alias: nam me discedere flevit
et longum 'formose, vale, vale,' inquit, 'Iolla.'
D. Triste lupus stabulis, maturis frugibus imbres,   80
arboribus venti, nobis Amaryllidis irae.
M. Dulce satis umor, depulsis arbutus haedis,
lenta salix feto pecori, mihi solus Amyntas.
D. Pollio amat nostram, quamvis est rustica, Musam:
Pierides, vitulam lectori pascite vestro.   85
M. Pollio et ipse facit nova carmina: pascite taurum,
iam cornu petat et pedibus qui spargat harenam.
D. Qui te, Pollio, amat, veniat quo te quoque gaudet;
mella fluant illi, ferat et rubus asper amomum.
M. Qui Bavium non odit, amet tua carmina, Maevi,   90
atque idem iungat vulpes et mulgeat hircos.
D. Qui legitis flores et humi nascentia fraga,
frigidus, o pueri, fugite hinc, latet anguis in herba.
M. Parcite, oves, nimium procedere: non bene ripae
creditur; ipse aries etiam nunc vellera siccat.   95
D. Tityre, pascentis a flumine reice capellas:
ipse, ubi tempus erit, omnis in fonte lavabo.
M. Cogite ovis, pueri: si lac praeceperit aestus,
ut nuper, frustra pressabimus ubera palmis.
D. Heu heu, quam pingui macer est mihi taurus in ervo!   100
idem amor exitium pecori pecorisque magistro.
M. His certe neque amor causa est; vix ossibus haerent.
nescio quis teneros oculus mihi fascinat agnos.
D. Dic quibus in terris—et eris mihi magnus Apollo—
tris pateat caeli spatium non amplius ulnas.   105
M. Dic quibus in terris inscripti nomina regum

nascantur flores, et Phyllida solus habeto.
P. Non nostrum inter vos tantas componere lites.
et vitula tu dignus et hic, et quisquis amores
aut metuet dulcis aut experietur amaros.   110
claudite iam rivos, pueri; sat prata biberunt.

ECLOGUE 4

Sicelides Musae, paulo maiora canamus!
non omnis arbusta iuvant humilesque myricae;
si canimus silvas, silvae sint consule dignae.
Vltima Cumaei venit iam carminis aetas;
magnus ab integro saeclorum nascitur ordo.   5
iam redit et Virgo, redeunt Saturnia regna,
iam nova progenies caelo demittitur alto.
tu modo nascenti puero, quo ferrea primum
desinet ac toto surget gens aurea mundo,
casta fave Lucina: tuus iam regnat Apollo.   10
teque adeo decus hoc aevi, te consule, inibit,
Pollio, et incipient magni procedere menses;
te duce, si qua manent sceleris vestigia nostri,
inrita perpetua solvent formidine terras.
ille deum vitam accipiet divisque videbit   15
permixtos heroas et ipse videbitur illis,
pacatumque reget patriis virtutibus orbem.
At tibi prima, puer, nullo munuscula cultu
errantis hederas passim cum baccare tellus
mixtaque ridenti colocasia fundet acantho.   20
ipsae lacte domum referent distenta capellae
ubera, nec magnos metuent armenta leones;
ipsa tibi blandos fundent cunabula flores.
occidet et serpens, et fallax herba veneni
occidet; Assyrium vulgo nascetur amomum.   25
at simul heroum laudes et facta parentis
iam legere et quae sit poteris cognoscere virtus,
molli paulatim flavescet campus arista,
incultisque rubens pendebit sentibus uva,
et durae quercus sudabunt roscida mella.   30
pauca tamen suberunt priscae vestigia fraudis,

quae temptare Thetim ratibus, quae cingere muris
oppida, quae iubeant telluri infindere sulcos.
alter erit tum Tiphys, et altera quae vehat Argo
delectos heroas; erunt etiam altera bella   35
atque iterum ad Troiam magnus mittetur Achilles.
hinc, ubi iam firmata virum te fecerit aetas,
cedet et ipse mari vector, nec nautica pinus
mutabit merces: omnis feret omnia tellus.
non rastros patietur humus, non vinea falcem;   40
robustus quoque iam tauris iuga solvet arator;
nec varios discet mentiri lana colores,
ipse sed in pratis aries iam suave rubenti
murice, iam croceo mutabit vellera luto;
sponte sua sandyx pascentis vestiet agnos.   45
   'Talia saecla' suis dixerunt 'currite' fusis
concordes stabili fatorum numine Parcae.
   Adgredere o magnos (aderit iam tempus) honores,
cara deum suboles, magnum Iovis incrementum!
aspice convexo nutantem pondere mundum,   50
terrasque tractusque maris caelumque profundum;
aspice venturo laetentur ut omnia saeclo!
o mihi tum longae maneat pars ultima vitae,
spiritus et quantum sat erit tua dicere facta!
non me carminibus vincat nec Thracius Orpheus,   55
nec Linus, huic mater quamvis atque huic pater adsit,
Orphei Calliopea, Lino formosus Apollo.
Pan etiam, Arcadia mecum si iudice certet,
Pan etiam Arcadia dicat se iudice victum.
   Incipe, parve puer, risu cognoscere matrem   60
(matri longa decem tulerunt fastidia menses)
incipe, parve puer: qui non risere parenti,
nec deus hunc mensa, dea nec dignata cubili est.

ECLOGUE 5

Menalcas   Mopsus

Me. Cur non, Mopse, boni quoniam convenimus ambo,
    tu calamos inflare levis, ego dicere versus,

hic corylis mixtas inter consedimus ulmos?
Mo. Tu maior; tibi me est aequum parere, Menalca,
    sive sub incertas Zephyris motantibus umbras,   5
    sive antro potius succedimus. aspice, ut antrum
    silvestris raris sparsit labrusca racemis.
Me. Montibus in nostris solus tibi certat Amyntas.
Mo. Quid, si idem certet Phoebum superare canendo?
Me. Incipe, Mopse, prior, si quos aut Phyllidis ignis   10
    aut Alconis habes laudes aut iurgia Codri.
    incipe: pascentis servabit Tityrus haedos.
Mo. Immo haec, in viridi nuper quae cortice fagi
    carmina descripsi et modulans alterna notavi,
    experiar: tu deinde iubeto ut certet Amyntas.   15
Me. Lenta salix quantum pallenti cedit olivae,
    puniceis humilis quantum saliunca rosetis,
    iudicio nostro tantum tibi cedit Amyntas.
    sed tu desine plura, puer: successimus antro.
Mo.   Exstinctum Nymphae crudeli funere Daphnin   20
    flebant (vos coryli testes et flumina Nymphis),
    cum complexa sui corpus miserabile nati
    atque deos atque astra vocat crudelia mater.
    non ulli pastos illis egere diebus
    frigida, Daphni, boves ad flumina; nulla neque amnem   25
    libavit quadripes nec graminis attigit herbam.
    Daphni, tuum Poenos etiam ingemuisse leones
    interitum montesque feri silvaeque loquuntur.
    Daphnis et Armenias curru subiungere tigris
    instituit, Daphnis thiasos inducere Bacchi   30
    et foliis lentas intexere mollibus hastas.
    vitis ut arboribus decori est, ut vitibus uvae,
    ut gregibus tauri, segetes ut pinguibus arvis,
    tu decus omne tuis. postquam te fata tulerunt
    ipsa Pales agros atque ipse reliquit Apollo.   35
    grandia saepe quibus mandavimus hordea sulcis,
    infelix lolium et steriles nascuntur avenae;
    pro molli viola, pro purpureo narcisso
    carduus et spinis surgit paliurus acutis.
    spargite humum foliis, inducite fontibus umbras,   40
    pastores (mandat fieri sibi talia Daphnis),
    et tumulum facite, et tumulo superaddite carmen:

'Daphnis ego in silvis, hinc usque ad sidera notus,
formosi pecoris custos, formosior ipse.'
Me. Tale tuum carmen nobis, divine poeta,   45
quale sopor fessis in gramine, quale per aestum
dulcis aquae saliente sitim restinguere rivo.
nec calamis solum aequiperas, sed voce magistrum:
fortunate puer, tu nunc eris alter ab illo.
nos tamen haec quocumque modo tibi nostra vicissim   50
dicemus, Daphninque tuum tollemus ad astra;
Daphnin ad astra feremus: amavit nos quoque Daphnis.
Mo. An quicquam nobis tali sit munere maius?
et puer ipse fuit cantari dignus, et ista
iam pridem Stimichon laudavit carmina nobis.   55
Me. Candidus insuetum miratur limen Olympi
sub pedibusque videt nubes et sidera Daphnis.
ergo alacris silvas et cetera rura voluptas
Panaque pastoresque tenet Dryadasque puellas.
nec lupus insidias pecori, nec retia cervis   60
ulla dolum meditantur: amat bonus otia Daphnis.
ipsi laetitia voces ad sidera iactant
intonsi montes; ipsae iam carmina rupes,
ipsa sonant arbusta: 'deus, deus ille, Menalca!'
sis bonus o felixque tuis! en quattuor aras: 65
ecce duas tibi, Daphni, duas altaria Phoebo.
pocula bina novo spumantia lacte quotannis
craterasque duo statuam tibi pinguis olivi,
et multo in primis hilarans convivia Baccho,
ante focum, si frigus erit, si messis, in umbra,   70
vina novum fundam calathis Ariusia nectar.
cantabunt mihi Damoetas et Lyctius Aegon;
saltantis Satyros imitabitur Alphesiboeus.
haec tibi semper erunt, et cum sollemnia vota
reddemus Nymphis, et cum lustrabimus agros.   75
dum iuga montis aper, fluvios dum piscis amabit,
dumque thymo pascentur apes, dum rore cicadae,
semper honos nomenque tuum laudesque manebunt.
ut Baccho Cererique, tibi sic vota quotannis
agricolae facient: damnabis tu quoque votis.   80
Mo. Quae tibi, quae tali reddam pro carmine dona?
nam neque me tantum venientis sibilus Austri

nec percussa iuvant fluctu tam litora, nec quae
saxosas inter decurrunt flumina vallis.
Me. Hac te nos fragili donabimus ante cicuta.   85
haec nos 'formosum Corydon ardebat Alexin,'
haec eadem docuit 'cuium pecus? an Meliboei?'
Mo. At tu sume pedum, quod, me cum saepe rogaret,
non tulit Antigenes (et erat tum dignus amari),
formosum paribus nodis atque aere, Menalca.   90

ECLOGUE 6

Prima Syracosio dignata est ludere versu
nostra neque erubuit silvas habitare Thalea.
cum canerem reges et proelia, Cynthius aurem
vellit et admonuit: 'pastorem, Tityre, pinguis
pascere oportet ovis, deductum dicere carmen.'   5
nunc ego (namque super tibi erunt qui dicere laudes,
Vare, tuas cupiant et tristia condere bella)
agrestem tenui meditabor harundine Musam.
non iniussa cano. si quis tamen haec quoque, si quis
captus amore leget, te nostrae, Vare, myricae,   10
te nemus omne canet; nec Phoebo gratior ulla est
quam sibi quae Vari praescripsit pagina nomen.
    Pergite, Pierides. Chromis et Mnasyllos in antro
Silenum pueri somno videre iacentem,
inflatum hesterno venas, ut semper, Iaccho;   15
serta procul tantum capiti delapsa iacebant,
et gravis attrita pendebat cantharus ansa.
adgressi (nam saepe senex spe carminis ambo
luserat) iniciunt ipsis ex vincula sertis.
addit se sociam timidisque supervenit Aegle,   20
Aegle Naiadum pulcherrima, iamque videnti
sanguineis frontem moris et tempora pingit.
ille dolum ridens 'quo vincula nectitis?' inquit;
'solvite me, pueri; satis est potuisse videri.
carmina quae vultis cognoscite; carmina vobis,   25
huic aliud mercedis erit.' simul incipit ipse.
tum vero in numerum Faunosque ferasque videres
ludere, tum rigidas motare cacumina quercus;

nec tantum Phoebo gaudet Parnasia rupes,
nec tantum Rhodope miratur et Ismarus Orphea.   30
Namque canebat uti magnum per inane coacta
semina terrarumque animaeque marisque fuissent
et liquidi simul ignis; ut his exordia primis
omnia et ipse tener mundi concreverit orbis;
tum durare solum et discludere Nerea ponto   35
coeperit et rerum paulatim.sumere formas;
iamque novum terrae stupeant lucescere solem
altius, atque cadant summotis nubibus imbres,
incipiant silvae cum primum surgere, cumque
rara per ignaros errent animalia montis.   40
hinc lapides Pyrrhae iactos, Saturnia regna,
Caucasiasque refert volucris furtumque Promethei.
his adiungit, Hylan nautae quo fonte relictum
clamassent, ut litus 'Hyla, Hyla' omne sonaret;
et fortunatam, si numquam armenta fuissent,   45
Pasiphaen nivei solatur amore iuvenci.
a, virgo infelix, quae te dementia cepit!
Proetides implerunt falsis mugitibus agros,
at non tam turpis pecudum tamen ulla secuta
concubitus, quamvis collo timuisset aratrum   50
et saepe in levi quaesisset cornua fronte.
a, virgo infelix, tu nunc in montibus erras:
ille latus niveum molli fultus hyacintho
ilice sub nigra pallentis ruminat herbas
aut aliquam in magno sequitur grege. 'claudite, Nymphae,
Dictaeae Nymphae, nemorum iam claudite saltus,   56
si qua forte ferant oculis sese obvia nostris
errabunda bovis vestigia; forsitan illum
aut herba captum viridi aut armenta secutum
perducant aliquae stabula ad Gortynia vaccae.'   60
tum canit Hesperidum miratam mala puellam;
tum Phaethontiadas musco circumdat amarae
corticis atque solo proceras erigit alnos.
tum canit errantem Permessi ad flumina Gallum
Aonas in montis ut duxerit una sororum,   65
utque viro Phoebi chorus adsurrexerit omnis;
ut Linus haec illi divino carmine pastor
floribus atque apio crinis ornatus amaro

dixerit: 'hos tibi dant calamos, en accipe, Musae,
Ascraeo quos ante seni, quibus ille solebat   70
cantando rigidas deducere montibus ornos.
his tibi Grynei nemoris dicatur origo,
ne quis sit lucus quo se plus iactet Apollo.'
Quid loquar aut Scyllam Nisi, quam fama secuta est
candida succinctam latrantibus inguina monstris   75
Dulichias vexasse rates et gurgite in alto,
a, timidos nautas canibus lacerasse marinis;
aut ut mutatos Terei narraverit artus,
quas illi Philomela dapes, quae dona pararit,
quo cursu deserta petiverit et quibus ante   80
infelix sua tecta super volitaverit alis?
omnia, quae Phoebo quondam meditante beatus
audiit Eurotas iussitque ediscere lauros,
ille canit (pulsae referunt ad sidera valles),
cogere donec ovis stabulis numerumque referre   85
iussit et invito processit Vesper Olympo.

ECLOGUE 7

Meliboeus   *Corydon*   *Thyrsis*

M. Forte sub arguta consederat ilice Daphnis,
   compulerantque greges Corydon et Thyrsis in unum,
   Thyrsis ovis, Corydon distentas lacte capellas,
   ambo florentes aetatibus, Arcades ambo,
   et cantare pares et respondere parati.   5
   huc mihi, dum teneras defendo a frigore myrtos,
   vir gregis ipse caper deerraverat; atque ego Daphnin
   aspicio. ille ubi me contra videt, 'ocius' inquit
   'huc ades, o Meliboee; caper tibi salvus et haedi;
   et, si quid cessare potes, requiesce sub umbra.   10
   huc ipsi potum venient per prata iuvenci,
   hic viridis tenera praetexit harundine ripas
   Mincius, eque sacra resonant examina quercu.'
   quid facerem? neque ego Alcippen nec Phyllida habebam
   depulsos a lacte domi quae clauderet agnos,   15
   et certamen erat, Corydon cum Thyrside, magnum.

posthabui tamen illorum mea seria ludo.
alternis igitur contendere versibus ambo
coepere, alternos Musae meminisse volebant.
hos Corydon, illos referebat in ordine Thyrsis.   20

C.   Nymphae, noster amor, Libethrides, aut mihi carmen,
quale meo Codro, concedite (proxima Phoebi
versibus ille facit) aut, si non possumus omnes,
hic arguta sacra pendebit fistula pinu.

T. Pastores, hedera crescentem ornate poetam,   25
Arcades, invidia rumpantur ut ilia Codro;
aut, si ultra placitum laudarit, baccare frontem
cingite, ne vati noceat mala lingua futuro.

C.   Saetosi caput hoc apri tibi, Delia, parvus
et ramosa Micon vivacis cornua cervi.   30
si proprium hoc fuerit, levi de marmore tota
puniceo stabis suras evincta coturno.

T. Sinum lactis et haec te liba, Priape, quotannis
exspectare sat est: custos es pauperis horti.
nunc te marmoreum pro tempore fecimus; at tu,   35
si fetura gregem suppleverit, aureus esto.

C.   Nerine Galatea, thymo mihi dulcior Hyblae,
candidior cycnis, hedera formosior alba,
cum primum pasti repetent praesepia tauri,
si qua tui Corydonis habet te cura, venito.   40

T. Immo ego Sardoniis videar tibi amarior herbis,
horridior rusco, proiecta vilior alga,
si mihi non haec lux toto iam longior anno est.
ite domum pasti, si quis pudor, ite iuvenci.

C.   Muscosi fontes et somno mollior herba,   45
et quae vos rara viridis tegit arbutus umbra,
solstitium pecori defendite: iam venit aestas
torrida, iam lento turgent in palmite gemmae.

T. Hic focus et taedae pingues, hic plurimus ignis
semper, et adsidua postes fuligine nigri.   50
hic tantum Boreae curamus frigora quantum
aut numerum lupus aut torrentia flumina ripas.

C.   Stant et iuniperi et castaneae hirsutae,
strata iacent passim sua quaeque sub arbore poma,
omnia nunc rident: at si formosus Alexis   55
montibus his abeat, videas et flumina sicca.

T. Aret ager; vitio moriens sitit aëris herba;
  Liber pampineas invidit collibus umbras:
  Phyllidis adventu nostrae nemus omne virebit,
  Iuppiter et laeto descendet plurimus imbri.   60
C. Populus Alcidae gratissima, vitis Iaccho,
  formosae myrtus Veneri, sua laurea Phoebo;
  Phyllis amat corylos; illas dum Phyllis amabit,
  nec myrtus vincet corylos, nec laurea Phoebi.
T. Fraxinus in silvis pulcherrima, pinus in hortis,   65
  populus in fluviis, abies in montibus altis;
  saepius at si me, Lycida formose, revisas,
  fraxinus in silvis cedat tibi, pinus in hortis.
M. Haec memini, et victum frustra contendere Thyrsin.
  ex illo Corydon Corydon est tempore nobis.   70

ECLOGUE 8

Pastorum Musam Damonis et Alphesiboei,
immemor herbarum quos est mirata iuvenca
certantis, quorum stupefactae carmine lynces,
et mutata suos requierunt flumina cursus,
Damonis Musam dicemus et Alphesiboei.   5
  Tu mihi seu magni superas iam saxa Timavi,
sive oram Illyrici legis aequoris,—en erit umquam
ille dies, mihi cum liceat tua dicere facta?
en erit ut liceat totum mihi ferre per orbem
sola Sophocleo tua carmina digna coturno?   10
a te principium, tibi desinet: accipe iussis
carmina coepta tuis, atque hanc sine tempora circum
inter victricis hederam tibi serpere lauros.
  Frigida vix caelo noctis decesserat umbra,
cum ros in tenera pecori gratissimus herba: 15
incumbens tereti Damon sic coepit olivae.
D. Nascere praeque diem veniens age, Lucifer, almum,
coniugis indigno Nysae deceptus amore
dum queror et divos, quamquam nil testibus illis
profeci, extrema moriens tamen adloquor hora.   20
  incipe Maenalios mecum, mea tibia, versus.
Maenalus argutumque nemus pinusque loquentis

semper habet, semper pastorum ille audit amores
Panaque, qui primus calamos non passus inertis.
  incipe Maenalios mecum, mea tibia, versus.   25
Mopso Nysa datur: quid non speremus amantes?
iungentur iam grypes equis, aevoque sequenti
cum canibus timidi venient ad pocula dammae.
  incipe Maenalios mecum, mea tibia, versus.   28ᵃ
Mopse, novas incide faces: tibi ducitur uxor.
sparge, marite, nuces: tibi deserit Hesperus Oetam.   30
  incipe Maenalios mecum, mea tibia, versus.
o digno coniuncta viro, dum despicis omnis,
dumque tibi est odio mea fistula, dumque capellae
hirsutumque supercilium promissaque barba,
nec curare deum credis mortalia quemquam.   35
  incipe Maenalios mecum, mea tibia, versus.
saepibus in nostris parvam te roscida mala
(dux ego vester eram) vidi cum matre legentem.
alter ab undecimo tum me iam acceperat annus,
iam fragilis poteram a terra contingere ramos: 40
ut vidi, ut perii, ut me malus abstulit error!
  incipe Maenalios mecum, mea tibia, versus.
nunc scio quid sit Amor: duris in cotibus illum
aut Tmaros aut Rhodope aut extremi Garamantes
nec generis nostri puerum nec sanguinis edunt.   45
  incipe Maenalios mecum, mea tibia, versus.
saevus Amor docuit natorum sanguine matrem
commaculare manus; crudelis tu quoque mater.
crudelis mater magis, an puer improbus ille?
improbus ille puer; crudelis tu quoque, mater.   50
  incipe Maenalios mecum, mea tibia, versus.
nunc et ovis ultro fugiat lupus, aurea durae
mala ferant quercus, narcisso floreat alnus,
pinguia corticibus sudent electra myricae,
certent et cycnis ululae, sit Tityrus Orpheus,   55
Orpheus in silvis, inter delphinas Arion.
  incipe Maenalios mecum, mea tibia, versus.
omnia vel medium fiat mare. vivite silvae:
praeceps aerii specula de montis in undas
deferar; extremum hoc munus morientis habeto.   60
  desine Maenalios, iam desine, tibia, versus.

Haec Damon: vos, quae responderit Alphesiboeus,
dicite, Pierides; non omnia possumus omnes.

A. Effer aquam et molli cinge haec altaria vitta,
verbenasque adole pinguis et mascula tura,   65
coniugis ut magicis sanos avertere sacris
experiar sensus; nihil hic nisi carmina desunt.
   ducite ab urbe domum, mea carmina, ducite Daphnin.
carmina vel caelo possunt deducere lunam,
carminibus Circe socios mutavit Vlixi,   70
frigidus in pratis cantando rumpitur anguis.
   ducite ab urbe domum, mea carmina, ducite Daphnin.
terna tibi haec primum triplici diversa colore
licia circumdo, terque haec altaria circum
effigiem duco; numero deus impare gaudet.   75
   ducite ab urbe domum, mea carmina, ducite Daphnin.
necte tribus nodis ternos, Amarylli, colores;
necte, Amarylli, modo et 'Veneris' dic 'vincula necto.'
   ducite ab urbe domum, mea carmina, ducite Daphnin.
limus ut hic durescit, et haec ut cera liquescit   80
uno eodemque igni, sic nostro Daphnis amore.
sparge molam et fragilis incende bitumine lauros.
Daphnis me malus urit, ego hanc in Daphnide laurum.
   ducite ab urbe domum, mea carmina, ducite Daphnin.
talis amor Daphnin qualis cum fessa iuvencum   85
per nemora atque altos quaerendo bucula lucos
propter aquae rivum viridi procumbit in ulva
perdita, nec serae meminit decedere nocti,
talis amor teneat, nec sit mihi cura mederi.   89
   ducite ab urbe domum, mea carmina, ducite Daphnin.
has olim exuvias mihi perfidus ille reliquit,
pignora cara sui, quae nunc ego limine in ipso,
terra, tibi mando; debent haec pignora Daphnin.
   ducite ab urbe domum, mea carmina, ducite Daphnin.
has herbas atque haec Ponto mihi lecta venena   95
ipse dedit Moeris (nascuntur plurima Ponto);
his ego saepe lupum fieri et se condere silvis
Moerim, saepe animas imis excire sepulcris,
atque satas alio vidi traducere messis.   99
   ducite ab urbe domum, mea carmina, ducite Daphnin.
fer cineres, Amarylli, foras rivoque fluenti

transque caput iace, nec respexeris. his ego Daphnin
adgrediar; nihil ille deos, nil carmina curat.
ducite ab urbe domum, mea carmina, ducite Daphnin.
aspice: corripuit tremulis altaria flammis   105
sponte sua, dum ferre moror, cinis ipse. bonum sit!
nescio quid certe est, et Hylax in limine latrat.
credimus? an, qui amant, ipsi sibi somnia fingunt?
parcite, ab urbe venit, iam parcite carmina, Daphnis.

ECLOGUE 9

Lycidas   Moeris

L. Quo te, Moeri, pedes? an, quo via ducit, in urbem?
M. O Lycida, vivi pervenimus, advena nostri
(quod numquam veriti sumus) ut possessor agelli
diceret: 'haec mea sunt; veteres migrate coloni.'
nunc victi, tristes, quoniam fors omnia versat,   5
hos illi (quod nec vertat bene) mittimus haedos.
L. Certe equidem audieram, qua se subducere colles
incipiunt mollique iugum demittere clivo,
usque ad aquam et veteres, iam fracta cacumina, fagos,
omnia carminibus vestrum servasse Menalcan.   10
M. Audieras, et fama fuit; sed carmina tantum
nostra valent, Lycida, tela inter Martia quantum
Chaonias dicunt aquila veniente columbas.
quod nisi me quacumque novas incidere lites
ante sinistra cava monuisset ab ilice cornix,   15
nec tuus hic Moeris nec viveret ipse Menalcas.
L. Heu, cadit in quemquam tantum scelus? heu, tua nobis
paene simul tecum solacia rapta, Menalca?
quis caneret Nymphas? quis humum florentibus herbis
spargeret aut viridi fontis induceret umbra?   20
vel quae sublegi tacitus tibi carmina nuper,
cum te ad delicias ferres Amaryllida nostras?
'Tityre, dum redeo (brevis est via) pasce capellas,
et potum pastas age, Tityre, et inter agendum
occursare capro (cornu ferit ille) caveto.'   25
M. Immo haec, quae Varo necdum perfecta canebat:

'Vare, tuum nomen, superet modo Mantua nobis,
Mantua vae miserae nimium vicina Cremonae,
cantantes sublime ferent ad sidera cycni.'

L. Sic tua Cyrneas fugiant examina taxos,   30
sic cytiso pastae distendant ubera vaccae,
incipe, si quid habes. et me fecere poetam
Pierides, sunt et mihi carmina, me quoque dicunt
vatem pastores; sed non ego credulus illis.
nam neque adhuc Vario videor nec dicere Cinna   35
digna, sed argutos inter strepere anser olores.

M. Id quidem ago et tacitus, Lycida, mecum ipse voluto,
si valeam meminisse; neque est ignobile carmen.
'huc ades, o Galatea; quis est nam ludus in undis?
hic ver purpureum, varios hic flumina circum   40
fundit humus flores, hic candida populus antro
imminet et lentae texunt umbracula vites.
huc ades; insani feriant sine litora fluctus.'

L. Quid, quae te pura solum sub nocte canentem
audieram? numeros memini, si verba tenerem: 45
'Daphni, quid antiquos signorum suspicis ortus?
ecce Dionaei processit Caesaris astrum,
astrum quo segetes gauderent frugibus et quo
duceret apricis in collibus uva colorem.
insere, Daphni, piros: carpent tua poma nepotes.'   50

M. Omnia fert aetas, animum quoque; saepe ego longos
cantando puerum memini me condere soles:
nunc oblita mihi tot carmina, vox quoque Moerim
iam fugit ipsa: lupi Moerim videre priores.
sed tamen ista satis referet tibi saepe Menalcas.   55

L. Causando nostros in longum ducis amores.
et nunc omne tibi stratum silet aequor, et omnes,
aspice, ventosi ceciderunt murmuris aurae.
hinc adeo media est nobis via; namque sepulcrum
incipit apparere Bianoris. hic, ubi densas   60
agricolae stringunt frondes, hic, Moeri, canamus:
hic haedos depone, tamen veniemus in urbem.
aut si nox pluviam ne colligat ante veremur,
cantantes licet usque (minus via laedet) eamus;
cantantes ut eamus, ego hoc te fasce levabo.   65

M. Desine plura, puer, et quod nunc instat agamus;
   carmina tum melius, cum venerit ipse, canemus.

ECLOGUE 10

Extremum hunc, Arethusa, mihi concede laborem:
pauca meo Gallo, sed quae legat ipsa Lycoris,
carmina sunt dicenda; neget quis carmina Gallo?
sic tibi, cum fluctus subterlabere Sicanos,
Doris amara suam non intermisceat undam,   5
incipe; sollicitos Galli dicamus amores,
dum tenera attondent simae virgulta capellae.
non canimus surdis, respondent omnia silvae.
   Quae nemora aut qui vos saltus habuere, puellae
Naides, indigno cum Gallus amore peribat?   10
nam neque Parnasi vobis iuga, nam neque Pindi
ulla moram fecere, neque Aonie Aganippe.
illum etiam lauri, etiam flevere myricae,
pinifer illum etiam sola sub rupe iacentem
Maenalus et gelidi fleverunt saxa Lycaei.   15
stant et oves circum; nostri nec paenitet illas,
nec te paeniteat pecoris, divine poeta:
et formosus ovis ad flumina pavit Adonis.
venit et upilio, tardi venere subulci,
uvidus hiberna venit de glande Menalcas.   20
omnes 'unde amor iste' rogant 'tibi?' venit Apollo:
'Galle, quid insanis?' inquit 'tua cura Lycoris
perque nives alium perque horrida castra secuta est.'
venit et agresti capitis Silvanus honore,
florentis ferulas et grandia lilia quassans.   25
Pan deus Arcadiae venit, quem vidimus ipsi
sanguineis ebuli bacis minioque rubentem.
'ecquis erit modus?' inquit 'Amor non talia curat,
nec lacrimis crudelis Amor nec gramina rivis
nec cytiso saturantur apes nec fronde capellae.'   30
tristis at ille 'tamen cantabitis, Arcades' inquit
'montibus haec vestris, soli cantare periti
Arcades. o mihi tum quam molliter ossa quiescant,

vestra meos olim si fistula dicat amores!
atque utinam ex vobis unus vestrique fuissem   35
aut custos gregis aut maturae vinitor uvae!
certe sive mihi Phyllis sive esset Amyntas,
seu quicumque furor (quid tum, si fuscus Amyntas?
et nigrae violae sunt et vaccinia nigra),
mecum inter salices lenta sub vite iaceret;   40
serta mihi Phyllis legeret, cantaret Amyntas.
hic gelidi fontes, hic mollia prata, Lycori,
hic nemus; hic ipso tecum consumerer aevo.
nunc insanus amor duri me Martis in armis
tela inter media atque adversos detinet hostis.   45
tu procul a patria (nec sit mihi credere tantum)
Alpinas, a! dura, nives et frigora Rheni
me sine sola vides. a, te ne frigora laedant!
a, tibi ne teneras glacies secet aspera plantas!
ibo et Chalcidico quae sunt mihi condita versu   50
carmina pastoris Siculi modulabor avena.
certum est in silvis inter spelaea ferarum
malle pati tenerisque meos incidere amores
arboribus: crescent illae, crescetis, amores.
interea mixtis lustrabo Maenala Nymphis,   55
aut acris venabor apros. non me ulla vetabunt
frigora Parthenios canibus circumdare saltus.
iam mihi per rupes videor lucosque sonantis
ire, libet Partho torquere Cydonia cornu
spicula—tamquam haec sit nostri medicina furoris,   60
aut deus ille malis hominum mitescere discat.
iam neque Hamadryades rursus neque carmina nobis
ipsa placent; ipsae rursus concedite silvae.
non illum nostri possunt mutare labores,
nec si frigoribus mediis Hebrumque bibamus,   65
Sithoniasque nives hiemis subeamus aquosae,
nec si, cum moriens alta liber aret in ulmo,
Aethiopum versemus ovis sub sidere Cancri.
omnia vincit Amor: et nos cedamus Amori.'
    Haec sat erit, divae, vestrum cecinisse poetam,   70
dum sedet et gracili fiscellam texit hibisco,
Pierides: vos haec facietis maxima Gallo,
Gallo, cuius amor tantum mihi crescit in horas

quantum vere novo viridis se subicit alnus.
surgamus: solet esse gravis cantantibus umbra,   75
iuniperi gravis umbra; nocent et frugibus umbrae.
ite domum saturae, venit Hesperus, ite capellae.

The Georgics

GEORGICS

BOOK 1

Quid faciat laetas segetes, quo sidere terram
vertere, Maecenas, ulmisque adiungere vitis
conveniat, quae cura boum, qui cultus habendo
sit pecori, apibus quanta experientia parcis,
hinc canere incipiam. vos, o clarissima mundi   5
lumina, labentem caelo quae ducitis annum;
Liber et alma Ceres, vestro si munere tellus
Chaoniam pingui glandem mutavit arista,
poculaque inventis Acheloia miscuit uvis;
et vos, agrestum praesentia numina, Fauni,   10
(ferte simul Faunique pedem Dryadesque puellae:
munera vestra cano); tuque o, cui prima frementem
fudit equum magno tellus percussa tridenti,
Neptune; et cultor nemorum, cui pinguia Ceae
ter centum nivei tondent dumeta iuvenci;   15
ipse nemus linquens patrium saltusque Lycaei
Pan, ovium custos, tua si tibi Maenala curae,
adsis, o Tegeaee, favens, oleaeque Minerva
inventrix, uncique puer monstrator aratri,
et teneram ab radice ferens, Silvane, cupressum;   20
dique deaeque omnes, studium quibus arva tueri,
quique novas alitis non ullo semine fruges,
quique satis largum caelo demittitis imbrem;
tuque adeo, quem mox quae sint habitura deorum
concilia incertum est, urbisne invisere, Caesar,   25
terrarumque velis curam, et te maximus orbis
auctorem frugum tempestatumque potentem
accipiat cingens materna tempora myrto,
an deus immensi venias maris ac tua nautae
numina sola colant, tibi serviat ultima Thule,   30
teque sibi generum Tethys emat omnibus undis,
anne novum tardis sidus te mensibus addas,

qua locus Erigonen inter Chelasque sequentis
panditur (ipse tibi iam bracchia contrahit ardens
Scorpius et caeli iusta plus parte reliquit)—   35
quidquid eris (nam te nec sperant Tartara regem,
nec tibi regnandi veniat tam dira cupido,
quamvis Elysios miretur Graecia campos
nec repetita sequi curet Proserpina matrem),
da facilem cursum atque audacibus adnue coeptis,   40
ignarosque viae mecum miseratus agrestis
ingredere et votis iam nunc adsuesce vocari.
    Vere novo, gelidus canis cum montibus umor
liquitur et Zephyro putris se glaeba resolvit,
depresso incipiat iam tum mihi taurus aratro   45
ingemere, et sulco attritus splendescere vomer.
illa seges demum votis respondet avari
agricolae, bis quae solem, bis frigora sensit;
illius immensae ruperunt horrea messes.
ac prius ignotum ferro quam scindimus aequor,   50
ventos et varium caeli praediscere morem
cura sit ac patrios cultusque habitusque locorum,
et quid quaeque ferat regio et quid quaeque recuset.
hic segetes, illic veniunt felicius uvae,
arborei fetus alibi atque iniussa virescunt   55
gramina. nonne vides, croceos ut Tmolus odores,
India mittit ebur, molles sua tura Sabaei,
at Chalybes nudi ferrum, virosaque Pontus
castorea, Eliadum palmas Epirus equarum?
continuo has leges aeternaque foedera certis   60
imposuit natura locis, quo tempore primum
Deucalion vacuum lapides iactavit in orbem,
unde homines nati, durum genus. ergo age, terrae
pingue solum primis extemplo a mensibus anni
fortes invertant tauri, glaebasque iacentis   65
pulverulenta coquat maturis solibus aestas;
at si non fuerit tellus fecunda, sub ipsum
Arcturum tenui sat erit suspendere sulco:
illic, officiant laetis ne frugibus herbae,
hic, sterilem exiguus ne deserat umor harenam.   70
    Alternis idem tonsas cessare novalis
et segnem patiere situ durescere campum;

aut ibi flava seres mutato sidere farra,
unde prius laetum siliqua quassante legumen
aut tenuis fetus viciae tristisque lupini   75
sustuleris fragilis calamos silvamque sonantem.
urit enim lini campum seges, urit avenae,
urunt Lethaeo perfusa papavera somno;
sed tamen alternis facilis labor, arida tantum
ne saturare fimo pingui pudeat sola neve   .   80
effetos cinerem immundum iactare per agros.
sic quoque mutatis requiescunt fetibus arva,
nec nulla interea est inaratae gratia terrae.
saepe etiam sterilis incendere profuit agros
atque levem stipulam crepitantibus urere flammis: 85
sive inde occultas viris et pabula terrae.
pinguia concipiunt, sive illis omne per ignem
excoquitur vitium atque exsudat inutilis umor,
seu pluris calor ille vias et caeca relaxat
spiramenta, novas veniat qua sucus in herbas,   90
seu durat magis et venas astringit hiantis,
ne tenues pluviae rapidive potentia solis
acrior aut Boreae penetrabile frigus adurat.
multum adeo, rastris glaebas qui frangit inertis
vimineasque trahit cratis, iuvat arva, neque illum   95
flava Ceres alto nequiquam spectat Olympo;
et qui, proscisso quae suscitat aequore terga,
rursus in obliquum verso perrumpit aratro
exercetque frequens tellurem atque imperat arvis.
    Umida solstitia atque hiemes orate serenas,   100
agricolae; hiberno laetissima pulvere farra,
laetus ager: nullo tantum se Mysia cultu
iactat et ipsa suas mirantur Gargara messis.
quid dicam iacto qui semine comminus arva
insequitur cumulosque ruit male pinguis harenae,   105
deinde satis fluvium inducit rivosque sequentis,
et, cum exustus ager morientibus aestuat herbis,
ecce supercilio clivosi tramitis undam
elicit? illa cadens raucum per levia murmur
saxa ciet, scatebrisque arentia temperat arva.   110
quid qui, ne gravidis procumbat culmus aristis,
luxuriem segetum tenera depascit in herba

cum primum sulcos aequant sata, quique paludis
collectum umorem bibula deducit harena?
praesertim incertis si mensibus amnis abundans 115
exit et obducto late tenet omnia limo,
unde cavae tepido sudant umore lacunae.
   Nec tamen, haec cum sint hominumque boumque
   labores
versando terram experti, nihil improbus anser
Strymoniaeque grues et amaris intiba fibris 120
officiunt aut umbra nocet. pater ipse colendi
haud facilem esse viam voluit, primusque per artem
movit agros, curis acuens mortalia corda
nec torpere gravi passus sua regna veterno.
ante Iovem nulli subigebant arva coloni; 125
ne signare quidem aut partiri limite campum
fas erat; in medium quaerebant, ipsaque tellus
omnia liberius nullo poscente ferebat.
ille malum virus serpentibus addidit atris,
praedarique lupos iussit pontumque moveri, 130
mellaque decussit foliis ignemque removit,
et passim rivis currentia vina repressit,
ut varias usus meditando extunderet artis
paulatim, et sulcis frumenti quaereret herbam,
et silicis venis abstrusum excuderet ignem. 135
tunc alnos primum fluvii sensere cavatas;
navita tum stellis numeros et nomina fecit
Pleiadas, Hyadas, claramque Lycaonis Arcton;
tum laqueis captare feras et fallere visco
inventum et magnos canibus circumdare saltus; 140
atque alius latum funda iam verberat amnem
alta petens, pelagoque alius trahit umida lina;
tum ferri rigor atque argutae lammina serrae
(nam primi cuneis scindebant fissile lignum),
tum variae venere artes. labor omnia vicit 145
improbus et duris urgens in rebus egestas.
   Prima Ceres ferro mortalis vertere terram
instituit, cum iam glandes atque arbuta sacrae
deficerent silvae et victum Dodona negaret.
mox et frumentis labor additus, ut mala culmos 150
esset robigo segnisque horreret in arvis

carduus; intereunt segetes, subit aspera silva
lappaeque tribolique, interque nitentia culta
infelix lolium et steriles dominantur avenae.
quod nisi et adsiduis herbam insectabere rastris   155
et sonitu terrebis avis et ruris opaci
falce premes umbras votisque vocaveris imbrem,
heu magnum alterius frustra spectabis acervum,
concussaque famem in silvis solabere quercu.
    Dicendum et quae sint duris agrestibus arma,   160
quis sine nec potuere seri nec surgere messes:
vomis et inflexi primum grave robur aratri,
tardaque Eleusinae matris volventia plaustra,
tribulaque traheaeque et iniquo pondere rastri;
virgea praeterea Celei vilisque supellex,   165
arbuteae crates et mystica vannus Iacchi.
omnia quae multo ante memor provisa repones,
si te digna manet divini gloria ruris.
continuo in silvis magna vi flexa domatur
in burim et curvi formam accipit ulmus aratri.   170
huic a stirpe pedes temo protentus in octo,
binae aures, duplici aptantur dentalia dorso.
caeditur et tilia ante iugo levis altaque fagus
stivaque, quae currus a tergo torqueat imos,
et suspensa focis explorat robora fumus.   175
    Possum multa tibi veterum praecepta referre,
ni refugis tenuisque piget cognoscere curas.
area cum primis ingenti aequanda cylindro
et vertenda manu et creta solidanda tenaci,
ne subeant herbae neu pulvere victa fatiscat,   180
tum variae inludant pestes: saepe exiguus mus
sub terris posuitque domos atque horrea fecit,
aut oculis capti fodere cubilia talpae,
inventusque cavis bufo et quae plurima terrae
monstra ferunt, populatque ingentem farris acervum   185
curculio atque inopi metuens formica senectae.
contemplator item, cum se nux plurima silvis
induet in florem et ramos curvabit olentis:
si superant fetus, pariter frumenta sequentur,
magnaque cum magno veniet tritura calore;   190
at si luxuria foliorum exuberat umbra,

nequiquam pinguis palea teret area culmos.
semina vidi equidem multos medicare serentis
et nitro prius et nigra perfundere amurca,
grandior ut fetus siliquis fallacibus esset,   195
et quamvis igni exiguo properata maderent.
vidi lecta diu et multo spectata labore
degenerare tamen, ni vis humana quotannis
maxima quaeque manu legeret. sic omnia fatis
in peius ruere ac retro sublapsa referri,   200
non aliter quam qui adverso vix flumine lembum
remigiis subigit, si bracchia forte remisit,
atque illum in praeceps prono rapit alveus amni.
    Praeterea tam sunt Arcturi sidera nobis
Haedorumque dies servandi et lucidus Anguis,   205
quam quibus in patriam ventosa per aequora vectis
Pontus et ostriferi fauces temptantur Abydi.
Libra dies somnique pares ubi fecerit horas
et medium luci atque umbris iam dividit orbem,
exercete, viri, tauros, serite hordea campis   210
usque sub extremum brumae intractabilis imbrem;
nec non et lini segetem et Cereale papaver
tempus humo tegere et iamdudum incumbere aratris,
dum sicca tellure licet, dum nubila pendent.
vere fabis satio; tum te quoque, Medica, putres   215
accipiunt sulci et milio venit annua cura,
candidus auratis aperit cum cornibus annum
Taurus et averso cedens Canis occidit astro.
at si triticeam in messem robustaque farra
exercebis humum solisque instabis aristis,   220
ante tibi Eoae Atlantides abscondantur
Cnosiaque ardentis decedat stella Coronae,
debita quam sulcis committas semina quamque
invitae properes anni spem credere terrae.
multi ante occasum Maiae coepere; sed illos   225
exspectata seges vanis elusit avenis.
si vero viciamque seres vilemque phaselum,
nec Pelusiacae curam aspernabere lentis,
haud obscura cadens mittet tibi signa Bootes:
incipe et ad medias sementem extende pruinas.   230
    Idcirco certis dimensum partibus orbem

per duodena regit mundi sol aureus astra.
quinque tenent caelum zonae: quarum una corusco
semper sole rubens et torrida semper ab igni;
quam circum extremae dextra laevaque trahuntur   235
caeruleae, glacie concretae atque imbribus atris;
has inter mediamque duae mortalibus aegris
munere concessae divum, et via secta per ambas,
obliquus qua se signorum verteret ordo.
mundus, ut ad Scythiam Riphaeasque arduus arces   240
consurgit, premitur Libyae devexus in Austros.
hic vertex nobis semper sublimis; at illum
sub pedibus Styx atra videt Manesque profundi.
maximus hic flexu sinuoso elabitur Anguis
circum perque duas in morem fluminis Arctos,   245
Arctos Oceani metuentis aequore tingi.
illic, ut perhibent, aut intempesta silet nox
semper et obtenta densentur nocte tenebrae;
aut redit a nobis Aurora diemque reducit,
nosque ubi primus equis Oriens adflavit anhelis   250
illic sera rubens accendit lumina Vesper.
hinc tempestates dubio praediscere caelo
possumus, hinc messisque diem tempusque serendi,
et quando infidum remis impellere marmor
conveniat, quando armatas deducere classis,   255
aut tempestivam silvis evertere pinum;
nec frustra signorum obitus speculamur et ortus,
temporibusque parem diversis quattuor annum.
     Frigidus agricolam si quando continet imber,
multa, forent quae mox caelo properanda sereno,   260
maturare datur: durum procudit arator
vomeris obtunsi dentem, cavat arbore lintres,
aut pecori signum aut numeros impressit acervis.
exacuunt alii vallos furcasque bicornis,
atque Amerina parant lentae retinacula viti.   265
nunc facilis rubea texatur fiscina virga,
nunc torrete igni fruges, nunc frangite saxo.
quippe etiam festis quaedam exercere diebus
fas et iura sinunt: rivos deducere nulla
religio vetuit, segeti praetendere saepem,   270
insidias avibus moliri, incendere vepres,

balantumque gregem fluvio mersare salubri.
saepe oleo tardi costas agitator aselli
vilibus aut onerat pomis, lapidemque revertens
incusum aut atrae massam picis urbe reportat.   275
    Ipsa dies alios alio dedit ordine Luna
felicis operum. quintam fuge: pallidus Orcus
Eumenidesque satae; tum partu Terra nefando
Coeumque Iapetumque creat saevumque Typhoea
et coniuratos caelum rescindere fratres.   280
ter sunt conati imponere Pelio Ossam
scilicet atque Ossae frondosum involvere Olympum;
ter pater exstructos disiecit fulmine montis.
septima post decimam felix et ponere vitem
et prensos domitare boves et licia telae   285
addere. nona fugae melior, contraria furtis.
    Multa adeo gelida melius se nocte dedere,
aut cum sole novo terras inrorat Eous.
nocte leves melius stipulae, nocte arida prata
tondentur, noctes lentus non deficit umor.   290
et quidam seros hiberni ad luminis ignis
pervigilat ferroque faces inspicat acuto.
interea longum cantu solata laborem
arguto coniunx percurrit pectine telas,
aut dulcis musti Volcano decoquit umorem   295
et foliis undam trepidi despumat aeni.
at rubicunda Ceres medio succiditur aestu,
et medio tostas aestu terit area fruges.
nudus ara, sere nudus. hiems ignava colono:
frigoribus parto agricolae plerumque fruuntur   300
mutuaque inter se laeti convivia curant.
invitat genialis hiems curasque resolvit,
ceu pressae cum iam portum tetigere carinae,
puppibus et laeti nautae imposuere coronas.
sed tamen et quernas glandes tum stringere tempus   305
et lauri bacas oleamque cruentaque myrta,
tum gruibus pedicas et retia ponere cervis
auritosque sequi lepores, tum figere dammas
stuppea torquentem Balearis verbera fundae,
cum nix alta iacet, glaciem cum flumina trudunt.   310
    Quid tempestates autumni et sidera dicam,

atque, ubi iam breviorque dies et mollior aestas,
quae vigilanda viris? vel cum ruit imbriferum ver,
spicea iam campis cum messis inhorruit et cum
frumenta in viridi stipula lactentia turgent?   315
saepe ego, cum flavis messorem induceret arvis
agricola et fragili iam stringeret hordea culmo,
omnia ventorum concurrere proelia vidi,
quae gravidam late segetem ab radicibus imis
sublimem expulsam eruerent; ita turbine nigro   320
ferret hiems culmumque levem stipulasque volantis.
saepe etiam immensum caelo venit agmen aquarum
et foedam glomerant tempestatem imbribus atris
collectae ex alto nubes; ruit arduus aether,
et pluvia ingenti sata laeta boumque labores   325
diluit; implentur fossae et cava flumina crescunt
cum sonitu fervetque fretis spirantibus aequor.
ipse pater media nimborum in nocte corusca
fulmina molitur dextra, quo maxima motu
terra tremit, fugere ferae et mortalia corda   330
per gentis humilis stravit pavor; ille flagranti
aut Athon aut Rhodopen aut alta Ceraunia telo
deicit; ingeminant Austri et densissimus imber;
nunc nemora ingenti vento, nunc litora plangunt.
hoc metuens caeli mensis et sidera serva,   335
frigida Saturni sese quo stella receptet,
quos ignis caelo Cyllenius erret in orbis.
in primis venerare deos, atque annua magnae
sacra refer Cereri laetis operatus in herbis
extremae sub casum hiemis, iam vere sereno.   340
tum pingues agni et tum mollissima vina,
tum somni dulces densaeque in montibus umbrae.
cuncta tibi Cererem pubes agrestis adoret:
cui tu lacte favos et miti dilue Baccho,
terque novas circum felix eat hostia fruges,   345
omnis quam chorus et socii comitentur ovantes,
et Cererem clamore vocent in tecta; neque ante
falcem maturis quisquam supponat aristis
quam Cereri torta redimitus tempora quercu
det motus incompositos et carmina dicat.   350
    Atque haec ut certis possemus discere signis,

aestusque pluviasque et agentis frigora ventos,
ipse pater statuit quid menstrua luna moneret,
quo signo caderent Austri, quid saepe videntes
agricolae propius stabulis armenta tenerent.   355
continuo ventis surgentibus aut freta ponti
incipiunt agitata tumescere et aridus altis
montibus audiri fragor, aut resonantia longe
litora misceri et nemorum increbrescere murmur.
iam sibi tum a curvis male temperat unda carinis,   360
cum medio celeres revolant ex aequore mergi
clamoremque ferunt ad litora, cumque marinae
in sicco ludunt fulicae, notasque paludes
deserit atque altam supra volat ardea nubem.
saepe etiam stellas vento impendente videbis   365
praecipitis caelo labi, noctisque per umbram
flammarum longos a tergo albescere tractus;
saepe levem paleam et frondes volitare caducas,
aut summa nantis in aqua conludere plumas.
at Boreae de parte trucis cum fulminat et cum   370
Eurique Zephyrique tonat domus, omnia plenis
rura natant fossis atque omnis navita ponto
umida vela legit. numquam imprudentibus imber
obfuit: aut illum surgentem vallibus imis
aeriae fugere grues, aut bucula caelum   375
suspiciens patulis captavit naribus auras,
aut arguta lacus circumvolitavit hirundo
et veterem in limo ranae cecinere querelam.
saepius et tectis penetralibus extulit ova
angustum formica terens iter, et bibit ingens   380
arcus, et e pastu decedens agmine magno
corvorum increpuit densis exercitus alis.
iam variae pelagi volucres et quae Asia circum
dulcibus in stagnis rimantur prata Caystri—
certatim largos umeris infundere rores,   385
nunc caput obiectare fretis, nunc currere in undas
et studio incassum videas gestire lavandi.
tum cornix plena pluviam vocat improba voce
et sola in sicca secum spatiatur harena.
ne nocturna quidem carpentes pensa puellae   390
nescivere hiemem, testa cum ardente viderent

scintillare oleum et putris concrescere fungos.
Nec minus ex imbri soles et aperta serena
prospicere et certis poteris cognoscere signis:
nam neque tum stellis acies obtunsa videtur, 395
nec fratris radiis obnoxia surgere Luna,
tenuia nec lanae per caelum vellera ferri;
non tepidum ad solem pennas in litore pandunt
dilectae Thetidi alcyones, non ore solutos
immundi meminere sues iactare maniplos. 400
at nebulae magis ima petunt campoque recumbunt,
solis et occasum servans de culmine summo
nequiquam seros exercet noctua cantus.
apparet liquido sublimis in aere Nisus,
et pro purpureo poenas dat Scylla capillo: 405
quacumque illa levem fugiens secat aethera pennis,
ecce inimicus atrox magno stridore per auras
insequitur Nisus; qua se fert Nisus ad auras,
illa levem fugiens raptim secat aethera pennis.
tum liquidas corvi presso ter gutture voces 410
aut quater ingeminant, et saepe cubilibus altis
nescio qua praeter solitum dulcedine laeti
inter se in foliis strepitant; iuvat imbribus actis
progeniem parvam dulcisque revisere nidos:
haud equidem credo, quia sit divinitus illis 415
ingenium aut rerum fato prudentia maior;
verum ubi tempestas et caeli mobilis umor
mutavere vias et Iuppiter umidus Austris
denset erant quae rara modo, et quae densa relaxat,
vertuntur species animorum, et pectora motus 420
nunc alios, alios dum nubila ventus agebat,
concipiunt: hinc ille avium concentus in agris
et laetae pecudes et ovantes gutture corvi.
Si vero solem ad rapidum lunasque sequentis
ordine respicies, numquam te crastina fallet 425
hora, neque insidiis noctis capiere serenae.
luna revertentis cum primum colligit ignis,
si nigrum obscuro comprenderit aëra cornu,
maximus agricolis pelagoque parabitur imber;
at si virgineum suffuderit ore ruborem, 430
ventus erit: vento semper rubet aurea Phoebe.

sin ortu quarto (namque is certissimus auctor)
pura neque obtunsis per caelum cornibus ibit,
totus et ille dies et qui nascentur ab illo
exactum ad mensem pluvia ventisque carebunt,   435
votaque servati solvent in litore nautae
Glauco et Panopeae et Inoo Melicertae.
sol quoque et exoriens et cum se condet in undas
signa dabit; solem certissima signa sequuntur,
et quae mane refert et quae surgentibus astris.   440
ille ubi nascentem maculis variaverit ortum
conditus in nubem medioque refugerit orbe,
suspecti tibi sint imbres: namque urget ab alto
arboribusque satisque Notus pecorique sinister.
aut ubi sub lucem densa inter nubila sese   445
diversi rumpent radii, aut ubi pallida surget
Tithoni croceum linquens Aurora cubile,
heu, male tum mitis defendet pampinus uvas;
tam multa in tectis crepitans salit horrida grando.
hoc etiam, emenso cum iam decedit Olympo,   450
profuerit meminisse magis; nam saepe videmus
ipsius in vultu varios errare colores:
caeruleus pluviam denuntiat, igneus Euros;
sin maculae incipiunt rutilo immiscerier igni,
omnia tum pariter vento nimbisque videbis   455
fervere: non illa quisquam me nocte per altum
ire neque ab terra moneat convellere funem.
at si, cum referetque diem condetque relatum,
lucidus orbis erit, frustra terrebere nimbis
et claro silvas cernes Aquilone moveri.   460
denique, quid vesper serus vehat, unde serenas
ventus agat nubes, quid cogitet umidus Auster,
sol tibi signa dabit. solem quis dicere falsum
audeat? ille etiam caecos instare tumultus
saepe monet fraudemque et operta tumescere bella.   465
ille etiam exstincto miseratus Caesare Romam,
cum caput obscura nitidum ferrugine texit
impiaque aeternam timuerunt saecula noctem.
tempore quamquam illo tellus quoque et aequora ponti,
obscenaeque canes importunaeque volucres   470
signa dabant. quotiens Cyclopum effervere in agros

vidimus undantem ruptis fornacibus Aetnam,
flammarumque globos liquefactaque volvere saxa!
armorum sonitum toto Germania caelo
audiit, insolitis tremuerunt motibus Alpes.   475
vox quoque per lucos vulgo exaudita silentis
ingens, et simulacra modis pallentia miris
visa sub obscurum noctis, pecudesque locutae
(infandum!); sistunt amnes terraeque dehiscunt,
et maestum inlacrimat templis ebur aeraque sudant.   480
proluit insano contorquens vertice silvas
fluviorum rex Eridanus camposque per omnis
cum stabulis armenta tulit. nec tempore eodem
tristibus aut extis fibrae apparere minaces
aut puteis manare cruor cessavit, et altae   485
per noctem resonare lupis ululantibus urbes.
non alias caelo ceciderunt plura sereno
fulgura nec diri totiens arsere cometae.
ergo inter sese paribus concurrere telis
Romanas acies iterum videre Philippi;   490
nec fuit indignum superis bis sanguine nostro
Emathiam et latos Haemi pinguescere campos.
scilicet et tempus veniet cum finibus illis
agricola incurvo terram molitus aratro
exesa inveniet scabra robigine pila,   495
aut gravibus rastris galeas pulsabit inanis,
grandiaque effossis mirabitur ossa sepulcris.
di patrii, Indigetes, et Romule Vestaque mater,
quae Tuscum Tiberim et Romana Palatia servas,
hunc saltem everso iuvenem succurrere saeclo   500
ne prohibete. satis iam pridem sanguine nostro
Laomedonteae luimus periuria Troiae;
iam pridem nobis caeli te regia, Caesar,
invidet atque hominum queritur curare triumphos,
quippe ubi fas versum atque nefas; tot bella per orbem,   505
tam multae scelerum facies, non ullus aratro
dignus honos, squalent abductis arva colonis,
et curvae rigidum falces conflantur in ensem.
hinc movet Euphrates, illinc Germania bellum;
vicinae ruptis inter se legibus urbes   510
arma ferunt; saevit toto Mars impius orbe;

ut cum carceribus sese effudere quadrigae,
addunt in spatia, et frustra retinacula tendens
fertur equis auriga neque audit currus habenas.

GEORGICS

BOOK 2

Hactenus arvorum cultus et sidera caeli;
nunc te, Bacche, canam, nec non silvestria tecum
virgulta et prolem tarde crescentis olivae.
huc, pater o Lenaee (tuis hic omnia plena
muneribus, tibi pampineo gravidus autumno   5
floret ager, spumat plenis vindemia labris),
huc, pater o Lenaee, veni, nudataque musto
tinge novo mecum dereptis crura coturnis.
    Principio arboribus varia est natura creandis.
namque aliae nullis hominum cogentibus ipsae   10
sponte sua veniunt camposque et flumina late
curva tenent, ut molle siler lentaeque genistae,
populus et glauca canentia fronde salicta;
pars autem posito surgunt de semine, ut altae
castaneae, nemorumque Iovi quae maxima frondet   15
aesculus, atque habitae Grais oracula quercus.
pullulat ab radice aliis densissima silva,
ut cerasis ulmisque; etiam Parnasia laurus
parva sub ingenti matris se subicit umbra.
hos natura modos primum dedit, his genus omne   20
silvarum fruticumque viret nemorumque sacrorum:
sunt alii, quos ipse via sibi repperit usus.
hic plantas tenero abscindens de corpore matrum
deposuit sulcis, hic stirpes obruit arvo
quadrifidasque sudes et acuto robore vallos.   25
silvarumque aliae pressos propaginis arcus
exspectant et viva sua plantaria terra.
nil radicis egent aliae summumque putator
haud dubitat terrae referens mandare cacumen.
quin et caudicibus sectis (mirabile dictu)   30
truditur e sicco radix oleagina ligno;
et saepe alterius ramos impune videmus

vertere in alterius, mutatamque insita mala
ferre pirum et prunis lapidosa rubescere corna.
  Quare agite o proprios generatim discite cultus,   35
agricolae, fructusque feros mollite colendo,
neu segnes iaceant terrae. iuvat Ismara Baccho
conserere atque olea magnum vestire Taburnum.
tuque ades inceptumque una decurre laborem,
o decus, o famae merito pars maxima nostrae,   40
Maecenas, pelagoque volans da vela patenti.
non ego cuncta meis amplecti versibus opto,
non, mihi si linguae centum sint oraque centum,
ferrea vox. ades et primi lege litoris oram;
in manibus terrae: non hic te carmine ficto   45
atque per ambages et longa exorsa tenebo.
  Sponte sua quae se tollunt in luminis oras,
infecunda quidem, sed laeta et fortia surgunt;
quippe solo natura subest. tamen haec quoque, si quis
inserat aut scrobibus mandet mutata subactis,   50
exuerint silvestrem animum, cultuque frequenti
in quascumque voces artis haud tarda sequentur.
nec non et, sterilis quae stirpibus exit ab imis,
hoc faciat, vacuos si sit digesta per agros;
nunc altae frondes et rami matris opacant   55
crescentique adimunt fetus uruntque ferentem.
iam quae seminibus iactis se sustulit arbos,
tarda venit seris factura nepotibus umbram,
pomaque degenerant sucos oblita priores
et turpis avibus praedam fert uva racemos.   60
scilicet omnibus est labor impendendus, et omnes
cogendae in sulcum ac multa mercede domandae.
sed truncis oleae melius, propagine vites
respondent, solido Paphiae de robore myrtus,
plantis edurae coryli; nascuntur et ingens   65
fraxinus Herculeaeque arbos umbrosa coronae,
Chaoniique patris glandes; etiam ardua palma
nascitur et casus abies visura marinos.
inseritur vero et fetu nucis arbutus horrida,
et steriles platani malos gessere valentis,   70
castaneas fagus; ornusque incanuit albo
flore piri, glandemque sues fregere sub ulmis.

Nec modus inserere atque oculos imponere simplex.
nam qua se medio trudunt de cortice gemmae
et tenuis rumpunt tunicas, angustus in ipso   75
fit nodo sinus; huc aliena ex arbore germen
includunt udoque docent inolescere libro.
aut rursum enodes trunci resecantur, et alte
finditur in solidum cuneis via, deinde feraces
plantae immittuntur: nec longum tempus, et ingens ·   80
exiit ad caelum ramis felicibus arbos,
mirata estque novas frondes et non sua poma.
  Praeterea genus haud unum nec fortibus ulmis
nec salici lotoque nec Idaeis cyparissis,
nec pingues unam in faciem nascuntur olivae,   85
orchades et radii et amara pausia baca,
pomaque et Alcinoi silvae, nec surculus idem
Crustumiis Syriisque piris gravibusque volemis.
non eadem arboribus pendet vindemia nostris
quam Methymnaeo carpit de palmite Lesbos;   90
sunt Thasiae vites, sunt et Mareotides albae,
pinguibus hae terris habiles, levioribus illae,
et passo psithia utilior tenuisque lageos
temptatura pedes olim vincturaque linguam,
purpureae preciaeque, et quo te carmine dicam   95
Rhaetica? nec cellis ideo contende Falernis.
sunt et Aminneae vites, firmissima vina,
Tmolius adsurgit quibus et rex ipse Phanaeus,
Argitisque minor, cui non certaverit ulla
aut tantum fluere aut totidem durare per annos.   100
non ego te, dis et mensis accepta secundis,
transierim, Rhodia, et tumidis, bumaste, racemis.
sed neque quam multae species nec nomina quae sint
est numerus: neque enim numero comprendere refert;
quem qui scire velit, Libyci velit aequoris idem   105
dicere quam multae Zephyro turbentur harenae,
aut ubi navigiis violentior incidit Eurus
nosse quot Ionii veniant ad litora fluctus.
  Nec vero terrae ferre omnes omnia possunt.
fluminibus salices crassisque paludibus alni   110
nascuntur, steriles saxosis montibus orni;
litora myrtetis laetissima; denique apertos

Bacchus amat collis, Aquilonem et frigora taxi.
aspice et extremis domitum cultoribus orbem
Eoasque domos Arabum pictosque Gelonos: 115
divisae arboribus patriae. sola India nigrum
fert hebenum, solis est turea virga Sabaeis.
quid tibi odorato referam sudantia ligno
balsamaque et bacas semper frondentis acanthi?
quid nemora Aethiopum molli canentia lana,   120
velleraque ut foliis depectant tenuia Seres?
aut quos Oceano propior gerit India lucos,
extremi sinus orbis, ubi aëra vincere summum
arboris haud ullae iactu potuere sagittae
(et gens illa quidem sumptis non tarda pharetris)?   125
Media fert tristis sucos tardumque saporem
felicis mali, quo non praesentius ullum,
pocula si quando saevae infecere novercae
[miscueruntque herbas et non innoxia verba,]
auxilium venit ac membris agit atra venena.   130
ipsa ingens arbos faciemque simillima lauro;
et, si non alium late iactaret odorem,
laurus erat: folia haud ullis labentia ventis,
flos ad prima tenax; animas et olentia Medi
ora fovent illo et senibus medicantur anhelis.   135
    Sed neque Medorum silvae, ditissima terra,
nec pulcher Ganges atque auro turbidus Hermus
laudibus Italiae certent, non Bactra neque Indi
totaque turiferis Panchaia pinguis harenis.
haec loca non tauri spirantes naribus ignem   140
invertere satis immanis dentibus hydri,
nec galeis densisque virum seges horruit hastis;
sed gravidae fruges et Bacchi Massicus umor
implevere; tenent oleae armentaque laeta.
hinc bellator equus campo sese arduus infert,   145
hinc albi, Clitumne, greges et maxima taurus
victima, saepe tuo perfusi flumine sacro,
Romanos ad templa deum duxere trumphos.
hic ver adsiduum atque alienis mensibus aestas:
bis gravidae pecudes, bis pomis utilis arbos.   150
at rabidae tigres absunt et saeva leonum
semina, nec miseros fallunt aconita legentis,

nec rapit immensos orbis per humum neque tanto
squameus in spiram tractu se colligit anguis.
adde tot egregias urbes operumque laborem,   155
tot congesta manu praeruptis oppida saxis
fluminaque antiquos subterlabentia muros.
an mare quod supra memorem, quodque adluit infra?
anne lacus tantos? te, Lari maxime, teque,
fluctibus et fremitu adsurgens Benace marino?   ·   160
an memorem portus Lucrinoque addita claustra
atque indignatum magnis stridoribus aequor,
Iulia qua ponto longe sonat unda refuso
Tyrrhenusque fretis immittitur aestus Avernis?
haec eadem argenti rivos aerisque metalla   165
ostendit venis atque auro plurima fluxit.
haec genus acre virum, Marsos pubemque Sabellam
adsuetumque malo Ligurem Volscosque verutos
extulit, haec Decios Marios magnosque Camillos,
Scipiadas duros bello et te, maxime Caesar,   170
qui nunc extremis Asiae iam victor in oris
imbellem avertis Romanis arcibus Indum.
salve, magna parens frugum, Saturnia tellus,
magna virum: tibi res antiquae laudis et artis
ingredior sanctos ausus recludere fontis,   175
Ascraeumque cano Romana per oppida carmen.
    Nunc locus arvorum ingeniis, quae robora cuique,
quis color et quae sit rebus natura ferendis.
difficiles primum terrae collesque maligni,
tenuis ubi argilla et dumosis calculus arvis,   180
Palladia gaudent silva vivacis olivae.
indicio est tractu surgens oleaster eodem
plurimus et strati bacis silvestribus agri.
at quae pinguis humus dulcique uligine laeta,
quique frequens herbis et fertilis ubere campus   185
(qualem saepe cava montis convalle solemus
despicere: huc summis liquuntur rupibus amnes
felicemque trahunt limum) quique editus Austro
et filicem curvis invisam pascit aratris:
hic tibi praevalidas olim multoque fluentis   190
sufficiet Baccho vitis, hic fertilis uvae,
hic laticis, qualem pateris libamus et auro,

inflavit cum pinguis ebur Tyrrhenus ad aras,
lancibus et pandis fumantia reddimus exta.
sin armenta magis studium vitulosque tueri,   195
aut ovium fetum aut urentis culta capellas,
saltus et saturi petito longinqua Tarenti,
et qualem infelix amisit Mantua campum
pascentem niveos herboso flumine cycnos;
non liquidi gregibus fontes, non gramina derunt,   200
et quantum longis carpent armenta diebus
exigua tantum gelidus ros nocte reponet.
nigra fere et presso pinguis sub vomere terra
et cui putre solum (namque hoc imitamur arando),
optima frumentis; non ullo ex aequore cernes   205
plura domum tardis decedere plaustra iuvencis;
aut unde iratus silvam devexit arator
et nemora evertit multos ignava per annos,
antiquasque domos avium cum stirpibus imis
eruit; illae altum nidis petiere relictis;   210
at rudis enituit impulso vomere campus.
nam ieiuna quidem clivosi glarea ruris
vix humilis apibus casias roremque ministrat;
et tofus scaber et nigris exesa chelydris
creta negant alios aeque serpentibus agros   215
dulcem ferre cibum et curvas praebere latebras.
quae tenuem exhalat nebulam fumosque volucris
et bibit umorem et, cum vult, ex se ipsa remittit,
quaeque suo semper viridi se gramine vestit,
nec scabie et salsa laedit robigine ferrum,   220
illa tibi laetis intexet vitibus ulmos,
illa ferax oleo est, illam experiere colendo
et facilem pecori et patientem vomeris unci.
talem dives arat Capua et vicina Vesaevo
ora iugo et vacuis Clanius non aequus Acerris.   225
    Nunc quo quamque modo possis cognoscere dicam.
rara sit an supra morem si densa requires
(altera frumentis quoniam favet, altera Baccho,
densa magis Cereri, rarissima quaeque Lyaeo),
ante locum capies oculis, alteque iubebis   230
in solido puteum demitti, omnemque repones
rursus humum et pedibus summas aequabis harenas.

si derunt, rarum pecorique et vitibus almis
aptius uber erit; sin in sua posse negabunt
ire loca et scrobibus superabit terra repletis,   235
spissus ager: glaebas cunctantis crassaque terga
exspecta et validis terram proscinde iuvencis.
salsa autem tellus et quae perhibetur amara
(frugibus infelix ea, nec mansuescit arando
nec Baccho genus aut pomis sua nomina servat)   240
tale dabit specimen: tu spisso vimine qualos
colaque prelorum fumosis deripe tectis;
huc ager ille malus dulcesque a fontibus undae
ad plenum calcentur: aqua eluctabitur omnis
scilicet et grandes ibunt per vimina guttae;   245
at sapor indicium faciet manifestus et ora
tristia temptantum sensu torquebit amaro.
pinguis item quae sit tellus hoc denique pacto
discimus: haud umquam manibus iactata fatiscit,
sed picis in morem ad digitos lentescit habendo.   250
umida maiores herbas alit, ipsaque iusto
laetior. a, nimium ne sit mihi fertilis illa,
nec se praevalidam primis ostendat aristis!
quae gravis est ipso tacitam se pondere prodit,   254
quaeque levis. promptum est oculis praediscere nigram,
et quis cui color. at sceleratum exquirere frigus
difficile est: piceae tantum taxique nocentes
interdum aut hederae pandunt vestigia nigrae.
   His animadversis terram multo ante memento
excoquere et magnos scrobibus concidere montis,   260
ante supinatas Aquiloni ostendere glaebas
quam laetum infodias vitis genus. optima putri
arva solo: id venti curant gelidaeque pruinae
et labefacta movens robustus iugera fossor.
at si quos haud ulla viros vigilantia fugit,   265
ante locum similem exquirunt, ubi prima paretur
arboribus seges et quo mox digesta feratur,
mutatam ignorent subito ne semina matrem.
quin etiam caeli regionem in cortice signant,
ut, quo quaeque modo steterit, qua parte calores   270
austrinos tulerit, quae terga obverterit axi,
restituant: adeo in teneris consuescere multum est.

collibus an plano melius sit ponere vitem
quaere prius. si pinguis agros metabere campi,
densa sere: in denso non segnior ubere Bacchus;   275
sin tumulis acclive solum collisque supinos,
indulge ordinibus; nec setius omnis in unguem
arboribus positis secto via limite quadret:
ut saepe ingenti bello cum longa cohortis
explicuit legio et campo stetit agmen aperto,   280
derectaeque acies, ac late fluctuat omnis
aere renidenti tellus, necdum horrida miscent
proelia, sed dubius mediis Mars errat in armis.
omnia sint paribus numeris dimensa viarum;
non animum modo uti pascat prospectus inanem,   285
sed quia non aliter viris dabit omnibus aequas
terra, neque in vacuum poterunt se extendere rami.
    Forsitan et scrobibus quae sint fastigia quaeras.
ausim vel tenui vitem committere sulco.
altior ac penitus terrae defigitur arbos,   290
aesculus in primis, quae quantum vertice ad auras
aetherias tantum radice in Tartara tendit.
ergo non hiemes illam, non flabra neque imbres
convellunt: immota manet multosque nepotes,
multa virum volvens durando saecula vincit,   295
tum fortis late ramos et bracchia tendens
huc illuc media ipsa ingentem sustinet umbram.
    Neve tibi ad solem vergant vineta cadentem,
neve inter vitis corylum sere, neve flagella
summa pete aut summa defringe ex arbore plantas   300
(tantus amor terrae), neu ferro laede retunso
semina, neve oleae silvestris insere truncos.
nam saepe incautis pastoribus excidit ignis,
qui furtim pingui primum sub cortice tectus
robora comprendit, frondesque elapsus in altas   305
ingentem caelo sonitum dedit; inde secutus
per ramos victor perque alta cacumina regnat,
et totum involvit flammis nemus et ruit atram
ad caelum picea crassus caligine nubem,
praesertim si tempestas a vertice silvis   310
incubuit, glomeratque ferens incendia ventus.
hoc ubi, non a stirpe valent caesaeque reverti

possunt atque ima similes revirescere terra;
infelix superat foliis oleaster amaris.
　　Nec tibi tam prudens quisquam persuadeat auctor   315
tellurem Borea rigidam spirante movere.
rura gelu tunc claudit hiems, nec semine iacto
concretam patitur radicem adfigere terrae.
optima vinetis satio cum vere rubente
candida venit avis longis invisa colubris,   320
prima vel autumni sub frigora, cum rapidus Sol
nondum hiemem contingit equis, iam praeterit aestas.
ver adeo frondi nemorum, ver utile silvis,
vere tument terrae et genitalia semina poscunt.
tum pater omnipotens fecundis imbribus Aether   325
coniugis in gremium laetae descendit, et omnis
magnus alit magno commixtus corpore fetus.
avia tum resonant avibus virgulta canoris,
et Venerem certis repetunt armenta diebus;
parturit almus ager Zephyrique tepentibus auris   330
laxant arva sinus; superat tener omnibus umor,
inque novos soles audent se germina tuto
credere, nec metuit surgentis pampinus Austros
aut actum caelo magnis Aquilonibus imbrem,
sed trudit gemmas et frondes explicat omnis.   335
non alios prima crescentis origine mundi
inluxisse dies aliumve habuisse tenorem
crediderim: ver illud erat, ver magnus agebat
orbis, et hibernis parcebant flatibus Euri,
cum primae lucem pecudes hausere, virumque   340
terrea progenies duris caput extulit arvis,
immissaeque ferae silvis et sidera caelo.
nec res hunc tenerae possent perferre laborem,
si non tanta quies iret frigusque caloremque
inter, et exciperet caeli indulgentia terras.   345
　　Quod superest, quaecumque premes virgulta per agros
sparge fimo pingui et multa memor occule terra.
aut lapidem bibulum aut squalentis infode conchas;
inter enim labentur aquae, tenuisque subibit
halitus, atque animos tollent sata. iamque reperti   350
qui saxo super atque ingentis pondere testae
urgerent: hoc effusos munimen ad imbris,

hoc, ubi hiulca siti findit Canis aestifer arva.
    Seminibus positis superest diducere terram
saepius ad capita et duros iactare bidentis,   355
aut presso exercere solum sub vomere et ipsa
flectere luctantis inter vineta iuvencos;
tum levis calamos et rasae hastilia virgae
fraxineasque aptare sudes furcasque valentis,
viribus eniti quarum et contemnere ventos   360
adsuescant summasque sequi tabulata per ulmos.
    Ac dum prima novis adolescit frondibus aetas,
parcendum teneris, et dum se laetus ad auras
palmes agit laxis per purum immissus habenis,
ipsa acie nondum falcis temptanda, sed uncis   365
carpendae manibus frondes interque legendae.
inde ubi iam validis amplexae stirpibus ulmos
exierint, tum stringe comas, tum bracchia tonde
(ante reformidant ferrum), tum denique dura
exerce imperia et ramos compesce fluentis.   370
    Texendae saepes etiam et pecus omne tenendum,
praecipue dum frons tenera imprudensque laborum;
cui super indignas hiemes solemque potentem
silvestres uri adsidue capreaeque sequaces
inludunt, pascuntur oves avidaeque iuvencae.   375
frigora nec tantum cana concreta pruina
aut gravis incumbens scopulis arentibus aestas
quantum illi nocuere greges durique venenum
dentis et admorso signata in stirpe cicatrix.
non aliam ob culpam Baccho caper omnibus aris   380
caeditur et veteres ineunt proscaenia ludi,
praemiaque ingeniis pagos et compita circum
Thesidae posuere, atque inter pocula laeti
mollibus in pratis unctos saluere per utres;
nec non Ausonii, Troia gens missa, coloni   385
versibus incomptis ludunt risuque soluto,
oraque corticibus sumunt horrenda cavatis,
et te, Bacche, vocant per carmina laeta, tibique
oscilla ex alta suspendunt mollia pinu.
hinc omnis largo pubescit vinea fetu,   390
complentur vallesque cavae saltusque profundi
et quocumque deus circum caput egit honestum.

ergo rite suum Baccho dicemus honorem
carminibus patriis lancesque et liba feremus,
et ductus cornu stabit sacer hircus ad aram,   395
pinguiaque in veribus torrebimus exta colurnis.
    Est etiam ille labor curandis vitibus alter,
cui numquam exhausti satis est: namque omne
    quotannis
terque quaterque solum scindendum glaebaque versis
aeternum frangenda bidentibus, omne levandum   400
fronde nemus. redit agricolis labor actus in orbem
atque in se sua per vestigia volvitur annus.
ac iam olim, seras posuit cum vinea frondes
frigidus et silvis Aquilo decussit honorem,
iam tum acer curas venientem extendit in annum   405
rusticus, et curvo Saturni dente relictam
persequitur vitem attondens fingitque putando.
primus humum fodito, primus devecta cremato
sarmenta, et vallos primus sub tecta referto;
postremus metito. bis vitibus ingruit umbra,   410
bis segetem densis obducunt sentibus herbae;
durus uterque labor: laudato ingentia rura,
exiguum colito. nec non etiam aspera rusci
vimina per silvam et ripis fluvialis harundo
caeditur, incultique exercet cura salicti.   415
iam vinctae vites, iam falcem arbusta reponunt,
iam canit effectos extremus vinitor antes:
sollicitanda tamen tellus pulvisque movendus,
et iam maturis metuendus Iuppiter uvis.
    Contra non ulla est oleis cultura: neque illae   420
procurvam exspectant falcem rastrosque tenacis,
cum semel haeserunt arvis aurasque tulerunt;
ipsa satis tellus, cum dente recluditur unco
sufficit umorem et gravidas, cum vomere, fruges.
hoc pinguem et placitam Paci nutritor olivam.   425
    Poma quoque, ut primum truncos sensere valentis
et viris habuere suas, ad sidera raptim
vi propria nituntur opisque haud indiga nostrae.
nec minus interea fetu nemus omne gravescit,
sanguineisque inculta rubent aviaria bacis.   430
tondentur cytisi, taedas silva alta ministrat,

pascunturque ignes nocturni et lumina fundunt.
et dubitant homines serere atque impendere curam?
quid maiora sequar? salices humilesque genistae,
aut illae pecori frondem aut pastoribus umbram   435
sufficiunt saepemque satis et pabula melli.
et iuvat undantem buxo spectare Cytorum
Naryciaeque picis lucos, iuvat arva videre
non rastris, hominum non ulli obnoxia curae.
ipsae Caucasio steriles in vertice silvae,   440
quas animosi Euri adsidue franguntque feruntque,
dant alios aliae fetus, dant utile lignum
navigiis pinus, domibus cedrumque cupressosque.
hinc radios trivere rotis, hinc tympana plaustris
agricolae, et pandas ratibus posuere carinas.   445
viminibus salices fecundae, frondibus ulmi,
at myrtus validis hastilibus et bona bello
cornus, Ituraeos taxi torquentur in arcus.
nec tiliae leves aut torno rasile buxum
non formam accipiunt ferroque cavantur acuto.   450
nec non et torrentem undam levis innatat alnus
missa Pado, nec non et apes examina condunt
corticibusque cavis vitiosaeque ilicis alvo.
quid memorandum aeque Baccheia dona tulerunt?
Bacchus et ad culpam causas dedit; ille furentis   455
Centauros leto domuit, Rhoetumque Pholumque
et magno Hylaeum Lapithis cratere minantem.
   O fortunatos nimium, sua si bona norint,
agricolas! quibus ipsa procul discordibus armis
fundit humo facilem victum iustissima tellus.   460
si non ingentem foribus domus alta superbis
mane salutantum totis vomit aedibus undam,
nec varios inhiant pulchra testudine postis
inlusasque auro vestis Ephyreiaque aera,
alba neque Assyrio fucatur lana veneno,   465
nec casia liquidi corrumpitur usus olivi;
at secura quies et nescia fallere vita,
dives opum variarum, at latis otia fundis,
speluncae vivique lacus, at frigida Tempe
mugitusque boum mollesque sub arbore somni   470
non absunt; illic saltus ac lustra ferarum,

et patiens operum exiguoque adsueta iuventus,
sacra deum sanctique patres; extrema per illos
Iustitia excedens terris vestigia fecit.
     Me vero primum dulces ante omnia Musae,   475
quarum sacra fero ingenti percussus amore,
accipiant caelique vias et sidera monstrent,
defectus solis varios lunaeque labores;
unde tremor terris, qua vi maria alta tumescant
obicibus ruptis rursusque in se ipsa residant,   480
quid tantum Oceano properent se tingere soles
hiberni, vel quae tardis mora noctibus obstet.
sin has ne possim naturae accedere partis
frigidus obstiterit circum praecordia sanguis,
rura mihi et rigui placeant in vallibus amnes,   485
flumina amem silvasque inglorius. o ubi campi
Spercheosque et virginibus bacchata Lacaenis
Taygeta! o qui me gelidis convallibus Haemi
sistat, et ingenti ramorum protegat umbra!
felix qui potuit rerum cognoscere causas,   490
atque metus omnis et inexorabile fatum
subiecit pedibus strepitumque Acherontis avari:
fortunatus et ille deos qui novit agrestis
Panaque Silvanumque senem Nymphasque sorores.
illum non populi fasces, non purpura regum   495
flexit et infidos agitans discordia fratres,
aut coniurato descendens Dacus ab Histro,
non res Romanae perituraque regna; neque ille
aut doluit miserans inopem aut invidit habenti.
quos rami fructus, quos ipsa volentia rura   500
sponte tulere sua, carpsit, nec ferrea iura
insanumque forum aut populi tabularia vidit.
sollicitant alii remis freta caeca, ruuntque
in ferrum, penetrant aulas et limina regum;
hic petit excidiis urbem miserosque penatis,   505
ut gemma bibat et Sarrano dormiat ostro;
condit opes alius defossoque incubat auro;
hic stupet attonitus rostris, hunc plausus hiantem
per cuneos geminatus enim plebisque patrumque
corripuit; gaudent perfusi sanguine fratrum,   510
exsilioque domos et dulcia limina mutant

atque alio patriam quaerunt sub sole iacentem.
agricola incurvo terram dimovit aratro:
hinc anni labor, hinc patriam parvosque nepotes
sustinet, hinc armenta boum meritosque iuvencos.   515
nec requies, quin aut pomis exuberet annus
aut fetu pecorum aut Cerealis mergite culmi,
proventuque oneret sulcos atque horrea vincat.
venit hiems: teritur Sicyonia baca trapetis,
glande sues laeti redeunt, dant arbuta silvae;   520
et varios ponit fetus autumnus, et alte
mitis in apricis coquitur vindemia saxis.
interea dulces pendent circum oscula nati,
casta pudicitiam servat domus, ubera vaccae
lactea demittunt, pinguesque in gramine laeto   525
inter se adversis luctantur cornibus haedi.
ipse dies agitat festos fususque per herbam,
ignis ubi in medio et socii cratera coronant,
te libans, Lenaee, vocat pecorisque magistris
velocis iaculi certamina ponit in ulmo,   530
corporaque agresti nudant praedura palaestra.
hanc olim veteres vitam coluere Sabini,
hanc Remus et frater, sic fortis Etruria crevit
scilicet et rerum facta est pulcherrima Roma,
septemque una sibi muro circumdedit arces.   535
ante etiam sceptrum Dictaei regis et ante
impia quam caesis gens est epulata iuvencis,
aureus hanc vitam in terris Saturnus agebat;
necdum etiam audierant inflari classica, necdum
impositos duris crepitare incudibus ensis.   540
  Sed nos immensum spatiis confecimus aequor,
et iam tempus equum fumantia solvere colla.

GEORGICS

BOOK 3

Te quoque, magna Pales, et te memorande canemus
pastor ab Amphryso, vos, silvae amnesque Lycaei.
cetera, quae vacuas tenuissent carmine mentes,
omnia iam vulgata: quis aut Eurysthea durum
aut inlaudati nescit Busiridis aras?   5
cui non dictus Hylas puer et Latonia Delos
Hippodameque umeroque Pelops insignis eburno,
acer equis? temptanda via est, qua me quoque possim
tollere humo victorque virum volitare per ora.
primus ego in patriam mecum, modo vita supersit,   10
Aonio rediens deducam vertice Musas;
primus Idumaeas referam tibi, Mantua, palmas,
et viridi in campo templum de marmore ponam
propter aquam, tardis ingens ubi flexibus errat
Mincius et tenera praetexit harundine ripas.   15
in medio mihi Caesar erit templumque tenebit:
illi victor ego et Tyrio conspectus in ostro
centum quadriiugos agitabo ad flumina currus.
cuncta mihi Alpheum linquens lucosque Molorchi
cursibus et crudo decernet Graecia caestu.   20
ipse caput tonsae foliis ornatus olivae
dona feram. iam nunc sollemnis ducere pompas
ad delubra iuvat caesosque videre iuvencos,
vel scaena ut versis discedat frontibus utque
purpurea intexti tollant aulaea Britanni.   25
in foribus pugnam ex auro solidoque elephanto
Gangaridum faciam victorisque arma Quirini,
atque hic undantem bello magnumque fluentem
Nilum ac navali surgentis aere columnas.
addam urbes Asiae domitas pulsumque Niphaten   30
fidentemque fuga Parthum versisque sagittis;
et duo rapta manu diverso ex hoste tropaea

bisque triumphatas utroque ab litore gentis.
stabunt et Parii lapides, spirantia signa,
Assaraci proles demissaeque ab Iove gentis   35
nomina, Trosque parens et Troiae Cynthius auctor.
Invidia infelix furias amnemque severum
Cocyti metuet tortosque Ixionis anguis
immanemque rotam et non exsuperabile saxum.
interea Dryadum silvas saltusque sequamur   40
intactos, tua, Maecenas, haud mollia iussa.
te sine nil altum mens incohat: en age segnis
rumpe moras, vocat ingenti clamore Cithaeron
Taygetique canes domitrixque Epidaurus equorum,
et vox adsensu nemorum ingeminata remugit.   45
mox tamen ardentis accingar dicere pugnas
Caesaris et nomen fama tot ferre per annos
Tithoni prima quot abest ab origine Caesar.
   Seu quis Olympiacae miratus praemia palmae
pascit equos, seu quis fortis ad aratra iuvencos,   50
corpora praecipue matrum legat. optima torvae
forma bovis cui turpe caput, cui plurima cervix,
et crurum tenus a mento palearia pendent;
tum longo nullus lateri modus: omnia magna,
pes etiam; et camuris hirtae sub cornibus aures.   55
nec mihi displiceat maculis insignis et albo,
aut iuga detrectans interdumque aspera cornu
et faciem tauro propior, quaeque ardua tota
et gradiens ima verrit vestigia cauda.
aetas Lucinam iustosque pati hymenaeos   60
desinit ante decem, post quattuor incipit annos;
cetera nec feturae habilis nec fortis aratris.
interea, superat gregibus dum laeta iuventas,
solve mares; mitte in Venerem pecuaria primus,
atque aliam ex alia generando suffice prolem.   65
optima quaeque dies miseris mortalibus aevi
prima fugit: subeunt morbi tristisque senectus
et labor, et durae rapit inclementia mortis.
semper erunt quarum mutari corpora malis:
semper enim refice ac, ne post amissa requiras,   70
ante veni et subolem armento sortire quotannis.
   Nec non et pecori est idem dilectus equino.

tu modo, quos in spem statues summittere gentis,
praecipuum iam inde a teneris impende laborem.
continuo pecoris generosi pullus in arvis   75
altius ingreditur et mollia crura reponit;
primus et ire viam et fluvios temptare minacis
audet et ignoto sese committere ponti,
nec vanos horret strepitus. illi ardua cervix
argutumque caput, brevis alvus obesaque terga,   80
luxuriatque toris animosum pectus, honesti
spadices glaucique, color deterrimus albis
et gilvo. tum, si qua sonum procul arma dedere,
stare loco nescit, micat auribus et tremit artus,
collectumque premens volvit sub naribus ignem.   85
densa iuba, et dextro iactata recumbit in armo;
at duplex agitur per lumbos spina, cavatque
tellurem et solido graviter sonat ungula cornu.
talis Amyclaei domitus Pollucis habenis
Cyllarus et, quorum Grai meminere poetae,   90
Martis equi biiuges et magni currus Achilli.
talis et ipse iubam cervice effundit equina
coniugis adventu pernix Saturnus, et altum
Pelion hinnitu fugiens implevit acuto.
    Hunc quoque, ubi aut morbo gravis aut iam segnior
        annis   95
deficit, abde domo, nec turpi ignosce senectae.
frigidus in Venerem senior, frustraque laborem
ingratum trahit, et, si quando ad proelia ventum est,
ut quondam in stipulis magnus sine viribus ignis,
incassum furit. ergo animos aevumque notabis   100
praecipue: hinc alias artis prolemque parentum
et quis cuique dolor victo, quae gloria palmae.
nonne vides, cum praecipiti certamine campum
corripuere, ruuntque effusi carcere currus,
cum spes arrectae iuvenum, exsultantiaque haurit   105
corda pavor pulsans? illi instant verbere torto
et proni dant lora, volat vi fervidus axis;
iamque humiles iamque elati sublime videntur
aëra per vacuum ferri atque adsurgere in auras;
nec mora nec requies; at fulvae nimbus harenae   110
tollitur, umescunt spumis flatuque sequentum:

tantus amor laudum, tantae est victoria curae.
primus Ericthonius currus et quattuor ausus
iungere equos rapidusque rotis insistere victor.
frena Pelethronii Lapithae gyrosque dedere   115
impositi dorso, atque equitem docuere sub armis
insultare solo et gressus glomerare superbos.
aequus uterque labor, aeque iuvenemque magistri
exquirunt calidumque animis et cursibus acrem,
quamvis saepe fuga versos ille egerit hostis,   120
et patriam Epirum referat fortisque Mycenas,
Neptunique ipsa deducat origine gentem.
  His animadversis instant sub tempus et omnis
impendunt curas denso distendere pingui
quem legere ducem et pecori dixere maritum;   125
florentisque secant herbas fluviosque ministrant
farraque, ne blando nequeat superesse labori
invalidique patrum referant ieiunia nati.
ipsa autem macie tenuant armenta volentes,
atque, ubi concubitus primos iam nota voluptas   130
sollicitat, frondesque negant et fontibus arcent.
saepe etiam cursu quatiunt et sole fatigant,
cum graviter tunsis gemit area frugibus, et cum
surgentem ad Zephyrum paleae iactantur inanes.
hoc faciunt, nimio ne luxu obtunsior usus   135
sit genitali arvo et sulcos oblimet inertis,
sed rapiat sitiens Venerem interiusque recondat.
  Rursus cura patrum cadere et succedere matrum
incipit. exactis gravidae cum mensibus errant,
non illas gravibus quisquam iuga ducere plaustris,   140
non saltu superare viam sit passus et acri
carpere prata fuga fluviosque innare rapacis.
saltibus in vacuis pascunt et plena secundum
flumina, muscus ubi et viridissima gramine ripa,
speluncaeque tegant et saxea procubet umbra.   145
est lucos Silari circa ilicibusque virentem
plurimus Alburnum volitans, cui nomen asilo
Romanum est, oestrum Grai vertere vocantes,
asper, acerba sonans, quo tota exterrita silvis
diffugiunt armenta, furit mugitibus aether   150
concussus silvaeque et sicci ripa Tanagri.

hoc quondam monstro horribilis exercuit iras
Inachiae Iuno pestem meditata iuvencae.
hunc quoque (nam mediis fervoribus acrior instat)
arcebis gravido pecori, armentaque pasces   155
sole recens orto aut noctem ducentibus astris.
  Post partum cura in vitulos traducitur omnis;
continuoque notas et nomina gentis inurunt,
et quos aut pecori malint summittere habendo
aut aris servare sacros aut scindere terram   160
et campum horrentem fractis invertere glaebis.
cetera pascuntur viridis armenta per herbas:
tu quos ad studium atque usum formabis agrestem
iam vitulos hortare viamque insiste domandi,
dum faciles animi iuvenum, dum mobilis aetas.   165
ac primum laxos tenui de vimine circlos
cervici subnecte; dehinc, ubi libera colla
servitio adsuerint, ipsis e torquibus aptos
iunge pares, et coge gradum conferre iuvencos;
atque illis iam saepe rotae ducantur inanes   170
per terram, et summo vestigia pulvere signent.
post valido nitens sub pondere faginus axis
instrepat, et iunctos temo trahat aereus orbis.
interea pubi indomitae non gramina tantum
nec vescas salicum frondes ulvamque palustrem,   175
sed frumenta manu carpes sata; nec tibi fetae
more patrum nivea implebunt mulctraria vaccae,
sed tota in dulcis consument ubera natos.
  Sin ad bella magis studium turmasque ferocis,
aut Alphea rotis praelabi flumina Pisae   180
et Iovis in luco currus agitare volantis,
primus equi labor est animos atque arma videre
bellantum lituosque pati, tractuque gementem
ferre rotam et stabulo frenos audire sonantis;
tum magis atque magis blandis gaudere magistri   185
laudibus et plausae sonitum cervicis amare.
atque haec iam primo depulsus ab ubere matris
audeat, inque vicem det mollibus ora capistris
invalidus etiamque tremens, etiam inscius aevi.
at tribus exactis ubi quarta accesserit aestas,   190
carpere mox gyrum incipiat gradibusque sonare

compositis, sinuetque alterna volumina crurum,
sitque laboranti similis; tum cursibus auras
provocet, ac per aperta volans ceu liber habenis
aequora vix summa vestigia ponat harena,   195
qualis Hyperboreis Aquilo cum densus ab oris
incubuit, Scythiaeque hiemes atque arida differt
nubila; tum segetes altae campique natantes
lenibus horrescunt flabris, summaeque sonorem
dant silvae, longique urgent ad litora fluctus;   200
ille volat simul arva fuga simul aequora verrens.
hic vel ad Elei metas et maxima campi
sudabit spatia et spumas aget ore cruentas,
Belgica vel molli melius feret esseda collo.
tum demum crassa magnum farragine corpus   205
crescere iam domitis sinito: nameque ante domandum
ingentis tollent animos, prensique negabunt
verbera lenta pati et duris parere lupatis.
    Sed non ulla magis viris industria firmat
quam Venerem et caeci stimulos avertere amoris,   210
sive boum sive est cui gratior usus equorum.
atque ideo tauros procul atque in sola relegant
pascua post montem oppositum et trans flumina lata,
aut intus clausos satura ad praesepia servant.
carpit enim viris paulatim uritque videndo   215
femina, nec nemorum patitur meminisse nec herbae
dulcibus illa quidem inlecebris, et saepe superbos
cornibus inter se subigit decernere amantis.
pascitur in magna Sila formosa iuvenca:
illi alternantes multa vi proelia miscent   220
vulneribus crebris, lavit ater corpora sanguis,
versaque in obnixos urgentur cornua vasto
cum gemitu, reboant silvaeque et longus Olympus.
nec mos bellantis una stabulare, sed alter
victus abit longeque ignotis exsulat oris,   225
multa gemens ignominiam plagasque superbi
victoris, tum quos amisit inultus amores,
et stabula aspectans regnis excessit avitis.
ergo omni cura viris exercet et inter
dura iacet pernox instrato saxa cubili   230
frondibus hirsutis et carice pastus acuta,

et temptat sese atque irasci in cornua discit
arboris obnixus trunco, ventosque lacessit
ictibus, et sparsa ad pugnam proludit harena.
post ubi collectum robur viresque refectae,   235
signa movet praecepsque oblitum fertur in hostem:
fluctus uti medio coepit cum albescere ponto,
longius ex altoque sinum trahit, utque volutus
ad terras immane sonat per saxa neque ipso
monte minor procumbit, at ima exaestuat unda   240
verticibus nigramque alte subiectat harenam.
    Omne adeo genus in terris hominumque ferarumque
et genus aequoreum, pecudes pictaeque volucres,
in furias ignemque ruunt: amor omnibus idem.
tempore non alio catulorum oblita leaena   245
saevior erravit campis, nec funera vulgo
tam multa informes ursi stragemque dedere
per silvas; tum saevus aper, tum pessima tigris;
heu male tum Libyae solis erratur in agris.
nonne vides ut tota tremor pertemptet equorum   250
corpora, si tantum notas odor attulit auras?
ac neque eos iam frena virum neque verbera saeva,
non scopuli rupesque cavae atque obiecta retardant
flumina correptosque unda torquentia montis.
ipse ruit dentesque Sabellicus exacuit sus   255
et pede prosubigit terram, fricat arbore costas
atque hinc atque illinc umeros ad vulnera durat.
quid iuvenis, magnum cui versat in ossibus ignem
durus amor? nempe abruptis turbata procellis
nocte natat caeca serus freta, quem super ingens   260
porta tonat caeli, et scopulis inlisa reclamant
aequora; nec miseri possunt revocare parentes,
nec moritura super crudeli funere virgo.
quid lynces Bacchi variae et genus acre luporum
atque canum? quid quae imbelles dant proelia cervi?   265
scilicet ante omnis furor est insignis equarum;
et mentem Venus ipsa dedit, quo tempore Glauci
Potniades malis membra absumpsere quadrigae.
illas ducit amor trans Gargara transque sonantem
Ascanium; superant montis et flumina tranant.   270
continuoque avidis ubi subdita flamma medullis

(vere magis, quia vere calor redit ossibus) illae
ore omnes versae in Zephyrum stant rupibus altis,
exceptantque levis auras, et saepe sine ullis
coniugiis vento gravidae (mirabile dictu)   275
saxa per et scopulos et depressas convallis
diffugiunt, non, Eure, tuos, neque solis ad ortus,
in Borean Caurumque, aut unde nigerrimus Auster
nascitur et pluvio contristat frigore caelum.
hic demum, hippomanes vero quod nomine dicunt   280
pastores, lentum destillat ab inguine virus,
hippomanes, quod saepe malae legere novercae
miscueruntque herbas et non innoxia verba.
    Sed fugit interea, fugit inreparabile tempus,
singula dum capti circumvectamur amore.   285
hoc satis armentis. superat pars altera curae,
lanigeros agitare greges hirtasque capellas.
hic labor, hinc laudem fortes sperate coloni.
nec sum animi dubius verbis ea vincere magnum
quam sit et angustis hunc addere rebus honorem;   290
sed me Parnasi deserta per ardua dulcis
raptat amor; iuvat ire iugis, qua nulla priorum
Castaliam molli devertitur orbita clivo.
nunc, veneranda Pales, magno nunc ore sonandum.
    Incipiens stabulis edico in mollibus herbam   295
carpere ovis, dum mox frondosa reducitur aestas,
et multa duram stipula filicumque maniplis
sternere subter humum, glacies ne frigida laedat
molle pecus scabiemque ferat turpisque podagras.
post hinc digressus iubeo frondentia capris   300
arbuta sufficere et fluvios praebere recentis,
et stabula a ventis hiberno opponere soli
ad medium conversa diem, cum frigidus olim
iam cadit extremoque inrorat Aquarius anno.
hae quoque non cura nobis leviore tuendae,   305
nec minor usus erit, quamvis Milesia magno
vellera mutentur Tyrios incocta rubores.
densior hinc suboles, hinc largi copia lactis;
quam magis exhausto spumaverit ubere mulctra
laeta magis pressis manabunt flumina mammis.   310
nec minus interea barbas incanaque menta

Cinyphii tondent hirci saetasque comantis
usum in castrorum et miseris velamina nautis.
pascuntur vero silvas et summa Lycaei,
horrentisque rubos et amantis ardua dumos,   315
atque ipsae memores redeunt in tecta suosque
ducunt et gravido superant vix ubere limen.
ergo omni studio glaciem ventosque nivalis,
quo minor est illis curae mortalis egestas,
avertes, victumque feres et virgea laetus   320
pabula, nec tota claudes faenilia bruma.
at vero Zephyris cum laeta vocantibus aestas
in saltus utrumque gregem atque in pascua mittet,
Luciferi primo cum sidere frigida rura
carpamus, dum mane novum, dum gramina canent,   325
et ros in tenera pecori gratissimus herba.
inde ubi quarta sitim caeli collegerit hora
et cantu querulae rumpent arbusta cicadae,
ad puteos aut alta greges ad stagna iubebo
currentem ilignis potare canalibus undam;   330
aestibus at mediis umbrosam exquirere vallem,
sicubi magna Iovis antiquo robore quercus
ingentis tendat ramos, aut sicubi nigrum
ilicibus crebris sacra nemus accubet umbra;
tum tenuis dare rursus aquas et pascere rursus   335
solis ad occasum, cum frigidus aëra Vesper
temperat, et saltus reficit iam roscida luna,
litoraque alcyonen resonant, acalanthida dumi.
   Quid tibi pastores Libyae, quid pascua versu
prosequar et raris habitata mapalia tectis?   340
saepe diem noctemque et totum ex ordine mensem
pascitur itque pecus longa in deserta sine ullis
hospitiis: tantum campi iacet. omnia secum
armentarius Afer agit, tectumque laremque
armaque Amyclaeumque canem Cressamque pharetram;   345
non secus ac patriis acer Romanus in armis
iniusto sub fasce viam cum carpit, et hosti
ante exspectatum positis stat in agmine castris.
   At non qua Scythiae gentes Maeotiaque unda
turbidus et torquens flaventis Hister harenas,   350
quaque redit medium Rhodope porrecta sub axem.

illic clausa tenent stabulis armenta, neque ullae
aut herbae campo apparent aut arbore frondes;
sed iacet aggeribus niveis informis et alto
terra gelu late septemque adsurgit in ulnas.   355
semper hiems, semper spirantes frigora Cauri.
tum Sol pallentis haud umquam discutit umbras,
nec cum invectus equis altum petit aethera, nec cum
praecipitem Oceani rubro lavit aequore currum.
concrescunt subitae currenti in flumine crustae,   360
undaque iam tergo ferratos sustinet orbis,
puppibus illa prius, patulis nunc hospita plaustris;
aeraque dissiliunt vulgo, vestesque rigescunt
indutae, caeduntque securibus umida vina,
et totae solidam in glaciem vertere lacunae,   365
stiriaque impexis induruit horrida barbis.
interea toto non setius aëre ningit:
intereunt pecudes, stant circumfusa pruinis
corpora magna boum, confertoque agmine cervi
torpent mole nova et summis vix cornibus exstant.   370
hos non immissis canibus, non cassibus ullis
puniceaeve agitant pavidos formidine pennae,
sed frustra oppositum trudentis pectore montem
comminus obtruncant ferro graviterque rudentis
caedunt et magno laeti clamore reportant.   375
ipsi in defossis specubus secura sub alta
otia agunt terra, congestaque robora totasque
advolvere focis ulmos ignique dedere.
hic noctem ludo ducunt, et pocula laeti
fermento atque acidis imitantur vitea sorbis.   380
talis Hyperboreo septem subiecta trioni
gens effrena virum Riphaeo tunditur Euro
et pecudum fulvis velatur corpora saetis.
    Si tibi lanitium curae, primum aspera silva
lappaeque tribolique absint; fuge pabula laeta,   385
continuoque greges villis lege mollibus albos.
illum autem, quamvis aries sit candidus ipse,
nigra subest udo tantum cui lingua palato,
reice, ne maculis infuscet vellera pullis
nascentum, plenoque alium circumspice campo.   390
munere sic niveo lanae, si credere dignum est,

Pan deus Arcadiae captam te, Luna, fefellit
in nemora alta vocans; nec tu aspernata vocantem.
At cui lactis amor, cytisum lotosque frequentis
ipse manu salsasque ferat praesepibus herbas: 395
hinc et amant fluvios magis, et magis ubera tendunt
et salis occultum referunt in lacte saporem.
multi etiam excretos prohibent a matribus haedos,
primaque ferratis praefigunt ora capistris.
quod surgente die mulsere horisque diurnis,   400
nocte premunt; quod iam tenebris et sole cadente,
sub lucem exportant calathis (adit oppida pastor),
aut parco sale contingunt hiemique reponunt.
Nec tibi cura canum fuerit postrema, sed una
velocis Spartae catulos acremque Molossum   405
pasce sero pingui. numquam custodibus illis
nocturnum stabulis furem incursusque luporum
aut impacatos a tergo horrebis Hiberos.
saepe etiam cursu timidos agitabis onagros,
et canibus leporem, canibus venabere dammas;   410
saepe volutabris pulsos silvestribus apros
latratu turbabis agens, montisque per altos
ingentem clamore premes ad retia cervum.
Disce et odoratam stabulis accendere cedrum,
galbaneoque agitare gravis nidore chelydros.   415
saepe sub immotis praesepibus aut mala tactu
vipera delituit caelumque exterrita fugit,
aut tecto adsuetus coluber succedere et umbrae
(pestis acerba boum) pecorique aspergere virus,
fovit humum. cape saxa manu, cape robora, pastor,   420
tollentemque minas et sibila colla tumentem
deice. iamque fuga timidum caput abdidit alte,
cum medii nexus extremaeque agmina caudae
solvuntur, tardosque trahit sinus ultimus orbis.
est etiam ille malus Calabris in saltibus anguis   425
squamea convolvens sublato pectore terga
atque notis longam maculosus grandibus alvum,
qui, dum amnes ulli rumpuntur fontibus et dum
vere madent udo terrae ac pluvialibus Austris,
stagna colit ripisque habitans hic piscibus atram   430
improbus ingluviem ranisque loquacibus explet;

postquam exusta palus terraeque ardore dehiscunt,
exsilit in siccum, et flammantia lumina torquens
saevit agris asperque siti atque exterritus aestu.
ne mihi tum mollis sub divo carpere somnos   435
neu dorso nemoris libeat iacuisse per herbas,
cum positis novus exuviis nitidusque iuventa
volvitur, aut catulos tectis aut ova relinquens,
arduus ad solem et linguis micat ore trisulcis.
    Morborum quoque te causas et signa docebo.   440
turpis ovis temptat scabies, ubi frigidus imber
altius ad vivum persedit et horrida cano
bruma gelu, vel cum tonsis inlotus adhaesit
sudor, et hirsuti secuerunt corpora vepres.
dulcibus idcirco fluviis pecus omne magistri   445
perfundunt, udisque aries in gurgite villis
mersatur, missusque secundo defluit amni;
aut tonsum tristi contingunt corpus amurca
et spumas miscent argenti vivaque sulpura
Idaeasque pices et pinguis unguine ceras   450
scillamque elleborosque gravis nigrumque bitumen.
non tamen ulla magis praesens fortuna laborum est
quam si quis ferro potuit rescindere summum
ulceris os: alitur vitium vivitque tegendo,
dum medicas adhibere manus ad vulnera pastor   455
abnegat et meliora deos sedet omina poscens.
quin etiam, ima dolor balantum lapsus ad ossa
cum furit atque artus depascitur arida febris,
profuit incensos aestus avertere et inter
ima ferire pedis salientem sanguine venam,   460
Bisaltae quo more solent acerque Gelonus,
cum fugit in Rhodopen atque in deserta Getarum,
et lac concretum cum sanguine potat equino.
quam procul aut molli succedere saepius umbrae
videris aut summas carpentem ignavius herbas   465
extremamque sequi, aut medio procumbere campo
pascentem et serae solam decedere nocti—
continuo culpam ferro compesce priusquam
dira per incautum serpant contagia vulgus.
non tam creber agens hiemem ruit aequore turbo   470
quam multae pecudum pestes. nec singula morbi

corpora corripiunt, sed tota aestiva repente,
spemque gregemque simul cunctamque ab origine gentem.
tum sciat, aërias Alpis et Norica si quis
castella in tumulis et Iapydis arva Timavi   475
nunc quoque post tanto videat, desertaque regna
pastorum et longe saltus lateque vacantis.
    Hic quondam morbo caeli miseranda coorta est
tempestas totoque autumni incanduit aestu
et genus omne neci pecudum dedit, omne ferarum,   480
corrupitque lacus, infecit pabula tabo.
nec via mortis erat simplex; sed ubi ignea venis
omnibus acta sitis miseros adduxerat artus,
rursus abundabat fluidus liquor omniaque in se
ossa minutatim morbo conlapsa trahebat.   485
saepe in honore deum medio stans hostia ad aram,
lanea dum nivea circumdatur infula vitta,
inter cunctantis cecidit moribunda ministros;
aut si quam ferro mactaverat ante sacerdos,
inde neque impositis ardent altaria fibris,   490
nec responsa potest consultus reddere vates,
ac vix suppositi tinguntur sanguine cultri
summaque ieiuna sanie infuscatur harena.
hinc laetis vituli vulgo moriuntur in herbis
et dulcis animas plena ad praesepia reddunt;   495
hinc canibus blandis rabies venit, et quatit aegros
tussis anhela sues ac faucibus angit obesis.
labitur infelix studiorum atque immemor herbae
victor equus fontisque avertitur et pede terram
crebra ferit; demissae aures, incertus ibidem   500
sudor et ille quidem morituris frigidus; aret
pellis et ad tactum tractanti dura resistit.
haec ante exitium primis dant signa diebus.
sin in processu coepit crudescere morbus,
tum vero ardentes oculi atque attractus ab alto   505
spiritus, interdum gemitu gravis, imaque longo
ilia singultu tendunt, it naribus ater
sanguis, et obsessas fauces premit aspera lingua.
profuit inserto latices infundere cornu
Lenaeos; ea visa salus morientibus una.   510
mox erat hoc ipsum exitio, furiisque refecti

ardebant, ipsique suos iam morte sub aegra
(di meliora piis, erroremque hostibus illum!)
discissos nudis laniabant dentibus artus.
ecce autem duro fumans sub vomere taurus   515
concidit et mixtum spumis vomit ore cruorem
extremosque ciet gemitus. it tristis arator
maerentem abiungens fraterna morte iuvencum,
atque opere in medio defixa relinquit aratra.
non umbrae altorum nemorum, non mollia possunt   520
prata movere animum, non qui per saxa volutus
purior electro campum petit amnis; at ima
solvuntur latera, atque oculos stupor urget inertis
ad terramque fluit devexo pondere cervix.
quid labor aut benefacta iuvant? quid vomere terras   525
invertisse gravis? atqui non Massica Bacchi
munera, non illis epulae nocuere repostae:
frondibus et victu pascuntur simplicis herbae,
pocula sunt fontes liquidi atque exercita cursu
flumina, nec somnos abrumpit cura salubris.   530
tempore non alio dicunt regionibus illis
quaesitas ad sacra boves Iunonis et uris
imparibus ductos alta ad donaria currus.
ergo aegre rastris terram rimantur, et ipsis
unguibus infodiunt fruges, montisque per altos   535
contenta cervice trahunt stridentia plaustra.
non lupus insidias explorat ovilia circum
nec gregibus nocturnus obambulat: acrior illum
cura domat; timidi dammae cervique fugaces
nunc interque canes et circum tecta vagantur.   540
iam maris immensi prolem et genus omne natantum
litore in extremo ceu naufraga corpora fluctus
proluit; insolitae fugiunt in flumina phocae.
interit et curvis frustra defensa latebris
vipera et attoniti squamis astantibus hydri.   545
ipsis est aer avibus non aequus, et illae
praecipites alta vitam sub nube relinquunt.
praeterea iam nec mutari pabula refert,
quaesitaeque nocent artes; cessere magistri,
Phillyrides Chiron Amythaoniusque Melampus.   550
saevit et in lucem Stygiis emissa tenebris

pallida Tisiphone Morbos agit ante Metumque,
inque dies avidum surgens caput altius effert.
balatu pecorum et crebris mugitibus amnes
arentesque sonant ripae collesque supini.   555
iamque catervatim dat stragem atque aggerat ipsis
in stabulis turpi dilapsa cadavera tabo,
donec humo tegere ac foveis abscondere discunt.
nam neque erat coriis usus, nec viscera quisquam   .
aut undis abolere potest aut vincere flamma;   560
ne tondere quidem morbo inluvieque peresa
vellera nec telas possunt attingere putris;
verum etiam invisos si quis temptarat amictus,
ardentes papulae atque immundus olentia sudor
membra sequebatur, nec longo deinde moranti   565
tempore contactos artus sacer ignis edebat.

GEORGICS

BOOK 4

Protinus aerii mellis caelestia dona
exsequar: hanc etiam, Maecenas, aspice partem.
admiranda tibi levium spectacula rerum
magnanimosque duces totiusque ordine gentis
mores et studia et populos et proelia dicam.   5
in tenui labor; at tenuis non gloria, si quem
numina laeva sinunt auditque vocatus Apollo.
    Principio sedes apibus statioque petenda,
quo neque sit ventis aditus (nam pabula venti
ferre domum prohibent) neque oves haedique petulci   10
floribus insultent, aut errans bucula campo
decutiat rorem et surgentis atterat herbas.
absint et picti squalentia terga lacerti
pinguibus a stabulis, meropesque aliaeque volucres
et manibus Procne pectus signata cruentis;   15
omnia nam late vastant ipsasque volantis
ore ferunt dulcem nidis immitibus escam.
at liquidi fontes et stagna virentia musco
adsint et tenuis fugiens per gramina rivus,
palmaque vestibulum aut ingens oleaster inumbret,   20
ut, cum prima novi ducent examina reges
vere suo, ludetque favis emissa iuventus,
vicina invitet decedere ripa calori,
obviaque hospitiis teneat frondentibus arbos.
in medium, seu stabit iners seu profluet umor,   25
transversas salices et grandia conice saxa,
pontibus ut crebris possint consistere et alas
pandere ad aestivum solem, si forte morantis
sparserit aut praeceps Neptuno immerserit Eurus.
haec circum casiae virides et olentia late   30
serpylla et graviter spirantis copia thymbrae
floreat, inriguumque bibant violaria fontem.

ipsa autem, seu corticibus tibi suta cavatis
seu lento fuerint alvaria vimine texta,
angustos habeant aditus: nam frigore mella   35
cogit hiems, eademque calor liquefacta remittit.
utraque vis apibus pariter metuenda; neque illae
nequiquam in tectis certatim tenuia cera
spiramenta linunt, fucoque et floribus oras
explent, collectumque haec ipsa ad munera gluten   40
et visco et Phrygiae servant pice lentius Idae.
saepe etiam effossis, si vera est fama, latebris
sub terra fovere larem, penitusque repertae
pumicibusque cavis exesaeque arboris antro.
tu tamen et levi rimosa cubilia limo   45
ungue fovens circum, et raras superinice frondes.
neu propius tectis taxum sine, neve rubentis
ure foco cancros, altae neu crede paludi,
aut ubi odor caeni gravis aut ubi concava pulsu
saxa sonant vocisque offensa resultat imago.   50
   Quod superest, ubi pulsam hiemem sol aureus egit
sub terras caelumque aestiva luce reclusit,
illae continuo saltus silvasque peragrant
purpureosque metunt flores et flumina libant
summa leves. hinc nescio qua dulcedine laetae   55
progeniem nidosque fovent, hinc arte recentis
excudunt ceras et mella tenacia fingunt.
hinc ubi iam emissum caveis ad sidera caeli
nare per aestatem liquidam suspexeris agmen
obscuramque trahi vento mirabere nubem,   60
contemplator: aquas dulcis et frondea semper
tecta petunt. huc tu iussos asperge sapores,
trita melisphylla et cerinthae ignobile gramen,
tinnitusque cie et Matris quate cymbala circum:
ipsae consident medicatis sedibus, ipsae   65
intima more suo sese in cunabula condent.
   Sin autem ad pugnam exierint—nam saepe duobus
regibus incessit magno discordia motu,
continuoque animos vulgi et trepidantia bello
corda licet longe praesciscere: namque morantis   70
Martius ille aeris rauci canor increpat, et vox
auditur fractos sonitus imitata tubarum.

tum trepidae inter se coeunt pennisque coruscant
spiculaque exacuunt rostris aptantque lacertos
et circa regem atque ipsa ad praetoria densae   75
miscentur magnisque vocant clamoribus hostem.
ergo ubi ver nactae sudum camposque patentis,
erumpunt portis; concurritur, aethere in alto
fit sonitus, magnum mixtae glomerantur in orbem
praecipitesque cadunt; non densior aëre grando,   80
nec de concussa tantum pluit ilice glandis.
ipsi per medias acies insignibus alis
ingentis animos angusto in pectore versant,
usque adeo obnixi non cedere dum gravis aut hos
aut hos versa fuga victor dare terga subegit.   85
hi motus animorum atque haec certamina tanta
pulveris exigui iactu compressa quiescunt.
    Verum ubi ductores acie revocaveris ambo,
deterior qui visus, eum, ne prodigus obsit,
dede neci; melior vacua sine regnet in aula.   Tves   90
alter erit maculis auro squalentibus ardens;
nam duo sunt genera: hic melior insignis et ore
et rutilis clarus squamis; ille horridus alter
desidia latamque trahens inglorius alvum.
ut binae regum facies, ita corpora plebis: 95
namque aliae turpes horrent, ceu pulvere ab alto
cum venit et sicco terram spuit ore viator
aridus; elucent aliae et fulgore coruscant
ardentes auro et paribus lita corpora guttis.
haec potior suboles, hinc caeli tempore certo   100
dulcia mella premes, nec tantum dulcia quantum
et liquida et durum Bacchi domitura saporem.
    At cum incerta volant caeloque examina ludunt
contemnuntque favos et frigida tecta relinquunt,
instabilis animos ludo prohibebis inani.   105
nec magnus prohibere labor: tu regibus alas
eripe; non illis quisquam cunctantibus altum
ire iter aut castris audebit vellere signa.
invitent croceis halantes floribus horti
et custos furum atque avium cum falce saligna   110
Hellespontiaci servet tutela Priapi.
ipse thymum tinosque ferens de montibus altis

tecta serat late circum cui talia curae;
ipse labore manum duro terat, ipse feracis
figat humo plantas et amicos inriget imbris.   115
    Atque equidem, extremo ni iam sub fine laborum
(vela traham) et terris festinem advertere proram,
forsitan et pinguis hortos quae cura colendi
ornaret canerem, biferique rosaria Paesti,
quoque modo potis gauderent intiba rivis   120
et virides apio ripae, tortusque per herbam
cresceret in ventrem cucumis; nec sera comantem
narcissum aut flexi tacuissem vimen acanthi
pallentisque hederas et amantis litora myrtos.
namque sub Oebaliae memini me turribus arcis,   125
qua niger umectat flaventia culta Galaesus,
Corycium vidisse senem, cui pauca relicti
iugera ruris erant, nec fertilis illa iuvencis
nec pecori opportuna seges nec commoda Baccho.
hic rarum tamen in dumis olus albaque circum   130
lilia verbenasque premens vescumque papaver
regum aequabat opes animis, seraque revertens
nocte domum dapibus mensas onerabat inemptis.
primus vere rosam atque autumno carpere poma,
et cum tristis hiems etiamnum frigore saxa   135
rumperet et glacie cursus frenaret aquarum,
ille comam mollis iam tondebat hyacinthi
aestatem increpitans seram Zephyrosque morantis.
ergo apibus fetis idem atque examine multo
primus abundare et spumantia cogere pressis   140
mella favis; illi tiliae atque uberrima tinus,
quotque in flore novo pomis se fertilis arbos
induerat totidem autumno matura tenebat.
ille etiam seras in versum distulit ulmos
eduramque pirum et spinos iam pruna ferentis   145
iamque ministrantem platanum potantibus umbras.
verum haec ipse equidem spatiis exclusus iniquis
praetereo atque aliis post me memoranda relinquo.
    Nunc age, naturas apibus quas Iuppiter ipse
addidit expediam, pro qua mercede canoros   150
Curetum sonitus crepitantiaque aera secutae
Dictaeo caeli regem pavere sub antro.

solae communis natos, consortia tecta
urbis habent, magnisque agitant sub legibus aevum,
et patriam solae et certos novere penatis;   155
venturaeque hiemis memores aestate laborem
experiuntur et in medium quaesita reponunt.
namque aliae victu invigilant et foedere pacto
exercentur agris; pars intra saepta domorum
narcissi lacrimam et lentum de cortice gluten   160
prima favis ponunt fundamina, deinde tenacis
suspendunt ceras; aliae spem gentis adultos
educunt fetus; aliae purissima mella
stipant et liquido distendunt nectare cellas.
sunt quibus ad portas cecidit custodia sorti,   165
inque vicem speculantur aquas et nubila caeli,
aut onera accipiunt venientum, aut agmine facto
ignavum fucos pecus a praesepibus arcent.
fervet opus, redolentque thymo fragrantia mella.
ac veluti lentis Cyclopes fulmina massis   170
cum properant, alii taurinis follibus auras
accipiunt redduntque, alii stridentia tingunt
aera lacu; gemit impositis incudibus Aetna;
illi inter sese magna vi bracchia tollunt
in numerum, versantque tenaci forcipe ferrum: 175
non aliter, si parva licet componere magnis,
Cecropias innatus apes amor urget habendi
munere quamque suo. grandaevis oppida curae
et munire favos et daedala fingere tecta.
at fessae multa referunt se nocte minores,   180
crura thymo plenae; pascuntur et arbuta passim
et glaucas salices casiamque crocumque rubentem
et pinguem tiliam et ferrugineos hyacinthos.
omnibus una quies operum, labor omnibus unus:
mane ruunt portis; nusquam mora; rursus easdem   185
vesper ubi e pastu tandem decedere campis
admonuit, tum tecta petunt, tum corpora curant;
fit sonitus, mussantque oras et limina circum.
post, ubi iam thalamis se composuere, siletur
in noctem, fessosque sopor suus occupat artus.   190
nec vero a stabulis pluvia impendente recedunt
longius, aut credunt caelo adventantibus Euris,

sed circum tutae sub moenibus urbis aquantur
excursusque brevis temptant, et saepe lapillos,
ut cumbae instabiles fluctu iactante saburram,   195
tollunt, his sese per inania nubila librant.
illum adeo placuisse apibus mirabere morem,
quod neque concubitu indulgent, nec corpora segnes
in Venerem solvunt aut fetus nixibus edunt;
verum ipsae e foliis natos, e suavibus herbis   ·   200
ore legunt, ipsae regem parvosque Quirites
sufficiunt, aulasque et cerea regna refingunt.
saepe etiam duris errando in cotibus alas
attrivere, ultroque animam sub fasce dedere:
tantus amor florum et generandi gloria mellis.   205
ergo ipsas quamvis angusti terminus aevi
excipiat (neque enim plus septima ducitur aestas),
at genus immortale manet, multosque per annos
stat fortuna domus, et avi numerantur avorum.
praeterea regem non sic Aegyptus et ingens   210
Lydia nec populi Parthorum aut Medus Hydaspes
observant. rege incolumi mens omnibus una est;
amisso rupere fidem, constructaque mella
diripuere ipsae et cratis solvere favorum.
ille operum custos, illum admirantur et omnes   215
circumstant fremitu denso stipantque frequentes,
et saepe attollunt umeris et corpora bello   ··
obiectant pulchramque petunt per vulnera mortem.
    His quidam signis atque haec exempla secuti
esse apibus partem divinae mentis et haustus   220
aetherios dixere; deum namque ire per omnis
terrasque tractusque maris caelumque profundum;
hinc pecudes, armenta, viros, genus omne ferarum,
quemque sibi tenuis nascentem arcessere vitas:
scilicet huc reddi deinde ac resoluta referri   225
omnia, nec morti esse locum, sed viva volare
sideris in numerum atque alto succedere caelo.
    Si quando sedem augustam servataque mella
thesauris relines, prius haustu sparsus aquarum
ora fove, fumosque manu praetende sequacis.   230
bis gravidos cogunt fetus, duo tempora messis:
Taygete simul os terris ostendit honestum

Pleas et Oceani spretos pede reppulit amnis,
aut eadem sidus fugiens ubi Piscis aquosi
tristior hibernas caelo descendit in undas.　　　　　235
illis ira modum supra est, laesaeque venenum
morsibus inspirant, et spicula caeca relinquunt
adfixae venis, animasque in vulnere ponunt.
sin duram metues hiemem parcesque futuro
contunsosque animos et res miserabere fractas,　　　240
at suffire thymo cerasque recidere inanis
quis dubitet? nam saepe favos ignotus adedit
stelio et lucifugis congesta cubilia blattis
immunisque sedens aliena ad pabula fucus;
aut asper crabro imparibus se immiscuit armis,　　　245
aut dirum tiniae genus, aut invisa Minervae
laxos in foribus suspendit aranea cassis.
quo magis exhaustae fuerint hoc acrius omnes
incumbent generis lapsi sarcire ruinas
complebuntque foros et floribus horrea texent.　　　250
　　Si vero, quoniam casus apibus quoque nostros
vita tulit, tristi languebunt corpora morbo—
quod iam non dubiis poteris cognoscere signis:
continuo est aegris alius color; horrida vultum
deformat macies; tum corpora luce carentum　　　255
exportant tectis et tristia funera ducunt;
aut illae pedibus conexae ad limina pendent
aut intus clausis cunctantur in aedibus omnes
ignavaeque fame et contracto frigore pigrae.
tum sonus auditur gravior, tractimque susurrant,　　260
frigidus ut quondam silvis immurmurat Auster,
ut mare sollicitum stridit refluentibus undis,
aestuat ut clausis rapidus fornacibus ignis.
hic iam galbaneos suadebo incendere odores
mellaque harundineis inferre canalibus, ultro　　　265
hortantem et fessas ad pabula nota vocantem.
proderit et tunsum gallae admiscere saporem
arentisque rosas, aut igni pinguia multo
defruta vel psithia passos de vite racemos,
Cecropiumque thymum et grave olentia centaurea.　　270
est etiam flos in pratis cui nomen amello
fecere agricolae, facilis quaerentibus herba;

namque uno ingentem tollit de caespite silvam
aureus ipse, sed in foliis, quae plurima circum
funduntur, violae sublucet purpura nigrae;   275
saepe deum nexis ornatae torquibus arae;
asper in ore sapor; tonsis in vallibus illum
pastores et curva legunt prope flumina Mellae.
huius odorato radices incoque Baccho
pabulaque in foribus plenis appone canistris.   .   280
   Sed si quem proles subito defecerit omnis,
nec genus unde novae stirpis revocetur habebit,
tempus et Arcadii memoranda inventa magistri
pandere, quoque modo caesis iam saepe iuvencis
insincerus apes tulerit cruor. altius omnem   285
expediam prima repetens ab origine famam.
nam qua Pellaei gens fortunata Canopi   ← Test end
accolit effuso stagnantem flumine Nilum   Quiz 2
et circum pictis vehitur sua rura phaselis,
quaque pharetratae vicinia Persidis urget,   290
et diversa ruens septem discurrit in ora   292
usque coloratis amnis devexus ab Indis,   293
et viridem Aegyptum nigra fecundat harena,   291
omnis in hac certam regio iacit arte salutem.
exiguus primum atque ipsos contractus in usus   295
eligitur locus; hunc angustique imbrice tecti
parietibusque premunt artis, et quattuor addunt,
quattuor a ventis obliqua luce fenestras.
tum vitulus bima curvans iam cornua fronte
quaeritur; huic geminae nares et spiritus oris   300
multa reluctanti obstruitur, plagisque perempto
tunsa per integram solvuntur viscera pellem.
sic positum in clauso linquunt, et ramea costis
subiciunt fragmenta, thymum casiasque recentis.
hoc geritur Zephyris primum impellentibus undas,   305
ante novis rubeant quam prata coloribus, ante
garrula quam tignis nidum suspendat hirundo.
interea teneris tepefactus in ossibus umor
aestuat, et visenda modis animalia miris,
trunca pedum primo, mox et stridentia pennis,   310
miscentur, tenuemque magis magis aëra carpunt,
donec ut aestivis effusus nubibus imber

erupere, aut ut nervo pulsante sagittae
prima leves ineunt si quando proelia Parthi.
   Quis deus hanc, Musae, quis nobis extudit artem?   315
unde nova ingressus hominum experientia cepit?
pastor Aristaeus fugiens Peneia Tempe,
amissis, ut fama, apibus morboque fameque,
tristis ad extremi sacrum caput astitit amnis
multa querens, atque hac adfatus voce parentem: 320
'mater, Cyrene mater, quae gurgitis huius
ima tenes, quid me praeclara stirpe deorum
(si modo, quem perhibes, pater est Thymbraeus Apollo)
invisum fatis genuisti? aut quo tibi nostri
pulsus amor? quid me caelum sperare iubebas?   325
en etiam hunc ipsum vitae mortalis honorem,
quem mihi vix frugum et pecudum custodia sollers
omnia temptanti extuderat, te matre relinquo.
quin age et ipsa manu felicis erue silvas,
fer stabulis inimicum ignem atque interfice messis,   330
ure sata et validam in vitis molire bipennem,
tanta meae si te ceperunt taedia laudis.'
   At mater sonitum thalamo sub fluminis alti
sensit. eam circum Milesia vellera Nymphae
carpebant hyali saturo fucata colore,   335
Drymoque Xanthoque Ligeaque Phyllodoceque,
caesariem effusae nitidam per candida colla,
[Nisaee Spioque Thaliaque Cymodoceque,]
Cydippe et flava Lycorias, altera virgo,
altera tum primos Lucinae experta labores,   340
Clioque et Beroe soror, Oceanitides ambae,
ambae auro, pictis incinctae pellibus ambae,
atque Ephyre atque Opis et Asia Deiopea
et tandem positis velox Arethusa sagittis.
inter quas curam Clymene narrabat inanem   345
Volcani, Martisque dolos et dulcia furta,
aque Chao densos divum numerabat amores.
carmine quo captae dum fusis mollia pensa
devolvunt, iterum maternas impulit auris
luctus Aristaei, vitreisque sedilibus omnes   350
obstipuere; sed ante alias Arethusa sorores
prospiciens summa flavum caput extulit unda,

et procul: 'o gemitu non frustra exterrita tanto,
Cyrene soror, ipse tibi, tua maxima cura,
tristis Aristaeus Penei genitoris ad undam   355
stat lacrimans, et te crudelem nomine dicit.'
huic percussa nova mentem formidine mater
'duc, age, duc ad nos; fas illi limina divum
tangere' ait. simul alta iubet discedere late
flumina, qua iuvenis gressus inferret. at illum   360
curvata in montis faciem circumstetit unda
accepitque sinu vasto misitque sub amnem.
iamque domum mirans genetricis et umida regna
speluncisque lacus clausos lucosque sonantis
ibat, et ingenti motu stupefactus aquarum   365
omnia sub magna labentia flumina terra
spectabat diversa locis, Phasimque Lycumque,
et caput unde altus primum se erumpit Enipeus,
unde pater Tiberinus et unde Aniena fluenta
saxosusque sonans Hypanis Mysusque Caicus   370
et gemina auratus taurino cornua vultu
Eridanus, quo non alius per pinguia culta
in mare purpureum violentior effluit amnis.
postquam est in thalami pendentia pumice tecta
perventum et nati fletus cognovit inanis   375
Cyrene, manibus liquidos dant ordine fontis
germanae, tonsisque ferunt mantelia villis;
pars epulis onerant mensas et plena reponunt
pocula, Panchaeis adolescunt ignibus arae.
et mater 'cape Maeonii carchesia Bacchi: 380
Oceano libemus' ait. simul ipsa precatur
Oceanumque patrem rerum Nymphasque sorores,
centum quae silvas, centum quae flumina servant.
ter liquido ardentem perfundit nectare Vestam,
ter flamma ad summum tecti subiecta reluxit.   385
omine quo firmans animum sic incipit ipsa:
    'Est in Carpathio Neptuni gurgite vates
caeruleus Proteus, magnum qui piscibus aequor
et iuncto bipedum curru metitur equorum.
hic nunc Emathiae portus patriamque revisit   390
Pallenen; hunc et Nymphae veneramur et ipse
grandaevus Nereus: novit namque omnia vates,

quae sint, quae fuerint, quae mox ventura trahantur;
quippe ita Neptuno visum est, immania cuius
armenta et turpis pascit sub gurgite phocas.   395
hic tibi, nate, prius vinclis capiendus, ut omnem
expediat morbi causam eventusque secundet.
nam sine vi non ulla dabit praecepta, neque illum
orando flectes; vim duram et vincula capto
tende; doli circum haec demum frangentur inanes.   400
ipsa ego te, medios cum sol accenderit aestus,
cum sitiunt herbae et pecori iam gratior umbra est,
in secreta senis ducam, quo fessus ab undis
se recipit, facile ut somno adgrediare iacentem.
verum ubi correptum manibus vinclisque tenebis,   405
tum variae eludent species atque ora ferarum.
fiet enim subito sus horridus atraque tigris
squamosusque draco et fulva cervice leaena,
aut acrem flammae sonitum dabit atque ita vinclis
excidet, aut in aquas tenuis dilapsus abibit.   410
sed quanto ille magis formas se vertet in omnis
tam tu, nate, magis contende tenacia vincla,
donec talis erit mutato corpore qualem
videris incepto tegeret cum lumina somno.'
Haec ait et liquidum ambrosiae diffundit odorem,   415
quo totum nati corpus perduxit; at illi
dulcis compositis spiravit crinibus aura
atque habilis membris venit vigor. est specus ingens
exesi latere in montis, quo plurima vento
cogitur inque sinus scindit sese unda reductos,   420
deprensis olim statio tutissima nautis;
intus se vasti Proteus tegit obice saxi.
hic iuvenem in latebris aversum a lumine Nympha
conlocat, ipsa procul nebulis obscura resistit.
Iam rapidus torrens sitientis Sirius Indos   425
ardebat caelo, et medium sol igneus orbem
hauserat; arebant herbae, et cava flumina siccis
faucibus ad limum radii tepefacta coquebant,
cum Proteus consueta petens e fluctibus antra
ibat; eum vasti circum gens umida ponti   430
exsultans rorem late dispergit amarum.
sternunt se somno diversae in litore phocae;

ipse, velut stabuli custos in montibus olim,
vesper ubi e pastu vitulos ad tecta reducit
auditisque lupos acuunt balatibus agni,   435
consedit scopulo medius, numerumque recenset.
cuius Aristaeo quoniam est oblata facultas,
vix defessa senem passus componere membra
cum clamore ruit magno, manicisque iacentem
occupat. ille suae contra non immemor artis   440
omnia transformat sese in miracula rerum,
ignemque horribilemque feram fluviumque liquentem.
verum ubi nulla fugam reperit fallacia, victus
in sese redit atque hominis tandem ore locutus
'nam quis te, iuvenum confidentissime, nostras   445
iussit adire domos? quidve hinc petis?' inquit. at ille:
'scis, Proteu, scis ipse; neque est te fallere quicquam:
sed tu desine velle. deum praecepta secuti
venimus hinc lassis quaesitum oracula rebus.'
tantum effatus. ad haec vates vi denique multa   450
ardentis oculos intorsit lumine glauco,
et graviter frendens sic fatis ora resolvit:
   'Non te nullius exercent numinis irae;
magna luis commissa: tibi has miserabilis Orpheus
haudquaquam ob meritum poenas, ni fata resistant,   455
suscitat, et rapta graviter pro coniuge saevit.
illa quidem, dum te fugeret per flumina praeceps,
immanem ante pedes hydrum moritura puella
servantem ripas alta non vidit in herba.
at chorus aequalis Dryadum clamore supremos   460
implevit montis; flerunt Rhodopeiae arces
altaque Pangaea et Rhesi Mavortia tellus
atque Getae atque Hebrus et Actias Orithyia.
ipse cava solans aegrum testudine amorem
te, dulcis coniunx, te solo in litore secum,   465
te veniente die, te decedente canebat.
Taenarias etiam fauces, alta ostia Ditis,
et caligantem nigra formidine lucum
ingressus, manisque adiit regemque tremendum
nesciaque humanis precibus mansuescere corda.   470
at cantu commotae Erebi de sedibus imis
umbrae ibant tenues simulacraque luce carentum,

quam multa in foliis avium se milia condunt,
vesper ubi aut hibernus agit de montibus imber,
matres atque viri defunctaque corpora vita   475
magnanimum heroum, pueri innuptaeque puellae,
impositique rogis iuvenes ante ora parentum,
quos circum limus niger et deformis harundo
Cocyti tardaque palus inamabilis unda
alligat et novies Styx interfusa coercet.   480
quin ipsae stupuere domus atque intima Leti
Tartara caeruleosque implexae crinibus anguis
Eumenides, tenuitque inhians tria Cerberus ora,
atque Ixionii vento rota constitit orbis.
iamque pedem referens casus evaserat omnis,   485
redditaque Eurydice superas veniebat ad auras
pone sequens (namque hanc dederat Proserpina legem),
cum subita incautum dementia cepit amantem,
ignoscenda quidem, scirent si ignoscere manes:
restitit, Eurydicenque suam iam luce sub ipsa   490
immemor heu! victusque animi respexit. ibi omnis
effusus labor atque immitis rupta tyranni
foedera, terque fragor stagnis auditus Averni.
illa 'quis et me' inquit 'miseram et te perdidit, Orpheu,
quis tantus furor? en iterum crudelia retro   495
fata vocant, conditque natantia lumina somnus.
iamque vale: feror ingenti circumdata nocte
invalidasque tibi tendens, heu non tua, palmas.'
dixit et ex oculis subito, ceu fumus in auras
commixtus tenuis, fugit diversa, neque illum   500
prensantem nequiquam umbras et multa volentem
dicere praeterea vidit; nec portitor Orci
amplius obiectam passus transire paludem.
quid faceret? quo se rapta bis coniuge ferret?
quo fletu manis, qua numina voce moveret?   505
illa quidem Stygia nabat iam frigida cumba.
septem illum totos perhibent ex ordine mensis
rupe sub aëria deserti ad Strymonis undam
flesse sibi, et gelidis haec evolvisse sub astris
mulcentem tigris et agentem carmine quercus;   510
qualis populea maerens philomela (sub umbra)
amissos queritur fetus, quos durus arator

observans nido implumis detraxit; at illa
flet noctem, ramoque sedens miserabile carmen
integrat, et maestis late loca questibus implet.   515
nulla Venus, non ulli animum flexere hymenaei:
solus Hyperboreas glacies Tanaimque nivalem
arvaque Riphaeis numquam viduata pruinis
lustrabat, raptam Eurydicen atque inrita Ditis
dona querens. spretae Ciconum quo munere matres   520
inter sacra deum nocturnique orgia Bacchi
discerptum latos iuvenem sparsere per agros.
tum quoque marmorea caput a cervice revulsum
gurgite cum medio portans Oeagrius Hebrus
volveret, Eurydicen vox ipsa et frigida lingua   525
a miseram Eurydicen! anima fugiente vocabat:
Eurydicen toto referebant flumine ripae.'
    Haec Proteus, et se iactu dedit aequor in altum,
quaque dedit, spumantem undam sub vertice torsit.
at non Cyrene; namque ultro adfata timentem: 530
'nate, licet tristis animo deponere curas.
haec omnis morbi causa, hinc miserabile Nymphae,
cum quibus illa choros lucis agitabat in altis,
exitium misere apibus. tu munera supplex
tende petens pacem, et facilis venerare Napaeas;   535
namque dabunt veniam votis, irasque remittent.
sed modus orandi qui sit prius ordine dicam.
quattuor eximios praestanti corpore tauros,
qui tibi nunc viridis depascunt summa Lycaei,
delige, et intacta totidem cervice iuvencas.   540
quattuor his aras alta ad delubra dearum
constitue, et sacrum iugulis demitte cruorem,
corporaque ipsa boum frondoso desere luco.
post, ubi nona suos Aurora ostenderit ortus,
inferias Orphei Lethaea papavera mittes   545
et nigram mactabis ovem, lucumque revises:
placatam Eurydicen vitula venerabere caesa.'
    Haud mora: continuo matris praecepta facessit;
ad delubra venit, monstratas excitat aras,
quattuor eximios praestanti corpore tauros   550
ducit et intacta totidem cervice iuvencas.
post, ubi nona suos Aurora induxerat ortus,

inferias Orphei mittit, lucumque revisit.
hic vero subitum ac dictu mirabile monstrum
aspiciunt, liquefacta boum per viscera toto   555
stridere apes utero et ruptis effervere costis,
immensasque trahi nubes, iamque arbore summa
confluere et lentis uvam demittere ramis.
    Haec super arvorum cultu pecorumque canebam
et super arboribus, Caesar dum magnus ad altum   560
fulminat Euphraten bello victorque volentis
per populos dat iura viamque adfectat Olympo.
illo Vergilium me tempore dulcis alebat
Parthenope studiis florentem ignobilis oti,
carmina qui lusi pastorum audaxque iuventa,   565
Tityre, te patulae cecini sub tegmine fagi.

Commentary

The Eclogues

ECLOGUE 1

The first *Eclogue* was composed in 41 BC or soon after, and is certainly later in time than some of the other poems. It is placed first in the collection because it is in a sense programmatic, that is to say it proclaims very clearly the nature of the new type of pastoral which Virgil was introducing, a type in which the real world and the imaginary Arcadia are intermingled. It proclaims too (through Tityrus) the hopes Virgil placed in Octavian (see note on 6), hopes soon to be reiterated in the *Georgics* and the *Aeneid*; yet there is deep uncertainty too, as is only too plain in the unhappy plight of Meliboeus.

Historical background
This poem is concerned with two shepherds whose farms have been confiscated for the settlement of soldiers (70f.); one of them has his farm restored after a petition to an unnamed *iuvenis* in Rome (42). This situation corresponds to the historical realities of the time. After the battle of Philippi in 42 BC it was agreed by the victors, Antony and Octavian, that land in northern Italy should be confiscated for the settlement of veterans; Octavian put Varus in charge of these operations, while Gallus was associated with tax-collection from the exempted farms. Cremona was one of the areas involved, and evidently Mantuan territory (where Virgil was born and brought up) was also included (9, 28; *Geo.* 2, 198). Cf. also Hor. *Sat.* 2, 2, 114f.

Allegory
There is some evidence (though most or even all of it probably stems from inferences drawn from *Eclogues* 1 and 9) that Virgil's farm was among those confiscated, but that it was restored to him through the help of powerful friends (Gallus and Varus) who pleaded his case with Octavian. It is probable that *Eclogue* 9 (a plea for restoration) was written before *Eclogue* 1 (thanks for restoration from Tityrus, and lamentation for loss from Meliboeus), so there is no need to assume (with Servius) that the restoration was subsequently annulled. It can be said with complete confidence that both these *Eclogues* spring from the personal experience of Virgil himself and of his friends.

Shall we then equate Tityrus allegorically with Virgil? Servius thought so (adding such suggestions as that Galatea was Mantua, Amaryllis Rome, and that *pinus* and *fontes* (lines 38-9) mean Rome and the senators respectively), and many since have followed him; but precise correspondence by allegory is not Virgil's method, and in any case Tityrus is old and a slave and a stranger to Rome, and Virgil none of these. Lejay is right in calling this eclogue a 'poem of allusion not of allegory', and so is Saint-Denis when he says that Tityrus and Meliboeus are both Virgil, and neither Virgil.

The new type of pastoral
Many of Virgil's pastorals not only use names, scenery and phrases from Theocritus' *Idylls* but also adapt aspects of their structure and content (especially 2, 3, 5, 7, 8); but this poem has no relationship with the content of any idyll of Theocritus, being concerned with a theme wholly personal to the country folk of Virgil's time. The scenery here (as in 9) is somewhat more specific (e.g. 46f., 67f) than the blend of Sicily, Arcadia and Italy which Virgil often uses, and we are led to feel (though we are not told so) that *nostra urbs* (line 20) is Mantua. Nevertheless the Arcadian element is also very strong: it could be said that Virgil has here defined his new type of pastoral by moving from Theocritus in two opposite directions. In one sense the *Eclogues* are far more remote, idealised and Arcadian than the relatively life-like realism of Theocritus' pastoral world; yet they sometimes come very close to the actualities of the Roman historical and literary scene, as in this poem and the ninth, and as in the fourth, fifth, sixth and tenth poems. Here then at the beginning of the collection we see the new concept of pastoral: an even remoter and more stylised world than ever before which can paradoxically embrace the historical realities of the Roman world. Here the outside world enters the private world of the shepherds; Roman actuality is blended with the Greek convention in a most remarkable way. On the one hand, the life of the shepherds becomes more clearly than ever before an escapist life of poetry and song, of private peace, of withdrawal from the chaos and violence and ambition of men seeking power and empire; and yet it must also confront reality. Tityrus has, through good fortune, come to terms with the outside world and may therefore continue to enjoy his pastoral bliss; Meliboeus has not, and at a stroke his fragile happiness is destroyed.

Literary qualities
In form the poem is carefully symmetrical: the individual lines are often patterned into memorable descriptive pictures, and the sections have a correspondence in length which is not too exact (5, 5; 8, 7, 1; 9, 4, 6; 13, 5; 15, 5). The content is wholly taken up with the tension between joy and sorrow, the latter expressed with moving poignancy and muted sympathy (as opposed for example to the dramatic intensity of the treatment of Dido's tragedy). This muted tone of sorrow was proper to the pastoral genre already in Theocritus (e.g. *Id.* 1, 3) but was so appropriate for Virgil's sensitive reactions towards suffering and unhappiness that it became a particular mark of his individual pastoral style (as for example especially in 2, 5, 8, 9, 10). It is in fact the sorrow of Meliboeus, the innocent victim, rather than the joy of Tityrus that lingers longest in the memory.
For discussion of this eclogue see R. Coleman *G.R.* 1966, pp. 79-97;

E.A. Fredricksmeyer *Hermes* 1966, pp. 208-18; L.P. Wilkinson *Hermes,* 1966, pp. 320-24; G. Williams *Tradition and Originality* . . . , pp. 307-12; V. Pöschl (cited in intro. to *Ecl.* 7); M. Winterbottom *G.R.* 1976, pp. 55-9.

1 f. The opening lines present Tityrus in the complete pastoral setting — shade, music, a beloved shepherdess; this sets up immediately a point of contrast for the references to the contemporary Roman world with which the poem is to deal.
1 Tityrus is the name of a shepherd in Theocritus *Id.* 3.2 (a poem addressed to Amaryllis) and *Id.* 7.72; cf. also *Ecl.* 3.20; 6, 4; 8.55. Most of Virgil's pastoral names are taken from Theocritus, but Meliboeus is not; it is however a Greek name meaning a cattle-minder. This line is recalled in the last line of the *Georgics* (4.566 *Tityre, te patulae cecini sub tegmine fagi*). The setting is idyllic and reminiscent of Theocritus; cf. *Id.* 7, 88-9 ('you sang sweetly beneath oak or pine') and *Id.* 12.8 ('beneath the shady beech').

tegmine: the word is unusual in this context; it normally means 'covering' in the sense of clothing, hence the parody in Numitorius' *Antibucolica* (Don. *Vit. Verg.* 43) *Tityre, si toga calda tibi est, quo tegmine fagi?*'
2 'practise your pastoral Muse on a slender pipe'; cf. *Ecl.* 6.8 and Lucr. 4.589 (of Pan) *fistula silvestrem ne cesset fundere musam.* For *silvae* indicating the pastoral setting, cf. *Ecl.* 4.3. Milton imitates the use of *meditari* (cf. Hor. *Sat.* 1.9.2) in *Lycidas* 66 ('meditate the thankless Muse'). *Avena* is literally an oat-stalk, and is commonly used, like *calamus* (10), *harundo* (6.8), of the shepherd's reed-pipe; cf. *Ecl.* 10.51, Milton, *Lycidas* 88, 'But now my Oat proceeds'; Collins, *Ode to Evening* 'If aught of oaten stop or pastoral song . . .'. Its epithet *tenuis* is both literal (of the instrument itself) and metaphorical (of the 'slender' style of the *Eclogues*). This line, like the previous one, has a patterned arrangement, in this case very near to a perfect golden line (which is composed of adjective, adjective, verb, noun, noun), and defined thus by Dryden, 'two substantives and two adjectives, with a verb betwixt them to keep the peace'.
3 **nos**: in very strong antithesis to *tu* (line 1), an antithesis reinforced by the repetition of *nos* and *patria* in the next line, and then of *tu.* Thus the whole theme of the poem's contrast between joy and sorrow

is expressed in the opening lines; we are compelled to ponder over the contrast between Tityrus' idyllic pastoral world and the real world so cruel to Meliboeus.
4 **lentus**: 'at ease', *'otiosus'* (Servius), cf. *Culex* 213.
5 **Amaryllida**: Greek form of the accusative, here cognate accusative after *resonare;* cf. (somewhat differently) *Geo.* 3.338 *litoraque alcyonen resonant, acalanthida dumi.* Amaryllis is a name from Theocritus (*Id.* 3.1; 4.36), well-known from Milton, *Lycidas* 68 'To sport with Amaryllis in the shade'. For the idea, with a different construction, cf. Prop. 1. 18. 31 *resonent mihi 'Cynthia' silvae,* Shakespeare *Twelfth Night* 1.5.293 'Holla your name to the reverberate hills, and make the babbling gossip of the air cry out "Olivia!"' '

deus: the word expresses the natural exaggeration of the grateful Tityrus. The benefactor of Tityrus is surely intended to suggest Octavian, though Virgil does not name him or give any other explicit indication. The extent to which Tityrus represents Virgil himself is discussed in the introduction to this *Eclogue*. The official deification of Octavian (Augustus) in his lifetime or after his death, and the fact that he was the adopted son of *divus Iulius* is not really relevant here; the expression is due to the personal exuberance (*mihi,* line 7) of Tityrus' vocabulary. Cf. 3.104, and compare the deification of Daphnis in the pastoral mode (5.64f.), with altars for his worship as in line 43 in this eclogue. This is a bucolic and not a political deification.

otia: cf. *Ecl.* 5.61 *amat bonus otia Daphnis;* the word here describes the peaceful pastoral life in contrast with worldly urban activity (*negotium*) and also in contrast with military life. See Coleman *ad loc.*
7 **illius**: the repetition emphasises the gratitude of Tityrus. Notice the pause after the fourth foot, called bucolic diaeresis because it was especially associated with Theocritus. It is quite common in the *Eclogues*; cf. lines 11, 74; and 2.15, 26, 42, 58.
9 **errare**: the infinitive after *permittere* is not uncommon in verse; cf. *Aen.* 9.240 and compare line 55, 2.43; 9.14. The word

indicates browsing and roaming around
without fear; cf. Theocr. *Id.* 9. 4; Hor.
Epod. 2. 12.

10 **ludere**: the verb suggests the carefree
life of the pastoral world; cf. *Ecl.* 6.1 and
Virgil's reference to his *Eclogues* in *Geo.* 4.
565 *carmina qui lusi pastorum.*
calamo: the word, taken from
Greek, means a reed, hence a reed-pipe; cf.
avena (line 2), *harundo* (6.8).

11 Meliboeus means that his natural
feelings of envy are outweighed by
astonishment that in such bad times
anyone can have such good luck.

12 **usque adeo turbatur**: 'there is such
complete chaos'; *turbatur* is impersonal
passive; cf. Ter. *Eun.* 649; Tac. *Ann.* 1.20.
The main MSS have *turbamur*, but
Quintilian read *turbatur* and Servius knew
the reading, and rightly preferred it.
Usque strengthens *adeo*.

12-13 'Look, I myself am driving my
goats along sick at heart, and this one,
Tityrus, I can indeed scarcely drag along.'
Protinus is more often used of time
('straight away') than of space, but cf.
Aen. 10. 340 *protinus hasta fugit* ('the
spear sped straight on').

14 **namque**: the word introduces the
explanation of why he has to drag one of
the goats. It is rare for *namque* to be
postponed from the beginning of its clause
(cf. 3.33; *Aen.* 5.733).

14-15 **gemellos . . . reliquit**: 'she gave
birth to twin kids, the hope of the flock,
but left them on the bare rock', i.e. they
were born dead or so weak that they could
not be saved. For *spem gregis*, cf. *Geo.*
4.162; Theocritus (*Id.* 1.25; 3.34) speaks of
a goat that has had twins as an especially
valuable present.

15 **laeva**: 'foolish'; cf. Hor. *AP* 302 *o ego
laevus*. There is a slight ellipse — I remember
omens warning me (and) if I hadn't been
stupid (I would have taken notice). The
phrase is repeated in *Aen.* 2.54 with a
rather different meaning.

17 **de caelo tactas**: 'struck by lightning',
an evil omen; cf. Cic. *Div.* 1.16f.

18 **qui**: perhaps 'what kind of a person',
rather than 'who' (cf. 2.19), but the point
cannot be pressed as Virgil varies between
qui and *quis* for reasons of euphony.

19f. Tityrus does not reply directly to the
question, but instead brings us out of the
fragile dream-world of the pastoral
convention very forcefully indeed by
referring to his experience of Rome, the
capital city of a very real world. The

spondaic movement of line 19 reinforces
the emphasis.

20 **huic nostrae**: the local market-town;
probably Virgil has Mantua in mind, but he
does not say so.

21 **depellere**: 'to drive'; *de-* has the sense
of destination, as in *deducere coloniam,
demittere naves*. The word is also a
technical term for 'to wean'; cf. Varro *RR*
2.2.17; *Ecl.* 3.82; 7.15; *Geo.* 3.187; but
the construction with *quo* ('whither')
necessitates the other meaning syntactically.

22-3 The simple attitude of Tityrus,
whose experience had never comprehended
anything like the city of Rome, is very
engaging.

24 **alias inter . . . urbes**: the order is not
unusual in verse (cf. a rarer example in
6.19), though *lenta . . . inter viburna* (25)
is more normal.

25 **lenta . . . viburna**: 'twining osiers'.
The word *lenta* (cf. 3.83) emphasises the
point of comparison: the cypresses stand
straight and high, the osiers bend and
interweave in bushes or hedges.

26 **tanta . . . causa**: 'the great reason',
for making the long journey for the first
time.

27 **libertas**: Tityrus is a slave who has at
last saved enough money (*peculium*, 32)
to go to Rome to buy his freedom. He had
not bothered to save (*iners*) while he loved
the extravagant Galatea, but the change of
his affections in favour of Amaryllis led
him to thriftier ways. Observe how
obliquely Virgil moves towards the theme
of land restoration: it was not the primary
reason for Tityrus' journey to Rome. See
note on 44.

sera tamen respexit: 'though late in
coming, did at last look on me with favour';
cf. Prop. 3.15.35 *sera, tamen pietas*; and for
respicere, cf. *Aen.* 5.689; Hor. *Odes* 1.2.36.

28 **candidior**: full-scale allegorical
interpretations find it embarrassing that
Virgil, when equated with Tityrus, should
be a slave and old. Servius suggests, to
avoid that latter difficulty, that *candidior*
should be taken with *libertas* and not with
barba! See the introduction to this
Eclogue.

30 **Galatea**: in Theocritus (*Id.* 6; *Id.* 11)
Galatea is a sea nymph who enters the
pastoral world because Polyphemus the
shepherd is in love with her.

34 **ingratae**: the countryman's
complaint that his wares are not sufficiently
appreciated or adequately paid for by the
people of the towns.

35 A rather humorous conflation of 'I never came home with much money' and 'my hand was never heavy with money'.

36 **Amarylli:** Greek vocative form with short final *i*; cf. *Alexi* (2.6); *Daphni* (5.25); *Moeri* (9.1).

37 'for whom you were letting the fruits hang on their trees'; Amaryllis was waiting for Tityrus to return so that the fruit could be picked fresh for him.

38 **aberat:** the final short syllable (which in archaic Latin was long) is here lengthened in arsis, i.e. by the ictus (beat) at the beginning of the foot; cf. 3.97; 6.53; 7.23; 9.66; 10.69; Page *ad loc.* and Austin's note on *Aen.* 4.64.

38-9 Notice how the effect of the 'pathetic fallacy' is reinforced by the slow spondees and the repetition of the name *Tityrus* and the word *ipse*. The attribution to inanimate things of feelings and emotions (πάθη) is generally called 'pathetic fallacy'. It occurs from earliest times in Greek literature (e.g. Hom. *Il.* 19.362) but its use, including the personification of animals, was greatly extended in pastoral poetry (cf. Theocr. *Id.* 1.71f; 7.74f. with Gow's note). Examples in the *Eclogues* are 5.27f. (see note on 5.20f.), 62f.; 10.13f.

40 **Quid facerem:** 'What (else) could I have done?' (cf. 7.14), i.e. his absence from Amaryllis was unavoidable as he had to go to Rome to purchase his freedom.

exire: supply *alibi* from the next line.

41 **praesentis ... divos:** i.e. Octavian (*iuvenem*, 42) and his friends. For the phrase, similarly employed, cf. Hor. *Odes* 3.5.2. The language (see note on 6) is again the excited exaggeration of a simple shepherd.

42 **iuvenem:** Octavian was in his early twenties at this time; cf. *Geo.* 1.500.

42-3 **quotannis ... fumant:** 'in whose honour our altars smoke twelve days a year', i.e. Tityrus is now making and proposing to make a monthly offering to his benefactor.

44 The repetition of *hic* ('here') from 42 emphasises that it was through the good fortune of being there in Rome (for a different reason, his manumission) that Tityrus was able to ask Octavian on his master's behalf for the restoration of his farm (see note on 27). *Primus* suggests the readiness with which Octavian himself replied to the request.

45 'Feed your cattle as before, boys; rear your bulls', i.e. your farm is restored. Notice the wholly pastoral phraseology

employed to express the official decision of the great man. *Pueri* is used of the humble personages of the pastoral world; cf. 3.111 and the Greek παῖς. For *submittere*, cf. *Geo.* 3.73, 159; other possible but less likely meanings are 'mate' (= *admittere*) or 'yoke' (*submittere iugo*).

46 **tua:** probably the meaning is that his master's farm belongs in some sense to Tityrus because that is where he tends the flocks and herds; it is also possible that Tityrus had a smallholding of his own on his master's farm.

47-8 'and they are big enough for you, although bare rock and swamp with its muddy rushes cover the whole pasture'; many editors prefer to punctuate so that the *quamvis* clause goes with what follows, but it is relevant to *magna*. Servius, perhaps rightly, sees a reference to the low-lying land around the river Mincius on which Mantua stands.

49-50 These are the disadvantages which Meliboeus pictures himself as having when he is forced out of his farm — pasturage to which the flocks and herds are unaccustomed and the likelihood of having neighbours with diseased animals. Notice the patterned nature of these lines.

49 **gravis ... fetas:** 'the sickly mothers', i.e. immediately after giving birth they are frail and need special attention; for *gravis*, cf. *Geo.* 3.95; Hor. *Epod.* 2.57. Others take it to mean 'the pregnant animals', with *gravis* in the sense of *gravidus;* cf. *Aen.* 1.274.

temptabunt: 'assail'; cf. *Geo.* 3.441.

51 **fortunate senex:** the repetition from 46 introduces the more positive aspect of Tityrus' fortune, and the spondaic rhythm of the rest of this line and the next reflects peace and security (*lentus in umbra,* 5).

52 **fontis sacros:** each fountain would have its nymph. Notice the emphasis on the religious aspect of the countryman's life; cf. Theocr. *Id.* 7.136.

frigus captabis opacum: 'you will seek out the cool shade'; cf. 2.8.

53-5 'On this side, as always before, the hedge on your neighbour's boundary, with Hyblaean bees feeding on its willow flowers, will often coax you with its gentle whispers to enjoy a siesta'. For *quae semper (suasit),* cf. 6.15; for the use of *ab,* cf. the normal idiom *a dextero cornu* ('on the right wing'). Hybla was famous for its honey (cf. 7.37); it was on the slopes of Mt Etna, and an oblique reference may be intended to Theocritus, whose pastorals are often set in Sicily; cf. 2.21; 4.1; etc.

54 florem depasta is an example of a retained accusative with a passive verb, a construction of which Virgil is fond. It arises from two different Greek constructions: the normal use of the middle voice with a direct object and the use of the accusative of respect ('fed on as to its flowers'); the second is dominant here. For fuller discussion see my note on *Aen.* 5.135 (Oxford edition); in the *Eclogues,* cf. 3.106; 6.15, 53, 68, 75; 7.32; 8.4.

55 Observe how the whispering leaves (cf. Theocr. *Id.* 1.1) are reflected onomatopoeically by the alliteration of *s*.

suadebit inire: the infinitive with *suadere* is not uncommon in verse; cf. *Geo.* 2.315-16; *Aen.* 3.364 and compare note on 9.

56 frondator: 'the pruner', the man who stripped the tree of leaves to prevent excessive shade; cf. 9.60-61; *Geo.* 2.400-401. In the light of these passages the suggestion that *frondator* is the name of a bird otherwise unknown cannot be sustained.

57 In Theocritus (*Id.* 5.96) a wood pigeon is promised as a present; cf. *Ecl.* 3.68-9. For the phrase *tua cura* (= *tuae deliciae*) in apposition, cf. *Ecl.* 10.22; Ov. *Trist.* 4.6.45 *absunt, mea cura, sodales.* The order of 57-8 is interwoven, so that *gemere cessabunt* is to be supplied in 57.

58 gemere . . . turtur: cf. Theocr. *Id.* 7.141 ἔστενε τρυγών ('the turtle-dove made moan'). Horace (*Odes* 1.2.9-10) speaks of doves in lofty elm-trees.

59f. This type of description, in which the normal procedures of nature are imagined to be reversed, is called adynaton (ἀδύνατον, 'impossibility'). Compare *Ecl.* 8.27-8; 53-57; Theocr. *Id.* 1.132-6 (with Gow's note); Hor. *Epod.* 5.79f.; 16.25f.; Ov. *Trist.* 1.8.1-7, especially line 5 *omnia naturae praepostera legibus ibunt.* It is particularly frequent in Ovid's elegiac verse.

59 leves . . . in aethere cervi: 'light-footed stags will pasture in the heavens'; some late MSS have *aequore* which has been adopted by some editors to make a contrast with line 60, but there is no need for such a contrast.

60 'and the seas will leave the fish uncovered on the shore'. This phenomenon does not seem very strange, but what Virgil means is that the seas will contract and withdraw from their usual levels, and fish will live their lives on dry land.

61-2 'roaming in exile over each other's territories the Parthians will drink of the

Arar or the Germans of the Tigris'; the idea is the total confusion of geography between east and west. The Arar is the modern Saône, in Eastern France, not far from Germany; the Tigris is in Mesopotamia. Tityrus' statement betrays (see note on 64f.) that in his ecstasy over his own good fortune he is oblivious of Meliboeus' plight.

63 quam: 'before', anticipated by *ante* of 59 and 61. The subjunctive (*labatur*) is normal with a temporal clause referring to the future.

64f. Meliboeus takes up Tityrus' point about the impossibility of Germans and Parthians changing places by lamenting that something comparable is in fact to happen to him as he goes into far exile from his farm. Compare Goldsmith, *The Deserted Village* (341f.):

Ah, no! To distant climes, a dreary scene,
Where half the convex world intrudes
    between,
Through torrid tracts with fainting steps
    they go,
Where wild Altama murmurs to their woe . .
Far different these from every former
    scene—
The cooling brook, the grassy-vested
    green. . . .

64 sitientis . . . Afros: 'to the thirsty land of the Africans', accusative of motion, like *Scythiam, Oaxen, Britannos.*

65 rapidum cretae . . . Oaxen: 'the Oaxes which churns up the chalk'. This is a much disputed passage, partly because of uncertainty about the whereabouts of the river Oaxes, and partly because *Cretae* may be the island of Crete. It seems on the whole best to accept the evidence for Oaxes as a river in Mesopotamia, a by-form of Oxus, in which case we get references to the south (Africans), to the north-east (Scythia), to the east (Mesopotamia), and to the north-west (Britain). The word *cretae* then will be an objective genitive (*rapiens cretam*) for which there is no parallel. The evidence for Oaxes as a river in Crete seems to derive from this passage (though there is the Cretan town Axos or Oaxos in Herod. 4.154 and the name Oiaxis for Crete in Ap. Rh. 1.1131), and the construction of *Cretae* would be strange.

66 Cf. Cat. 11.11-2 *ultimosque Britannos;* Hor. *Odes* 1.35.29-30 *in ultimos orbis Britannos;* Tac. *Agr.* 30; Dryden *Astr. Red.* 2 'a world divided from the rest'; Tennyson, *To Virgil,* 'I, from out the

Northern Island sundered once from all the human race, I salute thee, Mantovano ...'.

67-9 'shall I ever again a long time in the future see my homeland, the roof of my little cottage heaped high with turf, see and marvel one day at my kingdom, a few ears of corn?'. This is a very difficult sentence, especially in the adverbial use of *post* in 69, picking up the word from 67: the idea of the last line seems to be that the farm will go to rack and ruin, and instead of *has segetes* (72) he will see *aliquot aristas*. Some scholars have followed Servius' explanation, that *post aliquot aristas* means 'after a number of harvests' (i.e. years), a usage of *aristas* found otherwise only in Claudian (8.372 *decimas emensus aristas*); see U. Schindel, *Hermes* 1969, pp. 472f. Whichever version is preferred, the sentence is disjointed, perhaps deliberately to reflect Meliboeus' agitated and bitter state of mind.

70-72 Here the immediacy and personal impact takes us far from Arcadia into the realities of Virgil's own countryside, and his passionate wish that it shall not be defiled finds very powerful and direct expression.

70 This outburst of bitter indignation is made memorable by the powerfully exaggerated word *impius* ('godless'), the pathos in *tam culta* (so much work he had put in), and the unusual rhythm with the absence of main caesura in either third or fourth foot. Compare the angry tone of *Ecl.* 9.2f.

71 barbarus: again a violent exaggeration, not really with special reference to the possibility of non-Roman soldiers occupying the farm, but rather - like *impius* - a fierce execration against the new owner.

discordia: 'civil war'; cf. the personified figure *Discordia demens* amidst the ghastly shapes at the entrance to Hell (*Aen.* 6.280).

72 The unusual triple rhyme of *-os* (with none of the words in grammatical agreement) adds to the intensity.

73 nunc: highly ironical; cf. the fuller phrase *i nunc et:* the phrase *insere, Daphni, piros* occurs without irony in 9.50.

74 The formula is one normally used as the goats go home for the night (10.77); here of course it is used with the pathos of farewell to his home.

75 proiectus: 'lying'.

76 pendere: a very vivid image; the goats are 'hanging from', 'poised on the edge of', the cliff; cf. Ov. *Pont.* 1.8.51.

77 carmina nulla canam: notice the emphasis on song as part of the idyllic pastoral world, cf. 9.66f.

78 cytisum: 'clover', a frequently-used animal food in the ancient world; cf. 2.64; *Geo.* 2.431; Theocr. *Id.* 5.128.

79f. Tityrus offers generous hospitality in the hope of softening for the moment the disaster that has befallen Meliboeus. To some extent this perhaps modifies the sorrow that has been so dominant in the second half of the poem, and partially resolves the discord of the real world in the temporary harmony of Arcadian peace.

79 poteras: 'you could'; the imperfect is used in a polite and apologetic sense, meaning 'it was (and is) possible'; cf. Ov. *Met.* 1.679 *hoc poteras mecum considere saxo*.

80f. The offer of attractions is reminiscent in structure of those suggested to Galatea by Polyphemus in Theocr. *Id.* 11.45f.

81 molles: soft in the sense of 'ripe', 'mealy', 'floury'.

82-3 The final lines have a very gentle cadence, and the last line of all is patterned very like a golden line. For the imagery compare 2.67 and Milton, *Lycidas* 190 'And now the Sun had stretched out all the hills'.

ECLOGUE 2

This is one of Virgil's earliest eclogues, perhaps written in 43 BC or soon after, and his debt to Theocritus is particularly marked. He has based the poem largely on Polyphemus' lament for Galatea in *Idyll* 11, but has drawn also from other poems of Theocritus, especially *Idyll* 3, the lament of the love-lorn suitor of Amaryllis. Thus the poem is deliberately intended to challenge comparison with Theocritus; for all its similarities these are very considerable points of difference.

Structurally Virgil abandons Theocritus' introduction in which the poet tells
Nicias of the power of poetry in healing the wounds of love: Virgil goes straight,
to Corydon. He also omits the tail-piece of the Theocritean poem, which
comments on how Polyphemus cured his love by his song. He has moved the
setting from the mythological story of the legendary Polyphemus and Galatea
to a possibly real situation of a contemporary shepherd, Corydon, and his
beloved boy Alexis (on the theme of homosexual love in pastoral and elegy
see Coleman pp. 108-9). For the contrast in Theocritus between the sea (Galatea)
and the land (Polyphemus) Virgil has substituted a contrast between the town
(Alexis) and the country (Corydon); the country is seen in idyllic Arcadian
terms.

The tone of the poem is different from the Theocritean original, in the way
which is characteristic of Virgil. He abandons the realism and humour (*Id.*
11.30-33; 77-9) and concentrates more on the pathos (3 *tantum;* 5 *studio . . .
inani*). This difference is seen especially at the endings of the two poems:
Polyphemus is cheerful and rather offhand and quite confident that there are
plenty of other fish in the sea, but Corydon's reference to finding another
Alexis lacks such bravado, and is sad and plaintive. The muted notes of pathos
in Virgil are often reminiscent of Latin love-elegy, and we are reminded here of
the sorrowful tones of Tibullus (perhaps there is influence too from Virgil's
friend and patron the elegist Gallus, cf. *Ecl.* 10).

The structure of the poem is carefully organised, though not absolutely
symmetrical. The opening five lines are balanced by the closing section (69-73);
lines 6-18 with their plaintive tone correspond with lines 56-68 (though 60-62
interrupt the sequence), and the longer central section (19-55) is filled with
various kinds of appeals and arguments. Similarly there is a balance between the
noon-day setting of the early part, and the evening of the closing section; but
above all the symmetry is to be seen in the treatment of atmosphere and tone,
as the pathos and despair of Corydon is conveyed with a unity which contrasts
sharply with the variety of Polyphemus' moods in Theocritus.

The poem is in some sense a precursor of the sympathetic analysis of
unhappy love found later in *Ecl.* 10 and *Aen.* 4. For further discussion see
G. K. Galinsky, *C. Med.* 1965, pp. 161f.; E. W. Leach, *AJP* 1966, pp. 427f;
F. Robertson, *PVS* 1970-71, pp. 8f.

1 Corydon is a name from Theocritus
(*Id.* 4). Notice the patterned nature of the
line with which this elegant poem begins,
and the assonance of *o* and *a*.

ardebat Alexin: the transitive use
('burned with love for') is poetic; cf. Hor.
Odes 4.9.13 and the use of *deperire* in
Cat. 35.12. Alexis is a Greek name found
in Meleager (*Anth. Pal.* 12.127, an
epigram which has influenced Virgil in this
poem); the name does not occur in
Theocritus.

2 **delicias domini:** the boy Alexis was
the favourite slave (*puer delicatus*) of his
master (who was presumably Corydon's
master too); hence the hopeless nature of

Corydon's love.

3-4 **tantum . . . veniebat:** 'all he could do
was to keep on coming through the dense
beech-woods, the high overshadowing
trees'; the emphatic *tantum* conveys at this
early stage in the poem the pathos of
Corydon's loneliness.

3 **umbrosa cacumina:** in apposition to
fagos; cf. 9.9. The picture is wholly
pastoral, like the beginning of *Eclogue* 1;
but in this poem (unlike *Eclogue* 1) it
remains so throughout.

4 **incondita:** 'artless'; cf. Cic. *Orat.* 150;
Livy 4.20.2. The pastoral convention is
that the rustic shepherds sing rustic songs;
the contrast between the *rusticitas* of the

country (Corydon) and the *urbanitas* of the town (Alexis) is suggested here and developed later in the poem. The poem is not in fact 'artless', hence the suggestion that *incondita* means something like 'unpremeditated'; but the intention of the word is to contrast the simple shepherd with the sophisticated Alexis.

5 **iactabat**: 'uttered passionately'; cf. *Aen.* 1.102; 2.588.

inani: again there is emphasis on the pathos of Corydon's hopeless plight. *Inanis* is a favourite Virgilian word to express pathetic futility; cf. *Aen.* 10.465. There is a strong contrast here with Theocr. *Id.* 11, because by song Polyphemus heals his sorrow, as Theocritus emphasises both at the beginning (17) and at the end (80-81).

6 **O crudelis Alexi**: the rhythm recalls both the opening of the song of Polyphemus (ὦ λευκὰ Γαλάτεια, *Id.* 11.19) and that of the unnamed lover of Amaryllis (ὦ χαρίεσσ' Ἀμαρυλλί, *Id.* 3.6).

7 There is a sense pause after the trochee in the third foot for the third time in four lines (4, 6, 7). This is an unusual rhythm in the Latin hexameter, but much commoner in Greek; thus the metre as well as the subject-matter proclaims this poem as a variation on Theocritean themes. Cf. Theocr. *Id.* 3.9. ἀπάγξασθαί με ποησεῖς ('you will make me hang myself').

8f. This is an idyllic description of the pastoral world (cf. 1.52) set in sharp contrast (*at me*, 12) with Corydon's sufferings. Cf. Pope, *Past.* 2.85-8:

But see, the shepherds shun the noonday heat,
The lowing herds to murmuring brooks retreat,
To closer shades the panting flocks remove;
Ye gods! and is there no relief for Love?

9 Compare Theocr. *Id.* 7.22 καὶ σαῦρος ἐν αἱμασιαῖσι καθεύδει ('even the lizard sleeps in the walls'); Virgil has reversed the mode of expression.

10 **Thestylis et**: for the postponed conjunction, cf. 1.34, 68. Thestylis is the name of a serving-maid in Theocr. *Id.* 2.

rapido fessis . . . aestu: 'tired with the searing heat'; for *rapidus*, cf. *Geo.* 1.92; 4.425.

11 This describes the herbs of the dish known as *moretum* (the title of an extant poem which used to be attributed to Virgil); *alia* (garlic) and *serpyllum* (thyme)

are in apposition to *herbas*.

12 **at me**: in strong opposition to the previous four lines – Corydon is deprived, as he wanders around looking for Alexis, of the cool shade and peace of the noon-day scene. Most modern editors read *mecum* (i.e. the noise is company for Corydon), but the sentence is much neater if we take *me* as the object of *resonant* (cf. 1.5): 'the groves with their noisy cicadas echo my call'. This is supported by the imitation in Nemesianus (*Ecl.* 4.41-2). For the noise of cicadas, cf. *Geo.* 3.328 *cantu querulae rumpent arbusta cicadae*.

14 **satius**: 'preferable'; cf. *Aen.* 10.59.

15 **Menalcan**: a name from Theocritus (*Id.* 8), which recurs several times in the *Eclogues*. Here he is a young shepherd whom Corydon might have loved in preference to Alexis.

16 A fair complexion seems to have been generally preferred; cf. 10.38-9.

esses: the past tense is due to the influence of *fuit* (14).

17-18 Cf. Theocr. *Id.* 10.28-9 (violets and hyacinths are dark, but chosen first for garlands); 23.30-31 (white lilies wither, disappear like snow).

18 **ligustra cadunt**: *ligustrum* seems to have been a kind of privet, whose whiteness is mentioned also in Ov. *Met.* 13.789; Mart. 1.115.3. For *cadunt* (are left to fall, are not picked), cf. Theocr. *Id.* 23.30 (the lily) μαραίνεται ἀνίκα πίπτει ('it withers when it falls').

vaccinia: 'hyacinths'; cf. 10.39.

19 **qui sim**: 'what kind of a person I am'. In describing his wealth Corydon is probably speaking of what actually belongs to his master but is in his charge.

21f. Corydon's landscape is Sicilian, like that of Theocritus, and his account of his possessions very similar indeed to that of Polyphemus in Theocr. *Id.* 11.34-6.

22 **defit**: 'is lacking'.

23 **canto**: again this is reminiscent of Polyphemus (Theocr. *Id.* 11.38).

23-4 **quae solitus . . . Amphion**: 'songs like those which Amphion used to sing'.

24 A highly ornate, epic-sounding line, conveying Corydon's pride in his ability. The rhythm is very Greek, with a trochaic caesura in the third foot without main caesura in the fourth, a quadrisyllabic ending, and hiatus between *Actaeo* and *Aracyntho* (cf. 10.12, and see note on 3.6). Amphion was the legendary founder of Thebes (near which was the fountain Dirce) to whose song the walls built

themselves (Hor. *AP* 394f.); Aracynthus (cf. Prop. 3.15.42) was a mountain near (but not in) Attica, which used to be called Acte. Servius tells us that the geographical error was thought by some to be deliberate, in order to show that Corydon is a simple soul ignorant of geography; he also suggests, improbably, that *actaeus* is the Greek ἀκταῖος ('by the sea'). Amphion and Zethus, children of Antiope by Jupiter, were brought up amongst shepherds.

25-6 Again Virgil closely follows Theocritus, this time *Id.* 6.34-8 (a song about Polyphemus), where Polyphemus says he is not as ugly as people say, for when he looked into the smooth surface of the sea he seemed to himself very handsome. In *Idyll* 11 (which Virgil has been following in 21-3) Polyphemus admits his ugliness (30-34). Cf. Pope's imitation (*Past.* 2.27f.) 'As in the crystal spring I view my face . . .'.

26 placidum ventis: 'becalmed by the winds', i.e. because they were very gentle; cf. *Geo.* 4.484; *Aen.* 5.763; Hor. *Odes* 1.3.16.

Daphnin: the beautiful quasi-mythological god or prince of the shepherds, son of Hermes and a nymph; see introductory note to *Ecl.* 5.

27 iudice te: 'even if you were judge', prejudiced though you are against me.

si: equal to *siquidem*, 'since' (if it's true, as indeed it is, that . . .); cf. *Geo.* 1.7; *Aen.* 5.798; 6.530.

28f. Corydon's wish is similar in structure to that of Polyphemus in Theocr. *Id.* 11.65-6, but different in content: Polyphemus wants Galatea to be a shepherd with him and join in the milking and cheese-making. Compare Marlowe, *The Passionate Shepherd to his Love*:

Come live with me and be my love;
And we will all the pleasures prove
That hills and valleys, dales and fields,
Woods or steepy mountain yields.

28 sordida: self-deprecatory, like *rusticus* (56).

29 figere cervos: for the expression, cf. *Geo.* 1.308; for the association of hunting with the shepherd's life, which is not very common, cf. 3.12, 75; 10.56f.

30 viridi . . . hibisco: 'with a green switch', a branch of hibiscus (cf. 10.71); rather than, as some say, 'drive to the green hibiscus bushes'.

31-9 This passage about how they might sing to the shepherd's pipe together has

no parallel in Theocr. *Id.* 11.

31-3 The repetition *Pana . . . Pan . . . Pan* is characteristic of the pastoral style; cf. 5.25-30. *Pana* is Greek accusative. Pan was the rural god of shepherds and their music, strongly associated with the Arcadian countryside.

32 The reference is to the Pan-pipe or Syrinx; cf. 8.24; Theocr. *Id.* 8.18; Lucr. 4.588; Ov. *Met.* 1.698-712; this consisted of a number of reeds of different length fastened together side by side with wax. The one described by Corydon (36) had seven reeds of hemlock.

35 For Amyntas' skill in music, cf. *Ecl.* 5.8.

36f. Cf. Pope, *Past.* 2.39f: 'That flute is mine which Colin's tuneful breath Inspired when living, and bequeath'd in death . . .'.

36 disparibus . . . cicutis: 'formed of seven hemlock-stalks of different lengths joined together'; cf. Lucr. 5.1383 *cavas inflare cicutas*.

37 Damoetas is a pastoral name from Theocr. (*Id.* 6) which occurs again in *Ecl.* 3 and 5.

38 secundum: 'as its second owner', with the idea of 'worthy successor'; cf. Hor. *Odes* 1.12.18.

40-42 Virgil returns now to his Theocritean sources: in *Id.* 3.34 the lover says he is keeping for Amaryllis a white goat with two kids; in *Id.* 11.40-41 Polyphemus says he is bringing up eleven fawns and four bear-cubs for Galatea.

40 nec tuta: i.e. in a valley where it was unsafe for Corydon to go. Servius says *commendat a difficultate*.

41 Servius tells us that the white spots would change colour as the goats grew up, so the meaning here is that they are still very young.

42 bina . . . ubera: i.e. they are healthily hungry and well-fed.

43-4 An echo of Theocr. *Id.* 3.35-6 where the lover says that Mermnon's serving-girl wants the goat he is keeping for Amaryllis, and will get it as Amaryllis is so haughty with him.

43 abducere . . . orat: a poetic construction; cf. *Aen.* 6.313.

44 Cf. Theocr. *Id.* 3.33 'you care nothing for me'; for *sordent,* cf. Hor. *Epist.* 1.11.4.

45f. This idyllic passage is imitated by Columella in his book on gardens (10.96f.); there is a languorous aspect reminiscent of Meleager (*Anth. Pal.* 5.147).

50 'she sets off the delicate hyacinths

with pretty yellow marigolds'; this is a perfect golden line which aptly rounds off the highly descriptive passage. *Pingit* suggests that the hyacinths form the background which is decorated with the marigolds; the diminutive *luteolus* recalls the style of Catullus 64, of which the whole passage has been reminiscent.

51 **cana . . . mala:** i.e. quinces.

52 **mea . . . amabat:** a sentimental recollection of his previous love-affair (14).

53 This is a line of unusual rhythm: it is rare for each of the first two feet to be composed of a single word, and there is a hiatus after *pruna,* before the pause caused by the parenthesis. The only other certain instance of hiatus after a short vowel in Virgil is *Aen.* 1.405; for hiatus after a long vowel see note on 3.6.

54 The laurel and the myrtle are the emblems of poetry and love; combined (as they often are; cf. *Ecl.* 7.61f.) they represent Corydon's love song. Cf. Hor. *Odes* 3.4.19-20.

56 Corydon breaks off from his idyllic dream as he faces reality; for *rusticus es,* cf. Theocr. *Id.* 20.3.

57 **Iollas:** evidently the master of the slave-boy Alexis, cf. line 2; hence the futility for Corydon of such a competition. This line is reminiscent of the recurrent theme in elegy of the *dives amator.*

58-9 'I am ruined and have let the south wind get at my blossoms and wild boars into my pure streams'; this was perhaps a proverbial saying.

60 **di quoque:** perhaps especially Apollo, who was once a shepherd for King Admetus, and Venus who loved Adonis in the woods (Theocr. *Id.* 20.34f.). Cf. Pope *Past.* 2.59f: 'See what delights in sylvan scenes appear! Descending gods have found Elysium here. In woods bright Venus with Adonis stray'd. . . .'

61 **Dardaniusque Paris:** the Trojan prince Paris lived when young as a shepherd on Mt Ida; cf. Hor. *Odes* 1.15.

Pallas: Pallas Athena founded Athens, but Corydon would not even take Athens in exchange for the countryside.

62 Cf. *Geo.* 2.485-6.

63-4 These *exempla* are reminiscent of Theocr. *Id.* 10.30-31 where Bucaeus says to Bombyca 'The goat seeks the clover, the wolf the goat, the crane the plough, and I madly seek you'.

65 The Greek type of rhythm has

shortening in hiatus of the long vowel *o* (cf. *Ecl.* 3.79; 6.44; 8.108) and a pause after the trochee in the third foot (see note on 7).

66 **aratra . . . iuvenci:** 'the oxen bring home the plough hanging from the yoke', i.e. with its blade out of the ground; cf. Ov. *Fast.* 5.497 *versa iugo referuntur aratra;* Hor. *Epod.* 2.63-4 *videre fessos vomerem inversum boves collo trahentes languido.*

68 Though the day comes to its end, Corydon's love does not; cf. Theocr. *Id.* 2.38-40; Pope, *Past.* 2.89-92:

But soon the sun with milder rays descends
To the cool ocean, where his journey ends:
On me Love's fiercer flames for ever prey,
By night he scorches, as he burns by day.

69-73 The ending closely recalls Theocr. *Id.* 11.72f. where the Cyclops asks himself 'O Cyclops, Cyclops, where have your wits wandered' (ὦ Κύκλωψ Κύκλωψ πᾷ τὰς φρένας ἐκπεπότασαι;), and goes on to say that he would be better occupied making baskets and collecting fodder; he reflects that he will perhaps find another Galatea even more fair. On the variation in Virgil away from Theocritus' robust realism and light-hearted expansiveness in the direction of greater pathos and terseness see the introduction to this *Eclogue.*

69f. It has been suggested that these lines are not spoken by Corydon but are Virgil's own comment; this seems most unlikely especially in view of the Theocritean parallel (see previous note).

70 There are two points indicating Corydon's negligence here — the vine is only half-pruned, and the supporting elm has not had its leaves stripped off.

71-2 'why don't you rather get ready at least to plait something which your daily needs require from osiers and pliant reeds?'; i.e. Corydon urges himself to return from his preoccupation with hopeless love to the proper activities of the pastoral life. Compare 10.71 and perhaps Cat. 51.13-16.

73 Cf. Theocr. *Id.* 11.76 εὑρησεῖς Γαλάτειαν ἴσως καὶ καλλίον' ἄλλαν ('you will perhaps find another, a more beautiful Galatea'). The Idyll of Theocritus ends, as Virgil's poem does not, with an indication that Polyphemus' song has eased his unhappiness; see also notes on 5 and 69-73.

ECLOGUE 3

This is one of the earliest Eclogues (perhaps c. 42 BC) and one that shows the closest dependence on Theocritus. The first part of it is based on *Idyll* 4, in which Battus and Corydon exchange lively conversation, and the whole of it on *Idyll* 5 where Comatas and Lacon bandy insults and then have a contest in amoebaean song, which Morson judges in favour of Comatas. There are also close reminiscences of *Idylls* 1 and 8.

Amoebaean song in a pastoral setting is found also in Theocritus' eighth idyll: in this type of poem the second singer is required to balance and cap the verses of the first singer (cf. Hor. *Odes* 3.9; Cat. 45 and 62 for this technique in different settings). Virgil has amoebaean song again in *Eclogue* 7, while in *Eclogues* 5 and 8 each singer sings one song only (cf. Theocr. *Id.* 6). Many of Theocritus' bucolic idylls (7, 9, 10 in addition to 5, 6 and 8 already mentioned) are concerned with the song of shepherds, and Virgil constantly refers to song as a major aspect of the pastoral world (in this of course symbolising his own love of poetry); cf. 4.55f.; 5 passim; 6.31f., and especially 9.10f.

The first part of this poem differs from its Theocritean original in its tone. The shepherds in Theocritus are much more direct and real in their conversation: Virgil's are subtle and artificial, much more like literary figures than real shepherds. There is greater emphasis on description and elegance of phraseology, less on the realism and force of the banter and mutual insults. The theme of abuse in the first half of the poem does not lend itself so well to Virgil's smooth hexameter, or to the universalisation and wide symbolism which Virgil so often seeks to achieve, as does the amoebaean song of the second half; in this Virgil expresses through the shepherds' songs concepts of the importance of poetry, in particular as it deals with happy aspects and sad aspects of love (cf. the final lines of Palaemon, 109-10).

1-2 These lines are closely based on the opening of Theocritus' fourth idyll: 'Tell me, Corydon, whose cattle are these? Philondas's?' 'No, Aegon's; he gave them me to look after'.

1 cuium: the adjective *cuius* is an archaic form, common in Plautus and Terence. The form was parodied, according to Donatus (*Vita* 43) as follows:

dic mihi Damoeta: 'cuium pecus' anne Latinum?
Non. verum Aegonis nostri, sic rure loquuntur.

3 For the word order (*o oves, estis semper infelix pecus*), cf. *Geo.* 4.168 *ignavum fucos pecus a praesepibus arcent.*
3 Neaeram: evidently the beloved of both Aegon and Menalcas.
4 fovet: 'courts'.
5 'this hired shepherd milks the sheep twice an hour'; a wildly exaggerated

elaboration of Theocr. *Id.* 4.3 where Corydon is accused of secretly milking the flock he is looking after.

6 pecori et: there is hiatus at the caesura; cf. 63 and see note on 2.24.

7 'Just remember to be more careful about insulting men in that fashion': Damoetas is not a child to be ridiculed with impunity.

8 qui te: understand a verb like *amaverit, corruperit.* Theocritus in *Idyll* 5 (41f., 116f.) is much more explicit.

transversa: 'askance', adverbial accusative; cf. line 63; *Aen.* 5.19; 6.467.

9 faciles: 'tolerant'; cf. *Geo.* 4.535; Theocr. *Id.* 5.18. The Nymphs, local deities of the holy place (*sacellum*), were amused rather than angry.

10-11 'I suppose it was when they saw me cutting down Micon's trees and young vines with my wicked sickle'. Micon's vineyard is taken from Theocr. *Id.* 5.112.

Menalcas sarcastically attributes to himself something which he had seen Damoetas do.

10 arbustum: i.e. the rows of trees on which the vines were trained.

12f. Damoetas does not reply, but adds a new taunt, saying that Menalcas out of envy broke the bow and arrows (*calamus* is not uncommon in this sense) that were given to Daphnis (*puero*). Cf. 7.26; Theocr. *Id.* 5.12-13.

15 'and if you hadn't hurt him somehow, you'd have died'.

16 A reminiscence of Catullus' translation of Callimachus (66.47) *quid facient crines cum ferro talia cedant?* The reference is to what follows: people of thieving habits, like Damoetas, make life impossible for owners of flocks, such as Damon.

19 quo . . . ille: 'where's he off to?' Damoetas dashes out of his hiding-place to steal the goat, but on being seen goes back into hiding.

20 Tityre, coge pecus: i.e. round them up so that stragglers are not stolen. Tityrus is the shepherd looking after Damon's flock.

21 redderet: past jussive, a rare construction equivalent to *reddere debuit;* cf. *Aen.* 8.643.

24 posse negabat: for the omission of the reflexive *se* as subject to *posse,* cf. *Geo.* 2.234.

25f. The transition from the verbal altercations to the proposal of a contest in song is skilfully done.

25 tu illum: supply *vicisti* (21); this line and the next two are vigorous and sarcastic.

25-6 fistula cera iuncta: i.e. did he ever have a properly made Pan-pipe; cf. 2.32; Theocr. *Id.* 5.5f.

26 in triviis: 'at cross-roads', or as we should say 'at street-corners'. Cf. the adjective *trivialis* (trivial), Juv. 7.55.

27 'to murder the poor melody on a squeaky whistle'; cf. Milton, *Lycidas* 123-4 'their lean and flashy songs grate on their scrannel pipes of wretched straw'.

28f. Damoetas proposes a contest in song in terms which are surprisingly gentle after the previous bandying of insults. *Vicissim* indicates the balanced context (amoebaean, see note on 59) which follows at 60f.; cf. Theocr. *Id.* 5.21f.; 8.11f. for the proposal of a contest and the offering of stakes.

30 The heifer is milked twice a day

and has twins, an adaptation of Theocr. *Id.* 1.25-6; cf. *Id.* 8.86.

32f. The very close adaptation of Theocritus continues; cf. *Id.* 8.15f. Spenser imitates this passage, *Shepherd's Calender, March,* 40f.

For als at home I have a syre,
A stepdame eke as whott as fyre,
That dewly adayes counts mine.

35 id quod: 'a thing which·. . .', in apposition to *pocula ponam,* 'I will offer cups'.

36 insanire . . . tibi: 'since you want to enter a mad contest'; for the postposition of *quoniam,* cf. *qui* in 41.

pocula: i.e. a pair of cups, cf. 44. Virgil has in mind here the famous description (ecphrasis) of the cup in Theocr. *Id.* 1.27f.

37 fagina: wooden cups were traditionally associated with the simple life; cf. Tib. 1.10.8.

divini opus: the elision of a long syllable before a short is rare; cf. line 84. Alcimedon is not known.

38-9 'on which a pliant vine embossed upon them by the skilful chisel clothes the clusters spread by the pale ivy'. These are very highly poetical lines, the first patterned by the enclosing words in agreement, and the next an exact golden line. Cf. Spenser, *FQ* 2.9.24 'Over the which was cast a wandring vine,/Enchaced with a wanton yvie twine'.

40 The two embossed figures are of Conon, the famous astronomer of the third century BC mentioned in Catullus 66, and perhaps (according to one of Servius' suggestions) of Eudoxus, whose name Menalcas cannot remember. Eudoxus' prose work *Phaenomena* (fourth century BC) was versified by Aratus. Another possibility is Archimedes, who was a friend of Conon.

41 radio: 'with his rod', used for drawing geometrical figures; cf. *Aen.* 6.850. *Gentibus* means 'for the people', and draws attention to his scientific benefactions towards mankind.

42 The indirect question is a second object to *descripsit:* 'described the sky . . . , described what season the harvester should have, what season the bent ploughman.'

43 This line, like so many others in the passage, is a close imitation of Theocritus (*Id.* 1.59).

45 In Theocr. *Id.* 1.55 the cup is

decorated with acanthus, a flower very frequent in ancient art.

46 Orphea: Greek accusative; the idea of rocks and trees following the music of Orpheus is frequent in ancient literature. Cf. the well-known song in Shakespeare's *Henry the Eighth* 'Orpheus with his lute . . .'.

47 The irony of this speech reaches a climax in the repetition of Menalcas' remark (43); the implication is that such a cup is common, not to be compared with the calf (48). Cf. Theocr. *Id.* 5.25f.

49 veniam . . . vocaris: Menalcas means he will accept any conditions proposed, including the stake of a calf (cf. 109).

50 Menalcas is about to mention a particular judge that he has in mind, but breaks off in mid-sentence as Palaemon approaches and is seized upon as a convenient and suitable umpire. Cf. Theocr. *Id.* 5.61f; 8.25f.

52 si quid habes: contemptuously ironic; cf. Theocr. *Id.* 5.78.

53 nec quemquam fugio: this takes up Menalcas' remark in 49.

56-7 Palaemon shows his suitability as an umpire by throwing off a couple of elegant lines on his own account; cf. Meleager, *Anth. Pal.* 9.363.19f.

59 The contest is specified; it is to be in amoebaean style, cf. 28 and Theocr. *Id.* 8.61 δι' ἀμοιβαίων οἱ παῖδες ἄεισαν ('the boys sang in amoebaean song'), *Ecl.* 7.18-19.

60 Damoetas begins with a quotation from Theocr. *Id.* 17.1 (where see Gow's note) Ἐκ Διὸς ἀρχώμεσθα, which is also the beginning of Aratus' *Phaenomena,* written at about the same time as Theocritus' *Idyll. Musae* is best taken as a vocative (as in Theocr. *Id.* 17.1 and Ov. *Met.* 10.148f. *Ab Iove, Musa parens . . . carmina nostra move*), though as early as Servius the possibility of taking it as genitive was recognised (cf. Cicero's translation of Aratus *Ab Iove Musarum primordia*).

60-61 Damoetas' opening couplet is elegantly balanced with repetition (*Iove . . . Iovis; ille . . . illi*) in the Alexandrian style.

61 colit: 'looks after'; cf. *Aen.* 1.16.

62-3 Menalcas replies with a similar balance with repetition (*Phoebus . . . Phoebo*), setting up against the supreme god Jupiter the special god of poetry, Apollo (cf. Theocr. *Id.* 5.82f.). His final phrase is highly mannered with hiatus at the caesura after *lauri* (see note on 6), the

poetical adverbial accusative *suave* (cf. 4.43) and the quadrisyllabic ending of the Greek word *hyacinthus.*

Phoebo . . . munera sunt: 'I always have at home Phoebus' own special gifts for him': the laurel is always associated with Apollo, and the hyacinth is his special flower because of the myth about the youth Hyacinth, accidentally killed by Apollo, from whose blood the flower grew.

64-5 This couplet is based on Theocr. *Id.* 5.88-9 (cf. *Id.* 6.6-7), but Virgil has added the idea of hiding and wanting to be seen; cf. Aul. Gell. 9.9.

64 malo: the apple of Venus, symbol of love; cf. Cat. 65.19f.

66-7 Menalcas caps the previous couplet well: Galatea runs away from Damoetas, but Amyntas (the boy he loves; cf. *Ecl.* 2.35) comes of his own accord.

67 Delia: Diana, goddess of hunting, born on Delos (cf. 7.29), who would be well known to the hunting-dogs. Others take it to mean his girlfriend, Delia, but this has less point.

68-9 The promise of a present of a dove is from Theocr. *Id.* 5.96. *Veneri* means 'for my love' (i.e. Galatea); cf. Hor. *Odes* 1.33.13. Damoetas has noted the place where the doves nest, so that they are available (*parta*) for him to catch when he wishes. With *congessere* understand *nidum;* compare our use of 'build'.

70-71 This is based on Theocr. *Id.* 3.10: 'I bring you ten apples . . . and tomorrow will bring as many again'.

73 Damoetas means (as Servius says) that her words were so sweet as to be worthy of divine ears; cf. Theocr. *Id.* 7.93 ('beautiful songs, which report has perhaps taken to the throne of Zeus'). This is more likely than that Damoetas wishes the gods to hear her promises and hold her to them.

74-5 This time Menalcas does not cap Damoetas, but sadly complains of his separation from Amyntas on a menial task while they are out hunting (cf. Tib. 1.4.50).

76-9 These couplets are obscure: the best explanation seems to be that Damoetas asks a fellow-shepherd Iollas to send his beloved Phyllis to him because it is his birthday, a time for merrymaking, and humorously adds that he will be glad to welcome Iollas himself (*ipse venito*) not on his birthday but at the solemn and sober festival of the *Ambarvalia* (see note on 5.74-5) when lovemaking was

forbidden. This is capped by Menalcas
saying that for his part when he was
leaving Phyllis' company she wept and
said a long farewell not to him but to the
handsome Iollas, now rejected in favour
of Menalcas. The alternative is to suppose
that Menalcas speaks in the person of
Iollas.

77 **faciam:** 'sacrifice'; the word may
govern an accusative or an ablative in this
religious meaning; cf. Colum. 2.21.4.

79 **longum:** adverbial, perhaps best
taken with *inquit* ('spoke from afar'; cf.
Hor. *A.P.* 459) rather than with *vale* (so
Servius, cf. the Greek πολλὰ χαίρειν
λέγειν, used of rejection).

vale vale inquit: the second *vale*
has its final long vowel shortened in
hiatus; cf. 2.65; 6.44.

80-83 The listing of *exempla* is frequent
in pastoral poetry (as in elegy); cf.
2.63f., and Theocr. *Id.* 8.57f.

81 **Amaryllidis:** Damoetas appears to
switch his affections frequently (Galatea,
64; Phyllis 76), unlike Menalcas, who
remains true to his homosexual love.

82 **satis:** 'segetibus' (Servius).
depulsis: 'weaned'; cf. 7.15.

84 **Pollio:** a famous statesman and
literary figure, to whom *Eclogue* 4 is
dedicated; cf. Hor. *Odes* 2.1.; *Sat.* 1.10.42.
The introduction of real persons into the
imaginary pastoral world is a startling
feature of the *Eclogues:* cf. Gallus in
Ecl. 6 and 10 (where see intro.). It is true
that both Pollio and Gallus were poets, and
so might enter the shepherds' world like
the poets mentioned in Theocr. *Id.* 7.39f.;
but they were better known as prominent
political figures, and herein lies Virgil's
innovation.

quamvis est: the indicative with
quamvis (and the subjunctive with
quamquam) occurs not infrequently in
poetry, contrary to strict prose usage.

85 **Pierides:** a frequent epithet (cf.
6.13) for the Muses, who haunted Pieria,
the district around Mt Olympus.

vitulam: like *taurum* in the next
line this is a sacrificial victim for the welfare
of Pollio (*lectori vestro*).

86 The capping of the previous couplet
consists in saying that Pollio not only
likes reading poetry, but writes it. *Taurum*
goes one better than *vitulam*, especially
with the following descriptive line
(striking because of the long-postponed
qui) which is used again in *Aen.* 9.629:
'one to attack the sand with his horns and

scatter it with his hooves'.

88 'May the man who loves you,
Pollio, reach the point which he rejoices
you also have reached', i.e. pre-eminence in
poetry (rather than in political life,
which is less relevant here because of the
pastoral description in the following line).

90-91 Menalcas does not cap this second
couplet about Pollio, but instead offers a
curse to balance the happy prayer of
Damoetas. Bavius and Maevius were
evidently contemporary poets, the latter
of whom is also referred to very depreciat-
ingly by Horace (*Epod.* 10.1-2 *mala soluta
navis exit alite ferens olentem Maevium*).

91 'May the same man yoke foxes to
the plough and milk he-goats'; proverbial
expressions for the impossible.

92-3 Damoetas makes a fresh start,
changing the theme from personalities
to a generalised picture of the pastoral life
and its attendant perils. He expresses the
sudden approach of danger dramatically
with the long postponed *o pueri*, not only
placed after its relative clause (*qui . . .
fraga*) but actually inserted with its
imperative verb in the next clause. The
'cold snake' is taken from Theocr. *Id.*
15.58; cf. *Ecl.* 8.71.

94-5 The capping couplet depicts
another danger: even the ram fell in, and
the weaker sheep, if they went close to the
river, would be sure to do so. Servius
fantastically finds an allegory based on
Virgil's own experience, that he would have
been killed when his farm was taken over
by the centurion Arrius (= *aries*) if he had
not saved himself by jumping in the river.

96-7 Here for the first time Damoetas,
who has led off each time before, picks up
the idea of Menalcas, instructing the
imaginary shepherd Titytus (cf. 20) to keep
the sheep away from the river.

96 **reice:** scanned as a trochee by
synizesis; see note on 6.30.

97 **erit:** the final syllable is lengthened
in arsis at the caesura; see note on 1.38.

98 Menalcas replies with a warning of
the danger to the flock of too much sun:
hence they are to be rounded up (*cogere*)
into the shade.

lac praeceperit: 'gets at the milk
first', before the milker.

100 'Alas, alas, how rich the fodder,
yet how emaciated the bull!' The bull pines
with love's pangs, like Damoetas himself.

102-3 Menalcas caps this by com-
plaining that his flock is more emaciated
still, so that a deeper cause than love must

be sought, i.e. the evil eye.

102 The Latin here is difficult, and *neque* has to be taken as equivalent to *non*, a very rare and apparently colloquial usage. The alternative is to emend *his* to *hi* and read *hi certe — neque amor causa est — vix ossibus haerent.* The suggestion that *his* is an archaic nominative plural is unlikely.

vix ossibus haerent: i.e. they are all skin and bone; cf. Theocr. *Id.* 4.15.

103 **fascinat:** cf. Cat. 7.11-12 *quae nec pernumerare curiosi possint nec mala fascinare lingua,* Hor. *Epist.* 1.14.37.

104-7 The amoebaean contest ends with a riddle from each contestant. Damoetas' riddle has not yet been answered; the answer to Menalcas, known in Hellenistic times (Theocr. *Id.* 10.28), is given by Ovid (*Met.* 13.394f.) and Pliny (*NH* 21.66), namely that the hyacinth shows markings similar to the Greek letters AI, the first two letters of King Aias (Ajax); Servius was not satisfied with this, and said *tamen sciendum aenigmata haec, sicut fere omnia, carere aperta solutione.*

105 'the extent of the sky covers no more than three cubits'. Guesses at the answer to this range from the reflection of the sky in a well to the punning on a proper name Caelius, a spendthrift who got through all his property except six feet of earth (or four foot six) for his tomb. Servius gives both of these solutions, and ends with the story that Asconius Pedianus heard Virgil say that he had here produced a puzzle for critics to see who was most ingenious: there have been many contenders for the prize. For a fuller discussion see Coleman *ad loc.*

tris . . . non amplius ulnas: non amplius is often used absolutely — three cubits, no more'; cf. *Aen.* 1.683.

106 **inscripti nomina:** a most remarkable Greek construction, a retained accusative with a wholly passive verb, very much stranger than Virgil's normal retained accusative (see note on 1.53-5) where there is middle force to the verb, or an accusative of respect construction for the noun, or both. Compare Soph. *Trach.* 157-8 δέλτον ἐγγεγραμμένην ξυνθήματα ('a tablet inscribed with tokens').

108f. In Theocritus *Idyll* 5 the umpire succeeds in reaching a decision, in *Idyll* 6 the result is a draw.

108 **tantas componere lites:** 'to settle such a tremendous contest'.

109-10 **et quisquis . . . amaros:** i.e. as Servius says, *quicumque similis vestri est',* anyone who appreciates this poetry because they have (like Damoetas and Menalcas) experienced love, fearful when all is sweet, tortured when it is bitter. Cf. Cat. 64.95 and the anonymous poem once attributed to Sidney:

Faint amorist! what, dost thou think
To taste love's honey, and not drink
One dram of gall? Or to devour
A world of sweet, and taste no sour?

111 Servius discusses two possible meanings of this, one literal as Palaemon departs and gives instructions about irrigation, and the other metaphorical, as the stream (cf. Pind. *Nem.* 7.12) of pastoral poetry has flowed for long enough. The second is surely the dominant meaning. For this kind of ending to a poem cf. 10.77 and Cat. 61 fin. *claudite ostia virgines: lusimus satis. . . .*

ECLOGUE 4

This is the most famous of the *Eclogues* (indeed perhaps the most famous piece of Latin literature), and because of its prophetic tone — reminiscent in some ways of Isaiah (cf. Isaiah 9:6f.) — was in the Middle Ages and sometimes afterwards regarded as foretelling the birth of Christ. It is sometimes known as the Messianic Eclogue (see *Virgil's Messianic Eclogue* by J. B. Mayor, W. Warde Fowler, R. S. Conway, London, 1907; and T. F. Royds, *Virgil and Isaiah,* Oxford, 1918).

For modern scholars, few of whom hold the Messianic view, the identity of the child has presented a major topic of discussion. Some have followed Servius in thinking of Saloninus, a son of Pollio (for whom there is no firm

evidence) or another son Asinius Gallus (who was born too early). It seems
however impossible that a child of Pollio can be meant: Pollio was not of
sufficient eminence, and Virgil surely could not refer to the child as destined to
be born in Pollio's consulship without saying that it was to be Pollio's child.
Other suggestions are an expected child of the marriage of Antony and Octavia
(perhaps the most likely suggestion), or of Octavian and Scribonia; but the
plain fact remains that Virgil has not thought it necessary for his poem to
indicate what particular child, if any, he had in mind. Some scholars have
thought of the child as an allegory — no real child but a personification of the
new age, or a personification of Virgil's newly-born literary hopes as he began to
visualise writing his *Aeneid*. It seems best to conclude that Virgil did have a
particular child in mind who could act as a symbol for his optimistic hopes for
the future, but for the purposes of his poem did not wish to narrow his range
by being specific.

The poem can be dated to 40 BC, when Pollio was consul. He had served
with distinction in the previous year in Cisalpine Gaul, and was largely
instrumental in negotiating the Treaty of Brundisium between Antony and
Octavian. Thus his exploits as a soldier and statesman were considerable; but we
must not lose sight of the fact that the prime reason for dedicating the poem to
Pollio is to honour his literary achievements. These had been referred to in terms
of the highest praise in 3.84 (where see note), and the whole tone of the
Eclogue is literary and visionary rather than national and political.

What then is the literary type of the poem? It is introduced by the poet's
statement that he is going to sing a somewhat more elevated theme (*paulǫ
maiora*) than pastoral. There are indeed touches of pastoral in the poem, but
relatively few (as Servius rightly says), and only in this *Eclogue* and *Eclogue* 6
is there practically no direct debt to Theocritus' pastorals. It has perhaps certain
similarities of subject-matter with Theocritus' panegyric of Ptolemy (*Id.* 17):
it begins in the form of a panegyric for a consul, but the emphasis very soon
passes from the consul to the child. In some ways we may see the poem as a
genethliacon (a birthday poem) like e.g. Statius, *Silvae* 2.7, but it is closer to
that part of an epithalamium (a wedding song) which prophesies the birth of
glorious offspring for the happy pair, and it is very much inspired by Catullus
61.211f. and 64.320f.

Virgil's sources for his idyllic picture of the Golden Age are many and varied.
In particular the Sibylline oracle is mentioned (see note on 4) and this has led
to speculation about possible sources in Eastern prophetic literature, Jewish in
particular; but there is nothing in the poem which could not have come from
the Roman Sibylline tradition. Traces of Stoic cosmology occur (see note on 5),
and the long line of Golden Age legends in Greek and Latin literature helped to
shape Virgil's ideas, especially the Hesiodic description of the Five Ages of Man
(see note on 4). An interesting comparison can be made with Horace's *Epode*
16, where by contrast with Virgil's poem the life of the Golden Age lies far away
from Rome, only to be reached by a journey over the waves of Ocean. It cannot
be said for certain which of these poems preceded the other, but it seems on the
whole likely that *Eclogue* 4 was first.

The most important influence of all on Virgil was the sixty-fourth poem of
Catullus, the epyllion on the marriage of Peleus and Thetis which contains the

song of the Fates (Parcae, see note on 46-7) prophesying the birth of a child (Achilles, see note on 36), and ends with pessimistic reflections on the vanished Golden Age (see notes on 6 and 63). The diction and metre of Virgil's poem is very strongly reminiscent of the style of Catullus 64 with its end-stopped lines, its repetitions (note on 3), patterned lines (note on 4) and fondness for a word of three long syllables after the 2½ caesura (note on 28-30). What Virgil has given us in this poem is a variety of a Hellenistic epithalamium, based on Catullus but expressed optimistically rather than with a nostalgic pessimism. Unlike both Hesiod and Catullus, and indeed for the first time in Classical literature as far as we know, it proclaims a return to the lost Golden Age (cf. *Aen.* 6.791f.). It aims to convey the serenity of a perfect and idyllic world, anchored to real life in the sense that it is a proclamation that the real world is about to change, but employing imaginative poetic symbolism to convey its dream-like vision (see note on 43-4). It is presented with a verve and a joy which makes it a most memorable hymn of hope (see R. D. Williams, *PVS* 1974-5, pp. 1-6, and for a detailed literary analysis see Gordon Williams in *Quality and Pleasure in Latin Poetry,* ed. Tony Woodman and David West, 1974, pp. 31f.).

1 **Sicelides:** a reference to Virgil's usual model in the *Eclogues,* Theocritus of Sicily (see note on 2.21, and cf. 6.1; 10.1).

paulo maiora: with this phrase Virgil sets this *Eclogue* apart from the rest. As he explains in the next two lines, pure pastoral (*arbusta . . . humiles myricae*) does not satisfy all tastes, and though he is still writing in the pastoral mode (*silvas;* cf. 1.2) he is imparting to it a new dignity (*consule dignae*). Cf. Pope's *Messiah,* 2: 'To heavenly themes sublimer strains belong'.

3 **silvas, silvae:** the first of many repetitions of the kind beloved by Hellenistic poets and by Catullus; cf. 6-7, 21-3, 24-5, 32-3, 34-5, 50-52, 55-7, 58-9, 60-61, 60-62; and see Dover's *Theocritus,* Intro. pp. xlv f.

consule: i.e. Pollio, see note on 11.

4 This is a golden line, like line 29; lines 5, 14, 17, 20, 28, 30, 47 are similar in their symmetrical patterning. Virgil's metre in this poem is much closer to that of Catullus than in any other *Eclogue;* see the introduction to this poem.

Cumaei . . . carminis: a reference to the oracles of the Sibyl of Cumae, priestess of Apollo whose mystic characteristics evidently captured Virgil's imagination; cf. the long description of her in *Aen.* 6.9f.; 45f.; 77f.; 98f.; and the large part she plays in the *Aeneid* as Aeneas' guide through the underworld. For the importance of the Sibylline books in Roman religion, cf. Dion. Hal. 4.62.1f. We have no

certain knowledge of the nature of the prophecy referred to here, except that Virgil tells us (8-9) that it involves the return of the Golden Age to replace the Iron Age. There was of course a long line of authors, both Greek and Roman, who had dreamed of and written about a Golden Age; Virgil certainly has the Five Ages of Hesiod (*Works and Days* 109f.) in mind (hence some have even suggested that *Cumaei* refers to Cyme, home of Hesiod's father); compare also Aratus, *Phaen.* 98f. and especially the ending of Catullus' poem (64) about the marriage of Peleus and Thetis.

5 **magnus . . . ordo:** the phraseology perhaps suggests the Pythagorean and Stoic idea of the *magnus annus,* the cycle through which the universe passes to return again to its original state (Cic. *ND* 2.118).

saeclorum: this suggests the Etruscan idea of the epoch of 100 (or 110) years; Augustus celebrated *Ludi Saeculares* (and Horace wrote his *Carmen Saeculare;* cf. 5f. *quo Sibyllini monuere versus*) in 17 BC, to commemorate a new epoch. The child of this eclogue is to be the hero of the new *saeclum.* For the phraseology, cf. Cat. 64.22f. *o nimis optato saeclorum tempore nati heroes, salvete, deum genus.*

6 **Virgo:** Iustitia or Astraea; she was the last of the deities to quit the world when the previous Golden Age ended, and mankind's behaviour was such that the gods could no longer bear to be with them; she became the constellation Virgo. Cf. *Geo.* 2.473f. (where see note) *extrema per illos*

Iustitia excedens terris vestigia fecit; Cat.
64.397f.; Ov. *Met.* 1.150; Aratus, *Phaen.*
98f., Spenser *FQ* 7.7.37 'But after wrong
was lov'd, and Justice solde, She left the
unrighteous world, and was to heaven
extolled'; Pope, *Messiah* 18, 'Returning
Justice lift aloft her scale'.

Saturnia regna: the concept of the
Golden Age under Saturnus is frequent in
the *Aeneid;* cf. 6.792f. (with Austin's
note) *Augustus Caesar, divi genus, aurea
condet/saecula qui rursus Latio regnata per
arva/Saturno quondam;* 8.324f. *aurea quae
perhibent illo (sc. Saturno) sub rege
fuere/saecula; sic placida populos in pace
regebat, deterior donec paulatim ac
decolor aetas/et belli rabies et amor
successit habendi.*

7 **nova progenies:** 'a new race', i.e. of
gold and not of iron, sent from heaven
itself; or perhaps 'its first-born', referring
to the child.

8 **nascenti:** 'at his birth', whenever that
may be.

puero: see the introduction to this
poem.

ferrea: the last age of Hesiod's cycle,
Gold, Silver, Bronze, Heroic, Iron.

10 **Lucina:** goddess of childbirth,
identified sometimes with Juno, sometimes
(as here) with Diana, Apollo's sister
(Hor. *CS* 13f.).

Apollo: Apollo is the guardian deity
of the new age not only as the prophet who
through his priestess the Sibyl foretold it,
but also as the god of poetry who enables
Virgil to sing of it (cf. 57 and Tib. 2.5).
References to Apollo in Theocritus and in
Virgil's *Eclogues* are almost exclusively
concerned with his role as the divine patron
of pastoral song. Servius sees an allegorical
reference in Apollo and Lucina to Octavian
(whose special patron deity was Apollo)
and his sister Octavia.

11 **decus hoc aevi:** 'this glorious age';
cf. Lucr. 2.16, rather than 'this glory of his
time'; cf. Hor. *Odes* 3.16.20.

12 **Pollio:** Pollio was consul designate
in 41 BC for the following year. Virgil
does not mean that Pollio's statesmanlike
qualities were so great that as consul he
would be responsible for the return of the
Golden Age, but that it was a matter for
delight that his literary friend (see note
on 3.84) would be the person holding that
office at the time.

magni ... menses: the epithet is
emotive, more so than a word like *clari*
would be, and there is possibly an under-

tone of the Stoic *magnus annus* (see note
on 5).

13-14 'under your leadership any
traces of our sin which remain will be
rendered void and will free the lands of
fear for ever'. Virgil is thinking of the sin
of civil war which so preoccupied him in
the *Georgics* (e.g. 1.505f.); cf. Hor. *Epod.*
7 and 16, and *Odes* 1.2.29. Line 14 is a
patterned line; see note on 4.

15 **deum vitam:** cf. Hes. *WD* 112 where
he says the men of the Golden Age lived
like gods, ὥστε θεοὶ δ' ἔζωον.

16 The idea of the gods visiting the
heroes in person recalls the happy days of
Cat. 64.384f., as *sceleris ... nostri* in line 13
recalled the subsequent sin in Cat. 64.397.
This line is unusual metrically because of
the trochaic caesurae in third and fourth
foot without main caesura in either; the
passage is then rounded off by a line of a
very patterned type.

17 **patriis:** 'of his father' (cf. 26) rather
than, more generally, 'of his ancestors'.

18-45 This section of the poem describes
three stages in the advent of the Golden
Age: during the child's infancy (18-25),
during his adolescence (26-36), and in his
maturity (37-45).

18 **prima ... munuscula:** 'as her first
little gifts'; the diminutive *munuscula*, like
so much in this poem, is reminiscent of
Catullus: it is specially appropriate here
with *puero.*

19 **baccare:** a fragrant plant, with
magical properties (7.27).

20 **colocasia:** a large and splendid
Egyptian lily. For acanthus, cf. 3.45; for
ridere, cf. Cat. 64.284 ('the house smiles
with the fragrance of flowers').

21 **ipsae:** *sponte sua.* The spondaic word
filling the first foot receives a metrical
emphasis which prepares for the repetition
ipsa in 23.

22 **magnos ... leones:** notice the
threatening alliteration of *m.* The idyllic
vision extends beyond Italy, where there
were no lions; cf. *Geo.* 2.151f., a passage
reminiscent of this one in several ways —
see note on line 24. Cf. Isaiah 11:6 'the
wolf also shall dwell with the lamb'; Hor.
Epod. 16.51; Pope, *Messiah* 77f.

23 'your very cradle shall profusely
bloom with delightful flowers'; a return to
the theme of 19-20. Some editors transpose
this line to follow line 20 and alter *fundent*
to *fundet* ('the earth itself will pour
forth delightful flowers as your cradle').
But the case for this does not seem strong

enough to outweigh the unanimous
testimony of the MSS and the ancient
grammarians and scholiasts.

24 Cf. *Geo.* 2.152-4 *nec miseros fallunt
aconita legentis nec rapit immensos
orbis . . . anguis;* Hor. *Epod.* 16.52;
Isaiah 11:8.

25 **amomum:** a fragrant shrub; cf. 3.89.

26 **simul** = *simul ac (poteris legere et
cognoscere);* cf. *Geo.* 4.232.

parentis: see note on 17. Some
MSS read *parentum* which may be right.

28-30 These are three remarkably
patterned lines of symmetrical description,
each containing a verb in the future tense
in the same position of the line and two
nouns each with their adjective (except
only *campus*). The metrical movement is
very strongly reminiscent of Catullus'
hexameter, especially in the use of a word
of three long syllables after the caesura;
cf. especially Cat. 64.63-5; and see the
introduction to this poem.

28 **molli:** perhaps 'waving', 'yielding in
the wind'. The idea that the corn will be
produced without cultivation is to be
supplied from the context, especially from
incultis in the next line. For the idea, cf.
Hor. *Epod.* 16.43f.

30 The idea of honey flowing is of
course traditional in Golden Age
descriptions; cf. Hes. *WD* 232f.; Hor.
Epod. 16.47.

roscida: 'dewy' because honey was
thought normally to descend like dew on to
flowers for the bees to collect (cf. *Geo.*
4.1); in the idyllic Golden Age it will be
produced fully-made on oak trees.

31 **priscae vestigia fraudis:** an echo of
line 13, indicating that the Golden Age will
not immediately be complete; cf. 34f.

32-3 These activities are traditional
instances of man's degeneration from the
peace and serenity of the Golden Age:
cf. for ships Hes. *WD* 236-7; Aratus,
Phaen. 110-11; Hor. *Odes* 1.3.23-24 (with
Nisbet-Hubbard *ad loc.*); *Epod.* 16.57;
Tib. 1.3.37f.; *Geo.* 2.503; for fortifications
Ov. *Met.* 1.97; for ploughing *Geo.* 1.125.

32 **Thetim:** i.e. the sea; cf. Mart. 10.30.11
and the frequent use of Bacchus = *vinum*,
Ceres = *frumentum*, Vulcanus = *ignis*, etc.
Cf. Doris (= the sea) in *Ecl.* 10.5.

34 Again Virgil uses a trochaic caesura
in the third foot without a main caesura
in the fourth; cf. 16.

Tiphys . . . Argo: Tiphys was the
helmsman of the first ship Argo which sailed
with its complement of heroes under Jason

to Colchis; cf. Cat. 64.1-11. Cf. Shelley's
Hellas: 'A loftier Argo cleaves the main . . .'.

36 **magnus mittetur Achilles:** the
alliteration of *m* again indicates a mood of
menace (cf. 22). The choice of Achilles
and Troy to illustrate the renewal of war
is partly because of the eminence of
Achilles in legend, partly because Virgil
had a special interest in the Trojan war
(which was the background of the theme
of the *Aeneid*), but perhaps largely
because of the prophecy of Achilles' birth
by the Parcae in Catullus 64.338f. (see note
on 46-7).

37 **hinc:** 'hereafter', i.e. within a
generation or so.

38 **et ipse . . . vector:** 'even the
voyager', i.e. the trader mentioned in the
next phrase. Virgil very closely follows
Hesiod (*WD* 236-7) where he says of the
men who practise true justice that they do
not travel on ships, for the grain-giving
earth bears them fruit: οὐδ' ἐπὶ νηῶν
νίσσονται, καρπὸν δὲ φέρει ζείδωρος
ἄρουρα.

40-41 For the phraseology cf. Cat.
64.38f.

42 **mentiri:** 'counterfeit', a loaded word
suggesting that the process of dyeing wool
is an unnatural one inappropriate to the
Golden Age; cf. *Geo.* 2.465; Tib. 2.4.27f.;
Hor. *Odes* 3.5.27f.

43-4 'But the ram in the meadows of its
own accord will change its fleece now into
sweetly-blushing purple, now into saffron
yellow'. This highly chromatic description
has been harshly criticised (Page says
'there is only a step from the sublime to
the ridiculous, and Virgil has here decidedly
taken it'). But in fact these two lines
strengthen and confirm the wholly
idyllic and dream-like nature of the poetic
vision which Virgil offers in this poem.
It is indeed a poem of optimism for the real
world, but its whole point is that it is not
presented in real terms.

43 **suave:** adverbial accusative; cf. 3.63.

45 **sandyx:** 'scarlet'; cf. Prop. 2.25.45.

46-7 ' "Such an epoch hasten on", said
the Fates to their spindles, in concord with
the firm will of destiny'. These lines most
specifically recall the song of the Parcae
(the three fates) in Catullus 64.323f. with
its refrain *currite ducentes subtegmina,
currite, fusi.* The Parcae (Clotho,
Lachesis and Atropos) are described in
Spenser *FQ* 4.2.48. *Saecla* is surely
vocative, rather than cognate accusative
after *currite* ('run through such ages'), as

some suggest.

48f. This invocation is regarded by some as spoken by the Parcae, but it coheres better with what follows (53f.) if it is regarded as spoken in the poet's person; cf. *Geo.* 1.42.

49 **magnum Iovis incrementum**: a very remarkable phrase, meaning 'off-spring' in the sense of the biblical use of 'increase'. The spondaic fifth foot (cf. 5.38; 7.53) is again reminiscent of Catullus' hexameter: there are thirty instances in the four-hundred-odd lines of Catullus 64.

50 **convexo nutantem pondere**: 'trembling with its vaulted mass', reflecting the cosmic acceptance of the will of destiny.

51 **terrasque tractusque maris**: 'both the earth and the expanse of the sea . . .'; these phrases are in apposition to *mundum*. The *-que* of *terrasque* is lengthened in arsis, see note on 1.38. This particular instance (lengthening of *-que*) is in imitation of Homer, and occurs half a dozen times in the *Georgics* (e.g. 1.153). This line is repeated in *Geo.* 4.222.

52 **ut**: the postposition of the conjunction emphasises the words before it.

53f. Notice the emphasis on poetry in this final section: the poet longs for the new age to dawn, but above all wishes himself to celebrate it in verse. He pictures a time when he will really 'move out of the woods' and become a poet not of shepherds but of heroic deeds.

54 'and inspiration enough to sing of your deeds'; for *spiritus*, cf. Hor. *Odes* 4.6.29.

55-6 **non . . . nec . . . nec**: cf. 5.25; 10.64.

55 **Orpheus**: see note on 3.46.

56 **Linus**: in fable the son of Apollo, teacher of Orpheus; cf. 6.67.

57 **Orphei**: a spondee by synizesis; cf. 6.30.

Calliopea: one of the Muses; cf. *Aen.* 9.525.

58-9 The symmetrical repetition is very characteristic of the Hellenistic style; see note on 3.

58 **Arcadia**: the home of Pan, so that he would naturally be favoured. These two lines return to the pastoral world; cf. 2.31-3 and see note on 7.4.

60f. The poem ends in an intimate, almost lyric mood; cf. Cat. 61.216f., cited on 62.

60 **risu**: 'by smiling at her'; some take the meaning to be 'by her smile', but see note on 62.

61 **decem . . . menses**: the nine-month period of pregnancy, ten by lunar reckoning.

62 **incipe, parve puer**: the repetition of this phrase (and of *matrem . . . matri*) closes the poem in the Hellenistic style.

qui non risere parenti: the MSS have *cui . . . parentes*, but Quintilian (9.3.8) cites the passage as an example of the plural relative followed by a singular antecedent (*hunc*), and so this reading has much greater antiquity than the other. In addition to this evidence the reading is far better in itself: the repetition of *incipe parve puer* demands that action on the part of the baby should be described, and the decisive factor is the imitation of Catullus 61.216f. *Torquatus volo parvulus . . . dulce rideat ad patrem semihiante labello.* Many modern editors accept *cui . . . parentes*, but for the reasons given above this crux should be a crux no longer.

62-3 **qui . . . hunc**: Quintilian (9.3.8) comments on the use of this 'figure' of singular for plural: it is indeed strange, but rhetorically very effective here.

63 The commentators cite Homer *Od.* 11.601 where Hercules is described as feasting with the gods and enjoying the bed of Hebe. But the principal reference here, as so often in this poem, is to Catullus 64 where (*ad fin.*) the communion of gods and mortals in the Golden Age is described in a poem whose theme is the Golden Age wedding of the mortal Peleus to the goddess Thetis.

dignata: a final echo of Catullus (64.407, of the gods), *nec tales dignantur visere coetus*.

ECLOGUE 5

This poem illustrates very well the relationship of Virgil's poetry to that of Theocritus. Its setting is inspired by *Idyll* 8, where two shepherds meet and agree to a contest in song (cf. also *Idyll* 6), and part of its subject-matter is derived from *Idyll* 1, the second half of which is a lament for the death of Daphnis. But Virgil has adapted and expanded his source material, giving a greater intensity to the pathos, and then answering it with a serene and optimistic prophecy of the immortality of Daphnis. Death has not prevailed — the immortality of Daphnis counterbalances the poignant sorrow of the first part of the poem.

Daphnis is a major figure of the bucolic mythology, the leader or hero of the shepherds in the pastoral world, a semi-divine epitome of all that is most characteristic of this remote and dream-like world, the supreme singer, the personification of the peace and idyllic happiness of the idealised country existence, subject — like its other inhabitants — to the unhappiness of love and to death (as in Theocritus' first *Idyll*, where see Gow's notes), yet here in Virgil able to overcome the limitations of the human condition. See Coleman's note on 5.20.

The poem has been a favourite one for those who see allegory in the *Eclogues*, and from the time of Servius it has been suggested that Daphnis represents Julius Caesar, assassinated in 44 BC by the conspirators' daggers, yet immortalised by his deification (cf. 9.47). It is quite certain (see H.J. Rose, *The Eclogues of Vergil*, ch. 6)) that no elaborate correspondence of details is intended — Caesar did not introduce Bacchic rites (note on 29-31), did not die young, did not pre-decease his mother. But it is very possible that the death and deification of Caesar influenced Virgil's thoughts on the nature of mortality; it is better in the *Eclogues* to discard the term allegory and to think instead in terms of Virgil's own experience suggesting subjects for pastoral poetry.

This poem's simplicity of metre and diction is remarkable. The effects which Virgil achieves, in what is surely one of the finest of the *Eclogues*, are gained by direct writing of the most unelaborate kind — the themes of death and resurrection are handled with a gentle smoothness of metre and an elegant purity of diction which reflect in a most moving way the sorrows and joys of the pastoral world.

1-2 **boni . . . inflare . . . dicere:** 'skilled at'; the Greek epexegetic infinitive, used by Theocritus in the phrases which Virgil is imitating (*Id.* 8.4) ἄμφω συρίσδεν δεδαημένω, ἄμφω ἀείδεν ('both skilled in piping, both in singing'). Compare *Ecl.* 7.5 *cantare pares.* The beginning of this *Eclogue* recalls the setting of Theocr. *Id.* 8 where Menalcas and Daphnis meet and agree to a contest in song; see the introduction to this poem, and compare *Eclogues* 3 and 7.

3 **consedimus:** '(why) have we (not) sat down?'; the perfect tense expresses the idea that the action should already have taken place.

4 **maior:** '*id est vel natu vel merito*' (Servius). The former is certainly correct.

5 **incertas:** 'shifting', because of the wind.

6 **antro . . . antrum:** an example of the

simple repetition common in the pastoral style (see note on 4.3); there are many other examples in this poem.

6-7 **aspice ut . . . sparsit:** *sparsit* is indicative in parataxis; the *ut* clause is not subordinated but treated independently as a main clause; cf. *Aen.* 6. 855-6.

7 This is a golden line of a highly idyllic kind. *Labrusca* is the wild vine; cf. Hom. *Od.* 5.69 where a vine grows over Calypso's cave. For the descriptive effect, cf. Milton *PL* 4.257f.

> Umbrageous Grots and Caves
> Of cool recess, ore which the mantling Vine
> Lays forth her purple Grape, and gently creeps
> Luxuriant.

9 Mopsus' reply ironically indicates

Amyntas' conceit. Amyntas is mentioned
in 2.35f. as a rival to Corydon.

10-11 Phyllis, Alcon and Codrus are all
pastoral names, not to be identified (as
Servius tries to identify them) with
historical or legendary persons.

10 **Phyllidis ignis:** 'love-songs about
Phyllis'; cf. Hor. *Odes* 3.7.11.

12 **Tityrus:** a shepherd's name used not
infrequently in the *Eclogues* (e.g. 1.1;
3.20; etc.); cf. Theocr. *Id.* 3.2.

13 For the idea of carving songs on
trees, cf. 10.53f.

14 **modulans alterna notavi:** 'setting
them to music I indicated the changes',
i.e. the alternations between passages to be
sung and passages to be played on the flute.

15 Mopsus refers back to line 8,
indicating that his song will be proof that
Amyntas cannot really rival him.

iubeto ut certet: some MSS omit *ut* so
that the jussive subjunctive *certet* is in
parataxis, but the rhythm is better with
the fourth foot caesura. In prose *iubere*
prefers the infinitive construction.

16f. Cf. the similar comparisons in
32f., 46f.

16 **salix . . . olivae:** the willow and olive
have similarities in leaf-shape and colour,
but the olive is far more valuable.

17 **saliunca:** the Celtic wild reed.
Notice the patterned line (cf. 7) used to
reinforce the pictorial phraseology.

19 **desine plura** i.e. stop talking
(understand *loqui*) in readiness for the
song.

20f. This song for the death of
Daphnis, the divine prince of the
shepherds (cf. 2.26 and see introductory
note to this Eclogue), is presented very
simply with a dirge-like movement at the
beginning with spondaic rhythm, a heavy
pause after the first spondee in line 21,
strong alliteration in line 22; the wholly
spondaic rhythm of line 20 is echoed in
line 24. The personification of animals or
inanimate objects (pathetic fallacy, see
note on 1.38-9), which is frequent
throughout the song, is characteristic of
pastoral poetry, especially in passages of
pathos; it is one of the motifs in the lament
for Daphnis in Theocr. *Id.* 1.66f. Compare
also the later Greek pastorals, Bion's
Lament for Adonis, and Moschus' *Lament
for Bion;* and cf. Spenser, *Colin Clout*
22f.; Milton, *Lycidas* 37f.

But O the heavy change now thou art gon,
Now thou art gon and never must return!
Thee, Shepherd, thee the Woods and

desert caves
With wilde Thyme and the gadding Vine
oregrown,
And all their echoes mourn.

23 **atque . . . atque:** apparently 'both
. . . and', a variation on *et . . . et,* though
this usage is very rare, cf. Sil. 1.93-4
(*Geo.* 3.257; 4.343; 463; Tib. 2.5.73,
often cited as parallels, are different).
The alternative, to supply *est* to *complexa,*
seems very clumsy.

astra . . . crudelia: 'calls the stars cruel'
rather than 'invokes the cruel stars';
cf. *Geo.* 4.356.

24-5 **pastos . . . flumina:** i.e. the cattle
were not fed or watered. The rest of the
sentence is a variation on this theme.

25 **Daphni:** Greek vocative with short
-*i.*

nulla neque: for the doubled negative,
cf. 4.55, 10.64.

26 Compare Theocr. *Id.* 7.73-4 and
Spenser *Sheph. Cal. Nov.* 133-4.

The feeble flocks in field refuse their
former foode
And hang theyr heads as they would
learne to weepe.

27 **Poenos . . . leones:** there is a double
point here: even lions, fiercest of animals,
lamented (cf. Theocr. *Id.* 1.72), and even
in Africa Daphnis' death was known of.

28 **montesque . . . loquuntur:** 'both
the wild mountains and the forests say
that . . .'.

29-31 One of the attributes of Bacchus
was to yoke tigers to his chariot (cf. Hor.
Odes 3.3.13f.; *Aen.* 6. 804f); *thiasi* was a
technical term for the revels in his honour
(*Aen.* 7.581), and *hastae* refers to the
Bacchic wand, the *thyrsus (Aen.* 7.390);
cf. Eur. *Bacch.* 557-8. Line 31, rounding
the description of Bacchus' emblems, is a
golden line. The suggestion of Servius, that
we think here of Julius Caesar, because he
introduced Bacchic rites to Rome, is
wildly unlikely.

32-4 These phrases are based on
Theocr. *Id.* 8. 79-80: 'Acorns are the
glory of the oak, apples of the apple-tree,
the calf of the cow, and the cows
themselves of the cowherd'.

32 **arboribus:** the trees which support
the vines, cf. 2.70; *Geo.* 2.89.

34 **tulerunt:** 'took you', the simple
verb instead of the compound *abstulerunt.*

35 **Pales:** the god of pasture in whose
honour the festival *Palilia* was held;
cf. *Geo.* 3.1.

Apollo: in his capacity as Apollo
Nomios, Apollo of the pastures who once
served Admetus as a shepherd: see notes
on 2.60 and 4.10.

36 'often in the furrows to which we
have entrusted large grains of barley . . .'.
The biggest grains were preserved for
seed; cf. *Geo.* 1.197. The plural *hordea*
was criticised as improper; see note on
Geo. 1. 210.

37 'the weed darnel and wild oats
grow'; the two phrases are repeated in
Geo. 1.154. *Infelix* is a technical term
meaning 'not fruitful'.

38 **narcisso:** for the spondaic fifth foot
and polysyllabic ending, cf. 4.49; 7.53.

39 **paliurus:** 'thorn-bush'; Servius says
herba asperrima et spinosa.

40 Compare 9.19-20 (where the loss of
the singer Menalcas leads to the plaintive
question *quis caneret Nymphas? quis
humum florentibus herbis spargeret aut
viridi fontis induceret umbra?*) *Inducite
fontibus umbras* refers to putting foliage
and branches around the fountains.

43 Compare Theocr. *Id.* 1.120 Δάφνις
ἐγὼν ὅδε τῆνος ὁ τὰς βόας ὧδε νομεύων
('I am Daphnis, he who herded here his
cows'). Servius is probably right in
supplying *notus* to *in silvis:* 'well-known
in the forests and from there my fame
reaches to the stars above'.

43-4 The lapidary simplicity of the
epitaph ends the lament with a gentle
diminuendo; cf. Theocr. *Id.* 23. 43f.

45f. For the compliment, cf. Theocr.
Id. 8.82-3 ('your song is sweeter than
honey') and *Id.* 1.7-8 ('your song is
sweeter than the splashing stream').
Compare Milton, *PL* 8.210f.

For while I sit with thee, I seem in Heav'n,
And sweeter thy discourse is to my eare
Than Fruits of Palm-tree pleasantest to
thirst
And hunger both, from labour, at the hour
Of sweet repast.

46-7 'like quenching one's thirst in the
summer heat from a leaping stream of
sweet water'; the opening dactyls of
line 47 are imitative of the sense. Compare
Spenser, *FQ* 2.5.30.

48 Mopsus has already been praised for
his music (line 2); now his song is given
equal praise. *Magistrum* is of course
Daphnis.

49 **alter ab illo:** 'successor to him',
cf. 2.38.

50 **quocumque modo:** 'as best I can',

prout possumus (Servius).

52 This is a line of unusual rhythm
with trochaic caesurae in each of the first
three feet and no caesura at all in the
fourth.

54-5 **ista . . . carmina:** 'the songs you
mention'; i.e. the subject is worthy and
so is the song Menalcas has composed.
Stimichon is the name of another
shepherd.

56-7 Compare Pope, *Past.* 4.69-70:

But see! where Daphne wondering
mounts on high
Above the clouds, above the starry sky!

Cf. also Spenser, *Sheph. Cal. Nov.* 175f.:

She raigns a goddess now emong the
saintes,
That whilome was the saynt of shepheards
light . . .

and Milton, *Lycidas* 165f.:

Weep no more, woeful shepherds, weep
no more
For Lycidas your sorrow is not dead,
Sunk though he be beneath the watry
floore . . .
There entertain him all the Saints above
In solemn troops and sweet Societies . . .

56 **candidus:** 'shining', 'radiant', i.e. as
a god; cf. Hor. *Odes* 1.2.31; 1,18.11;
Epod. 3.9.

58 **alacris . . . voluptas:** 'a thrill of
pleasure', because Daphnis is deified. The
pathetic fallacy of Mopsus' song is here
reiterated in reverse: all nature now feels
joy instead of sorrow.

59 **Dryadasque puellas:** the Dryads
(wood-nymphs), now rejoicing in
Daphnis' deification, correspond with the
Nymphs (line 20) who wept at his death.

60-61 The universal peace of this
vision is reminiscent of the Golden Age of
Eclogue 4; cf. 4.22f., and for *otia* see
note on 1.6.

62-4 **ipsi . . . ipsae . . . ipsa:** cf. 1.
38-9 *ipsae te, Tityre, pinus, ipsi te fontes,
ipsa haec arbusta vocabant.*

63 **intonsi:** 'shaggy', i.e. forest-clad, a
most unusual epithet, in this metaphorical
sense only elsewhere applied to trees
(e.g. *Aen.* 9.681), but very appropriate
here to point the personification.

64 **deus . . . Menalca:** in apposition to
carmina. For the phraseology, cf. Lucr.
5.8 *deus ille fuit, deus, inclute Memmi.*

65 **sis . . . felixque:** a religious formula;
cf. *Aen.* 1.330; 12.647.

66 **duas altaria:** 'two others as high altars'; *altaria,* according to Servius, were confined to *dei superi.*

67-8 Compare Theocr. *Id.* 5. 53-4 where Lacon promises to the Nymphs a bowl of milk and another of olive oil, and for the whole of the passage Theocr. *Id.* 7.63f.

69 **hilarans convivia Baccho:** 'making the feast glad with wine'.

71 'I will pour from goblets the fresh nectar of Ariusian wine'; Ariusia, famous for its wine, was in Chios. *Calathus* generally means a basket, but is used of a bowl in *Geo.* 3.402 and of a cup in Mart. 9.59.15.

72-3 Compare Theocr. *Id.* 7.71-2, where at a celebration, two shepherds will play the pipe, one from Acharnae and one from Lycope.

72 **Lyctius:** from Lyctos, in Crete.

74-5 The reference here is first to an unspecified festival to the Nymphs, and secondly to the Ambarvalia in honour of Ceres (cf. 3.76-9; *Geo.* 1.338f.; Tib. 2.1).

77 The idea that cicadas feed on dew is mentioned in Theocr. *Id.* 4.16.

78 This line occurs again in *Aen.* 1.609 in a very similar context (*in freta dum fluvii current, dum montibus umbrae lustrabunt convexa, polus dum sidera*

pascet...).

79 Cf. Lucr. 5.14f.; *Geo.* 1. 7f.

80 **damnabis tu quoque votis:** 'you too will hold men to their vows'; the idea is that when a man makes a vow he becomes a prisoner of his vow, he is *voti reus (Aen.* 5.237). Cf. Livy 10.37,16 *voti damnata republica.*

81f. The singing contest in Theocr. *Id.* 6 ends with interchange of gifts.

84 A patterned line reminiscent in sense of lines 45-6 and the passage from Theocr. *Id.* 1 quoted there.

85 **ante:** before you give your gift (line 81).

cicuta: a pipe of a single hemlock stalk; contrast 2.36 where seven *cicutae* are joined to make a Pan-pipe.

86-7 Menalcas refers first to the opening words of *Eclogue 2* and then to the opening of *Eclogue 3.*

88 **pedum:** in Theocr. *Id.* 7.43 (cf. 128f.) the goatherd promises a gift of a shepherd's crook; cf. Hes. *Theog.* 30.

89 **non tulit:** cf. 2.35f., where Amyntas did not get the pipe he wanted.

90 **paribus nodis atque aere:** 'with its symmetrical knots and its bronze'; the hand of man had added the bronze to the natural beauty of the selected piece of wood.

ECLOGUE 6

The sixth *Eclogue* is a most remarkable poem, one which extends the normal boundaries of pastoral (as *Eclogue* 4 does, but in a very different way). Like *Eclogue* 4 but unlike the other eclogues it has little resemblance to Theocritus, either in whole or part. It begins with a typical Alexandrian *recusatio* (cf. Callim. *Aet.* 1.1.17f.; Prop. 3.3), as Virgil proclaims his unreadiness to sing of kings and battles, and therefore his inability to sing the praises of Varus, to whom none the less the poem is a tribute. It continues with the tale of Silenus the satyr being caught asleep and forced to sing a song; and the majority of the poem is concerned with Silenus' song.

The song covers an astonishing span of subjects, beginning with the creation of the world and continuing with brief allusive references (in the epyllion style) to nine mythological stories into which is inserted a song in honour of Gallus, Virgil's contemporary (see note on 64-73). It is plain that the stories are those which were favourite themes with Alexandrian poets such as Callimachus, Euphorion, Nicander (see J.P. Elder, *HSCP* 1961, 109f. and O. Skutsch, *Rh. Mus.* 1956, 193f.). It has been argued (F. Skutsch, *Aus Vergils Frühzeit,* 1901 and *Gallus und Vergil,* 1906) that they constitute a catalogue of Gallus' poetry or (Z. Stewart, *HSCP* 1959, 179f.) that they illustrate all the different genres which were favourite with the Alexandrians. Brooks Otis (*Virgil*, pp. 136f., and pp. 406f.) has argued that there is a pessimistic element here (all the stories are concerned with *amor indignus*, indicating a degeneration from the Golden Age) which contrasts with the optimism of a returning Golden Age expressed in *Eclogue* 4. We may say with certainty that these were the themes with which the neoteric poets in Rome, followers of the Alexandrians, often concerned themselves, and that Virgil's poem is a list of favourite contemporary subjects, presented in a neoteric style. But whatever fascination such subjects may once have had for his young mind, he would, before long, renounce them (cf. *Geo.* 3.6f.).

The presence of the contemporary statesman and poet Gallus in the song of Silenus is startling, and the effect comparable to his appearance as a shepherd in the pastoral world of *Eclogue* 10. The idea of a poet being consecrated to the Muses, as Gallus is, is very typical of the Alexandrians and of their model Hesiod (note on 69–70); it seems certain that Virgil is paying a high compliment to his friend, and very likely that the subject-matter of Silenus' song is chosen with reference to the material about which Gallus liked to write, though it is not essential to argue that he did in fact write about all these subjects. They were the myths, often associated with metamorphosis and with unnatural or frustrated love, which the Alexandrians (and after them the Roman elegists) used to illustrate human emotions. It is interesting that the story which is given the longest treatment (that of Pasiphae and the bull) was especially typical of the strange world of which the Alexandrians loved to write, and that it exercised a continuing fascination upon Virgil, as we see from *Aen.* 6.24f.

1-8 **Virgil's Muse** (for the Muse Thalea, cf. Hor. *Odes* 4.6.25) first sported (for the verb used of pastoral poetry, cf. 1.10 and *Geo.* 4.565) in Syracusan verse (a reference to Theocritus of Sicily; cf. 4.1, 10.1) in the woods (cf. 4.3): when he turned to epic poetry he was dissuaded by Apollo, so now he returns to pastoral.

2 **erubuit ... habitare:** the infinitive with *erubescere* ('blush to dwell in') occurs first in Virgil.

3 **reges et proelia:** Servius gives a number of suggestions to explain this phrase, of which the two most convincing are that Virgil made an early attempt to start the *Aeneid* or that he began an epic poem on the kings of Alba. Donatus (*Vita* 19) says that Virgil began a Roman theme but disliking the subject turned back to the *Eclogues* instead. The intervention of Apollo is imitated by Hor. *Odes* 4.15. 1f.; Prop. 3. 3. 13f.; Ov. *AA* 2. 493f.; and Milton *Lycidas* 76f. 'But not the praise, Phoebus replied, and touched my trembling ears'.

Cynthius: an epithet of Apollo from Mt Cynthus on the island of Delos, his birth-place (cf. *Geo.* 3.36).

4 **Tityre:** Apollo addresses Virgil by the name of one of his shepherds (*Ecl*

1.1; 3.20; 5.12; etc.).

4-5 **pinguis ... deductum:** the two words are in strong antithesis; the sheep should be fat, but the song slender, thin-spun. The metaphor is from spinning wool; cf. Hor. *Epist.* 2.1.225 *tenui deducta poemata filo;* Prop. 1.16.41; Callim. *Aet.* 1.1.22f. 'Apollo said to me ... "Fatten the beast you offer to the gods, but keep your style lean" '. On this see Clausen, *GRBS* 1964, pp. 181f.

6 **super ... erunt:** tmesis, (cf. 8.17; *Aen.* 2.567) of *superesse* in its sense of 'be in abundance', cf. Livy 2.27.12.

7 **Vare:** Alfenus Varus was a prominent statesman and soldier; cf. 9.26f. Servius suggests that the wars referred to were against the Germans; the adjective *tristia* is a standing epithet.

condere: 'write' or 'write about'; cf. 10.50; Hor. *Epist.* 1.3.24. *seu condis amabile carmen;* Ov. *Trist.* 2.335-6 *Caesaris acta condere.*

8 The statement of Virgil's return to pastoral poetry contains favourite epithets of the pastoral genre: *agrestis* (cf. 1.10), *tenuis* (cf. 1.2, a very similar line), and is presented in a perfect golden line (cf. 17).

9 **non iniussa cano:** i.e. the poet has Phoebus' authority (lines 4-5) to write

pastoral.

tamen: i.e. although I cannot sing Varus' praises, yet he is commemorated in this pastoral poem dedicated to him.

11-12 'nor is any page more pleasing to Phoebus than one which has at its beginning the name of Varus': for *praescripsit*, cf. Tac. *Ann.* 3.57; *Hist.* 3.13. Servius says *Vari nomen gestat in titulo.*

13 After the preface and dedication, Virgil now asks the Muses (cf. 3.85; 9.33; 10.72) to lead him into the subject-matter.

Chromis et Mnasyllos: perhaps two satyrs or fauns, semi-divine personages like Aegle, or perhaps two shepherds.

14 Silenum: the most famous of the satyrs, attendant of Bacchus, generally comically portrayed (cf. Plato *Symp.* 216 d; Hor. *AP* 239; Ov. *Met.* 11.90f.). The idea of his being caught and compelled to tell a story goes back perhaps to Hom. *Od.* 4.382f. (Proteus caught by Menelaus, cf. *Geo.* 4.387f.), and Servius refers to a passage in Theopompus about how Silenus was caught in a drunken sleep, bound in chains, and made to reveal ancient stories. Cf. also Cic. *TD* 1.114.

15 inflatum ... venas: 'his veins swollen', retained accusative; cf. 53; 68; 75; and see note on 1.53-5.

Iaccho: = *Baccho* (7.61) = *vino*.

16 procul tantum: 'just a little distance away', apparently (as Conington suggests) a rendering of Theocr. *Id.* 1.45 τυτθὸν δ᾿ ὅσσον ἄπωθεν.

capiti: for the dative, cf. 7.47; Ov. *Met.* 6.592.

17 'and the heavy tankard was hanging from his hand by its well-worn handle'; a golden line. Both the epithets add to the picture of the habitual drunkard.

19 ipsis ... sertis: 'fetters made of the actual garlands'; the placing of the preposition is not uncommon in Lucretius (e.g. 1.841), but unusual in Virgil (cf. 1.24 for a dissyllabic preposition so placed). Servius compares *Aen.* 5.663 *transtra per et remos.*

20 timidisque supervenit: 'came to join them as they hesitated', i.e. gave them confidence by her support of their trick.

21 iamque videnti: 'though he was now awake'.

22 moris: *morum* is the mulberry, a fruit with abundant dark red juice.

24 potuisse videri: 'that you are seen to have been able to do it', i.e. he confesses that he has been caught, and no further

compulsion is called for. Cf. *Aen.* 5.231 *possunt quia posse videntur.* Others take the meaning to be 'that I could be seen' (gods, and presumably demi-gods, are not normally seen), but this is less likely.

25 cognoscite: 'listen to', 'get to know'; cf. Juv. 3.288 *cognosce prooemia rixae.*

26 huic ... erit: 'for her there will be something different as payment'; the periphrasis of the neuter followed by a genitive in place of the straightforward *alia merces* adds to the comic effect. Servius comments *Nymphae minatur stuprum latenter, quod verecunde dixit Vergilius.*

27 in numerum: 'in rhythm'; cf. Lucr. 2.631; *Aen.* 8.453.

Faunosque ferasque: 'both Fauns and wild animals'; the doubled *-que* gives a trochaic lilt imitative of the dance. Fauns are rustic deities often associated with Pan; the mention of wild animals anticipates the mention of Orpheus (30), whose music made even animals fall under its sway.

29 Mt Parnassus in northern Greece was sacred to Phoebus Apollo and the Muses; cf. 10.11.

30 Orpheus was especially associated with Thrace; cf. 4.55. Rhodope and Ismarus were mountains in Thrace. *Orphea* (Greek accusative) scans as a dissyllable by synizesis of the last two vowels; cf. 42, 4.57 and *Geo.* 1.279.

31f. On the subject-matter of Silenus' song, partly Lucretian science and partly Alexandrian mythology, see the introduction.

31-40 The phraseology of this passage is often Lucretian (*magnum per inane, semina, animae, liquidi ignis, concreverit*); see specifically Lucr. 5.416-508. The content is similar also to Orpheus' song in Ap. Rh. 1.496f., and not unlike Iopas' song in *Aen.* 1.740f; cf. also Ov. *Met.* 1.5f.

31-3 'For he sang how atoms of earth and air and sea and also of streaming fire had collected together in the mighty void': the idea of the four elements as the source of all matter goes back to Empedocles (fifth century BC). For *liquidus ignis*, cf. Lucr. 6.205; 349: the meaning is liquid in the sense of not solid.

33-4 his exordia primis omnia: 'all beginnings came from these things first'. The reading here is doubtful: P has *ex omnia*, R and other MSS have *exordia*, and this is attested by Macrobius (6.2.22) and is a Lucretian word. The phrase in

Lucr. 1.61, where he talks of atoms *quod ex illis sunt omnia primis,* supports P, but the difficulty over *omnia* repeated in line 34 would be considerable (Sabbadini conjectured *omnis*). Nettleship conjectured *his ex ordia primis* (cf. Lucr. 4.28).

34 'and the newly-formed circle of the universe of itself took shape'. *Tener* suggests that at this early stage everything was young and soft, till it took shape (*concreverit*) and was hardened (*durare*); cf. Lucr. 5.780f. *mundi novitatem et mollia terrae arva.*

35 The subject is *mundi orbis:* the universe began to harden that part of itself which was to be land and to confine Nereus in the ocean. Others take *solum* as the subject, with *durare* intransitive. The sea god Nereus (*Nerea* is Greek accusative) is given his specific domain; for *discludere,* cf. Lucr. 5.438. The passage is reminiscent of Lucr. 5.432f.; cf. Ov. *Met.* 1.21f.

37 **terrae stupeant:** 'how the lands marvelled'; the construction is still governed by *uti.* For the subject-matter, cf. Lucr. 2.1105f.; 5.471f. Virgil's idea (cf. Ov. *Met.* 1.21f., esp. 70-71) is that the various parts of the universe separate out from the general mass which is the earth.

38 The clouds are now moved further away so that showers can fall. I have punctuated after *altius,* so that it goes with the previous line; many editors take it with what follows, so that *atque* is postponed, but such a postposition is not Virgilian. There is something to be said for R's reading *utque.*

39-40 'While forests first began to rise up, and a few animals to roam over the mountains which had known none before'; cf. Lucr. 5.824. *Ignaros,* read by R, means that the mountains had not previously known animals; P has *ignotos,* ('strange') which would mean that the animals had not yet had time to become familiar with the places which would become their 'haunts'. The former is preferable because of the parallelism with *terrae stupeant* (37); the emphasis is on the reaction of the already existing mountains, not on that of the newcomers. Notice how this section ends with a golden line (cf. 8, 17).

41f. Silenus now moves from his Epicurean cosmogony to mythological stories of early times; cf. Ap. Rh. 1.496f.; Ov. *Met.* 1.89f.

41 **lapides Pyrrhae iactos:** 'the stones which Pyrrha threw', a reference to the re-peopling of the world after the flood by Deucalion and Pyrrha, when they threw stones which turned into men and women; the story is told at length by Ovid (*Met.* 1.313f.); see also note on *Geo.* 1.62.

Saturnia regna: i.e. the Golden Age under Saturnus, see note on 4.6. This is a second item in the enumeration; it is not in apposition to the previous words. In Ovid, and in most versions of the legend, it occurs before the flood, which was sent by Jupiter, Saturnus' successor.

42 The reference is to the theft of fire from heaven by Prometheus, and his subsequent punishment when he was fettered on the Caucasus mountains and an eagle preyed on his liver. This story also usually precedes that of the flood.

Promethei: the last two vowels are pronounced as a single syllable by synizesis; cf. 30 and 78.

43f. The story of how during the voyage of the Argonauts Hylas was lost, captured by the nymphs of the fountain while he was fetching water, and of Hercules' vain efforts to find him, is told in Theocr. *Id.* 13 and Ap. Rh. 1.1207f., and referred to as a trite theme in *Geo.* 3.6. A feature in some versions of the story was that when Hercules shouted Hylas' name the nymphs who had captured him shouted it back as an echo.

43-4 **his adiungit . . . clamassent:** 'to these he added the story of the fountain at which Hylas was lost and how the sailors shouted his name', literally 'at what fountain Hylas was left behind'; it is an unusual way of introducing the subject, as the emphasis must be on Hylas not the fountain, but it seems very awkward to take *quo* as *quomodo,* as Servius does. Cf. *quibus . . . alis* (80-81).

44 Cf. Theocr. *Id.* 13.58 where Hercules shouts Hylas' name in vain; Spenser, *FQ* 3.12.7 'And every wood and every valley wyde He filld with Hylas' name; the nymphs eke Hylas cryde'.

Hyla, Hyla: for the scansion, cf. 3.79; while the final *a* in the first word remains long in hiatus, it is shortened in hiatus in the second word.

45-6 'and in song he consoles Pasiphae for her love of the snow-white bullock, Pasiphae, happy if cattle had never existed'. The reference is to the story of King Minos' wife who was caused by Poseidon to fall in love with a bull and became the mother of the Minotaur (cf. Cat. 64, *Aen.* 6.24f.).

48 The daughters of Proetus were
punished for their pride by being made to
imagine they were cows (hence *falsis
mugitibus,* 'feigned mooing'); cf. Callim.
Hymn. 3.233f., Ov. *Met.* 15.326. Notice
the epyllion technique of inserting a story
within a story, as in Cat. 64; the narrative
method is also of the epyllion type, with
emphasis on dramatic and pictorial details
rather than the logical flow of events.
Proetides: Greek nominative plural with
a short final syllable.

49-51 'yet not one of them sought such
base union with cattle (as Pasiphae did),   ·
even though they feared the plough on
their necks and often felt for their horns
on their smooth foreheads'; i.e. they
certainly thought they were cows, but
did not — as Pasiphae did — seek the love
of bulls.

52 The repetition of the opening phrase
(cf. 47) takes us back to Pasiphae after
the parenthesis and gives a sense of pathos.

53 'the bull, resting his snow-white
body on soft beds of hyacinth . . .';
for the retained accusative *latus,* cf. 15; for
the lengthening of the second syllable of
fultus and the quadrisyllabic ending,
cf. *Geo.* 4.137. Here the bull seems to enjoy
the idyllic pleasures of the pastoral world
in which Pasiphae has no part.

55f. Silenus now reports the words of
Pasiphae, beginning her speech at the
bucolic diaeresis (cf. 21; 25; 58).

56 **Dictaeae:** Dicte was a well-known
mountain in Crete, the kingdom of King
Minos and Queen Pasiphae. Pasiphae is
appealing to the Nymphs to prevent the
bull from getting away, so that she can
find him by following his hoof-prints; he
may be still in the area cropping the grass
or chasing the cows.

60 **Gortynia:** Gortyna was a town in
Crete.

61 Atalanta was promised in marriage
to any suitor who could beat her in a race;
Hippomanes (Milanion) was given by Venus
one of the golden apples of the
Hesperides and during the race threw it
in front of Atalanta. She could not
resist the temptation to stop to pick it up,
and Hippomanes won the race; see Ov.
Met. 10.560f.

62-3 The sisters of Phaethon, weeping
for their brother who had been burnt to
ashes by flying too near the sun, were
metamorphosed (Ov. *Met.* 2.340f.) into
alder trees or poplars (Ap. Rh. 4.595f.;
Aen. 10.190). The patronymic *-ides* is

here used in an extended sense, 'kinsfolk
of'; cf. Mart. 4.32.1.

62 **circumdat:** the singer is represented
as doing what he sings about.

64-73 The introduction of a real
person into this list of mythological
stories is extremely striking; compare
Eclogue 10, where Gallus enters the
pastoral world as a shepherd. Gallus was a
famous soldier and statesman of Virgil's
day, and in addition a writer of elegy and
epyllia mentioned as one of the four
important elegists by Quintilian (10.1.93)
and Ovid (*Tr.* 4.10.53). His distinguished
political career culminated in his appoint-
ment by Augustus as prefect of Egypt, but
his behaviour there caused him to fall into
disgrace and he committed suicide. There
was a story (almost certainly false) that
originally *Geo.* 4 ended with his praises
but was subsequently altered by Virgil; see
note on *Geo.* 4.315-424.

64 **Permessi ad flumina:** Permessus was
a river whose source was on Mt Helicon
sacred to the Muses (*sorores*) in Aonia
(Boeotia); cf. Prop. 2.10.26 where it seems
to be especially associated with love-elegy.

65 **Aonas:** the word scans as a dactyl,
the final syllable being short (Greek third
declension).

67 **Linus:** the great singer of legend
(cf. Prop. 2.13.8), son of Apollo and
teacher of Orpheus, was mentioned in
4.56-7; here he is called a shepherd to
associate him with pastoral poetry.

68 **crinis ornatus:** retained accusative,
cf. 15.

69-70 'The Muses give you these reeds —
look, take them — which they gave once to
the old poet of Ascra'. The poet is Hesiod,
and the reference is to the beginning of his
Theogony where he tells how the Muses
came to him and taught him song. The
mention of Hesiod is very significant, as
the Alexandrian poets, in whose tradition
Gallus followed, regarded Hesiod as their
great model (cf. Callim. *Aet.* 1.2),
especially because of the idea of divine
inspiration associated with him. Thus
Gallus is said to have reached the highest
point of poetry.

71 This accomplishment is generally
attributed to Orpheus.

72 'With the reeds let the origin of the
Grynean grove be proclaimed by you'.
Apollo had a famous oracle at Grynium in
Asia Minor; cf. *Aen.* 4.345. Servius tells
us that Euphorion, an Alexandrian poet
imitated by the Roman elegists, had sung

of Grynium. Note the emphasis on origins (*aetiae*), a type of poetry especially favoured by Hesiod and the Alexandrians.

74 **Scyllam Nisi**: supply *ut narraverit* from 78. The reference is to Scylla daughter of Nisus who cut the purple lock from her father's hair to give to her lover. As a result she and her father were turned into birds, she into a sea-bird called *ciris* and he into a sea-eagle, for ever pursuing her. The pseudo-Virgilian *Ciris* tells of this legend; cf. also *Geo.* 1.404f.

75f. The description of Scylla which now follows is of the other more famous Scylla, the monster who occupied the rock opposite Charybdis. The same conflation of the two occurs in Prop. 4.4.39f. and Ov. *Fast.* 4.500; *AA* 1.331f. For line 75, cf. Lucr. 5.892; *Aen.* 3.424f. (where see my note, Oxford edition); Ov. *Met.* 13. 732f.; and Milton's description of Sin (*PL* 2.653-4) 'about her middle round/A cry of Hell Hounds never ceasing barked . . .'. *Inguina* is retained accusative after *succinctam;* see note on 15.

76 **Dulichias**: i.e. the ships of Odysseus of Ithaca, with which the little island Dulichium was associated; cf. Hom. *Od.* 12.73f.

vexasse: the apparent understatement is discussed by Aul. Gell. 2.6.

77 In Homer it was the six mouths of Scylla, rather than her sea-dogs, which carried off her victims.

78f. This version of the story is that Tereus raped the sister (Procne) of his wife Philomela, who took vengeance on her husband by serving up at a banquet the flesh of their son Itys. Tereus pursued Philomela but was metamorphosed into a hoopoe, and she into a nightingale, and Procne into a swallow. In other versions Philomela was the sister and Procne the wife; cf. *Geo.* 4.15; Ov. *Met.* 6.424f.

78 **Terei**: scanned as a dissyllable by synizesis; cf. 42. Notice the heavy spondees of the line.

80 **quo cursu**: 'by what method', i.e. by flying.

deserta petiverit: 'she (the nightingale) made for a hidden retreat'.

80-81 'how before that, unhappy one, she fluttered on her wings above the house she had possessed': *ante* is adverbial, referring to her last look at her palace before she flew away for ever. *Quibus . . . alis* is literally 'upon what wings', in the sense of 'how on wings'; cf. *quo fonte* (43).

82 **meditante**: 'singing'; cf. 1.2.

83 **Eurotas**: the river on which Sparta stood; the reference is to Apollo's songs to the Spartan boy Hyacinthus there. Page quotes Pope, *Past.* 4.13:

Thames heard the numbers as he flowed along,
And bade his willows learn the moving song.

84 **pulsae referunt**: 'echo'; cf. 5.62; *Aen.* 7.702.

86 **invito . . . Olympo**: 'the evening star climbed into the reluctant heavens'; even Olympus is listening to the song and does not wish it to end.

ECLOGUE 7

This graceful and charming little poem is very closely modelled on Theocritus (*Idyll* 8, an amoebaean contest; there are also echoes of other *Idylls*, especially 6, 7, 9, 11). It aims to use the Theocritean subject-matter to create pictures of idyllic lyricism, expressed in gentle cadences appropriate to its simple themes. The setting described in the first twenty lines is varied from Theocritus *Idyll* 8 where there are only two characters altogether, but the method of the singing contest and many of the phrases are borrowed and transmuted into Latin song. The sole aim of the eclogue is to present the grace and beauty of pastoral song. It is much more successful than *Eclogue* 3 in adapting Theocritus to something new and specially Virgilian.

The reasons for Corydon's victory have been a subject of dispute among scholars; the discussion ranges from a detailed analysis of all the faults of Thyrsis' verses compared with the excellence of those of Corydon to the view that there is nothing to justify Corydon's victory except that dramatically someone had to win, as we have already had one dead-heat (in *Eclogue* 3). But it is surely the case that Corydon's subjects are more attractively pastoral and his lyricism more gentle; there is a harsher and even arrogant air about Thyrsis which accords less well with the pastoral world and the aim of sheer beauty in song. For further discussion and summary of other views see F.H. Sandbach, *CR* 1933, 216f.; S.V.F. Waite, *CP* 1972, 121f.; and the full treatment in V. Pöschl, *Die Hirtendichtung Virgils*, 1964, p. 93f.

1 arguta: 'whispering'; cf. 8.22, and Theocr. *Id.* 1.1; the poem begins with (and maintains throughout) the idyllic peace of a pastoral landscape. The opening scenes resemble those of Theocr. *Id.* 6 and 8.

Daphnis: for Daphnis, the legendary bucolic hero, see the introduction to *Eclogue* 5; here, however, (as sometimes in Theocritus) he appears as an ordinary shepherd.

2 Corydon et Thyrsis: for Corydon, cf. *Ecl.* 2; for Thyrsis, Theocr. *Id.* 1.64f.

4 Arcades: Arcadia was the home of Pan (4.58) and in Virgil takes on a special significance as the idyllic location of the pastoral genre (cf. *Ecl.* 10). It does not occur in this sense in Theocritean pastoral, and is one of Virgil's particular innovations in the genre, presenting an idealised other-worldly setting for the life of the shepherds. See the masterly treatment by B. Snell, *The Discovery of the Mind,* trans. Rosenmeyer, 1953, pp. 281f. Here then the meaning is not so much that both shepherds came from Arcadia (they are presented as Italians), but that they were both worthy representatives of the ideal world because of their ability in song. See further Coleman *ad loc.*

5 cantare pares: for the construction, cf. 5.1-2; for the subject-matter, cf. Theocr. *Id.* 8.4 (the poem on which much of this eclogue is based) 'both skilled at piping, both at singing'.

6 mihi: ethic dative, reminding us that the whole eclogue is narrated by Meliboeus.

defendo: presumably Meliboeus was occupied in protecting his myrtles against the possibility of frost (perhaps with straw or the like), and while thus engaged lost sight of the leader of his goats and had to go off to find him (and the rest, who would have followed him; cf. line 9).

7 vir gregis: a personification of the he-goat, based on Theocr. *Id.* 8.49 (ἁνερ); cf. Hor. *Odes* 1.17.7.

deerraverat: the first and second

syllables coalesce into one by an easy synizesis, normal e.g. with *deest.*
atque: = *et subito;* cf. *Aen.* 4.663.

12 The description of Mincius (the river which flows into Lake Benacus; cf. *Geo.* 3.15) is idyllically given in a golden line (cf. 24); this is Virgil's own country, set within the pastoral framework.

13 The oak was especially sacred to Jupiter because of his shrine amidst the oak groves at Dodona (*Geo.* 2.16; 3.332). For the bees, cf. Theocr. *Id.* 1.107 (5.46).

18-19 Cf. Theocr. *Id.* 8.30-31: 'first Menalcas sang, then Daphnis took up the answering song'. For amoebaean verse see the introduction to *Ecl.* 3, and especially 3.59 *amant alterna Camenae.*

19 alternos . . . volebant: 'the Muses wished to remember answering verses'; a strange phrase influenced by the association of the Muses with memory (*Aen.* 7.645).

21 Libethrides: an allusive epithet (from Euphorion) to show Corydon's literary learning; Libethra was a fountain on Mt Helicon, mountain of the Muses, who are here called Nymphs. The declension is Greek, so that the final syllable is short; cf. *Arcades* (4).

22 Codro: another shepherd (cf. 5.11), here standing for eminence in song; many allegorical interpretations (Messalla, Cornificius, Cinna) have been offered.

proxima Phoebi: cf. 5.9.

23 facit: the last syllable is lengthened in arsis at the caesura; see note on 1.38.

24 He means that he will retire; for the hanging-up of the tools of one's trade on retirement, cf. Hor. *Odes* 3.26; Tib. 2.5.29f. The pine was sacred to Pan, god of the shepherds (Prop. 1.18.20).

25 crescentem . . . poetam: 'the rising poet'; some MSS have *nascentem,* but cf. Euphorion in *Anth. Pal.* 6.279 where Apollo is asked to give his ivy to the poet as he grows (ἀεξομένῳ). *Crescentem* is also more appropriate for Thyrsis' self-confident attitude.

26 The reply of Thyrsis 'caps' Corydon

by picking up his reference to Codrus, and arrogantly surpassing Corydon's prayer.
rumpantur ut ilia: a coarse phrase; cf. Cat. 11.20.

27 The meaning is that if Codrus praises Thyrsis too much it will lay Thyrsis open to the evil eye (cf. 3.103); therefore this must be prevented by the herb *baccar* (4.19) which was thought to have the magical property of warding off spells. Cf. Cat. 5 and 7.

29 **Delia:** Diana, goddess of hunting, sister of Phoebus (22); cf. 3.67.

29-30 **parvus . . . Micon:** understand the verb *dedicat;* it is frequently omitted in inscriptions and dedications; cf. *Aen.* 3.288. Corydon here speaks in the person of a youthful hunter; Micon *(parvus)* clearly echoes Theocritus' Menalcas (8.64) where he refers to himself as little (μικκός). Others take Micon to be a son or young friend of Corydon.

31-2 'If this is mine to keep, you will stand all in smooth marble, your ankles girt in purple buskins'; i.e. he will erect a full-scale statue of Diana. In the phrase *si proprium hoc fuerit* the pronoun *hoc* seems to refer to success in hunting of the kind implied in the previous two lines; for *proprium,* cf. *Aen.* 6.871. The buskin *(coturnus)* was a large boot associated both with tragedy; cf. 8.10; and with hunting; cf. *Aen.* 1.337; for the retained accusative *suras,* see note on 1.53-5.

33f. Thyrsis responds to Corydon's invocation to Diana by his own invocation to Priapus, the rustic deity of gardens and vineyards *(Geo.* 4.111).

33 **sinum:** a somewhat colloquial word for 'bowl', appropriate to the modest nature of the offering of milk and cakes.

37-40 These are fine lines, beginning with a long and colourful build-up of Galatea's charms, passing to a time-clause made emphatic by heavy alliteration of *p,* then to an if-clause as simple and direct as could be, and concluding with a main clause of only one word, the emphatic imperative *venito,* summarising the love and desire of the whole little song.

37 **Nerine:** 'daughter of Nereus', a Greek form of the patronymic, a learned and literary type of diction; cf. Cat. 64.28. The famous Galatea was a sea-nymph, and Corydon thus associates his shepherdess with legendary beauty.

thymo . . . Hyblae: again a colourful literary allusion, referring to the honey made by the bees from the thyme-covered

mountain of Hybla; cf. 1.54.

38 So Polyphemus (Theocr. *Id.* 11.20) calls his Galatea whiter than milk (cf. Ov. *Met.* 13.789f.); for white ivy, cf. 3.39; Pliny *NH* 16.145.

41 **immo ego:** 'but what about me?'; the words emphatically introduce Thyrsis' riposte, a statement of his love parallel to Corydon's but expressed more urgently and impatiently, emphasised with alliteration of *r.*

Sardoniis . . . herbis: honey from the flowers of Sardinia (cf. Hor. *AP* 375) and Corsica (cf. 9.30) was proverbially bitter; hence our phrase 'sardonic laughter'.

44 **si quis pudor:** i.e. the cattle should feel ashamed at prolonging the day's work for Thyrsis and preventing him from returning home to his loved one.

45-7 The invocation to nature is based on Theocr. *Id.* 8.33f; 37f; cf. also *Geo.* 3.143f. Notice the slow spondees of line 45, conveying the idea of peace.

45 **somno mollior herba:** 'grass softer than sleep'; cf. Theocr. *Id.* 5.51 'fleeces softer than sleep', ὕπνω μαλακώτερα, and the same phrase of coverlets *(Id.* 15.125).

46 'and the green arbute which gives you shade with its chequered shadow'; *vos* refers back to *fontes* and *herba.* Corydon's phrases again are very idyllic — he is concerned much more than Thyrsis with the world of pure pastoral beauty.

47 **pecori:** 'from the flock'; for the dative, cf. 6.16.

49f. Thyrsis' reply contrasts the comforts of winter indoors with Corydon's description of summer out-of-doors. Cf. Theocr. *Id.* 9.19f.; 11.51.

52 **numerum lupus:** 'as much as the wolf cares about numbers', i.e. the predatory wolf is not concerned that there may be too many sheep for him to dare to attack, any more than the river in flood cares about the presence of the banks which cannot confine it. Conington refers to the story that Alexander the Great, when told of the numbers of the Persian army, replied that a single butcher is not afraid of a number of sheep.

53-6 Compare Theocr. *Id.* 8.41f.: 'everywhere there is spring . . . where the lovely Nais walks; but if she departs, the cowherd and the cows lose their bloom'.

53 Corydon now tries a line of extremely unusual metre, with hiatus both at the caesura and in the spondaic fifth foot; see notes on 2.24; 3.6; 5.38; and cf. also *Aen.* 3.74; 9.647. Other instances of this rare

type of line ending are with proper nouns or Greek words. No other line in Virgil has this combination of unusual features.

54 **sua . . . poma:** the phrase *sua quaeque poma sub arbore* is unusual for *quaeque sub arbore sua,* but the suggestion that *sua* is ablative scanned as a monosyllable should not be entertained for a moment.

55 **Alexis:** Corydon's beloved in *Ecl.* 2.

57 The dactylic line conveys agitation at the idea of hostile nature.

vitio . . . aeris: 'because of the poisoned air'; cf. *Geo.* 3.478 *morbo caeli;* and compare Lucr. 6.1090f. for a description of 'diseases' of the air.

58 'Bacchus grudges the shade of the vine to the hills'; i.e. the vine leaves are shrivelled up or fallen off.

59-60 This is a very neat reversal of Corydon's image; Thyrsis must have won this round, but he is by now too far behind.

60 'and Jupiter will descend in full measure in sweet rain'; for the identification of Jupiter with features of the weather, cf. *Geo.* 1.418; 2.325f.

61f. For the first time in the contest Corydon alludes to Thyrsis' reply, first by

reintroducing Bacchus (Iacchus) and his vines, and then by singing of Thyrsis' Phyllis.

61 The poplar was traditionally associated with Hercules; cf. Theocr. *Id.* 2. 121; *Geo.* 2.66; *Aen.* 8.276.

62 The myrtle (cf. *Geo.* 1.28) was said to have sheltered Venus when she rose from the sea; the laurel of course is always associated with Phoebus (cf. Ovid's story, in *Met.* 1.452f., of Daphne).

65-8 Thyrsis balances Corydon's song by the mention of the trees, and as Corydon had used the name of Phyllis which he had introduced he matches Corydon's Alexis (55) with his Lycidas. His last line echoes his first, a variant on Corydon's last line echoing his second.

69-70 'Those songs I remember, and that Thyrsis contended in vain and was beaten: ever since then it's Corydon, Corydon, for us'. The last line is an adaptation of Theocr. *Id.* 8.92, where after the end of the contest in which Daphnis was the winner Theocritus says: 'ever since then Daphnis was first among the herdsmen'.

ECLOGUE 8

This poem (like *Eclogues* 3, 5 and 7) is composed of answering songs; like 5 it is not set in the form of a contest (cf. Theocr. 7, 9, 10). The songs are prefaced by an introductory section of sixteen lines; they balance each other in length (45 lines) and in the number of verses in each section for the first seven sections, but not in the last three. The refrains are based on Theocr. *Id.* 1 and 2; the subject-matter on Theocr. *Id.* 1, 3 and 11 in the first half, and Theocr. *Id.* 2 in the second half. As will be seen from the notes, the frequency of reminiscence of Theocritus is very great, yet Virgil has produced something quite original out of his material. The song of Damon is given greater depth of pathos (compare Corydon in *Ecl.* 2) than either that of Polyphemus (Theocr. *Id.* 11) or the lover of Theocr. *Id.* 3; and the song of Alphesiboeus (based on Simaetha's song which forms the whole of Theocr. *Id.* 2) is set in contrast with what has gone before, treating of the same theme (unhappy love) but with the difference that, while Damon's situation is tragic and hopeless, Alphesiboeus' heroine has success with her magic spells and the poem ends on a dramatic note of optimism.

The introduction stresses firstly the power of song and then invokes the unnamed person to whom it is dedicated. The majority opinion, that this is Pollio, seems correct; the reference to Illyria fits Pollio's campaigns against the Parthini in 39 BC, and the mention of tragedies fits well with what we know of Pollio's literary activities (see note on 10). He was mentioned in *Eclogue* 3, and *Eclogue* 4 was dedicated to him by name. Servius however says that the dedica-

tion of this poem is intended for Augustus (Octavian), and this has been
supported by Bowersock, *HSCP* 1971, 73f.; he argues that the reference is to
Octavian's campaigns in Illyria and along its coast in 35 BC, and points out
that Octavian's tragedy, *Ajax*, is mentioned by Suetonius (*Aug.* 85.2).
For a full discussion of the symmetry and narrative style of the poem, see
Otis, pp. 105f.

1 **Musam:** 'the song', object of *dicemus*
(5), where it is repeated. The names of the
two shepherds have both occurred before
(3.17; 5.73).

2 Cf. Theocr. *Id.* 6.45 and Tennyson,
Gardener's Daughter, 'the steer forgot to
graze'; for pathetic fallacy see note on
1.38-9; and cf. especially 5.25-6. The
power of song is strongly emphasised at the
beginning of a poem entirely about song;
indeed even the dedication (6f.) is
postponed while Virgil speaks of the
miraculous effects of poetry.

3 **lynces:** there were no lynxes in Italy,
so that the imaginary setting of the poetry
is emphasised.

4 **cursus:** retained accusative after the
passive verb *mutata* used in a Greek middle
sense; see note on 1.53-5. Others take it as
the object of *requiescere* in a transitive
sense, comparing Prop. 2.22.25; *Ciris* 2.33.
Cf. Milton, *Comus* 493-4 (of Thyrsis)
'Whose artful strains have oft delayd
The hudling brook to hear his madrigal'.

6 **Tu mihi:** in this invocation *mihi* is
left without construction, as a sort of
ethic dative (cf. 7.6). *Tu* is surely Pollio,
as is apparent from the description of his
deeds (see intro.). For Pollio, cf. 3.84,
4 intro.

magni . . . Timavi: 'you are passing the
cliffs of mighty Timavus'; for *superare* in
this nautical sense and for Timavus (at the
north end of the Adriatic) cf. *Geo.* 3.475;
Aen. 1.244. Virgil refers to Pollio's
homeward journey from his Illyrian
campaigns in 39 BC (Hor. *Odes* 2.1.15f.;
Dio 48.41).

7 **oram Illyrici . . . aequoris:** i.e. further
south than Timavus.

8-10 Virgil asks whether the day will
ever come when he can worthily celebrate
(i) Pollio's military deeds (ii) his poetic
achievements. Compare 6.6f. for a similar
recusatio.

10 Pollio was a tragic poet (Hor. *Sat.*
1.10.42; *Odes* 2.1.9f.); the buskin
(*coturnus;* cf. 7.32) was a high boot worn
in tragic performances (cf. Juv. 6.634-6,
where also Sophocles is mentioned as the
Greek tragedian *par excellence*).

11 'From you comes the beginning, for
you the conclusion'; imitated from Theocr.
Id. 17.1, ἐκ Διὸς ἀρχώμεσθα καὶ ἐς Δία
λήγετε Μοῖσαι, like *ab Iove principium*
(3.60, where see note). Cf. also Hom. *Il.*
9.97; Hes. *Theog.* 34. Most modern editors
read *desinam* with P, but the shortened
-am in hiatus is quite unparalleled in
Virgil, and M and Servius (and other
ancient authorities) read *desinet.*

11-12 **iussis . . . tuis:** 'because you
asked'; cf. 6.9.; *Geo.* 3.41 *tua, Maecenas,
haud mollia iussa.* 'Commands' is too
strong a word in this poetic context, and
misleading.

12-13 'and let this ivy intertwine
around your temples mingling with your
victor's laurels'; ivy refers to Virgil's
poetry (cf. 7.25) which Pollio may take as
a tribute along with the conquering
general's laurels. Pollio celebrated a
triumph in 39 BC.

15 This idyllic line is repeated in *Geo.*
3.326.

16 **incumbens tereti . . . olivae:** 'leaning
against a smooth olive tree' (cf. Theocr.
Id. 3.38), rather than 'leaning on his peeled
olive staff' (cf. Theocr. *Id.* 7.18). The
objection that olive trees are not usually
smooth only lends point to the fact that
this one was relatively so; for the adjective
applied to trees, cf. *Aen.* 6.207.

17 **praeque . . . veniens age:** 'herald the
day and bring it in'; the verb *prae . . .
veniens* is separated by tmesis; cf. 6.6.

18 **indigno:** 'unrequited'; cf. 10.10; the
postposition of the conjunction and verb,
dum queror, emphasises the words in this
line.

19-20 **nil . . . profeci:** i.e. he has not
had his previous pleas answered, when he
called the gods to witness his suffering.

21 The refrain is based on Theocr.
Id. 1.64 'Begin, beloved Muses, begin the
pastoral song'. *Maenalios* refers to the
mountains in Arcadia sacred to Pan; cf.
Theocr. *Id.* 1.123-4.

22 **argutumque . . . pinusque:** 'both
. . . and'; for *argutum*, 'whispering',
cf. 7.1; here it has the added point that
Arcadia is the land of song.

24 **Panaque:** object of *audit,* Greek accusative.

qui . . . inertis: i.e. Pan was the inventor of the pipe's music; cf. 2.32f.

26 **Mopso:** another shepherd, Damon's rival for Nysa's love; the diaeresis after the first spondee and the juxtaposition of the names emphasise his indignation.

quid . . . amantes: 'what may we lovers not expect', i.e. anything can happen.

27 **grypes:** 'griffins', fabulous monsters. Such a prophecy of the reversal of nature, called adynaton, is characteristic of the diction of pastoral and elegiac poetry; see notes on 52f. and on 1.59f.

28 **timidi . . . dammae:** for the masculine *damma* ('deer'), cf. *Geo.* 3.539; Quint. 9.3.6.

pocula: 'water'; literally it means 'goblets', and is here used in an artificial high style of diction; cf. *Geo.* 1.9; 3.529.

29 **faces:** for the wedding ceremony, like *nuces* in the next line (cf. Cat. 61. 128f.), see Coleman *ad loc.* Damon speaks with bitter irony.

30 **tibi . . . Oetam:** 'for you the evening star leaves Oeta', i.e. rises above it (cf. Cat. 62.7; Oeta was a mountain in Thessaly). Damon visualises the oncoming of Mopsus' wedding night.

32 **digno:** highly ironical; she despises everyone else and has picked a worthless person who is thoroughly worthy of her.

33-4 **dumque . . . barba:** supply *odio sunt.*

34 Cf. Theocr. *Id.* 3.7-8 and Polyphemus' self-criticism in Theocr. *Id.* 11. 31f.; Virgil, however, has removed the element of comedy and has heightened the pathos.

37f. This is a fine section, with a gentle pathos that is very effective. Page quotes Macaulay: 'I think that the finest lines in the Latin language are those five which begin — *saepibus in nostris . . .* I cannot tell you how they struck me'. The lines are closely modelled on the moving passage in Theocr. *Id.* 11.25f., the love of Polyphemus for Galatea: 'I fell in love with you, my love, when first you came with my mother to gather hyacinths from the hill, and I led you on the way'; but the idea of the reminiscence of childhood days is original in Virgil, and immensely effective.

38 **cum matre:** Virgil has varied Theocritus so that Nysa is with her mother, not Mopsus' mother, as *dux vester* shows.

39 **alter ab undecimo:** 'the next after the eleventh', i.e. the twelfth.

41 'When I saw, how I fell in love, how a fatal mistake carried me away'; because she will not requite his love. The construction is a translation of Theocr. *Id.* 2.82 χώς ἴδον, ὡς ἐμάνην, 'and when I saw, so I became mad' (cf. also *Id.* 3.42); in greek the word ὡς may be used demonstratively but in Latin *ut* cannot, so that Virgil has given a different syntax from his model, with the second *ut* exclamatory.

perii, ut: there is hiatus at the caesura; cf. 44 and see note on 3.6.

43-5 These lines are based on Theocr. *Id.* 3.15f. 'now I know Love . . . he was suckled by a lioness and his mother brought him up in the wild places'.

43 **scio:** the shortened -o occurs elsewhere in Virgil only with *nescio.*

44 **Tmaros . . . Rhodope:** Tmaros was a mountain in Epirus, Rhodope (cf. 6.30) a mountain in Thrace. For the denial of human parentage, cf. *Aen.* 4.365f.; Hom. *Il.* 16.34f.

Rhodope aut: there is hiatus at the caesura, cf. 41.

Garamantes: a people of Africa, cf. *Aen.* 6.794. For the quadrisyllabic ending, cf. 2.24; 3.63.

45 'produced him, no child of our race or blood', i.e. inhuman, cf. Hom. *Il.* 16.33f. The use of the present tense *edunt* is idiomatic ('are his parents'), like the Greek τίκτουσι, cf. *Geo.* 1.279 (*creat*); *Aen.* 8.141 (*generat*); 10.518 (*educat*).

47 The reference is to Medea who killed her children to take vengeance on Jason who had deserted her.

48 **crudelis . . . mater:** Damon apportions blame both to the divine agent Cupid, and to the mortal mother Medea.

49 **improbus:** cf. *Aen.* 4.413 *improbe Amor, quid non mortalia pectora cogis?*

50 The repetition is 'precious', very much in the Alexandrian style, and of the kind beloved by Ovid; see Coleman *ad loc.*

52f. The reversal of nature (adynaton) occurs for the second time in Damon's song; cf. 27f., and in particular Theocr. *Id.* 1.132f. Compare Pope, *Dunciad* 3.245-6 'The forests dance, the rivers upwards rise, Whales sport in woods, and dolphins in the skies'.

54 'let the tamarisks ooze rich amber from their barks'; amber was rare, and generally associated with alder trees, certainly not with a humble shrub like the tamarisk.

55 **cycnis ululae:** cf. Theocr. *Id.* 5.136-7.

55-6 'let Tityrus be Orpheus, Orpheus in the woods and Arion among the dolphins', i.e. let the humble shepherd be equal to the legendary musician Orpheus in pastoral surroundings, and to Arion amidst the waves (Arion was saved from drowning by charming the dolphins with his music and riding on the back of one of them).

56 delphinas: Greek accusative plural with short final syllable.

58 omnia . . . mare: 'let everything indeed become mid-ocean', a very strange phrase meaning that the world is no good to him; it might as well be drowned by a universal flood. Virgil is still imitating Theocr. *Id.* 1.132f., where in line 134 Thyrsis says πάντα δ' ἔναλλα (or ἄναλλα) γένοιτο — 'may everything turn upside down'. It seems possible that the word ἔναλλα suggested the sea to Virgil (Greek ἐνάλια); he may also have been influenced by a passage in Archilochus (74.8) where (in a 'reversal of nature' passage) the poet speaks of wild animals taking up the marine life (νομὸν ἐνάλιον) of dolphins.

fiat: attracted to the singular number of the predicate; cf. 67 and Ov. *Met.* 1.292.

vivite: 'farewell', based on the Greek χαίρετε; cf. Theocr. *Id.* 1.115-16.

59-60 This is based on Theocr. *Id.* 3.25-7 where the lover says, 'I will jump into the sea, and if I die, that will be pleasant to you'; cf. also *Id.* 23.21f.

59 specula de montis: for the word order, cf. *Geo.* 4.333 *thalamo sub fluminis.*

61 Similarly towards the end of his song in Theocr. *Id.* 1. Thyrsis changes the refrain from 'Begin . . .' to 'Cease . . .' (*Id.* 1.127).

63 The poet asks the Muses (*Pierides;* cf. 6.13) to sing Alphesiboeus' reply, for he himself cannot.

64f. The song of Alphesiboeus is based on Simaetha's laments over her unhappy love for Delphis in Theocr. *Id.* 2. The speaker in Alphesiboeus' song is a woman lamenting her love for Daphnis, and trying to win him by magic (as Simaetha did).

65 adole: a technical word in sacrifices, sometimes meaning 'worship' (as *Aen.* 1.704) sometimes 'offer', (especially by burning) as here (cf. Ov. *Fast.* 3.803).

mascula: 'masculine' incense (cf. Pliny *NH* 12.61) was the name of a particular kind.

66-7 sanos avertere . . . sensus: i.e. to make him insane with love; cf. Cat. 83.4.

67 nihil . . . desunt: i.e. all else is prepared, and only a magic chant is now needed: it is supplied in the refrain of the next line.

68 The refrain recalls that in Theocr. *Id.* 2.17f. ἴυγξ, ἕλκε τὺ τῆνον ἐμὸν ποτὶ δῶμα τὸν ἄνδρα: 'Magic wheel, draw that man to my house'.

69f. Notice the repetition *carmina . . . carminibus,* picking up the use of the word in each of the two previous lines and finally varied to *cantando* in line 71.

69 For the power of magic compare Tib. 1.8.19f.; Hor. *Epod.* 5.45f.; 17.4f.; Ov. *Am.* 2.1.23f.; and more generally *Aen.* 4.487f.

70 The witch Circe by her spells changed men into pigs: Odysseus (Ulixes) however succeeded in getting his crew changed back again (Hom. *Od.* 10.203f.).

Ulixi: a form of the genitive; cf. *Aen.* 2.7; *Aen.* 1.30 (*Achilli*).

71 Conington quotes a fragment of Lucilius (575) *Marsus colubras disrumpit cantu* and Ov. *Met.* 7.203, *Am.* 2.1.25. For *frigidus,* stock epithet of a snake, cf. 3.93.

73-4 'First I put round you these three threads, contrasting with their three different colours'; i.e. round the effigy of Daphnis (as the next line shows). The number three was important in magic; cf. Theocr. *Id.* 2.43 (with Gow's note); *Aen.* 4.511; Spenser, *FQ* 3.2.50; Shakespeare, *Macbeth* 4.1.1. 'Thrice the brinded cat hath mewed'.

75 effigiem: cf. Dido's use in magic of an effigy of Aeneas in *Aen.* 4.508.

impare: a poetic form for the usual ablative *impari.*

77 tribus . . . ternos: i.e. each of the three knots will have three colours; notice the emphasis on binding, as is frequent in magic (Theocr. *Id.* 2.3.10).

Amarylli: the name of her attendant, who was addressed at the beginning of the song (64f.).

78 necte . . . modo: 'just tie them'; cf. *Aen.* 1.401 *perge modo,* 'just press on'.

80 The jingling rhyme of the two halves of the line clearly is intended to reproduce the sound of a magic chant; cf. 'Double double, toil and trouble . . .'. For the melting of wax, cf. Theocr. *Id.* 2.28.

81 eodemque: the first two vowels coalesce by synizesis; cf. *Aen.* 10.487 and note on 6.30.

sic: i.e. may Daphnis be hard to others and soft to her.

82 molam: 'salted meal'; cf. *Aen.* 4.517; Theocr. *Id.* 2.18.

fragilis: 'crackling'; cf. Theocr. *Id.* 2.24; Tib. 2.5.81 (where the loud crackling of

burning laurel is a good omen). For
bitumine, cf. Hor. *Epod.* 5.81-2.

83 **urit:** she burns the laurel as a magical
compensation for the way Daphnis 'burns'
her. Again the line is very closely based on
Theocr. *Id.* 2 (23-4 Δέλφις ἔμ' ἀνίασεν
ἐγὼ δ' ἐπὶ Δέλφιδι δάφναν αἴθω: 'Delphis
has angered me, and I burn this laurel for
Delphis'). The phrase *in Daphnide* is based
on the Greek ἐπὶ Δέλφιδι; compare also *Aen.*
2.541 *talis in hoste fuit.*

85 **Daphnin:** governed by *teneat* (89).

qualis cum: = *qualis amor tenet
buculam cum* . . . On the whole it seems
that the traditional interpretation of this
passage (that the heifer is passionately
seeking her mate) is correct; cf. Theocr.
Id. 2.48 (where Simaetha prays that
Daphnis may be maddened with love as
mares are maddened by the drug
hippomanes). But the interpretation of
Rose is interesting; comparing Lucr. 2.355f.
(the famous passage about the cow seeking
its lost calf) he takes the diminutive *bucula*
as indicating pathos not youth and
considers that Virgil too is speaking of a
cow and its lost calf. Support is perhaps
lent to this by the Lucretian echo in
propter aquae rivum (Lucr. 2.30).

88 **'helpless through love, and forgets**
to withdraw from night's late hours'; for
perdita, cf. 2.59; and for *decedere nocti,*
cf. *Geo.* 3.467 (the same phrase);
4.23 *decedere . . . calori.* For the image of
withdrawing from night's domain
Conington aptly compares Gray's 'And
leaves the world to darkness and to me'.
According to Macrobius (*Sat.* 6.2.20) the
whole of this line was taken from Varius'
poem *De Morte* where it described a
hunted deer.

89 **talis amor:** the reiteration after a
long subordinate clause is like that of the
first sentence of the eclogue.

91f. This is based on Theocr. *Id.* 2.53f.
where a fringe from Delphis' cloak is cast
on to the flames; *exuviae* and *perfidus* are
recalled — like much else from this
eclogue — in Dido's magical spells against
Aeneas (*Aen.* 4.496; 421).

92 **limine in ipso:** presumably her own
threshold (cf. 107), rather than that of
Daphnis, as in Theocr. *Id.* 2.60.

93 **debent . . . Daphnin:** 'these tokens

owe Daphnis to me', i.e. must, if the magic
works, bring him back, because they bind
him to her.

95 **Ponto:** a reference to Colchis on the
Black Sea, home of the arch-magician
Medea (cf. Hor. *Epod.* 17.35).

96 **Moeris:** a shepherd, skilled in magic
(cf. the following lines); the name is used
again in the next eclogue.

97-9 These are attributes of a magician:
for werewolves, cf. Ov. *Met.* 1.209f.; Pliny
NH 8.80; for necromancy, cf. *Aen.* 4.490;
Tib. 1.2.45-6; Hor. *Epod.* 17.79; Ov. *Met.*
7.206; for the charming of corn crops
(forbidden in the Twelve Tables), cf. Tib.
1.8.19; Sen. *NQ* 4.7; Pliny *NH* 28.17.
Cf. Shakespeare, *Tempest* 5.1.48-50 'graves
at my command Have wak'd their sleepers,
oped and let them forth By my so potent
art'.

101f. These instructions are based on
Theocr. *Id.* 24.91f. (burn serpents, gather
the ashes, and throw them beyond the
boundaries without looking back).

101-2 **rivoque . . . iace:** 'and throw them
into a flowing stream and over your head';
the metre and alliterations of line 102 are
urgent and agitated, with the emphatic verb
iace giving a strong conflict of word accent
with ictus.

105f. The dramatic ending to the poem,
with an indication of the success of the
magic, differs from Theocr. *Id.* 2, which
ends with no indication of success. The
drama is emphasised by the unusual pause
in the fifth foot of line 106.

105-6 'the ash itself has caught the
altar with its flickering flames all by
itself, while I was hesitating to bring it',
i.e. the altar has blazed up of its own
accord; Plutarch (*Cic.* 20) relates a similar
good omen. Servius, followed by Ribbeck,
regards these verses as spoken by the
attendant Amaryllis, but this would be an
unnecessary interruption of the song.

107 'There is certainly something going
on, and Hylax is barking at the door';
the dog thinks it hears someone approach-
ing.

108-9 The element of doubt slows the
poem to a gentle end, as does the variation
of the refrain.

108 **qui amant:** for the shortening of
the vowel in hiatus, cf. 2.65; *Aen.* 6.507.

ECLOGUE 9

This poem is a companion to the first *Eclogue:* both are concerned with the dispossession of shepherds from their farms. It seems likely that this poem is prior to the first, expressing as it does an almost wholly unhappy situation (with even the famous singer Menalcas unable to save their farms for Lycidas and Moeris) compared with the joy of Tityrus in *Eclogue* 1, when his farm is restored to him through the intervention of a young man (probably Octavian). The theory that it is later than *Eclogue* 1, and refers to a second dispossession, seems disproved by line 3. Like *Eclogue* 1 this poem is anchored to historical reality (there were indeed confiscations at this time; see the introductory note to *Eclogue* 1), but to equate Virgil allegorically with Menalcas is to interpret the poem more directly and precisely than Virgil's method justifies. The poem is surely based on his personal experience; it has more precise geographical location (7-9; 26-9) than most of the *Eclogues;* but it is universalised in song rather than offered as veiled history.

The essence of the poem is the assault upon the idyllic pastoral world by outside influences; the peace and gentle song of the shepherds are shattered by the intrusion of arrogant strangers, possessed of the power to destroy the very essence of their existence (line 3-6). The tone of the poem is alarmed, dramatic, angry; the serenity of the pastoral world is absent. The relationship of this poem to Theocritus is less close than in most of the other *Eclogues* — naturally enough, as its theme is so closely connected with the personal experience of Virgil or of his friends; but it is essentially based on Theocritus' seventh idyll (which tells how Simichidas met Lycidas and they sang songs to each other) with the vital difference that the songs in Theocritus bring joy, but in Virgil they have lost their joy because of the disaster. It is noteworthy that this idyll of Theocritus, unlike any other, contains explicit references to the real literary world (*Id.* 7.37f., a passage which Virgil adapts, 32-6). Other passages from this idyll which Virgil uses are referred to in the notes on lines 1, 42, 59-60, 64; and two of the songs (23-5; 39-43) are adaptations of different idylls of Theocritus, unlike the replies to them (27-9, 46-50) which are both essentially Roman.

1 **Quo . . . pedes** understand *ducunt* (cf. Theocr. *Id.* 7.21). *Moeri,* with short final syllable, is a Greek vocative; cf. *Amarylli, Daphni,* etc.
urbem: probably Mantua (cf. 27f.; 1.20), the nearest city to his farm.
2 Moeris does not reply to the question, but bursts out with the unexpected and unbelievable disaster which has befallen him. Notice the dislocated order of his phrases, with *advena nostri* separated from *possessor agelli* both by the parenthetical *quod* clause and by the postponed *ut* of its own clause. The juxtaposition of *advena nostri* is rhetorically powerful — a stranger, *my* land.
vivi pervenimus: understand *eo:* 'we

have lived to come to such a point that . . .'; he means he would have expected to die before such a disaster should befall him.
3 **agelli:** the diminutive conveys not only a humble reference to his little domain, but also a sentimental attachment to it; it stands in powerful antithesis to the crude words of the new owner — *haec mea sunt.*
5 **nunc victi tristes:** the slow spondees, with the echo of alliteration of *v* that is dominant throughout these lines, helps to convey his despondency.
6 'we are sending to market these kids on his behalf, and may it turn out ill for him'; for the archaic use of *nec = ne,* cf. 10.46.

7-8 qua . . . clivo: 'that from the spot where the hills begin to retreat and slope from their summits in a gentle descent . . .', i.e. the whole flat area from the hills to the river Mincius.

11 Audieras: 'yes, you had heard that', picking up Lycidas' *audieram* (7) and thus giving great emphasis to the antithesis introduced by *sed . . .*

11-13 tantum . . . columbas: 'are as effective among weapons of war as men say Chaonian doves are when the eagle comes'; doves are called Chaonian from the famous oak groves of Dodona in Chaonia (Epirus) which were haunted by doves.

14 quacumque . . . lites: 'to stop the sudden dispute by any means'; for *incidere*, cf. Hor. *Epist.* 1.14.36. It is a poetic infinitive after *monuisset;* cf. 25 and see note on 1.9.

15 ante: 'beforehand', adverbial; cf. 63.

sinistra . . . cornix: 'a crow on the left', i.e. an omen favouring his action; cf. Cic. *Div.* 1.85 *cur a sinistra cornix faciat ratum.*

17 cadit in quemquam: 'happen to anyone'; the use of *quemquam* implies the negative answer.

19 caneret: 'would sing of' (if you had been killed).

19-20 Lycidas asks who else would be able to sing songs about flowers or shady fountains – cf. 5.40, and Ben Jonson, *Pan's Anniversary:* 'Strew, strew the glad and smiling ground with every flower'. The poet is here said to do what he sings about; cf. 6.62.

21 'Or what about the songs which I secretly overheard from you the other day?' For *sublegi* Servius says *intercepi.*

22 delicias . . . Amaryllida nostras: 'to Amaryllis, whom we all love'; the name Amaryllis occurs fairly often in the *Eclogues.*

23-5 These lines are very closely modelled on Theocr. *Id.* 3.3-5, where the love-sick shepherd goes to serenade Amaryllis and entrusts his goats in the meantime to Tityrus, with instructions to water them and beware of being butted by the he-goat.

24 potum: supine; 'to drink'.

inter agendum: 'as you drive them'; *agendum* is a gerund, and the expression has an archaic tinge.

25 occursare . . . caveto: the infinitive with *cavere* is mainly poetical, see note on 14.

26 immo haec: 'but what about this?': Moeris adds another quotation from

Menalcas. Lycidas' quotation (23-5) was from Theocritus; this is wholly Roman. The same is true of the other pair of songs (39-43 and 46-50).

Varo: cf. 6. 7, and the introduction to *Ecl.* 1; Varus was in charge of the land confiscations for the veteran soldiers of Antony and Octavian.

27 superet . . . nobis: 'only let Mantua survive for us', concessive subjunctive; *superare* is in the sense of *superesse;* cf. *Geo.* 2.235; *Aen.* 5.519.

28 Cremona, which had supported the Republicans, was a centre for confiscations of land, and Mantua, Virgil's birthplace, was only some 65 km away; cf. *Geo.* 2.198.

29 sublime: in agreement with *nomen* (27), the object of *ferent,* rather than adverbial.

cycni: the swans of Mantua are mentioned in *Geo.* 2.199; there is also a suggestion of swans symbolising song.

30 'So may your bees avoid Cyrnean yews . . .'; for the use of *sic* in prayers of this sort, cf. 10.4f.; Hor. *Odes* 1.3.1f.; Tib. 1.4.1f. Cyrnos was a name of Corsica; for the ill-effects of yew, cf. *Geo.* 4.47, and for the bitterness of plants from that area, cf. Ov. *Am.* 1.12.10 and see note on 7.41 (Sardinia).

33 Pierides: the Muses; cf. 3.85.

33-4 Cf. Theocr. *Id.* 7. 37-41, where Simichidas says that everyone calls him the best of singers, but he does not believe them, as he cannot compare with Sicelidas or Philetas, any more than a frog can compare with a grasshopper.

34 vatem: i.e. an inspired poet, something more than *poeta* (32).

35 Vario . . . Cinna: Varius was a leading epic poet (cf. Hor. *Sat.* 1.10.43-4; *Epist.* 2.1.245f.; *Odes* 1.6.1 and see note on 8.88); he and Tucca were Virgil's posthumous literary executors. Some MSS have *Varo,* but that would be wholly inappropriate after Varus' mention as a statesman (not a poet) in line 26, and Servius attests *Vario.* Cinna was a neoteric poet, mentioned by Catullus (95) as author of a poem called *Zmyrna:* he figures in Shakespeare's *Julius Caesar* where he is killed in mistake for the conspirator Cinna.

36 'but I make a noise like a goose among tuneful swans'; cf. the passage from Theocritus cited on 32-4. Servius makes much play with a supposed reference here to a poet called Anser (Ov. *Trist.* 2.435), but this seems very unlikely.

37 **id ... ago:** 'yes, that's what I'm
busy with', i.e. trying to remember one of
Menalcas' songs as requested (32).
39-43 The song is imitated from Theocr.
Id. 11.42f. where Polyphemus sings to
Galatea: 'Come to me ... leave the grey
sea to beat on the shore ... here are
laurels and slender cypresses, dark ivy,
the sweet-berried vine ... who would
prefer the sea?'
39 **nam:** cf. *Geo.* 4.445 for the tmesis of
quisnam.
42 Cf. Theocr. *Id.* 7.8: 'the poplars and
elms wove a shady bower'.
43 **feriant sine:** 'let them strike'; for
sine in parataxis with the jussive
subjunctive, cf. *Geo.* 4.90; *Aen.* 5.163.
44 **quid, quae:** 'what of the words which
...?'; cf. *Geo.* 1.111.
45 **numeros ... tenerem:** 'I remember
the rhythm, if only I could recall the
words', an attractively phrased elliptical
condition, where the true main clause is
suppressed ('if only I could recall the
words, I would have it all'). Another way of
expressing this is to say that the *si* clause
is an independent wish.
46-50 Some MSS and editors attribute
these lines to Moeris, but Lycidas' reply
(44-50) balances the previous words of
Moeris (37-43).
46 **antiquos:** the ancient constellations,
as opposed to the novel apparition of
Caesar's comet; the epithet is transferred
from *signorum* to *ortus.*
47 **Dionaei ... astrum:** Caesar was
descended, according to tradition, through
Iulus and Aeneas from Venus and her
mother Dione. The reference is to the
comet which appeared at the games in
July after Julius Caesar's death and was
supposed to carry his soul to heaven (Hor.
Odes 1.12.47; cf. *Aen.* 8.681).
48 **astrum:** the repetition of the word,
with a pause after the first spondee (cf.
8.26), is very emphatic.
quo ... gauderent: 'under whose
influence the crops might rejoice'; the
subjunctive is final (*quo = ut eo*).
49 **duceret:** 'took on', 'drew in'; cf. Ov.
Met. 3.484-5.
50 The transition of thought is that if
Daphnis grafts his pears under the benign
influence of Caesar's comet they will be
fruitful and bear crops for future
generations. The context contrasts sharply
with that of the similar phraseology in
1.73.

51 **fert:** 'takes away'; cf. 5.34.
animum quoque: 'etiam memoriam'
(Servius).
51-2 'I remember how often as a boy I
used to bring long summer days to their
end as I sang'; cf. Callim. *Epigr.* 2. 3 'we
put the sun to rest'; *Geo.* 1.458; Hor.
Odes 4.5.29.
53 **oblita:** 'forgotten', passive, a very
rare usage; cf. Prop. 1.19.6.
53-4 **Moerim ... Moerim:** the use of his
own name and the repetition of it adds to
the pathos; cf. Catullus' use of his own
name (e.g. 72.1).
54 This is a proverbial expression: if
wolves saw a person before he saw them,
he lost his voice; cf. Theocr. *Id.* 14.22;
Pliny *NH* 8.80.
56 'By your excuses you are putting
off my passionate desire'; i.e. by saying
you cannot remember your songs you are
frustrating (but not removing) my longing
to hear them; cf. Lucr. 1.398.
57 **tibi:** ethic dative, 'I want you to
know'. He means that the weather is now
suitable for pausing to sing songs: *ut possis
canere, cuncta siluerunt* (Servius); cf.
Theocr. *Id.* 2.38.
aequor: perhaps Lake Garda, possibly
the Sicilian sea of Theocritus, certainly not,
as Servius says, *spatium campi* (both
stratum and *silet* are appropriate for
water).
58 **ventosi ... murmuris aurae:** 'the
breezes with their rustling sound', a strange
and vivid phrase.
59-60 The idea is from Theocr. *Id.*
7.10-11 'we had not yet reached half-way,
and the tomb of Brasilas was not yet in
sight'; Bianor was, according to Servius,
another name for Ocnus the founder of
Mantua.
61 **stringunt:** 'strip', to use as fodder;
cf. *Geo.* 1.305.
62 **tamen veniemus in urbem:** 'we will
still get to the city', even if we stop now
for song.
63 **colligat ante:** 'may bring the rain
first'; *ante* is adverbial; cf. 15.
64 **usque:** 'all the way'; cf. *Aen.* 6.487;
for the verse, cf. Theocr. *Id.* 7.35-6.
65 For the repetition, cf. 8.49-50.
fasce: the burden of the goats, carried
perhaps under his arms, perhaps on his
shoulders or in some sort of container.
66 **puer:** the second syllable is lengthened
in arsis; see note on 1.38.
67 **ipse:** i.e. Menalcas.

ECLOGUE 10

There is every reason to think that this poem, which concludes the collection of *Eclogues,* was the latest in composition (perhaps 37 BC), and it is certainly the most original and in many ways the strangest of all the *Eclogues:* Virgil introduces into the pastoral world the real person of Gallus, prominent statesman, military leader and elegiac poet. We have had in the other *Eclogues* glimpses of the real world (Pollio, Varus, Gallus himself in 6), and there have been oblique references to events such as land-confiscation, the death of Julius Caesar, the birth of a child; but here the whole poem is taken up with the attempt to assimilate Gallus into the idyllic world of Arcadia. The artificiality of the poem has alienated some critics; others (such as Putnam, pp. 342f.) have been deeply excited by its symbolism, seeing it as an exploration of the tension between the world of action and the world of dreams, or between the world of elegy and the pastoral world. Macaulay's judgment is famous, that he preferred the *Georgics* to the *Aeneid* and the *Eclogues* to the *Georgics,* and of the *Eclogues* the second and tenth.

In its poignant exploration of unhappy love the poem reminds us often of *Eclogues* 2 and 8, and its chief literary similarity is with the first idyll of Theocritus, where the poet sings of the unhappy love of Daphnis (see notes on 9f.; 13-16; 19-21). Thus the continuity of the pastoral genre is secured in a poem which gives it a wholly different direction, one which was to have enormous influence on subsequent pastoral poetry in Latin and later in modern European languages (Milton's *Lycidas* is the best known example, but there are many more — see W. Leonard Grant, *Neo-Latin Literature and the Pastoral* and T.G. Rosenmeyer, *The Green Cabinet,* passim).

A good deal is known about the public life of Gallus — see note on *Ecl.* 6.64-73 — but we have sadly little information about his poetic achievement. He is mentioned by Ovid and by Quintilian as one of the four prominent Roman elegists, but virtually nothing of his work survives. Servius (see note on 46f.) tells us that Virgil's verses in this part of the *Eclogue* are taken from Gallus' own poetry, and it is indeed probable that there are references and allusions which we cannot now recognise. What is certain is that Virgil expresses, within a remarkable and quite new convention, his private and personal affection for Gallus, and in doing so explores in a strange synthesis the different levels on which the life of men works itself out, the real world of action, the half-conventional emotional world of elegiac love poetry and the wholly conventional imaginary world of an idyllic pastoral Arcadia.

1 **Arethusa:** a famous fountain in Sicily (cf. *Aen.* 3.694f.; Cic. *Verr.* 2.4.118), here symbolising Virgil's debt to his Sicilian model Theocritus; cf. 4.1 and 6.1. Compare Milton, *Lycidas* 85f: 'O Fountain Arethuse, and thou honour'd Flood, Smooth-sliding Mincius . . .'; Shelley's poem *Arethusa arose . . .;* Moschus, *Lament for Bion* 77; and Theocr. *Id.* 1.117f., where the dying Daphnis says goodbye to Arethusa.

2 **Gallo:** the famous statesman and poet; cf. 6 intro. and note on 6.64-73.
sed . . . Lycoris: 'but such that Lycoris herself may read them'; *legat* is final subjunctive. Lycoris was the name of Gallus' mistress, for whom he wrote elegies; cf. Prop. 2.34.91; Ov. *Am.* 1.15.30; Ov. *AA* 3.537 *Vesper et Eoae novere Lycorida terrae.* Servius identifies her with one Volumnia, known as Cytheris (who sang

Virgil's sixth *Eclogue* in the theatre), and says that she left Gallus and went off with Antony to Gaul.

4-5 The story was that the river Alpheus in southern Greece pursued the nymph Arethusa, who was changed by Diana into a fountain, and passing under the sea united his river with the fountain: here Virgil evidently thinks of the lovers making journeys under the sea to meet each other.

4 **sic**: for this idiomatic use, see note on 9.30.

5 **Doris**: daughter of Oceanus, mother of Arethusa, here by metonymy meaning the sea.

7 **simae**: 'blunt-nosed', like a monkey (simian); cf. Theocr. *Id.* 8.50 (of goats) σιμαί . . . ἔριφοι and 7.80 (of bees).

8 **respondent omnia silvae**: 'the woods re-echo all our songs'; i.e. nature responds to the shepherd's songs; cf. 1.5 and see note on 1. 38-9. For this use of *respondere*, cf. Ov. *Met.* 11.53. Compare Milton, *Lycidas* 42-4:

The Willows and the Hazel Copses green
Shall now no more be seen
Fanning their joyous Leaves to thy soft
  lays.

9f. These lines are closely modelled on the beginning of Thyrsis' lament for Daphnis in Theocr. *Id.* 1.66f.: 'Where were you, nymphs, where were you when Daphnis was wasting away? In the beautiful valleys of Peneius or of Pindus? For you were not by the mighty river of Anapus or on the peak of Etna or by the sacred water of Acis'. Virgil has altered the emphasis: in Theocritus the local Sicilian nymphs were away, perhaps in Thessaly, from the scene of Daphnis' death in Sicily: but here the Nymphs were away from their usual places in Thessaly where the Muses dwelt and therefore were unaware of human affairs, like the gods in Homer when they go off to visit the Ethiopians (*Il.* 1.423; *Od.* 1.22). Milton's imitation (*Lycidas* 50f.) has the Theocritean emphasis, with the local Nymphs absent from the scene of Lycidas' death off the coast of Wales:

Where were ye Nymphs when the remorse-
  less deep
Clos'd ore the head of your lov'd Lycidas?
For neither were ye playing on the steep,
Where your old Bards, the famous Druids
  lie,
Nor on the shaggy top of Mona high,
Nor yet where Deva spreads her wizard
  stream . . .

10 **Naides**: 'water-nymphs'; cf. 6.21. The specific word (rather than *Nymphae* as in Theocritus) makes a connexion with Arethusa, the fountain of pastoral song. The word scans in Greek fashion as a dactyl.

indigno: 'unhappy' because unrequited; cf. 8.18.

11 **Parnasi . . . Pindi**: mountains in northern Greece, sacred to the Muses; cf. 6.29.

11-12 **vobis . . . moram fecere**: 'held you', 'delayed you'; cf. *Aen.* 3.473.

12 **Aonie Aganippe**: Aganippe was a fountain near Mt Helicon, sacred to the Muses, in Boeotia (Aonia); cf. 6.65. *Aonie* is a Greek feminine form of the adjective; for the hiatus in the fifth foot with polysyllabic ending, cf. 2.24.

13-16 This is one of the most famous examples in Latin poetry of the lamentation of inanimate nature (pathetic fallacy, see note on 1.38-9 and cf. 5.24f.). It is based on the same passage (see note on 9f.) of Theocritus (*Id.* 1.71f.: 'for him the jackals, for him the wolves lamented, even the lions of the forest bewailed his death; . . . cattle and bulls, heifers and calves made lamentation'); and it is imitated in Milton's *Lycidas* (39f.):

Thee Shepherd, thee the Woods and
  desert Caves,
With wilde Thyme and the gadding Vine
  oregrown,
And all their echoes mourn. . . .

13 **lauri, etiam**: there is hiatus at the caesura (see note on 3.6), here perhaps — immediately after the hiatus in the previous line — helping to convey metrically the idea of lamentation.

14-15 The repetitions from line 13 show this device of pastoral poetry at its most effective as they slow down and reiterate the expression of sorrow.

15 **Maenalus . . . Lycaei**: mountains in Arcadia (cf. 8.21; *Geo.* 1.16), indicating that the locale of this poem is imaginary, and preparing the way for Gallus to be transformed into a shepherd of the pastoral world. There is nothing like this concept of an idyllic Arcadia before Virgil, but after him (as for example in Milton's *Lycidas*) it became a frequent feature of pastoral.

16-18 This is a powerful expression of the unity of Nature, its animals, and its shepherds in the pastoral world, comparable in some ways with Virgil's concept in the *Georgics* of the unity of the elements in the real world of the Italian countryside, Nature, its animals, its farmers. Compare Pope, *Past.* 2.5-6:

Soft as he mourn'd the streams forgot to flow,
The flocks around a dumb compassion show.

18 This pastoral aspect of the legend about Adonis, the beautiful youth beloved of Venus and killed while hunting, occurs in Theocr. *Id.* 1.109; 3.47.

19-21 This is based on Theocr. *Id.* 1.80-82: 'the cowherds came, the shepherds came, the goatherds came, and all asked him what was wrong. Priapus came . . . and Venus came . . .'. Virgil has changed the divinities so that his have much more direct reference to pastoral.

20 'Menalcas too came, dripping from the winter acorns'; he had been preparing acorns for winter fodder by soaking them in water (Cato, *Agr.* 54). Menalcas is the name of a cowherd, specified as a variation on the generalised reference in the previous line to shepherds and pig-keepers, perhaps with some regard to *Ecl.* 9 where he is the great singer.

21 Apollo is god both of poetry and of shepherds (see notes on 4.10, 5.35).

23 perque . . . perque: 'both through . . . and through'; cf. 65-6; 8.22. The word *alium* (see note on 2) is emphasised by its position between these two phrases.

24 agresti . . . honore: 'Silvanus with the glory of the countryside crowning his head', i.e. wearing a crown of flowers and leaves. Silvanus was a god of the country-side, in some ways the Roman equivalent of Pan; cf. *Geo.* 1.20.

25 ferulas . . . quassans: 'shaking the fennel . . .'; i.e. which he wore on his head, as is seen from Lucr. 4.587 (of Pan) *pinea semiferi capitis velamina quassans.*

26 quem vidimus ipsi: to see the gods is rarely granted, and in the case of Pan associated with danger (cf. Theocr. *Id.* 1.16); hence the word 'panic'.

27 ebuli . . . minioque: *ebulum* was a plant with berries that stained red, and *minium* a metal with the same property. Compare 6.22; Ov. *Fast.* 1.415.

28 Amor non talia curat: i.e. Love is not won over by tears; the thought is elaborated in the next two lines.

31 tamen: 'in spite of that', i.e. that Love does not show pity; cf. 9.62.

Arcades: see note on 15.

32 cantare periti: 'skilled at singing', epexegetic infinitive; cf. 5.1-2.

33-4 'O how gently then my bones would rest if your pipe would one day sing of my love'; the expression has an elegiac ring. *Olim* can mean 'away in the future'; cf. *Geo.* 2.94, as well as 'away in the past'.

38 seu . . . furor: 'or whatever passion'; cf. *Aen.* 4.101.

quid . . . Amyntas?: Gallus answers an imaginary objection to his love for the dark Amyntas; cf. 2.16f. and Theocr. *Id.* 10.26f. where Bucaeus justifies his love for the dark-skinned Bombyca by saying that the violet is dark, and the hyacinth, yet they are sought first for garlands.

40 iaceret: some MSS have *iaceres,* which is adopted by many editors, but the second-person verb does not fit the sentence well.

42 hic: i.e. in Arcadia, as opposed to his real life (*nunc,* 44).

43 ipso . . . aevo: 'here with you I would waste away only through old age', i.e. not for any other reason like unhappiness or war.

44f; The reference to Gallus' military campaigns cannot for certain be identified; it could be to those of 37 BC against Sextus Pompeius; see Coleman *ad loc.* The word *Martis* goes with *amor* as well as with *armis.*

46f. Servius tells us that all these verses are taken from Gallus' own poetry; much of the phraseology is certainly that of elegy (cf. for example Prop. 1.8.5f.).

46 nec . . . tantum: 'and be it not mine to believe such a thing'; for *nec (= ne),* cf. 9.6.

47 Servius' suggestion is that she is going on a campaign with Antony: see note on 2, and cf. 22-3.

48 me sine sola: 'all alone without me': *sola* is not to be taken in its strict sense, but as emphasising *sine me.*

50-51 'I will depart and play on the pipe of a Sicilian shepherd the songs which I have made in Chalcidian verse'; the reference is to the Alexandrian poet Euphorion of Chalcis (see 6 intro. and cf. Quint. 10.1.56), a model of the Roman elegists. Gallus is saying that he will abandon the world of elegy for that of pastoral; the adjective *Siculi* refers to Theocritus.

52 spelaea: a Greek word for cave, rare in Latin; Gallus is emphasising the Greek nature of his poetic inspiration.

53 pati: 'endure my love'; cf. Theocr. *Id.* 1.93.

53-4 tenerisque . . . arboribus: for the idea of carving songs on trees, cf. 5.13-14; Theocr. *Id.* 18.47; Prop. 1.18.22; Ov. *Her.* 5.23; Shakespeare, *As You Like It,* 3.2; and Spenser, *Colin Clout* 632:

Her name in every tree I will endosse,
That, as the trees do grow, her name may grow.

55 'I will mingle with the Nymphs and wander over Maenalus'; *Maenala* is an alternative form for *Maenalus* (15). M has *lymphis,* which Geymonat surprisingly accepts.

56f. For the association of hunting with the pastoral life, see note on 2.29.

57 Parthenios: Parthenius was, like Maenalus, a mountain in Arcadia.

58f. Gallus' imaginary entry into Arcadia becomes more vivid and compelling to him as he dwells enthusiastically on the prospect; the phraseology here is similar to Hor. *Odes* 3.4.6f.

59 Partho . . . Cydonia: the literary epithets are very obtrusive as Gallus puts his thoughts into poetic form. Both Parthians and Cretans (Cydonea was a town in Crete) were famous archers; cf. *Geo.* 3.31; 345.

60 Again an elegiac touch; cf. Prop. 1.5.28 *cum mihi nulla mei sit medicina mali.*

61 'or as if that god would learn to be gentle towards the sufferings of mortals'; *deus ille* is Cupid (*Amor,* 28).

62 Hamadryades: the nymphs of line 55, now more precisely defined as wood-nymphs.

rursus: his mood changes back again to despondency.

64 illum: the god Cupid; observe the heavy spondaic rhythm conveying hopelessness.

65-6 Hebrumque . . . Sithoniasque: 'both . . . and'; cf. 23. The river Hebrus was in Thrace, proverbial for cold winters (cf. Theocr. *Id.* 7.112) and the adjective *Sithonius* means Thracian (Hor. *Odes* 3.26. 10).

66 nives hiemis . . . aquosae: 'the snows of their soaking winter'.

67 moriens . . . liber aret: 'the bark dries up and dies'.

68 'we were to drive the sheep of the

Aethiopians beneath the constellation Cancer'; Gallus at the end is indeed thinking of himself as a shepherd. The Aethiopians exemplify the far south; cf. Theocr. *Id.* 7.113. Horace (*Odes* 1.22.17f.) in less serious mood ends his Lalage poem with the picture of his love continuing to be the same if he were transported to the extreme north or the extreme south.

69 Gallus' song ends on a note of despair as he finally rejects the pastoral world, realising that Amor is merciless and all powerful; cf. *Aen.* 4.412 *improbe Amor.* The last words are reminiscent of the theme of the lover's servitude so often described in surviving Roman elegy, and doubtless in the lost elegy of Gallus too.

Amor: et: there is lengthening in arsis at the caesura; see note on 1.38.

70-77 These lines form an epilogue not only for this poem but for all the *Eclogues.*

71 gracili . . . hibisco: 'wove a basket of simple hibiscus flowers'; the proper pastoral occupation when the shepherd is not out of doors; cf. 2.72. There is probably a metaphorical reference, as Servius suggests, to the *gracilitas* (simplicity) of pastoral poetry.

72 haec facietis maxima: 'will make these words famous'; the success of the poem depends on the favour of the Muses (*divae Pierides*).

73-4 These lines are very personal and emotional, and show that in addition to his respect for Gallus' achievements in practical life and poetry Virgil was also deeply attached to him. The repetition of the word *Gallo* has added emphasis because of the pause after the spondaic first foot; cf. 5.21; 8.26.

76 The repetition of *gravis umbra . . . umbrae* brings the poem towards its close by a feature of diction especially characteristic of pastoral poetry; cf. 2. 31-3 and 8. 48-50, and see note on 4.3.

77 The closing line is phrased in actual terms, referring to the end of the shepherd's day, but also has the metaphorical sense of concluding the pastoral song; cf. 3.111. It is reminiscent of lines used earlier in the *Eclogues,* e.g. 1.74, 7.44, and so rounds the book of *Eclogues* in familiar phraseology.

The Georgics

GEORGICS 1

The first book deals with tilling the land, with the varying kinds of treatment necessary for different soils and different crops, the need to control weeds and pests and in particular the necessity for observing the 'farmer's calendar', the correct times of year for the various operations, and the ways of foretelling the weather. Its didactic material is based on Greek and Latin handbooks, such as Theophrastus, Cato and Varro, and much of its information about seasons and weather comes from the Alexandrian poet Aratus (especially 351f.); there is some too from Hesiod's *Works and Days* (43-203 *Works*; 204-350 *Days*).

To these factual sources Virgil has added a deep poetic insight into the marvels of the countryside and the beauty of well-ordered nature, an intense insistence on the dignity of the farmer's hard work, and a rich texture of musical movement and descriptive imagery, with evocative references to far-off places, to mythology, to the ceremonies of country religion. The poet's love of his subject is underlined by the frequent use of personal phrases, and by the constant personification of nature's animals and plants; in fact the didactic material forms a framework for the presentation of a complete ethical and religious viewpoint, in which Nature is seen as part of the total world made and organised by divine powers. (See especially note on 118-46).

The book is framed in a historical setting, with reference to the future emperor Augustus at the beginning and the end. After its introductory section (1-42) it falls into two parts: advice and encouragement about farming tasks (43-203) and information about the seasons and the forecasting of the weather (204-463). It ends with a tremendous peroration of protest against the present unhappy state of Italian farmland because of the ruinous civil wars.

1-42 *The subject of the poem is described, followed by an invocation first to the gods especially concerned with agriculture, and then to Octavian Caesar, urging him to support the poet's undertaking.*

1-42 Virgil begins by sketching the subject of his four books (crops, trees, cattle, bees) and then invokes a large number of rural deities to assist him. This is based on Varro's invocation (*RR* 1.1.5f.) to the twelve gods *qui maxime agricolarum*

duces sunt, but with very marked variations; Virgil leaves out less well-known deities like Robigus and Lympha and Bonus Eventus, substitutes Greek divinities (Dryads, Aristaeus, Pan, Triptolemus) and adds a Greek literary flavour by the use of words such as *Chaoniam, Acheloia, Ceae, Tegeaee.* For fuller discussion see Wilkinson, pp. 146f.

This is followed by a fulsome invocation to Octavian (Augustus) Caesar, who is allocated as much space as all the other divinities put together. Comparable prophecies of his deification (for which the deification of Julius Caesar after his death had set a precedent) are to be found in *Aen.* 1.286f.; Hor. *Odes* 1.2; 3.3; 3.5. Page well points out (in his note on *Geo.* 1.24) that (i) deification of mortal heroes was not uncommon in Roman legend (Hercules, Bacchus, Romulus); (ii) the hope which farmers would place in a leader who could give them peace after generations of devastation was very great and very sincere; (iii) poets frequently embellish their subject in a fashion which would seem exaggerated in prose. To these considerations may be added the practice in the Greek world of excessive praise and of deification of heroes, and the fact that Virgil does not directly suggest deification in Octavian's lifetime. But even when all this is taken into account, it still remains true that modern convention is not sympathetic to this kind of amplified panegyric. For further discussion see Wilkinson, pp. 162f.

1-5 Virgil begins by summarising the subjects of the *Georgics:* the first book is largely about cultivation of the soil and the right seasons for the various operations (line 1); the second book is about trees (line 2); the third about cattle (lines 3-4); the fourth about bees (line 4).

1-2 faciat . . . vertere: this first book is concerned with the work of the land at different times of the year, and the phraseology recalls the title of Hesiod's didactic poem on agriculture, *Works and Days:* Virgil's debt to Hesiod is explicitly acknowledged in 2.176, where see note.

1 laetas: Roman agricultural vocabulary possessed elements of personification ('joyful' crops) which Virgil uses to give vividness to his subject. Servius tells us that manure was commonly called *laetamen* (bringing joy to the plants). *Laetus* is a favourite word of Virgil in the *Georgics*, e.g. 69; 101; 325. Cicero comments on metaphorical usage of this kind in *De Orat.* 3.155 . . . *luxuriem esse in herbis, laetas segetes etiam rustici dicunt.* Martyn quotes Psalm 65:13 '. . . the valleys also are covered over with corn; they shout for joy, they also sing.'

sidere: the rising and setting of the constellations was a normal method of indicating the time of year in Roman agriculture (cf. 73). From lines 204 onwards this topic forms a major part of the

subject-matter of Book 1.

2 Maecenas: the chief patron of letters in this period, a right-hand man of Octavian; all four books of the *Georgics* are dedicated to him (2.41; 3.41; 4.2).

ulmisque . . . vitis: the elm was a tree much used for the support of vine tendrils; cf. *Ecl.* 2.70; *Geo.* 2.221. The metaphor of 'marrying' the vine to the elm was frequent (e.g. Cat. 62.54); cf. Milton, *PL* 5.215f. 'Or they led the vine To wed her Elm', and Shakespeare, *Comedy of Errors* 2.2.178f. 'Thou are an elm, my husband, I a vine Whose weakness, married to thy stronger state, Makes me with thy strength to communicate'. The plane tree is called *caelebs* ('bachelor') because it was not used as a support for vines, its foliage being too dense.

3-4 quae cura . . . pecori: 'the proper attention for oxen, the care needed for keeping flocks'; probably *pecori* here refers to sheep rather than being a repetition of *boves.*

4 pecori, apibus: there is hiatus at the pause; see note on *Ecl.* 3.6.

parcis: 'thrifty', *quae mella custodiunt* (Servius); cf. Mart. 14.222. Supply *habendis.*

5 hinc: 'now'; cf. Varro *RR* 2 Intro. 6 *incipiam hinc.*

5f. The long invocation is addressed to a large number of deities concerned with agriculture before finally focusing on Octavian Caesar (24-42). See note on 1-42.

5-6 The reference is to the sun and moon; whether they are here identified with Liber (Bacchus) and Ceres is difficult to determine. Servius and Macrobius (*Sat.* 1.18. 23) think so, and certainly the invocation is abrupt otherwise (*vos . . . Liber et alma Ceres . . . et vos . . . tuque*); on the other hand Varro (*RR* 1.1.5) invokes 'in the second place the Sun and Moon and in the third Bacchus and Ceres'. It therefore seems preferable to regard Liber and Ceres as different from the sun and moon.

6 ducitis annum: 'guide the year', i.e. cause the seasons; cf. Milton *Comus* 112-14 'the Starry Quire Who in their nightly watchful Spheres Lead in swift round the Months and Years'.

7 Liber et alma Ceres: Liber (cf. Ecl. 7.58) is a frequent term for Bacchus (the one who frees), god of wine (line 9); the gift of Ceres, goddess of corn, the goddess who nourishes (*alma, alo*) is described in line 8. The two are linked in *Ecl.* 7.59 and Lucr. 5.14.

si = *siquidem*, 'as surely as'; cf. line 17 and *Ecl.* 2.27.

8-9 Notice the patterned arrangement (ABACB) of these two descriptive lines, each quite close to a golden line (see note on *Ecl.* 1.2); they refer to Ceres and Liber in chiastic order (line 7 Liber ... Ceres, line 8 Ceres, line 9 Liber).

8 'changed the Chaonian acorn for the nourishing corn-stalk'; this construction with *mutare* is normal. The 'ornate' epithet *Chaonian* enriches the imagery of the line by associating the acorn with the famous oak-groves sacred to Zeus (cf. 2.67) at Dodona (cf. line 149) in Chaonia (Epirus, cf. *Ecl.* 9.13). For acorns as the food of primitive man, cf. 147f.; Lucr. 5. 939f.; Juv. 6.10.

9 **pocula ... Acheloia:** *pocula* ('goblets') is used by the poets for 'water' (see note on *Ecl.* 8.28); *Acheloia* is another 'ornate' epithet, referring to the river Achelous in central Greece, said to be the oldest of all rivers.

10 **praesentia:** 'present to help', cf. *Ecl.* 1.41.

Fauni: rustic deities often associated with Pan (16f.) and with guarding flocks; cf. *Ecl.* 6.27.

11 The sudden interjection conveys a feeling of excitement and rejoicing to be expressed in dance (*ferte ... pedem*); it is reinforced by the dactylic rhythm.

Faunique ... Dryadesque: the doubled *-que* ('both ... and') is a feature of the high style; cf. 52 and *Ecl.* 6.27. The Dryads were tree-nymphs; cf. *Ecl.* 5.59.

12-13 **cui ... equum:** 'for whom the earth first produced a neighing horse'; *prima* has an adverbial sense. Poseidon (Neptune) was from very early times associated with horses, and had the epithet Hippios; here the reference may be to the story of how Neptune and Athene (Minerva) both wished to give their name to the city of Athens, and it was decided that the right to do so should go to the one who gave mortals the most valuable gift. Neptune with a blow of his trident produced a horse from the earth; Athene however won the contest by producing an olive-tree. Cf. Spenser, *Muiopotmos* 305f.

14 **cultor nemorum:** 'guardian of the groves'; the phrase is used of Diana in *Aen.* 11.557. The reference here is to Aristaeus, who figures largely in the fourth book of the *Georgics* (4.317f.) as the hero who taught men how to produce new swarms of bees; he was particularly

associated with the Aegean island Cea (Ceos).

15 **ter centum:** of an indefinite large number, cf. Hor. *Odes* 3.4.79.

16-18 Pan was associated with Arcadia (*Ecl.* 4.58) in which Lycaeus and Maenalus were high mountains (*Ecl.* 10.15; Theocr. *Id.* 1.123-4); Tegea was a famous town there.

18-9 **oleaeque Minerva inventrix:** see note on 12-13.

19 The discoverer of the plough is Triptolemus, a king of Eleusis in Attica; cf. Ov. *Fast.* 4.507f. Servius suggests Osiris as an alternative (cf. Tib. 1.7.29) but this is less likely in the Greek context of Pan and Athene.

20 Silvanus (*Ecl.* 10.24; *Geo.* 2.494) was a Roman rural deity; in mythology he was the lover of the youth Cyparissus (Servius *ad loc.*): hence the association with the cypress tree.

21 **studium ... tueri:** 'whose love it is to look after the fields'; for the infinitive after *studium*, cf. 2.195.

22-3 **quique ... quique:** 'both you who ... and you ...'; the relatives are in apposition to *dique deaeque omnes*.

22 **non ullo semine:** i.e. those which naturally sow themselves, as opposed to *satis* in the next line, 'crops sown by man'.

24 **tuque adeo:** the climax of the invocation is marked by the intensifying *adeo;* cf. 94; *Ecl.* 4.11.

24-5 **quem ... incertum est:** 'and we do not know which assemblies of the gods will soon have you amongst them'; the combination of relative clause and indirect question is used to hold in suspense the identity of this last future divinity to be invoked.

25f. **urbisne ... an deus ... maris ... anne novum ... sidus:** the long sentence elaborates the possibility of a divinity on earth, or on the sea, or in the heavens – but not (36f.) in the underworld.

25 **Caesar:** i.e. Octavian (Augustus), not (as has been argued) Julius Caesar. For this fulsome invocation see note on 1-42.

27 This line of only four words, with spondaic rhythm, helps the impressiveness of Virgil's invocation.

28 **materna ... myrto:** the myrtle was sacred to Venus, ancestral mother of the Julian *gens* (*Ecl.* 9.47); cf. *Ecl.* 7.62; *Aen.* 5.72.

30 **Thule:** an island to the north of Britain, thought of as beyond the encircling Ocean; it is not certain which island was meant.

31 Tethys: mother of the sea-nymphs; the implication is another marriage like that of Thetis to Peleus.

32 The suggestion is that Caesar would become a constellation, a sign of the zodiac indicating the movement of the 'slow months', i.e. the longer summer months (cf. Manil. 2.102).

33 Erigonen . . . sequentis: 'between Erigone and the pursuing claws', i.e. the claws of the constellation Scorpion (35); Erigone in mythology became the constellation Virgo.

35 iusta plus parte: 'more than a fair share'; the Scorpion will retard his claws (which projected into the constellation Libra; cf. Manil. 2.557f.). Suetonius (*Aug.* 5) gives September 23 as Augustus' birthday – this was within the period dominated by Libra, though later it was officially transferred to Capricorn.

38 The Elysian fields were part of the underworld (*Tartara*) in Greco-Roman mythology, and thought of as the land of the blessed (Hom. *Od.* 4.565f.; *Aen.* 6.637f.).

39 Proserpina was abducted by Pluto, king of the Underworld, (Claud. *De Rapt. Pros., passim*) and according to this version did not wish to return (cf. Lucan 6.699f.); the common version was that she returned for six months each year (Ov. *Met.* 5.391f.).

40 cursum: for the metaphor (a poetic journey) cf. 2.39.

41 ignarosque viae: cf. Lucr. 2.10 *viam palantis quaerere vitae.*

42 ingredere: 'come forward', i.e. accompany me on the beginning of my journey.

votis . . . vocari: i.e. in anticipation of future deification, cf. *Aen.* 1.290 (of Augustus) *vocabitur hic quoque votis,* and note on 1-42.

43-70 *The need for early ploughing and for determining the nature of the land; different places vary in their characteristics by a fixed law of nature. So with fertile soils plough first in spring; but with sandy soils a single ploughing in autumn will suffice.*

43-70 The theme of hard work, characteristic of the whole poem, is vividly presented in this first didactic section (45f.; 63f.), and the personal tone towards the reader at which Virgil always aims occurs often (45; 56; 63), along with instances of the personification of inanimate things

(46; 48; 53). There are literary reminiscences of Hesiod and Lucretius, and the didactic material – mostly from Varro – is subordinated to poetic imagination, both by the methods of personal involvement and personification already mentioned and by the use of richly emotive geographical place-names (56-59) and of mythology (61-3).

43 Virgil begins his instructions at the beginning (*vere novo*) of the farmer's year (7 February according to Varro); cf. Hes. *WD* 383f.; 458f. The passing of winter's cold is emphasised by the placing of the two chilly words *gelidus canis* before the word which begins the clause (*cum*).

44 Zephyro putris se glaeba resolvit: 'the clod is thawed by the west wind and crumbles', cf. 2.204; 262f.; 330; *putris* is proleptic, cf. 70.

45-6 Virgil is recalling Lucr. 5.207f. *vis humana . . . consueta . . . ingemere et terram pressis proscindere aratris;* he transfers the verb *ingemere* from the farmer to the ox, the farmer's trusty servant.

45 iam tum mihi: Virgil aims at a sense of urgency first by emphasising the need for speed (*iam tum*), and then by associating himself with the work (*mihi* is ethic dative, 'I urge you'; cf. *mecum*, 41).

46 splendescere: the ploughshare is in fact made shiny by the soil, and the image is chosen to emphasise the beauty of successful work.

48 Servius takes this to mean two ploughings, each one exposing the earth to sun (in the day) and cold (at night). On the other hand Varro speaks of three ploughings (*RR* 1.29) and Pliny (*NH* 18.181) definitely interpreted Virgil's passage as meaning four ploughings. It seems on the whole more likely that Servius is right because of the contrast with one ploughing for light soil (67-8).

49 illius . . . messes: 'the harvests from this crop' (*illa seges* 47).

ruperunt: gnomic aorist expressing a general truth: 'have always . . . and will in the future . . .'; cf. 84; 161; 287.

50 ignotum . . . aequor: 'a previously unploughed plain'; *aequor* is not uncommon in this sense in the *Georgics*, e.g. 1.97; 2.105; 205;541.

51-2 'let it be our concern to learn first about the prevailing winds and the varying nature of the climate, and both the local cultivation and the condition of the area': *cultus* refers to previous cultivation of the

land, and *habitus* to its natural features.
Cf. Cato *Agr.* 34-5.

53 Cf. Varro *RR* 1.3 *quae sint in quoque
agro serenda ac facienda;* Virgil has added a
touch of personification with the verb
recuset (cf. *sensit* in 48).

56 The sudden diversion generalises the
theme of variety from agriculture to the
products of the whole wide world; cf.
2.114f. It is emphasised with the personal
didactic phrase *nonne vides;* cf. Lucr.
2.207 *et saep.*

56-7 Tmolus in Lydia was famous for
wine (cf. 2.98): this is the earliest passage
where it is associated with saffron for which
Cilicia was a well-known source. Saffron
was used for perfume, e.g. in the theatre
(Lucr. 2.416). The ivory of Indian elephants
was much sought after (cf. Cat. 64.48),
and the Arabians (Sabaei) were famous for
spices and perfumes (2.117, Tib. 2.2.4);
hence their epithet *molles* ('luxury-loving').

ut . . . **mittit:** the clause is left in
parataxis after *nonne vides* rather than
being subordinated; cf. the use after *aspice
(Ecl.* 5. 6-7).

58 The Chalybes, in the region of the
Black Sea, were famous as iron-workers,
cf. *Aen.* 8.421; Pontus (the Black Sea) sent
its 'stinking beaver-oil' (Lucr. 6.794) for
medicinal purposes.

59 Epirus was an area of north-western
Greece well-known for its racehorses
(3.121), which frequently won the Olympic
games (held in the Greek province of Elis,
3.202). *Palmas equarum* is a heightened
poetic expression for *equas palmares.*

60-61 **continuo . . . quo tempore:** 'right
from the time when . . .', i.e. right from the
creation of man after the flood. Cf. Lucr.
5.916f., a passage recalled several times in
this section. *Foedera* also has a Lucretian
ring, cf. 1.586 *foedera naturai.*

62 The story of how Deucalion and
Pyrrha re-peopled the earth after the flood
by throwing stones which turned into men
and women is told in Ov. *Met.* 1.313f.
Cf. *Ecl.* 6.41; Milton *PL* 11.12f. . . .
'Deucalion and chaste Pyrrha, to restore
The Race of Mankind drown'd, before the
Shrine of Themis stood devout'.

63 **durum genus:** an aetiological
explanation of why men are hardy; cf. 2.
340f.: Lucr. 5.926. Pindar (*Ol.* 9.68f.),
referring to Deucalion and Pyrrha, linked
the Greek words λαός (people) and λᾶας
(stone).

ergo age: by the use of the imperative
Virgil again conveys immediacy; cf. 45 and 56.

64 **pingue solum:** 'if the soil is rich',
contrasted with *at si non fuerit tellus
fecunda* (67).

64-5 **primis . . . tauri:** note the spondaic
movement conveying the effort of the
oxen, an effect reinforced by the single
spondaic word *fortes* filling the first foot
and the alliteration of *t.*

65-6 Cf. Philips, *Cyder* 2.401-2 'with
vehement suns When dusty summer bakes
the crumbling clods'; Thomson, *Seasons,
Autumn,* 4f. 'whate'er . . . summer suns
concocted strong'; Keats, *Ode to Autumn*
'close bosom-friend of the maturing sun'.

67-8 'it will be enough to raise the earth
in a shallow furrow at the rising of
Arcturus', i.e. in September.

69-70 **illic . . . hic:** 'in the former case
. . . in the latter'. The postposition of *ne*
in both these lines puts emphasis on the
words brought forward.

70 'in case the infrequent rainfall should
run away from the barren sand': *sterilem* is
proleptic – the sandy soil will be barren
unless the moisture in it is conserved.
Virgil is wrong in thinking that frequent
stirring of light soil causes moisture to be
lost (see K. D. White, *Proc. Virg. Soc.*
1967-8 p. 14).

71-99 *It is sometimes desirable to leave
fields fallow, often desirable to rotate
crops. Burning of stubble is useful, and so is
harrowing and second ploughing.*

71-99 Here Virgil gives didactic
precepts often based on Cato or Varro, but
he presents them in such a way as to
elevate the factual information into poetic
imagery. This is especially apparent in his
use of adjectives (e.g. 72 *segnem;* 73 *flava;*
75 *tristis;* 76 *fragilis,* etc.), and of personification (74 *laetum;* 83 *gratia;* 95 *iuvat;*
99 *exercet, imperat*), and in the touches of
mythology (78 Lethe; 96 Ceres). For a full
analysis of the poetic diction of this
passage see Wilkinson, p. 200-202.

71 **alternis:** 'alternately', 'in
alternation'.

idem: 'likewise', literally 'you the same
man . . .'.

tonsas . . . novalis: 'your land when
harvested to lie idle and fallow'; *novalis*
is predicative. The word basically means
land worked for the first time, but is also
used of land left fallow; cf. Varro *RR*
1.29.1.

73 **mutato sidere:** 'at a different time of
the year'.

75 **viciae:** 'vetch'. Like beans and lupin

this is a leguminous plant, and would
increase the nitrogen content of the soil,
so that corn would do well; cf. Cato *Agr.*
37.2; Colum. 2.13.1.

tristis 'bitter'; cf. 2.126.

77 **enim:** the connection of thought is
that you should rotate (or alternate, 79)
especially such crops as those mentioned and
those about to be mentioned.

urit: 'exhausts'; cf. *effetos* (81).

78 The triple phrase (tricolon) with
repetition (*urit . . . urit . . . urunt*) is a
favourite device of diction with Virgil (cf.
266-7); notice how the first two phrases are
technical and factual while the third is given
mythological imagery (Lethe was the river
of forgetfulness in the underworld; cf.
Geo. 4.545); Huxley quotes Keats, *Ode to
Autumn:* 'Drows'd with the fumes of
poppies'.

79-80 **arida . . . sola:** 'provided that you
are not reluctant to feed dry soil with rich
manure'; cf. Cato *Agr.* 5.8; Varro *RR* 1.38;
Colum. 2.14.

80 **pudeat sola neve:** this type of line
ending — two dissyllables not preceded by a
monosyllable, causing conflict of word
accent and ictus — is very rare in Virgil;
cf. 2.153 and my note (Oxford edition) on
Aen. 5.731.

82 **sic quoque:** 'in this way too': by
rotation as well as by letting them lie fallow
(71-2) the fields recover their fertility.

83 **nec nulla . . . terrae:** 'and you do not
have the nil return (*nulla . . . gratia*) of land
left unploughed'. The land is personified;
cf. Colum. 2.2.7.

84 The connection of thought is with
the feeding (80-81) of land after crops have
been taken (*sterilis*); they should be
manured (80), or given wood ash (81) or
have the stubble set on fire, a procedure still
followed even though the stubble now is
much more low-cut than in ancient times
(Varro *RR* 1.50.2).

85 Notice how the dactylic rhythm
reproduces the image of dancing and
crackling flames.

86f. The presentation of alternative
reasons (the last two of which are mutually
exclusive) is in the tradition of Lucretius'
didactic method, e.g. Lucr. 5.519f. The
first two of the four reasons given have
some truth in them; the stubble by being
burnt is converted into chemicals valuable
for the soil, and the soil is to some extent
sterilised.

88 **vitium:** i.e. viruses and disease spores.

exsudat: 'is sweated out', the verb is

found intransitively only here.

89-90 **caeca . . . spiramenta:** 'opens up
hidden channels'; the fire would make
cracks in the soil, but this would have no
long-term effect upon its friability.

91 **venas . . . hiantis:** 'closes up open
channels'.

92 **rapidi:** 'parching'; cf. 424; 4.425;
Ecl. 2.10.

93 **penetrabile:** 'penetrating', in an
active sense, cf. Lucr. 1.494 *penetraleque
frigus; Aen.* 10.481 *penetrabile telum.*

adurat: 'should burn it up'; the verb is
appropriate for the last two subjects (*sol,
Boreas*), though not for the first (*pluviae*)
for which an idea like 'penetrate' must be
supplied. For *adurere* of cold, cf. Ov. *Met.*
14.763, and compare Shakespeare, *The
Tempest* 1.2.255 'in the veins of the earth
when it is bak'd with frost'.

94-9 The references to hoeing and
harrowing and cross-ploughing return to the
general theme of the preparation of the
ground begun at 45f.

94 **glaebas . . . inertis:** 'lumps of soil';
inertis refers to the uselessness of large heavy
lumps in which seed cannot germinate
(*nihil creantes,* Servius).

95 **vimineasque . . . cratis:** 'harrows made
of osiers', i.e. of pliant wood; cf. 166.

96 **nequiquam:** 'without favour'.

97-8 'and the man who turns his plough
at an angle and breaks up again the ridges
which he raises when he first cuts the
land'. This seems to be a reference to
reploughing with the angle of the ploughshare altered (Colum. 2.2.25; Pliny *NH*
18.178) rather than to cross-ploughing at an
angle to the original furrows.

99 **exercet:** 'works', cf. 1.220; 2.356;
Hor. *Epod.* 2.3 *paterna rura bubus exercet
suis;* both this verb and *imperat* contain
a military metaphor indicating the battle
which the farmer must wage (cf. *comminus
. . . insequitur,* 104-5; 125; 155; 2.369f.
dura exerce imperia*).

100-117 *The farmer should pray for wet
summers and mild winters. For conditions
of drought he should have irrigation
channels; he should see that the young
corn is grazed down if too luxuriant; he
should drain off flood-water.*

100-117 This section consists of a series
of precepts urging the need to counteract
excess of drought or of water. It is
presented urgently, with a continuation of
the military metaphors begun in line 99
(cf. 104f.) and with much personification
(*laetissima* 101; *supercilium* 108; *elicit*

109) and compelling rhetorical devices (*quid dicam* 104; *ecce* 108; *quid qui* 111). The geography of distant lands adds to the poetic impact (102-3) and the descriptive effect is very vivid (107; 109-10; 117).

100 solstitia: the solstice (when the sun seems to stand still) is either the longest day or the shortest day, but most commonly used in Latin (as here; cf. *Ecl.* 7.47) of the longest day. This would normally be hot and dry, and rain at this time would be valuable for the crops.

101 hiberno ... pulvere: compare our saying 'A peck of March dust is worth a king's ransom'; Macrobius (*Sat.* 5.20) quotes an old Latin poem *hiberno pulvere, verno luto, grandia farra, camille, metes.* Virgil's passage is discussed by Pliny, *NH* 17.14.

102-3 'under no other conditions of cultivation does Mysia have so much to boast about and Gargara itself marvels at its own harvests', i.e. when these proverbially fertile places have wet summers and warm winters they surpass themselves in fertility. The sentence is somewhat elliptical, and another possible interpretation is 'it is without cultivation that Mysia can boast so much ...', i.e. because the summers are wet and the winters warm cultivation is hardly necessary at all. For the personification *mirantur*, cf. 2.82.

Mysia ... Gargara: Mysia was an area of north-west Asia Minor, and Gargara a mountain and a town in the same area.

104f. 'Why should I mention the man who ...?' The transition is abrupt after 100-103, though it follows well enough on 99.

104-5 comminus ... insequitur: a strong military metaphor, see note on 99.

105 cumulosque ... harenae: 'levels the heaps of unfertile sand'; for *ruit*, cf. *Aen.* 9.516; for *male*, cf. *Aen.* 2.23.

106 satis: 'to the crops'.

sequentis: 'flowing', following the channels made, *quia qua duxeris sequuntur* (Servius).

108-9 ecce ... elicit: 'just look, he coaxes water from the ridge of a sloping path'; notice the devices of diction used in order to present the image vividly, *ecce, supercilio* (literally 'brow', a personification based on the Greek use of ὀφρῦς, cf. Livy 34.29.11). *Elicit* according to Servius is a technical term, but (as often in Latin) the technical term can have a vivid impact (cf. *laetus*, etc.); this is increased by the pause

after the first dactyl; cf. 326; 333; 3.516.

109-10 Virgil pauses on the visual aspects of the irrigation streams, using a high proportion of dactyls in the early parts of the lines, and a subtle pattern of alliteration (*c, u, c, a*). The passage is based on a brilliant simile in Homer (*Il.* 21.257f.); cf. also Cat. 68.57f.

110 scatebrisque ... temperat: 'slakes with bubbling water'; this is the earliest occurrence of *scatebra,* always a very rare word.

111 quid qui: supply *dicam de eo*; the construction is parallel to 104.

procumbat: 'droop', as would happen if the stalk were so long as not to be able to support the ear of corn at the top.

112 depascit: 'grazes down', i.e. the farmer gets the tops nibbled off the growing plants by letting the sheep in as soon as the corn is as high as the ridges of the furrows.

113 quique paludis: the transition from grazing down corn to draining marshland is abrupt, as Virgil presents a series of precepts all designed to emphasise the need for constant action.

115 incertis ... mensibus: i.e. in spring or autumn (Servius).

116 exit: 'overflows its banks'; cf. *Aen.* 2.497.

116-17 'and covers the whole wide area with a layer of mud, causing sloping hollows to steam with the warm water'. For *sudare,* cf. Lucr. 6.943. The picture is very characteristic of the Po valley which Virgil knew well from childhood.

118-46 *Birds, weeds, overhanging trees will all cause problems. This is because Jupiter decided that agriculture should be difficult, in order to sharpen men's faculties. For this reason he abolished the Golden Age, when the earth bore fruit without men's endeavours. The result was that men gradually learned the necessary skills for civilisation; hard work and the need for survival prevailed over all obstacles.*

118-46 This famous passage provides a religious and moral foundation to the whole poem as Virgil gives an explanation of the conditions of human life. He begins by listing the difficulties of the farmer in addition to those already mentioned (ploughing, irrigation, drainage etc.); and against this background tells how Jupiter in his benevolence ended the Golden Age in order to make men employ their skills and their labour. The Golden Age is described first positively (125-8) and then negatively (129-32); the passage may be

compared with Hesiod *WD* 90f.; 109f. Cf. also 2.536f.; *Ecl.* 4.28f.; 5.60-61; *Aen.* 8. 324f.; Tib. 1.3.35.; Ov. *Met.* 1.89f. (where see Lee's note); Hor. *Epod.* 16.41f.
Man's inventiveness forms the subject of the rest of the section, and here the main source is Lucretius 5.206f.; 1361f. Virgil's account has many similarities with Lucretius, but differs essentially in the concept that man made these advances because of the divine will: in Lucretius they are entirely achieved by man himself against all the odds. Virgil also differs very significantly from Hesiod's account of the fall from the Golden Age, in that Hesiod is wholly gloomy about the degeneration of man while Virgil considers that the hard work (*labor*) involved in this new situation was beneficial in itself, and a proof of the benevolence of Jupiter. On the whole subject, especially the Stoic background to this concept of providence, see Wilkinson pp. 134-41; he quotes Milton, *PL* 10.1054-6 where Adam says 'With labour must I earn My bread? What harm? Idleness had been worse; My labour will sustain me'. We may compare *Geo.* 2.433 *et dubitant homines serere atque impendere curam?* with *Aen.* 6.806-7 *et dubitamus adhuc virtutem extendere factis,/aut metus Ausonia prohibet consistere terra?* Both questions summarise the main moral theme of their poems: in the case of the *Aeneid* the need to found Rome in spite of all difficulties, and in the case of the *Georgics* the need to work unceasingly in order to win Nature's bounties.

118-21 'And yet, even when the hard toil of men and oxen alike has made all these efforts in ploughing the soil the accursed geese and Strymonian cranes or chicory with its bitter roots still do damage or else overhanging trees cause trouble'. The double negative *nec . . . nihil* conveys the idea that the farmer might have hoped to have coped with all the difficulties by following the injunctions so far, but it is not the case that there are no more.

119 improbus: 'accursed', a half-playful expletive (*insatiabilis,* Servius) as in 388; *Ecl.* 8.49. It is a favourite word with Virgil, often more seriously intended than here (e.g. *Aen.* 2.356; 4.386). Cf. 146, and see Austin's note on *Aen.* 4.386.

120 Strymoniaeque: the epithet, referring to Thrace, is ornamental, cf. lines 8 and 9, and compare *Aen.* 10.265. Huxley quotes Shelley (*Hellas* 480) 'cranes upon the cloudless Thracian wind'. The crane

migrated south to Greece and Africa for the winter (Hes. *WD* 448).

121 umbra nocet: cf. *Ecl.* 10.76 *nocent et frugibus umbrae.*

pater ipse: Jupiter, who succeeded his father Saturnus under whom the mythological Golden Age had prevailed on earth (125f.), wishes to impose hard work upon mankind for their own benefit; cf. Aratus, *Phaen.* 5f.; and note on 118-46.

122-3 primusque . . . agros: 'and first caused the land to be cultivated by men's skill' – before that, Nature had produced all that was needed (127-8).

125f. For descriptions of the Golden Age see note on 118-46.

127 in medium quaerebant: 'men's efforts were for the benefit of all' (*in commune,* Servius); cf. 4.157.

128 liberius: 'more generously', than it now does for all the farmer's toil; cf. Hes. *WD* 117-18; Lucr. 2.1158f.

129-32 The series of very short main clauses (five in four lines) conveys by means of rapid images (snakes, wolves, stormy sea, no honey dripping from the trees, no fire, no wine) the sudden total change in the way of life.

131 mellaque: for honey dripping from the trees in the Golden Age cf. *Ecl.* 4.30; Ov. *Met.* 1.112.

ignemque removit: Hesiod (*WD* 1.47f) tells of how Jupiter took fire away from mortals, and of his anger against Prometheus for stealing it back again.

133 'so that experience by taking thought might devise the various arts'; for the metaphor in *extundere* (literally 'strike out'), cf. 4.315; 328. For *usus,* cf. 2.22; Lucr. 5.1452-3 *usus et impigrae simul experientia mentis paulatim docuit pedetemptim progredientes.* At this point Virgil's description of the development of civilisation is very reminiscent of the second half of Lucretius 5, but with the difference that in Virgil it is divinely motivated.

135 'and strike out fire, hidden in the veins of flint'; for the phrase, cf. *Aen.* 1.174; 6.6-7. I have preferred *et* (read by A) to *ut* of the other MSS because the clause is parallel with the previous one introduced by *et,* giving two examples of the general statement in 133 (*et* in both cases is epexegetic).

136 alnos . . . cavatas: 'hollowed out alder trees', i.e. roughly made into the shape of boats; the alder grows best near water. Notice the personification in *sensere;* cf. *mirantur* (103).

137 **numeros ... fecit:** 'classified and named'.

138 The Pleiades are a group of seven stars in Taurus which at their spring rising marked the beginning of navigation and at their autumn setting the end of navigation, cf. 221 and 4.233; the nearby Hyades, which rose and set a little later than the Pleiades are the 'rainers'; cf. Hom. *Il.* 18.486; *Aen.* 1.744. Callisto, the daughter of Lycaon, was turned into a bear by Juno and became part of the northern constellation Arctos, the Great Bear; cf. Cat. 66.66 and, for Lycaon, Ov. *Met.* 1.163f.

Pleiadas: Greek accusative plural; the last syllable is short by nature and is here lengthened in arsis, cf. 153 and see note on *Ecl.* 1.38.

139 **fallere visco:** the reference is to trapping animals by means of birdlime, an adhesive substance made of mistletoe berries.

140 **inventum:** sc. *est,* impersonal passive — 'men found out how to ...' For the rest of the line, cf. Lucr. 5.1251.

142 **alta petens:** the picture is of a man casting a weighted net on the river so that it sinks deeply enough to catch the fish; the next phrase refers to a drag-net used at sea. Observe how the visual presentation of men using the new techniques varies the list of the actual inventions.

143 **ferri rigor:** supply *venit* from *venere* (145). Iron now replaces bronze.

argutae lammina serrae: 'the blade of the shrill saw'; for *argutus,* cf. 377; *Ecl.* 9.36.

144 The process of splitting wood with wedges is similarly described in *Aen.* 6.181-2.

145-6 'Grim toil conquered all the difficulties, and poverty pressing hard when life is harsh'. This is the generally accepted meaning of these famous phrases: *improbus* is used with its full force (contrast 119); cf. *Aen.* 2.356 *improba ventris ... rabies* (of wolves); *Aen.* 10.727-8 *improba ... ora* (of a lion), and its use of angry warriors in *Aen.* 9.62; 11.767. There is something to be said for an alternative rendering: 'Grim hardship (the tyranny of hardship) prevailed everywhere ...'; this would give a summarising picture of how different things were under Jupiter from the idyllic ease of the Golden Age, and perhaps a more usual meaning for *improbus* (cf. *Aen.* 4.412); but it would not bring out the glorification of hard work which is a major theme of the *Georgics* throughout. Otis is right

(p. 157) in maintaining that *improbus* cannot have a favourable sense ('unremitting, untiring' work); what Virgil is doing here is presenting both sides of his picture — *labor* is indeed an essential and praiseworthy aspect of the human condition, but it can be grim and overpowering. The same ambivalence is found in the *Aeneid* as Virgil explores the grim aspects of the mission of Aeneas (especially the deaths of Dido and Turnus) as well as its glories and triumphs.

147-59 Ceres first taught man how to grow corn, but very soon diseases and weeds attacked the crops: so you must hoe, frighten the birds, prune the undergrowth, pray for rain if you want a good harvest.

147-59 This brief paragraph returns from the theme of the lost Golden Age to man's present situation: *labor* again is stressed as essential, and the final lines (155f.) return quite precisely to the dangers mentioned at the beginning of the section (118f.).

147 **Ceres:** goddess of corn; cf. 7; Lucr. 5.14-15; Ov. *Fast.* 4.401-402; *Met.* 5.341f.

148-9 **glandes ... Dodona:** Dodona was the sacred grove of Zeus, famed for its oak-trees; see note on 8, and cf. Lucr. 5.939f.; Varro *RR* 2.1.4.

148 **arbuta:** a wild tree with edible berries often referred to in the Roman world, the 'strawberry-tree'; there is no relationship between arbutes and the modern strawberry other than a slight visual similarity; cf. Lucr. 5.965; *Geo.* 2.69; 520; 3.301; 4.181.

149 **deficerent silvae:** 'failed the forest', i.e. was no longer available in the forest; it seems more idiomatic to regard *silvae* as dative after *deficere* than as genitive after the nouns.

150-51 'so that hateful mould consumed the stalks'; *esset* is imperfect subjunctive of *edere;* the word *robigo* is a technical term of crop-production. The Romans worshipped the god *Robigus* (Varro *RR* 1.1.6) who would keep away this disease; cf. Ov. *Fast.* 4.911f.

151-2 **segnisque horreret ... carduus:** 'the unproductive thistle stood high'; for *segnis* Servius rightly says *inutilis, infecundus.* The word *horrere* (cf. 314) suggests both 'bristling', 'spiky' (very appropriate for the flower of the thistle) and also in this context 'roughness', 'lack of cultivation' (*horridus*); see my note on *Aen.* 5.37 (Oxford edition).

152 **silva:** commonly used of under-growth, here referring to the choking weeds

around the corn.

153 **lappaeque tribolique:** in apposition
to *silva (-que . . . -que* is 'both . . . and');
cf. 3.385. The first *-que* is lengthened in
the arsis of the foot; cf. 164; 352; 371 and
note on *Ecl.* 4.51

nitentia: cf. Lucr. 1.252 *nitidae surgunt
fruges.*

154 **infelix:** a metaphor which became a
technical term meaning unproductive; cf.
Ecl. 5.37 (almost the same line); *Geo.*
2.314. Compare Shakespeare, *Henry V*
5.2.51-3 'and nothing teems, But hateful
docks, rough thistles, kecksies, burs,
Losing both beauty and utility'.

155f. Virgil now returns to the problems
mentioned in 119f. (weeds, birds, shade),
thus symmetrically rounding off this
section of the work.

155 **insectabere:** 'attack', another
military metaphor; see note on 99.

157 **premes umbras:** 'prune away
overshadowing branches'; cf. 121.

158 **heu . . . spectabis:** again the vivid
personal touch, see note on 56; cf. Hes.
WD 394-5; Lucr. 2.2.

160-75 *The necessary implements —
ploughs, wagons, drags, harrows, hoes,
baskets, winnowing-fans. Instructions for
constructing a plough.*

160-75 This section is partly based on
Varro *RR* 1.22.1, and on Hesiod *WD* 427f.
Virgil has adapted the material to his own
purpose by renewal of the military metaphor
which he has used so frequently (*arma,*
160); by the religious connexion of the
implements (163-6); and by another
memorable expression of the richness of
the eventual reward (168).

160 **arma:** 'implements'; the word is not
necessarily military (cf. *Aen.* 1.177), but in
the context after *insectabere* (155) it
conveys something of a military metaphor.
Cf. Varro *RR* 1.22.1 and for full discussion
of all these implements see K.D. White,
*Agricultural Implements of the Roman
World.*

161 **quis sine:** = *sine quibus;* the postposition of the preposition with a relative
pronoun is found in prose.

potuere: gnomic aorist (cf. 49), 'never
could have been and cannot be now'.

162 **vomis . . . aratri:** *vomis* (or *vomer,*
46) is the ploughshare, *aratrum* the whole
plough. The epithet 'curved' is a stock
description of the plough; cf. 19.

163 The slow-rolling wagons (cf. 2.206;
3.536) of the Eleusinian mother refer to the

rites of Demeter (Ceres) whose worship at
Eleusis in Greece was famous; the Romans,
according to Servius, celebrated her cult
with a procession of wagons. Notice how
the religious associations of the implements
are stressed here and in the next few lines.
For the adjective *tarda* in an adverbial
sense with a participle, cf. 2.377 and 4.370.

164 'and threshing-sledges and drags';
the first *-que* is lengthened in arsis; see note
on 153.

165 'also the cheap wicker-work
implements of Celeus'. Celeus was a king of
Eleusis, father of Triptolemus (see note
on 19) who showed hospitality to Ceres
and became the first priest of her cult. The
reference here is to baskets and the like.

166 **crates:** 'hurdles' or 'harrows' (cf.
95), here made of arbute branches.

mystica vannus Iacchi: 'the ritual
winnowing fan of Bacchus'; the winnowing-
fan had long been associated with Bacchus
(Iacchus; cf. *Ecl.* 6.15; 7.61) and was carried
in his procession.

167-8 These lines were the motto of
Book 2 of Smart's *Hop-Garden;* cf. Hes.
WD 457.

168 Here Virgil's passion for the
countryside, its order and beauty when
properly looked after, finds memorable
expression. *Digna* means 'appropriately' for
its potential glory, 'in full measure'.

169f. Hesiod *(WD* 427f.) describes the
construction of a plough at some length.
For full discussion of this passage see K.D.
White, *Agricultural Implements of the
Roman World,* pp. 123f., 213f., with
references given there. Huxley (note on
175) well says 'we have here an impres-
sionist painting, not a blueprint for an
agricultural engineer'.

169 **continuo in silvis:** this seems to
mean that the elm is bent into the required
shape while still growing in the woods.

170 **in burim:** 'to form the plough-beam'.

171 **temo:** the pole to which the oxen
would be attached by a yoke.

172 **aures:** 'pin-ears', rather than
'mould-boards', attached on each side of
the share to throw up ridges; on this see
R. Aitken, *JRS* 1956, pp. 101f.

dentalia: the share-beam, the sole, the
piece into which the share was fitted, and
on to which the mould-boards would go.
The 'double back' probably refers to the
bifurcated shape of the share-beam behind
the share.

173 **iugo:** 'for the yoke', dative of
purpose.

174 **stivaque**: 'a plough-handle' or 'stilt', for steering. The word is in apposition to *fagus, -que* being explanatory.

currus: a very poetical expression for the plough with its oxen drawing it, seen as a sort of chariot; it does not imply wheels, as Servius thinks. Cf. Cat. 64.9, where he uses *currus* of the ship *Argo*.

175 The meaning is that these parts of the plough will have been cut in good time (*ante*, 173) so that they can be seasoned by means of smoke.

176-203 *I can tell you some old adages, unless you think them beneath notice. You must make your threshing-floor solid so that weeds or pests do not destroy it. You should watch the fruit and blossom on the nut-tree as a sign of the future harvest. You should soak your beans before sowing them. You should always choose the largest seeds; otherwise your crop will degenerate as everything does by nature.*

176-203 It is interesting to consider the reasons which led Virgil to choose these particular unconnected precepts. The preparation of the threshing-floor is described in Cato and Varro (note on 180-81), and Virgil has used it in order to give a most attractive description of the little animals that may ruin it, presented from the animal's point of view with personification and mock-heroic phraseology that makes them seem no insignificant part of Nature's total world (see note on 181f.). The nut-tree affords an opportunity for descriptive writing of an idyllic kind; the treatment of seeds suggests the conquest of difficulties (*siliquis fallacibus*, 195); finally the selection of the largest seeds each year gives occasion for a reflection on how everything naturally deteriorates unless human foresight and planning prevent it and for one of the memorable similes of the poem, as the man rowing upstream is pictured swept backwards the moment that he relaxes his efforts.

The whole passage is presented in Virgil's direct didactic method (compare note on 100-117), with emphasis on the person addressed (176-7; 187), and on the poet himself as preceptor (176; 193; 197).

176-7 **possum . . . refugis**: cf. Lucr. 1.400 *multaque praeterea tibi possum commemorando . . .*; Lucr. 1.410 *quod si pigraris. . . .*

177 **tenuis**: 'slight', 'small'; cf. 4.6 (on the subject of bees) *in tenui labor*.

178 **cum primis**: 'especially', literally

'along with your first actions'; *in primis* is commoner (Aul. Gell. 17.2.5).

180-81 'in case weeds grow through, or in case it crumbles away and becomes cracked and dusty and then all sorts of pests may mock your efforts'. On the threshing-floor, cf. Cato *Agr.* 91; 129; Varro *RR* 1.51. For *inludant*, cf. 2.375.

181f. Virgil's description of these little animals is characterised by personification, and is very sympathetic towards the small creatures which form part of Nature's great scheme; cf. *domos* (the mouse has a house, not a hole), *horrea* (the mouse's little pile is as crucial for it as a great barn is for humans), *cubilia* (the mole has its bedroom), *inopi metuens . . . senectae* (the ant is making provision for its old age, cf. Hor. *Sat.* 1.1.33f.). This Disneyesque attitude is seen in its fullest form in the description of the society of bees in Book 4. The same kind of personification is frequent in Phaedrus' fables; Huxley speaks of the 'mock-epic exaggeration of this catalogue of criminals'.

181 **exiguus mus**: the monosyllabic ending, generally used to convey majesty or great size (cf. 247; 313; and see my note on *Aen.* 5.481, Oxford edition), is here employed with mock-heroic effect, reinforced by the assonance of *-us mus*. Horace uses it in a wholly mocking sense, *Ars Poet.* 139 *parturient montes, nascetur ridiculus mus*. See Quint. 8.3.20.

182 **posuitque . . . atque**: a rare method of coordination ('both . . . and') which adds to the mock-elevated impression of the diction.

183 **oculis capti**: 'blind', cf. Livy 22.2.11 *altero oculo capitur*.

184-5 **quae plurima . . . ferunt**: all the many strange things which the earth produces'; cf. *Aen.* 6.729. Here again the effect is mock-heroic.

186 **curculio**: on the damage done to corn by weevils, cf. Varro *RR* 1.63.

187 **contemplator**: emphatic form of the imperative (*contemplare*); cf. 4.61; Lucr. 2.114; 6.189.

187-8 **nux . . . florem**: 'when in the woods the nut-tree in full profusion clothes itself in blossom'; for this use of *plurima* cf. 2.166; 183; *Ecl.* 7.60. There is a strong pictorial element in the personification of *se induet*; cf. 4.143. For the construction, cf. *Aen.* 7.20.

189 **si superant fetus**: 'if the fruit is abundant'; this is a good sign for the future corn harvest. The nut-tree can be used for

forecasting because it flowers early in the season.

190 This is a golden line (see note on *Ecl.* 1.2); these are less common in the *Georgics* than in the *Eclogues* (cf. 222; 468; 497).

192 **pinguis palea:** 'rich only in chaff'; cf. Milton, *PL* 4.983-5 'The careful plowman doubting stands, Lest on the threshing-floore his hopeful sheaves Prove chaff'.

193 **vidi equidem:** again the personal touch, picked up at 197 (*vidi*).

medicare: 'treat': it becomes evident in 195 that the reference here is to leguminous plants, presumably beans.

194 'and to steep them first in sodium nitrate and black olive oil'. *Amurca* is the dregs or lees of olives after they have been pressed; it is referred to frequently in Cato and Varro. This passage (cf. Theophr. *HP* 2.4.2) is taken up by Columella (2.10.11).

195-6 These explanations seem unlikely: the beneficial effect would be in quicker and perhaps stronger germination, and protection of the seed against pests.

195 **fallacibus:** if not treated, the pods would 'deceive' by not being packed with beans.

197 **spectata:** 'tested' (*probata,* Servius); supply *semina* (193).

198-9 **ni vis . . . legeret:** 'had not human effort picked out by hand each year all the biggest'; the relationship of the conditional sentence to the main sentence is rather elliptical. For the phrase, cf. Lucr. 5.207 (also of Nature's encroachment) *ni vis humana resistat.* This passage of Lucretius was very much in Virgil's mind here; cf. also Varro *RR* 1.52.1.

199f. This statement of the inevitable degeneration of Nature unless man intervenes (cf. Colum. 2.9.11f.) stresses once again *labor,* the main theme of the *Georgics.* The simile makes it one of the most memorable passages in the poem.

200 **ruere . . . referri:** 'historic' infinitive of habitual action, cf. *Aen.* 2.98. For the phrase, cf. *Aen.* 2.169. The alliteration of *r* helps to emphasise the gnomic reflexion.

203 **atque:** Servius, Nonius and Aulus Gellius (10.29) take this to be a non-coordinating usage of *atque (= statim).* It seems better however to regard the construction of the sentence as being *non aliter quam is refertur qui . . . si remisit . . . atque illum rapit:* ('just as the rower is swept back who is rowing upstream, if he relaxes and the current whirls him back'). Notice the emphatic pattern of

alliteration in this line (*p, r, a*); it is reminiscent of Cat. 65.23 *atque illud prono praeceps agitur decursu.*

204-30 *The farmer must observe the proper dates for sowing various crops by observing the rising and setting of the constellations.*

204-30 Here Virgil begins a major new section of his work, as he describes the farmers' calendar. Such a calendar, based on the constellations, was traditional in agricultural writing (Varro *RR* 1.29-36; cf. Colum. 11.2); Virgil also uses the account in Hesiod (*WD* 618-94) of the constellations as a guide to seafarers, and for technical details he is indebted to Aratus, *Phaen.* passim. He has constructed the passage in four sections, dealing with autumn (barley, etc.), spring (beans, etc.), autumn (wheat, etc.), late autumn (vetch, etc.). The material is given variety by means of geographical names (207; 228), mythology (212; 221-2) and an occasional flash of high poetic description (217-18; 221-2, the latter a golden line).

204-7 The argument is that the seasons of the year, as indicated by the rising and setting of constellations, are as important to farmers as to sailors; cf. Hes. *WD* 618f.

204 **Arcturi sidera:** Arcturus (cf. line 68 and Arat. *Phaen.* 94) is the brightest star in the constellation Bootes; its setting in October portended the advent of stormy weather (cf. Plaut. *Rud.* 70). *Sidera* refers to the whole constellation Bootes whose stars are said to belong to Arcturus which dominates the constellation; cf. 229.

205 **Haedorumque dies:** 'the dates of the Kids', i.e. their rising and setting; the setting of the Haedi, which like Arcturus are near the Pole Star, portended wet weather; compare *Aen.* 9.668 *pluvialibus Haedis,* and Arat. *Phaen.* 166.

Anguis: the Snake, sometimes called Draco, is also near the Pole Star; cf. 244.

206 **quam quibus:** = *quam eis quibus,* 'as by those by whom . . .', understand *eis* (dative of agent like *nobis,* 204).

vectis: 'sailing', the timeless use of the perfect participle; cf. 293.

207 **Pontus:** the Black Sea was proverbially stormy; cf. Hor. *Odes* 3.4.30.

ostriferi . . . Abydi: cf. Ennius *Hed.* 2 *ostrea plurima Abydi,* and Cat. 18.3-4 *ora Hellespontia ceteris ostriosior oris.* Abydus was on the Hellespont opposite to Sestos; it was famous in mythology for Leander's swim.

208 **Libra:** the Balance; the reference is to the autumn equinox; at the spring equinox the sun is in Aries. Cf. Thomson, *Seasons, Autumn* 24 'And Libra weighs in equal scales the year'; Lucan 8.467.
dies: an archaic form of the genitive; cf. Aul. Gell. 9.14.7 (who quotes Enn. *Ann.* 413 and Cic. *Sest.* 28). The MSS have *die* or *diei,* and Servius supports *die;* I have preferred *dies* on the authority of Aulus Gellius.

209 'and now divides the circle of the heavens in half between light and darkness'; a variation on the theme of the previous line.

210 **hordea:** 'barley', poetic plural; cf. 317 and *Ecl.* 5.36: Servius quotes a parody of this plural — *hordea qui dixit, superest ut tritica dicat:* 'who talks of barleys may as well say wheats'. Cf. also *Quint.* 1.5.16.

211 **usque sub extremum . . . imbrem:** 'right up to the very verge of the rains of winter which prevents work'; that this is the meaning seems to be proved by 214 *dum sicca tellure licet.* For *intractabilis,* cf. *Aen.* 4.53.

212 **Cereale papaver:** Servius gives a number of reasons why the poppy is associated with Ceres, of which the most interesting is that she used it as a tranquilliser when she had lost her daughter Proserpina (Ov. *Fast.* 4.547).

213 **iamdudum:** 'high time', literally 'time to have started ploughing long ago'; cf. *Aen.* 2.103.

214 **pendent:** i.e. are not yet descending in rain.

215 **vere fabis satio:** Seneca (*Ep. Mor.* 86) disagrees with this statement but it may have been true for Virgil's own area of Italy (Pliny *NH* 18.120).
Medica: a kind of lucerne or clover said to have been introduced into Greece from Persia, and subsequently into Italy; cf. Pliny *NH* 18.144. The use of the vocative (apostrophe) is here convenient metrically.

217-18 The assonance of words beginning with *a* and *c* in these two descriptive lines is remarkable.
The sun enters the constellation Taurus in April; *aperit* refers to the derivation of *Aprilis* (cf. Ov. *Fast.* 4.87). For Taurus, cf. Thomson, *Seasons, Spring* 26-7 'At last from Aries rolls the bounteous Sun, And the bright Bull receives him'; Milton, *PL* 1.769 'In spring time, when the Sun with Taurus rides'.

217 **auratis . . . cornibus:** a reference to the Roman practice of gilding the horns of bulls for triumphal processions.

218 **et averso . . . astro:** 'and the Dog yields, turning its star away, and sets'; i.e. the Dog (Sirius) cannot face the onset of Taurus and disappears below the horizon. Another possible rendering of this much disputed passage is to take *averso . . . astro* as dative, referring to Taurus — 'the Dog yields to the reversed constellation', because the Bull seems to move backwards towards Sirius. One MS (M) has *adverso:* 'the Dog yields to the constellation which confronts it'. On the confusion between *aversus* and *adversus* in astronomical contexts see Housman on Manil. 1.264.

219-20 Wheat (*triticum*) and spelt (*far*) are linked together as types of corn which produce ears (*aristae*) and are to be sown in the autumn (like barley, 210), unlike the leguminous crops mentioned in 215-16.

221 'first, I tell you, let the Eastern daughters of Atlas depart from view': the reference is to the Pleiades (see note on 138) whose morning setting (*Eoae*) was in November. The Pleiades are called daughters of Atlas in Hes. *WD* 383. The scansion of this line presents several unusual features; there is a hiatus at the 2½ caesura (see note on *Ecl.* 3.6), and a polysyllabic ending with a spondaic fifth foot (see note on *Ecl.* 4.49). The word *Atlantides* is a Greek nominative plural with a short final syllable; the word *Eous* sometimes has a short first syllable (288).

222 'and let the Cretan star of the blazing Crown disappear'; this is the constellation called Corona from the crown of Ariadne (princess of Cnossos in Crete) which was put in the heavens by Bacchus; cf. Arat. *Phaen.* 71; Manil. 5.21. The date of its setting is variously given; Virgil follows a tradition which placed it in November. This densely pictorial phrase is presented in a golden line.

223 **debita . . . semina:** cf. Cowper, *Task* 3.649-50 '. . . ere he gives the beds The trusted treasure of their seeds'.

225 **Maiae:** one of the seven stars of the Pleiades (221); cf. Varro *RR* 1.34.
The trochaic pause in the fifth foot is rare and puts emphasis on *sed illos;* cf. 242.

226 **vanis . . . avenis:** 'with useless wild oats'; cf. 154. The cultivated corn has degenerated into wild oats; cf. Theophr. *HP* 8.7.1.

227-8 Vetch, *phaselus* (a bean with an

edible pod), and lentils were sown for
cattle-food, hence *vilem*.

228 **Pelusiacae . . . lentis:** Pelusium was
in the Nile delta (Mart. 13.9).

229 **Bootes:** this is a constellation very
near the Pole Star; its evening setting is in
October; cf. 204.

230 **sementem:** an abstract word
meaning 'sowing'.

231-58 *Providence has arranged the zones
of the sky, and the corresponding zones
on earth, so that the two temperate zones
between the poles and the equator are
habitable by mortals and are given the
varying seasons necessary for agriculture.*

231-58 This passage about the zones of
the sky is closely based on a passage from
Eratosthenes (note on 233), and is in parts
quite close to Lucretius (5.650f.). But the
tone is very different from that of
Lucretius: the latter describes a universe
without divine governance, while Virgil
emphasises the providential care of the gods
for mortals (*idcirco*, 231; *munere
concessae divum*, 238). The astronomical
part is based on Aratus (as in the previous
section); see note on 244-5. Virgil has
produced a strange mixture of mythology
(242-3) with contemporary Stoic scientific
doctrine about the geography of the world
(see Richter's notes on this passage).

231 **idcirco:** i.e. to help the farmer; the
gods have organised the universe so that man
has aids for his task (cf. 238 *munere . . .
divum*).

232 **duodena . . . astra:** the twelve signs
of the zodiac (cf. Ov. *Met.* 13.618-19; Manil.
1.255f.); the distributive number is used
instead of the cardinal *duodecim* which is
impossible metrically. *Mundi* is dependent
on *astra*.

233 The zones of the sky are thought of
as corresponding with the zones of the
earth; the whole description is based on a
passage from Eratosthenes' Hermes, quoted
in full by Conington, who also cites Ov.
Met. 1.45f.; Tib. 4.1.151f.; Macrob. *Somn.*
2.7. Cf. also Varro *RR* 1.2.3-4; Lucr. 5.
650f.

233f. The description of the five zones
begins in the middle area with the torrid
zone, moves to the two outside ice-bound
zones and finally dwells on the two
temperate zones where man can flourish.

234 **ab igni:** the unexpected use of the
preposition probably arises from the phrase
ἐκ πυρός in Eratosthenes.

235-6 'round which on the outside on left

and right extend (two) zones blue with cold'.

237 **has inter mediamque:** 'between
these two and the middle zone'.

mortalibus aegris: cf. *Aen.* 2.268; 10.274;
Lucr. 6.1. The phrase is a translation of
Homer's δειλοῖσι βροτοῖσιν.

239 'in which the slanting array of the
signs of the zodiac could revolve'; the slant
(the ecliptic) is to explain the varying seasons
of the year in the temperate zones, as
opposed to everlasting summer in the torrid
zone and everlasting winter in the polar
zones.

240f. Virgil's picture seems to be of the
earth 'rising up' to the North Pole and
'descending' to the South Pole: the
underworld is located in the south, while
in the south temperate zone (247f.) it may
be always dark, or may be daytime when it
is night-time in our zone.

240 **Scythiam Riphaeasque . . . arces:**
used of the far north; cf. 3.197; 349;
382; 4.518.

241 **premitur . . . devexus:** 'sinks down
as it slopes away'.

Libyae: the sea-coast of Libya was well-
known to the Romans; here Virgil uses the
term to suggest enormous extent southwards.

242-3 'Here (i.e. in the north) is our pole
always high above us, but that other pole
black Styx and the deep shades look upon
beneath their feet'. Virgil seems to picture
the underworld as being below us, but above
the inhabitants (if any) of the southern
temperate zone; contrast Lucr. 3.25f.
Virgil's picture is a curious mixture of
mythology and geography.

244-5 The constellation Anguis is
between the Great Bear and the Little Bear,
in the area of the Pole Star; cf. 205. Virgil
is very closely following Aratus (*Phaen.*
45f.). *Arctos* (feminine) is the Greek word
for a bear; our word arctic derives from it.

245-6 **Arctos . . . Arctos:** for this
rhetorical device of repetition, cf. *Ecl.* 9.
47-8.

246 This line is imitated from Homer
(*Il.* 18.489 — the Bear never dips down into
Ocean); cf. also Aratus *Phaen.* 48; Ov. *Met.*
13.293. The constellations when they set
were thought of as disappearing into the
stream of Ocean: the constellations around
the Pole Star never set in Mediterranean
latitudes.

247-51 The same alternative explanations
are given by Lucretius (5.650f.; cf. also
1.1065f.).

247 **intempesta silet nox:** for the monosyllabic ending see note on 181; for

intempesta ('timeless' night), cf. Enn. *Ann.* 102; 167; Lucr. 5.986; *Aen.* 3.587.

250 Cf. *Aen.* 5.739, a very similar line; for *adflare* used transitively, cf. also *Aen.* 2.649.

252 **tempestates . . . caelo:** 'forecast the season's weather even when the sky is uncertain', i.e. by getting dates from the constellations.

254 **marmor:** a common poetic word for the sea, cf. Enn. *Ann.* 384.

255 'launch our ready ships', a variation on the theme of the previous clause, not a reference to military operations by sea, as some have thought. For *arma* of a ship's tackle, cf. *Aen.* 4.290.

256 **tempestivam:** 'at the right time'; cf. Cato *Agr.* 31 for various precepts about the right time for felling trees.

259-310 *There are various things that can be done in winter when the weather is unfavourable. There are various days in the lunar calendar which are favourable or otherwise for different activities. Again there are things better done at night-time. The harvest is the occupation of summer-time, but in winter the farmer is on holiday or hunting.*

259-310 This section consists of a miscellaneous collection of precepts, reminiscent of the manner of Hesiod upon whom some of it is based; cf. *WD* 493f.; 765f. Some comes from Cato (*Agr.* 2.3; 39) and some from Varro (*RR* 1.37). According to Pliny (*NH* 18.321) Virgil followed Democritus as well as Hesiod in the section on the auspicious days of the lunar month.

The list of precepts is varied by various Virgilian devices: favourite rhetorical turns (266-7; 289-90), geographical terms (265; 309), the simile of the rejoicing sailors (303-4), the extended mythology of 277-83 (which occupies most of the superstitious section about lucky days), and in particular by the two descriptive vignettes – the donkey going to market (273-5) and the domestic scene of man and wife busy on a winter night (291-6).

260-61 'It is possible to get ahead with many tasks which would soon have to be done in a hurry in the good weather'. Aulus Gellius (10.11) comments on the difference between *maturare*, 'to do in good time' and *properare* 'to hurry'.

261-2 **procudit . . . dentem:** 'sharpens the point of the share', see note on 172; cf. Lucr. 5.1264-5. The end of the share has become blunted through frequent use.

262 **lintres:** Servius says this means either boats or troughs for wine; the second seems certainly correct; cf. Cato *Agr.* 11; Tib. 1.5.23.

263 For branding of cattle (the technical word is *character*), cf. 3.158; piles or sacks of corn were labelled with *tesserae* (Servius). The verb *impressit* is more appropriate for the first phrase than the second (zeugma); cf. 93.

264 For *vallos* ('stakes') cf. 2.25; for *furcae* (used as pronged supports, especially for vines), cf. 2.359.

265 **Amerina . . . retinacula:** 'supports from Ameria', i.e. flexible branches (of willow or the like) which grew especially in Ameria (in Umbria); cf. Colum. 4.30.4.

266 'Now pliant baskets should be woven from switches of bramble'; *facilis* refers to the comparative ease of making baskets from flexible material. Servius takes *Rubea* as a proper noun (from Rubi; cf. Hor. *Sat.* 1.5.94), but cf. Pliny *NH* 16.176.

268-9 The connexion of thought is that you can do some jobs indoors in bad weather (259) and likewise some jobs are permissible even on festal days when most tasks would be forbidden by religious scruples (*fas*) or actual legislation (*iura*); cf. Cato *Agr.* 2.4; Colum. 2.21.

269 **deducere:** Macrobius (*Sat.* 3.3.10) suggests this means to make drainage channels serviceable by cleaning them out, rather than to dig new channels; cf. Cato *Agr.* 2.4.

270 **religio:** Virgil allows the first syllable to be long, otherwise the word would not fit in hexameter verse; cf. *reliquiae.*

272 Dipping sheep against scabies was permissible on festal days (Macrob. *Sat.* 3.3), but not washing them simply to clean the wool (Colum. 2.22.2).

273-5 'Often the driver loads the flanks of his slow donkey with oil or cheap fruit and brings back on his return from the city an indented millstone or a mass of black pitch'. *Lapis incusus* is a stone worked into the shape of a millstone and indented by a stonemason; pitch could be used for sealing wine, making repairs, etc. Servius quotes Varro as saying that markets could be held on festal days; cf. Cato, *Agr.* 138.

276 **alios alio . . . ordine:** 'various days in various categories', i.e. the days of the lunar month are ranked as more or less appropriate for different activities.

277 **felicis operum:** 'as lucky in regard to undertakings'; the genitive of respect is a

Grecism; cf. *Aen.* 11.416 *fortunatusque laborum.*

277-8 This is taken from Hesiod (*WD* 802f.) 'Avoid the fifth days ... they say that on the fifth day the Furies attended the birth of Horcus whom Strife bore to trouble the perjured'. Virgil has varied this, perhaps conflating it with another source or perhaps through imperfect recollection of the passage of Hesiod: in particular he has changed Horcus, the god of oaths, to Orcus, the god of the underworld (unless we read *Horcus* here with P, as Celsus did, according to Servius).

278-9 This refers to the Giants and Titans produced by Mother Earth who were destroyed by Jupiter; cf. *Aen.* 4.178f. (where the offspring mentioned are Coeus and Enceladus and Fama); *Aen.* 6.580f.; Hor. *Odes* 3.4.49f.; *Ov. Met.* 1.151f. Coeus and Iapetus are sons of Earth and Heaven in Hesiod (*Theog.* 134).

279 **creat:** 'became the mother of', an idiomatic use of the present tense, see note on *Ecl.* 8.45.

Typhoea: a Titan (cf. Hes. *Theog.* 821) mentioned again in *Aen.* 8.298; 9.716. The word scans with a long *o* and the *ea* reduced to a single syllable by synizesis; see note on *Ecl.* 6.30 (*Orphea*).

280 **rescindere:** for the infinitive after *coniurare*, cf. Hor. *Odes* 1.15.7.

280-88 The brothers are Otus and Ephialtes, sons of Aloeus; cf. Hom. *Od.* 11.305f.; *Aen.* 6.582f. They attempted to storm Jupiter in heaven by piling Ossa on Pelion and Mt Olympus on top of both. Notice the metrical effects in this passage: spondees in line 280 and the first part of 281; hiatus at the caesura in 281 (see note on *Ecl.* 3.6) and shortening in hiatus with the word *Pelio* (cf. 437 and see note on *Ecl.* 2.65); three elisions in line 282 and then the smooth effortless line (283) expressing Jupiter's easy triumph.

284 In Hesiod (*WD* 805f.) the seventeenth day is referred to immediately after the fifth, but Hesiod says it is the time for threshing and timber-cutting. The items given by Virgil for the seventeenth are all given by Hesiod for various different days.

felix ... ponere: 'lucky for planting', an epexegetic infinitive of a Greek type. See note on *Ecl.* 5.1-2.

285 **prensos domitare:** 'to take in hand and tame'; cf. 3.207.

285-6 **licia ... addere:** 'to join the warp-threads to the loom', in readiness for

weaving; cf. Hes. *WD* 779; Ov. *Met.* 6.54.

286 The ninth day in Hesiod is said to be generally a favourable one; Virgil's *fugae melior* presumably refers to runaway slaves and indicates to the farmer that on this day he should be on his guard for the possibility of slaves running away (though he need not fear theft).

287 'Many problems yield more easily in the cold of night'; *dedere* is gnomic aorist ; cf. 49.

288 **Eous:** 'the morning star'; cf. *Aen.* 3.588.

289-90 This arrangement of three parallel clauses with repetition of *nocte ... nocte ... noctis* is a favourite device of Virgilian diction; cf. 266-7 and see note on 78.

290 **noctes:** object of *deficit*; cf. 4.281.

291 **quidam:** 'someone I know', a device for indicating personal involvement, like the use of the first or the second person (see note on 176-203).

292 **inspicat:** 'splits the top of', so that the torches may kindle more easily. *Inspicare* is a very rare word, connected with *spica*, 'a spike'.

294 'his wife runs through the web with the shrill shuttle', cf. the description of Circe weaving (*Aen.* 7.14, the same words). For singing at the loom to while away the toil, cf. Ov. *Tr.* 4.1.13-14; Tib. 2.1.65-6. The domestic touch adds to the intimate mood in this passage; notice the spondaic movement in this line and the next, conveying perhaps (as Huxley says) the patient performance of routine.

295 'or distills the liquid of sweet must on a fire'; *mustum* is unfermented grape juice; for *Vulcano = igne,* cf. *Ceres* (corn) in 297; for the hypermetric elision of *umorem* (sometimes equal to convey the boiling over of the must), cf. 2.69; 3.449; and instances with *-que* in 2.344; 443; 3.242; 377. See my note on *Aen.* 5.422 (Oxford edition).

296 'and skims off the surface of the bubbling cauldron with leaves'; for *trepidi,* cf. *tremulus* in *Aen.* 8.22; for this operation, cf. Colum. 12.19-20.

298 **tostas:** 'ripened', by the sun.

299 **nudus ... nudus:** 'plough naked, sow naked', i.e. do so in the warm season, because winter is the inactive time (*ignava*). The phrase is a direct translation of Hesiod (*WD* 391) γυμνὸν σπείρειν, γυμνὸν δὲ βοωτεῖν.

300 **frigoribus:** 'in the cold times', ablative of time when.

parto: 'what they've produced'; cf.
Aen. 8.317.
302 **genialis:** 'festive' (cf. *Aen.* 6.603),
the time for relaxing.
303 **pressae:** 'heavy-laden', making the
parallel with the farmer whose harvest is
gathered.
304 **puppibus:** with the following clause;
et is postponed (cf. *aut* in 274). The line is
repeated in *Aen.* 4.418.
305 **sed tamen:** in spite of the general
relaxation in winter (*plerumque* 300), there
are tasks to be done.
306 The berries of bay and myrtle were
used for flavouring.
307-8 These lines refer to hunting, not
to the protection of crops; cf. Hor. *Epod.*
2.35f.
308 **auritos:** 'long-eared'; applied by
Ovid (*Am.* 2.7.15) to donkeys.
309 'as you whirl the hempen thongs
of the Balearic sling'; this type of catapult
was especially associated with the Balearic
islands where it was supposed to have been
invented; cf. Ov. *Met.* 2.727.

311-50 *In autumn and spring particularly,
but also in high summer, storms may
destroy the farmer's work: this makes it
vital to watch for weather-signs and
especially to observe the due religious
ceremonies in honour of Ceres, goddess of
agriculture.*
311-50 In this passage Virgil makes his
transition from the subject of the farmer's
calendar to his next subject, signs of the
weather. It separates these two sections of
didactic material with descriptive writing
of an extraordinary impact. It begins with a
detailed and vividly coloured picture of a
storm, with diction in the grand style and
metrical effects to reinforce the mood (see
notes on 313; 320; 326; 326-7; 334).
There are reminiscences of Homer, Hesiod
and in particular Lucretius (see note on
316f.); but the passage ends with a
message wholly un-Lucretian as Virgil
stresses the need for proper religious
observances and describes the festivals of
the countryside with a deep personal
affection.
311-15 Virgil begins with mention of
storms in autumn and spring, when they are
most frequent; he then passes to a summer
storm at harvest-time (316f.) and enlarges
the description into a vast generalised
picture of havoc (322f.).
311 **tempestates . . . sidera:** 'the storms
and the climate of autumn'; the 'stars' are
responsible for the climatic conditions of

the particular part of the year; cf. 335 and
Aen. 11.260.
312 **breviorque ... et:** -*que ... et* is a
rarer variant for -*que . . que* or *et . . . et,*
'both . . . and'.
mollior: 'less oppressive', as the summer
changes to autumn.
313 **vel cum ruit:** i.e. *vel quae vigilanda
sint viris cum ruit;* the *cum* clause parallels
the *ubi* clause in 312. Notice the alliteration
of *v* in this line, suggestive of dramatic
effect; cf. *Aen.* 6.833 *neu patriae validas
in viscera vertite viris.*
ruit imbriferum ver: 'spring descends with
its torrential rain'; for *ruit,* cf. 324; *Aen.* 5.
695. *Imbrifer* is a poetic compound; cf. Ov.
Met. 13.725. The monosyllabic ending
conveys violence; see note on 181 and
compare 247.
314 'when the spiky harvest has already
begun to bristle on the plains'; for *spicea,*
cf. 292; for *inhorruit,* cf. Hom. *Il.* 23.599;
and see note on 151.
316f. For the storm description cf.
Hom. *Il.* 16.385f. (a simile); Hes. *WD* 507f.
(the north wind); and especially Lucr.
1.271f.; 6.253f.
316 **saepe ego:** the personal element
(cf. 45; 193; 197, and note on 100-17)
produces an added vividness for this highly
wrought description of storm.
317 **hordea:** for the plural see note on
210.
320 **sublimem expulsam eruerent:** 'tore
it off and whirled it skywards'; the subjunctive is consecutive. The elisions help to
convey the turmoil, especially with the
conflict of accent and ictus in the first four
feet.
320-21 **ita . . . volantis:** 'so fiercely did the
storm snatch in its black whirlwind both the
light straw and the flying stalks'. The
subjunctive *ferret* seems to be due to
attraction from *eruerent.* For *ita,* cf. Lucr.
1.275; 286 (a passage describing a storm).
322 **agmen:** used of rivers in Enn. *Ann.*
173 and Lucr. 5.271 (cf. *Aen.* 2.782), and
of clouds in Lucr. 6.100.
323 Compare Lucr. 6.253f., esp. 259
with the similar unusual elision.
324 **ruit arduus aether:** 'the high
heavens descend'; cf. 313 and *Aen.* 1.129
caelique ruina.
325 **sata . . . labores:** repeated in a simile
in *Aen.* 2.306; cf. Hes. *WD* 46 ἔργα βοῶν.
326 **diluit:** the pause after the run-on
dactylic verb emphasises the dramatic
action; cf. 109; 333; 2.210; 3.516.
326-7 At the climax of the sentence

Virgil uses patterned initial alliteration of *f*, *c*, *f* again; he continues this effect in 328-30 (*n*, *m*, *t*, *f*).

327 **fervetque . . . aequor:** 'the sea seethes with heaving waters'; cf. Lucr. 6.427; Virgil pictures the storm sweeping in from the sea.

328 **corusca:** better taken with *fulmina*, not *dextra* (as many commentators say); cf. Lucr. 5.295-6 *coruscis fulguribus;* with the other rendering the juxtaposition of *nocte corusca* not in agreement would be awkward.

332 The first half of the line is taken from Theocr. 7.77; Athos and Rhodope are mountains in northern Greece; Ceraunia is in north-west Greece; cf. *Aen.* 3.506. Compare Thomson's use of geographical names in the storm-scene in *Seasons, Summer* 1161f.:

Amid Carnarvon's mountains rages loud
The repercussive roar; with mighty crush
Into the flaming deep from the rude rocks
Of Penmanmaur heaped hideous to the sky
Tumble the smitten cliffs; and Snowdon's
  peak
Dissolving instant yields his wintry load.

Athon: a false Greek form of the accusative; some editors read *Atho* (as in Theocr. 7.77) with shortening in hiatus.

334 **plangunt:** 'wail', intransitive; cf. *Aen.* 11.145; notice the alliteration of *n* in this line, conveying the menacing roar of the wind.

336-7 The planets Saturn (cold, because outermost from the sun of the known planets, cf. Pliny *NH* 2.34) and Mercury (in mythology Mercury was born and brought up on Mt Cyllene in southern Greece) would vary in their position (*errare*) with regard to the constellations and fixed stars, and thus add a further element to weather forecasting, more concerned with astrology (as Servius' explanations suggest) than likely seasonal climate.

338 **in primis venerare deos:** 'above all, worship the gods'; this simply-expressed phrase summarises the basic theme of the *Georgics,* that the farmer can succeed only with the help of the gods of the country-side, which he will have if his attitude is religious and worshipful.

339 **operatus:** 'making sacrifices', a technical word in religion; cf. *Aen.* 3.136. The references in what follows are to the *Cerealia* (April) and the *Ambarvalia* (May); cf. Tib. 2.1, and to another festival of Ceres at the beginning of harvest-time.

341-2 The movement becomes spondaic to express serenity; there is hiatus at the caesura in 341, see note on *Ecl.* 3.6.

341 Cf. Hes. *WD* 585 (of summer): 'then the goats are fattest and wine at its best'.

344 'and for her you must drench honeycombs with milk and mellow wine'; observe the emphasis given by *tu* (picking up *tibi* in the previous line) – each individual must make his offerings.

345 **felix:** 'auspicious', without involving any ill omen that would mar the efficacy of the sacrifice.

347 **in tecta:** 'to their houses', i.e. to associate her with each family individually as well as with all collectively.

349 **torta redimitus tempora quercu:** 'his brows encircled with a wreath of oak'; the construction is retained accusative with a passive verb; see note on *Ecl.* 1.53-5 and cf. *Aen.* 3.81.

350 'he dances his primitive dance and sings his chants'; *incompositos* refers to the simple traditional nature of the movements. The rhythm of the line, with no break between 1½ and 3½ caesura is relatively unusual and conveys something of the idea of the unsophisticated rhythm of the dance.

351-92 *Jupiter has decreed that there should be signs by which men can forecast the weather; storms and rain can be foreseen in many ways, for example by signs from birds, shooting-stars, cattle, frogs, fungus on lamp-wicks.*

351-92 This passage about weather-signs is closely based on the miscellaneous collection of such lore in Aratus, perhaps with some reference to Theophrastus, *De Signis;* much of the material is repro-duced in Pliny, *NH* 18.359f. Aratus' work was a didactic hexameter poem of the third century BC called *Phaenomena:* the first part of it was used in the astronomical section of this book (see note on 204-30) and the last section is concerned with weather signs and sometimes given the separate title of *Diosemiae.* Some fragments of Cicero's translation survive, and Servius quotes lines from Varro of Atax (note on 375f.) suggesting that Virgil may have used his adaptation of Aratus. But out of the heterogeneous and excessively detailed lists of Aratus Virgil has made a passage of superb poetry, partly by rigorous selection of material rather than exhaustive lists, partly by his emphasis on the care of Jupiter for mankind in organising the cosmos (note on 353), partly by his intense interest in the creatures of nature (birds, ants, cattle, frogs), but chiefly by his vivid imagery (e.g. the frogs, the crow, the girl weaving by lamplight) and his musical mastery of the hexameter. For full analysis of this section see L. A. S. Jermyn, *Greece and Rome*, 1951 pp. 27f. and Wilkinson pp. 234f.

352 'both the heat and the rains, and the winds which bring cold weather'; the nouns are in apposition to *haec* in the previous line. The first *-que* is lengthened in arsis; cf. 371 and see note on 153.

353 **ipse pater statuit:** notice the insistence on divine providence, see note on 231-58.
Examples of the moon's weather indications are given in 395f., 427f.; *moneret* is indirect deliberative subjunctive, 'what signs she was to give'.

356f. The first 'sign', that of impending wind, is not so much a forecast as a series of indications that a gale is already beginning (the same is true of some of the later signs). Cf. Aratus, *Phaen.* 909f.; Cic. *De Div.* 1.13. Notice the alliteration of the hard consonant *t*.

357-8 **aridus ... fragor:** 'a dry sound', i.e. harsh, cracking, an evocative image taken from Lucr. 6.119 (of thunder) *aridus ... sonus;* cf. the imitation by Thomson, *Seasons, Summer* 1117f., 'the dull sound/That from the mountain previous to the storm/Rolls o'er the muttering earth'.

359 **misceri:** 'give a confused noise' (*perturbari*, Servius), a favourite word of Virgil; cf. *Aen.* 1.124; 4.160; 411. The alliteration of *m* in this line is imitative of the sense.

360-61 'Then too the wave does not spare the curved ships at the time when ...'. The construction of *temperare* here is unusual (literally 'does not restrain itself from the ships'); but there does not seem sufficient reason for accepting Stanford's *iam subitum* or Phillimore's *tibi tum.* For *male*, almost = *non*, cf. 105.

361f. The signs from birds are based on Aratus, *Phaen.* 913f.; cf. Cic. *De Div.* 1.14; Pliny *NH* 18.361-2; and compare the imitation in Thomson, *Seasons, Winter* 144f.

364 The heron, a land bird, flies high away from its usual pools which will be roughened by the gale.

365f. The passage about shooting stars is based on Aratus, *Phaen.* 926f.; cf. Theophr. *De Signis* 13; Pliny *NH* 18.352.

For the diction cf. Lucr. 2.206-7 *faces ... nonne vides longos flammarum ducere tractus?* Thomson (*Seasons, Winter* 127f.) imitates closely: 'The stars obtuse emit a shivering ray; Or frequent seem to shoot athwart the gloom And long behind them trail the whitening blaze'.

368-9 Again Thomson imitates (*Seasons, Winter* 130-31) 'Snatched in short eddies plays the withered leaf; And on the flood the dancing feather floats'. Cf. Aratus, *Phaen.* 921-3, Theophr. *De Signis* 37, Pliny *NH* 18.360. Virgil's *conludere* is a vivid personification of his own.

370f. Again Virgil is following Aratus closely (*Phaen.* 933f.) 'But when the lightning comes from the east and the south ... the sailor is fearful ...'.

371 **Eurique Zephyrique:** *-que ... -que* is 'both , , , and'; the first *-que* is lengthened in arsis before the double consonant *z;* see note on 352.

373-4 **imprudentibus ... obfuit:** 'has never caused damage to people not warned'; for *imprudentibus* Servius says *ignaris*, i.e. there is no reason to be caught unaware, because of all the signs available. M has *prudentibus*, 'careful'.

375f. Servius quotes seven lines from Varro of Atax (an older contemporary of Virgil) based on Aratus (*Phaen.* 942f.) of which line 373 is a direct quotation and lines 375-6 and 385 a very close adaptation. Cf. also Aratus, *Phaen.* 1031f.; Theophr. *De Signis* 38.

375-6 For the cow sniffing the air, cf. Aratus, *Phaen.* 954-5 ('The cattle before rain from heaven look up at the sky and sniff the air'); Varro of Atax quoted by Servius *et bos suspiciens caelum, mirabile visu, naribus aerium patulis decerpsit odorem;* Cicero (*De Div.* 1.15, translating Aratus) *mollipedesque boves, spectantes lumina caeli, naribus umiferum duxere ex aere sucum.* Thomson, *Seasons, Winter* 132f. has 'With broadened nostrils to the sky upturned The conscious heifer snuffs the stormy gale'.

377 A quotation from Varro of Atax (see note on 375f.); *arguta* means 'shrill'; cf. 294. For the swallow flying low, cf. Arat. *Phaen.* 944, Pliny *NH* 18.363.

378 Cf. Cicero (translating Aratus, *De Div.* 1.15) *vos quoque signa videtis, aquai dulcis alumnae, cum clamore paratis inanes fundere voces, absurdoque sono fontes et stagna cietis;* Ov. *Met.* 6.376 with similar onomatopoeia of *q* sounds) *quamvis sint sub aqua, sub aqua*

maledicere temptant. The onomatopoeia is reminiscent of the frogs in Aristophanes, βρεκεκεκὲξ κοὰξ κοάξ.

379 tectis penetralibus: the ant is personified as having its 'innermost shrine'; cf. the mouse in 181f. The ant as a weather forecaster is again from Aratus, *Phaen.* 956f. 'ants swiftly carry up all their eggs from their hollow nests'; cf. Theophr. *De Signis* 22; Pliny *NH* 18.364.

380-81 bibit ingens arcus: 'the mighty rainbow drinks up the moisture'; for this belief in ancient times, cf. Plaut. *Curc.* 131; Prop. 3.5.32; Ov. *Met.* 1.271. Aratus (*Phaen.* 940) says a double rainbow indicates imminent rain.

382 corvorum . . . exercitus: again a personification, of the crows in an 'army'; for crows as weather prophets, cf. Arat. *Phaen.* 963f.; Pliny *NH* 18.362.

383 variae . . . volucres: this is the reading of the best MSS; it involves an anacoluthon (break in construction) — 'then there are the various birds of the sea . . . you can see them dipping their heads in the water'. Other MSS have *varias* and Servius supports them, but it seems that this is an alteration to make the sentence more precisely grammatical.

383-4 'and those which grub up the Asian meadows of Cayster all around in the swamps they love'; cf. *Aen.* 7.701-2 *Asia . . . palus;* Hom. *Il.* 2.461 'in the Asian meadow around the streams of Cayster'. *Circum* is adverbial.

385f. Cf. Varro of Atax (note on 375f.) *tum liceat pelagi volucres tardaeque paludis cernere inexpletas studio certare lavandi et velut insolitum pennis infundere rorem;* Arat. *Phaen.* 942f.

387 incassum . . .gestire: 'rejoice for no reason'; cf. Varro (note on 385f.). *Incassum* seems to be an enlargement of Varro's *inexpletas studio* (Aratus has ἄπληστον, 'insatiably'): Servius wildly says it is 'in vain' because the water can't get through their feathers.

388-9 This is one of Virgil's most memorable cameos; the descriptive effect is heightened by the alliteration of *p, v,* and then in full measure *s.*

388 improba: see note on 119. The impact here, humorous as in 119, is centred on the unceasing noise. Cf. Arat. *Phaen.* 949f.; Cic. *De Div.* 1.14 *fuscaque non nunquam cursans per litora cornix Demersit caput et fluctum cervice recepit.* Compare also Lucr. 5.1084f.

390-92 Another memorable cameo:

even at night (and indoors) — note the position of *nocturna* between *ne* and *quidem* — girls at their spinning see the signs of storm when their lamps spit and mould appears. Again there is marked alliteration (*n, p*). Cf. Arat. *Phaen.* 1034f.; Thomson, *Seasons, Winter* 134-8 'E'en as the matron, at her nightly task, With pensive labour draws the flaxen thread The wasted taper and the crackling flame Foretell the blast.'

393-423 *Signs of fair weather given by the sky and by birds and animals.*

393-423 This section about indications of fair weather is, like the previous section, quite closely based on Aratus' *Phaenomena.* The two striking features of Virgil's treatment of the subject are first the glimpses of mythology (399; 404-9), and secondly the sympathetic presentation of nature's creatures, especially 411-12, 413-14, 422-3. See further L.A.S. Jermyn, *Greece and Rome,* 1951, pp. 49f. and Wilkinson pp. 239-42.

393 ex imbri: 'after rain', a not uncommon use of *ex.*

soles: 'sunny days', cf. 2.332.

serena: used as a noun, 'fine weather'; cf. *Aen.* 5.851; Lucan 1.530.

395 acies: 'edge', 'outline'; cf. 2.365.

396 'Nor the moon to rise dominated by her brother's rays', i.e. not dim, but as if with her own light; this is due to the dryness of the atmosphere. The moon (Phoebe) is the sister of Phoebus, the Sun.

397 tenuia: scanned as a dactyl with the *u* acting as a consonant, cf. Lucr. 3.383; *Geo.* 2.121; 4.38; and compare *genua Aen.* 5.432. This line refers to cirrhus cloud; cf, Arat. *Phaen.* 938-9 'often when rain is coming clouds very like fleece are to be seen beforehand'; Lucr. 6.504; Pliny *NH* 18.356.

399 Halcyons (kingfishers) are beloved by the sea-nymph Thetis because in mythology Alcyone, when her husband had been shipwrecked, threw herself into the sea and was changed into a kingfisher; cf. Ov. *Met.* 11.384f. In Theocr. 7.59 the halcyons are beloved of the Nereids.

399-400 ore solutos . . . maniplos: 'lumps (of straw) which they have loosened with their snouts'; i.e. to prepare a bed for themselves; cf. Pliny *NH* 18.364.

401 The low clouds are presumably early morning mist; cf. Pliny *NH* 18.357; and Arat. *Phaen.* 988-90 'if a misty cloud extends along the bottom of a high mountain when the topmost peaks show forth clear, then the weather will be fair'.

403 'the owl fruitlessly practises his late song', fruitlessly perhaps because he wants rain and is not going to get it. Cf. Arat. 'Phaen. 999f.; Thomson, *Seasons, Winter* 143-4 'Assiduous in his bower the wailing owl Plies his sad song'.

404-5 **Nisus . . . Scylla**: Nisus is a sea-hawk, Scylla a bird called *ciris;* the reference is to the mythological story, told in the pseudo-Virgilian *Ciris,* of how Scylla cut the purple lock from her father Nisus' head, on which the safety of the realm depended, because of her love for Minos. They were both transformed into birds, the father pursuing, the daughter fleeing. See note on *Ecl.* 6.74, and cf. Ov. *Met.* 8.8f.; Prop. 3.19.21f.; Pope, *Rape of the Lock,* 3.122f. 'Think of Scylla's fate! Changed to a bird, and sent to flit in air She dearly pays for Nisus' injured hair'.

405 Notice the intense alliteration of *p,* emphasising Scylla's suffering.

406-9 These lines are reproduced exactly in *Ciris,* 538-41; the repetition is a device of Alexandrian style.

406 The dactylic movement represents flight, as in 409.

410f. Compare Aratus, *Phaen.* 1003-9, where the rooks utter two cries followed by a babel of sound, and then happily make for their nests.

411 **cubilibus**: another example of Virgil's personification of living things, see note on 379. The next lines continue to express Virgil's interest in and insight into the ways of nature's creatures; for the phrase *nescio qua . . . dulcedine laeti,* cf. 4.55 (of the bees).

413 **actis**: 'finished' (= *peractis*).

415-16 'not, I think, because they have by divine gift a greater talent or a greater prophetic power given by fate'; *divinitus* is an adverb; with *ingenium* supply *maius* from *maior.* This passage is often contrasted with 4.219f., where Virgil reports the Stoic view that the bees have a share in divinity; here however he is not denying the divinity of the birds, merely their prophetic powers.

417-18 **caeli . . . vias**: 'the changing humidity of the sky alters direction'.

419 'thickens what was thin before and thins out what was thick'; i.e. when Jupiter alters the weather to wet (*umidus austris*) from fine, or again from fine to wet, the rooks are sensitive to it.

420 **species animorum**: 'the images in their minds'.

420-21 **motus nunc alios, alios . . .;** 'feelings now different from when . . .', a condensed phrase avoiding the expected comparative clause, influenced by Lucr. 5.1081.

422 **avium concentus**: cf. Spenser, *FQ* 2.5.31 'Therein the merry birds of every sorte Chaunted aloud their chearfull harmonie And made amongst themselves a sweete consort'.

424-63 *The moon and the sun give signs of future weather by their aspects at different times.*

424-63 In this section Virgil has selected certain weather signs from the much larger list given by Aratus (*Phaen.* 778-891). He has added occasional touches of mythology (437; 447), and arranged his material so as to lead in to the portents given by the sun (and in many other ways) in connexion with the death of Julius Caesar with which the great peroration of this book is concerned.

424-5 **sequentis ordine**: 'following in fixed phases'.

426 **hora**: 'tomorrow's hour' means, in this context, the weather to be expected.

428 'if she encircles black air with a dim crescent'.

430 'if she spreads a maidenly blush over her face'; cf. Arat. *Phaen.* 803; Pliny *NH* 18.347; the personification of the moon (Phoebe) is mock-heroic, reinforced by the repetition *ventus . . . vento.*

433 **neque obtunsis . . . cornibus**: 'with her horns not blurred'; cf. Arat. *Phaen.* 785; 806f.

436 **votaque . . . solvent**: 'shall pay their vows'; cf. *Aen.* 3.404; 12.766f.

437 Aulus Gellius (13.26) says this is a line adapted from the Greek author Parthenius, Virgil's teacher; Virgil's scansion is on the Greek model with a hiatus after *Glauco* (see note on *Ecl.* 2.24, but this hiatus in thesis is unparalleled) and shortening in hiatus after *Panopeae* (see note on 280-83, and cf. 4.461), no main caesura, and a quadrisyllabic ending. Glaucus was a sea deity (cf. *Aen.* 5.823), Panopea a sea-nymph (cf. *Aen.* 5.825), and Melicertes, son of Ino, also called Palaemon (*Aen.* 5.823), another sea deity (cf. Ov. *Met.* 4.416f.).

438-9 Virgil now passes to the second of the two subjects set out in 424. He proceeds to lay greater emphasis on the sun, especially with regard to the portents at the time of Julius Caesar (463f.); and he emphasises the importance of this part of his theme with the strong alliteration (of *s*) in 439, and the repetition *sol . . . solem.*

440 'both those signs which he brings in the morning and those when the stars are rising'; cf. Arat. *Phaen.* 820-21.

441 maculis: i.e. flecks of cloud; cf. Arat. *Phaen.* 822f.

442 medioque . . . orbe: i.e. seems concave, cf. Arat. *Phaen.* 828f. (κοῖλος); Pliny *NH* 18.342 (*concavus*).

443-4 'for the south wind is pressing onwards from the ocean, bad both for the trees and the crops and also for the cattle'; the second line is wholly dactylic, an effect conveying speed reinforced by the triple *-que* and the trochaic caesurae.

446 diversi rumpent radii: 'the rays shoot forth in different directions', i.e. the sun itself is obscured; cf. Arat. *Phaen.* 846f.; Plin. *NH* 18.346.

447 A mythological line, based on Homer (*Il.* 11.1) and repeated in *Aen.* 4.585; 9.460. Aurora, the dawn goddess, was married to the mortal Tithonus.

448 pampinus: the vine leaves, thought of as protecting the grapes.

449 'So much bounding hail cracks and leaps on the rooftops'; *in tectis* gives the visual impact necessary to the picture; *horridus* suggests the 'bristling' effect of rebounding hail (cf. Pind. *Pyth.* 4.81), as well as the idea of causing fear. For the general picture, cf. *Aen.* 5.458-9; 9.669-71. The alliteration of *t* and the dactylic movement of the second half of the line are imitative of the sense.

450 hoc etiam: referring forward to 453f., and explained by the parenthetic phrase in 451-2.

451 magis: i.e. the evening signs are more important; cf. Arat. *Phaen.* 890f., where the word μᾶλλον is used of them.

453 caeruleus: i.e. cloudy, greyish; cf. Arat. *Phaen.* 835-9.

454 immiscerier: archaic form of the passive infinitive, cf. *Aen.* 4.493.

457 ire . . . moneat: 'persuade me to go', for the poetic use of the infinitive cf. *Ecl.* 9.14. M has *moveat* in the first hand, which might well be correct; I have preferred *moneat,* read by R and the second hand of M, and attested by Priscian.

458 Virgil now combines morning and evening signs; *-que . . . -que* is 'both . . . and'. For *condere* cf. *Ecl.* 9.;52.

459 frustra . . . nimbis: 'there will be no point in being fearful of storms'; cf. Arat. *Phaen.* 858f.

461-3 These lines summarise (*denique*) the importance of the sun in giving weather signs of all kinds.

461 serenas: 'bright', i.e. not portending rain.

463-97 *The sun gave signs of disaster at the time of Julius Caesar's assassination; there were many other terrifying portents too to prophesy the horrors of the civil wars.*

463-97 Virgil here develops a formidable list of portents of disaster which occurred during the civil wars after the death of Julius Caesar. Many of them are attested by the historians (Plut. *Caes.* 69.4; Dio. 45.17.5) and they are imitated from Virgil by Tibullus (2.5.71f.), Ovid (*Met.* 15.783f.) and Lucan (1.522f). Virgil's sources seem wholly Roman (except perhaps for Ap. Rh. 4.1280f.) and parallels for the portents may be found frequently in Livy (notes on 476, 478) and Cicero (notes on 480; 484-6). The passage is handled in a highly rhetorical style, and its concluding lines (493-7) present a memorable image in carefully patterned hexameters.

463 solem: the repetition prepares for the transition from the sun giving weather signs to the sun giving portents of historical events.

466 ille etiam: again the repetition emphasises a transition, this time from general historical events to the death of Julius Caesar.

miseratus: sc. *est,* the main verb.

467-8 Two highly patterned lines, the second a perfect golden line; cf. 190, 497. For the dimness of the sun in the year of Caesar's assassination, cf. Ov. *Met.* 15.785f.; the passage is elaborated by Lucan 1.522f. (cf. especially 540-43) describing the portents before the civil war between Pompey and Caesar. Cf. Gay, *Trivia,* 3.378f. 'mighty Caesar's doom, When the sun veil'd in rust his mourning head, And frightful prodigies the skies o'erspread', and Shakespeare, *Hamlet,* 1.1.114f. 'A little ere the mightiest Julius fell . . .'.

468 impia: a word especially applied to civil war; cf. 511 and Hor. *Epod.* 16.9, and for the general theme Hor. *Odes* 1.2; *Epod.* 7.

469 quamquam: 'and yet', used here as a coordinating conjunction (= *tamen*); the transition is that besides the eclipse of the sun there were many other indications of divine disfavour.

470 'accursed dogs and ill-omened birds', a powerful line composed of only four words, two adjectives with their two nouns; cf. 27. For *importunus*, cf. *Aen.* 11.305, 12.864; for these omens, cf. Dio 45.17; Ov. *Met.* 15.791; 797; Lucan 1.549; 558; Shakespeare, *Julius Caesar* 1.3.26-8 'And yesterday the bird of night did sit Even at noonday upon the market-place, Hooting and shrieking'.

471-3 'How often did we see Etna gushing from its broken furnaces overflow into the fields of the Cyclopes, rolling balls of fire and molten rock'. The Cyclopes in their capacity as blacksmiths were located near the 'furnaces' of Mt Etna; cf. 4.170f.; *Aen.* 3.571f. where several of these phrases are repeated; *Aen.* 8.424f.; and Lucr. 6.680f. Observe the alliteration in *liquefacta . . . saxa*.

474 The sound of warfare in the sky as a prodigy in times of crisis occurs in Tib. 2.5.73f.; Ov. *Met.* 15.783f. Cf. *Aen.* 8.524-9 and Shakespeare, *Julius Caesar* 2.2.19f. 'Fierce fiery warriors fought upon the clouds, In ranks and squadrons and right form of war. . . . The noise of battle hurtled in the air'. Germany is specified as adjacent to or part of Julius Caesar's conquests in Gaul; likewise the Alps have special reference to Caesar's campaigns and his invasion of Italy.

476 **vulgo exaudita:** 'heard by many'; for this prodigy, cf. Livy 1.31.3; 2.7.2; 5.32.6; Ov. *Met.* 15.792f.; Lucan 1.569.

477 **ingens:** 'a mighty voice'; the run-on adjective filling the first spondee takes great emphasis; cf. *Aen.* 4.185; 6.590.

simulacra . . . miris: 'phantoms pale in wondrous wise'; cf. Lucr. 1.123; *Aen.* 1.354.

478 **obscurum noctis:** 'the darkness of the night'; the neuter of an adjective used as a noun and followed by a genitive is a favourite turn of Virgilian diction; cf. 4.159 and see my note on *Aen.* 5.695 (Oxford edition).

pecudesque locutae: cf. Livy 3.10.6; 24.10.10.; 27.11.4; Tib. 2.5.78.

480 'and the sad ivory weeps in temples and the bronze images sweat'; cf. Milton, *On the Morning of Christ's Nativity* 195 'and the chill marble seems to sweat'; Dio 46.33; Tib. 2.5.77; Ov. *Met.* 15.792; Cic. *De Div.* 1.98; Ap. Rh. 4.1280f.

482 **fluviorum rex Eridanus:** the river Po; cf. 4.372; *Aen.* 6.659. *Fluviorum* scans as three long syllables, the *i* being taken as a consonant; see note on 397.

483 Compare Dio 45.17 and the description of flood in Hor. *Odes* 3.29.36f.

484 **tristibus aut:** the postponement of *aut* puts strong emphasis on the word preceding it; *tristibus* ('ill-omened') summarises the whole mood of the passage.

484-6 For the portents of inauspicious sacrificial victims, blood in wells, wolves howling, cf. Dio 46.33; Ov. *Met.* 15.794f.; Cic. *De Div.* 1.98; Claud. 18.2f.

486 The alliteration of *u* reproduces the sound of howling.

487-8 A thunderbolt from a clear sky was one of the most frequently mentioned portents; cf. Hor. *Odes* 1.34.5f.

487 **alias:** adverb, 'at any other time'.

488 **cometae:** for comets as ill-omened cf. Tib. 2.5.71; Lucan 1.529; Suet. *Ner.* 36.

489 **paribus . . . telis:** 'with matching armour', i.e. soldiers of the same nationality; cf. *Aen.* 6.826 of the wars between Caesar and Pompey, Lucan 1.7.

490 **iterum videre Philippi:** the battle of Philippi was fought in 42 BC between the republicans, Brutus and Cassius, on the one side and Antony and Octavian on the other. The reference in *iterum* is to the battle of Pharsalia, also in northern Greece but some distance from Philippi, between Pompey and Caesar. There has been much controversy about the precise meaning of this line because Philippi is not the same as Pharsalia, and there have been suggestions that Virgil is referring to two separate battles at Philippi (twenty days apart), or that his geography is confused; but *iterum* need not be interpreted so narrowly — Virgil is saying that the now-familiar catastrophe of civil war occurred yet again, this time at Philippi.

492 Emathia is used vaguely for the area of Thessaly and Macedonia containing both Pharsalia and Philippi and the mountain Haemus; cf. Ov. *Met.* 15.824. For *sanguine nostro . . . pinguescere*, cf. Hor. *Odes* 2.1.29.

494-7 As Virgil comes to the conclusion of this section he uses a series of very tightly patterned lines, ending with an exact golden line; cf. 468.

495 **scabra robigine:** cf. Lucan 1.243, and the metaphorical use of the phrase in Cat. 68.151.

pila: i.e. Roman weapons.

497 **grandiaque:** probably, as Servius says, because they would be men of bygone times and therefore thought to be larger in stature (cf. Juv. 15.69f.; Lucr. 2.1150f.).

498-514 *An appeal to the Roman gods to permit Octavian to save his people from the disasters of the civil wars: farming is gone to rack and ruin and the country is rushing to disaster like a chariot out of control.*

498-514 Virgil returns at the end of the book to the theme with which he began in his invocation, the hopes which are placed in the young Octavian. His picture of the grim state of the Roman world is highly coloured and deeply pessimistic, a pessimism which is finally resolved at the end of the fourth book. In particular he lays emphasis on the wretched state of Italian farming, contrasting the miserable condition of the battle-ravaged country-side (506-8) with the potential beauty and glory of ordered agriculture, the theme with which so much of this book has been concerned.

498f. For this passage compare Hor. *Odes* 1.2; Ov. *Met.* 15.861f.

498 **Indigetes:** 'divine heroes of our land'; the word is an emotional one, used of great national heroes who are deified, such as Aeneas (*Aen.* 12.794; Livy 1.2.6). The invocation in this line is to the native divinities of Rome and Italy, first in general terms, then specifically Romulus the founder and Vesta, goddess of the hearth and home, always associated with the *Lares et Penates*.

499 The Tiber (often called Tuscan as it flowed from Etruria, cf. *Aen.* 8.473) and the Palatine Hill were two of the most evocatively patriotic features of Rome.

500 **hunc . . . iuvenem:** the young Octavian, see note on 1-42.

saltem: 'at least', i.e. at long last; till now no Roman has been able to save Virgil's generation from civil wars, not even Julius Caesar.

501 **ne prohibete:** the unusual pause after a trochee in the second foot increases the impact of the prayer.

502 The idea of paying (*luere*) for the sins of ancestors is elaborated in Hor. *Odes* 3.6.

Laomedonteae: the sonorous adjective gives weight to the line; Laomedon, an early Trojan king, had cheated the gods of the promised reward for building Troy (*Aen.* 3.248; 4.542; Hor. *Odes* 3.3.21f.; Ov. *Met.* 11.200f.),

503-5 'Now for a long time, Caesar, the realm of heaven has begrudged us your presence, and complains that you care for triumphs among men; for here

among us right and wrong are overturned'. Caesar is Octavian, and the exaggerated sentiment (cf. 24f. where Virgil discusses the future deification of Octavian) suggests that the gods wish Octavian to join them straightaway, but Octavian is still concerned with the critical situation of the Romans in the mortal world.

505 **fas versum atque nefas:** cf. Cat. 64.397f., especially 405 *omnia fanda nefanda malo permixta furore.*

506-7 'there is no proper respect for the plough; the fields go to waste when the farmers are taken away from them'; these phrases summarise Virgil's hatred for the effect of civil war on the Italian countryside. *squalere* means 'to be overgrown', 'to be ugly' (with overtones of mourning), and is the antithesis of the beauty of ordered nature which has so often been praised in this book. Cf. Pope, *Windsor Forest* 65-6, 'The fields are ravish'd from the industrious swains, From men their cities and from gods their fanes'; Shakespeare, *Henry V* 5.2.39f. 'And all her husbandry doth lie on heaps, Corrupting in its own fertility.'

508 Cf. Lucr. 5.1293-4 *inde minutatim processit ferreus ensis, versaque in opprobrium species est falcis aeni,* *Aen.* 7.635 (on the outbreak of war) *vomeris huc et falcis honos, huc omnis aratri cessit amor; recoquunt patrios fornacibus enses,* Ov. *Fast.* 1.699f. See Huxley's note *ad loc.* on 'swords into pruning-hooks'.

509 The reference is too indefinite to permit of precise dating: by the Euphrates Virgil means the Parthians against whom the Romans were constantly fighting during this period, and frontier troubles with the Germans were also frequent. Clearly the date is well before the battle of Actium; contrast the more optimistic note at the end of *Geo.* 4.

511 **impius:** with reference to civil wars, cf. 468.

512f. The simile of the chariot (cf. 3.103f.; *Aen.* 5.144f.; Hor. *Sat.* 1.1.114f.) out of control gives a most striking and dramatic end to the book.

512 **carceribus:** *carceres* is a technical term for the starting-pens in chariot races; cf. 3.104; *Aen.* 5.145.

513 **addunt in spatia:** a much disputed phrase; the meaning evidently is 'speed on from lap to lap'. The MSS vary, some omitting *in* and others having *spatio*, and some later ones insert *se* after *addunt*, but the imitation by Silius (16.373 *in spatia addebant*) adds antiquity to the reading *addunt in spatia*. For the construction of *in spatia*, cf. *in dies* ('from day to day').

513-14 'and the charioteer vainly clinging to the reins is carried away by the horses and the chariot no longer heeds his guidance'. The runaway effect which the diction presents is reflected in the metre, with no main caesura in third or fourth foot.

GEORGICS 2

Book 2 deals with trees, most especially the vine, and is presented in a joyful manner, ending with the famous panegyric of the farmer's life (458f. *O fortunatos nimium* . . .) in which the richness of the rewards is idyllically described, and contrasted with the mad rush and corrupt behaviour of city life. The book also contains the equally famous praises of Italy (136f. *sed neque Medorum* . . .), a paradise more favoured by nature than any other part of the world. But the beauty and fertility of Italy is not achieved by nature alone, but by man's constant toil (61 *scilicet omnibus est labor impendendus* . . .) and watchfulness.

One of the frequently recurring themes of this book, as of the others, is the personification of nature (see notes on 82; 177; 346-70). We see the whole of man's environment as a unified entity, part of the divine organisation of our world; this is emphasised by the constant references to the religion of the countryside by which men acknowledge their part in a total cosmos much greater than themselves (notes on 9-34; 259-287; 371-96).

In the more didactic sections Virgil has followed prose sources (Theophrastus, Cato, Varro) but always enlivened them by the methods mentioned above and by reminiscences of the poetic descriptions of Lucretius (e.g. in the description of spring, note on 315-45). Finally his incredible mastery of the music of the Latin hexameter has enabled him to colour the countryside with the golden glow of its natural beauty transformed into words.

For botanical discussions see the attractive edition of Martyn (1741) and J. Sargeaunt, *The Trees, Shrubs and Plants of Virgil* (Oxford, 1920).

1-8 *Come to my aid, Bacchus, as I sing of trees, especially the vine.*

1-8 The beginning of the new book strikes the same excited and happy note as the beginning of Book 1, and is in very marked contrast with the atmosphere of gloom and pessimism with which the first book ended. The invocation to Bacchus is separated by the first didactic passage (9-34) from the second invocation (39f.) to Maecenas.

1 This line summarises the content of the first book, cultivation and climate, and is a variation on *Geo*. 1.1.

2-3 The subject of this book is to be vines, saplings, including those which support vines (cf. 1.2), and olives.

3 Olives were proverbially slow-growing; Pliny (*NH* 15.3) cites Hesiod as saying that no one who sows an olive will ever

himself pick fruit from it; cf. Varro *RR* 1.41.4.

4 **Lenaee**: a frequent epithet of Bacchus, meaning 'god of the wine-press' (ληνός); cf. 529.

5-6 **pampineo . . . ager**: 'the fields blossom, heavy with the autumn's vines'; notice the lengthening in arsis of the final syllable of *gravidus* (see note on *Ecl.* 1.38), and the spondaic fifth foot (see note on *Ecl.* 4.49).

7-8 'with me dip your bare legs in the new must, taking off your buskins'; the reference is to the treading of the grapes to bring out the juice (must). Bacchus would wear the high boot or buskin (*coturnus*) either in his capacity as god of tragedy or as a god associated with hunting; see note on *Ecl.* 7.31-2.

9-34 *There are various ways in which*

trees are propagated; in some cases they reproduce their species by natural means, and in others the agricultural skill of farmers produces the best results.

9-34 The didactic subject-matter here is based on material derived (perhaps through intermediate sources) from Theophrastus (*HP* 2.1f.). Virgil has made his own arrangement, dividing the headings into two main groups (those that reproduce themselves in the wild state, 10-21; and those which man cultivates 22-34); then each group is sub-divided, the first into three sections – *sponte sua, de semine, ab radice,* and the second into six –*plantae, stirpes* etc., *plantaria, summum cacumen, caudicibus sectis, insita.*

The noticeable feature of the whole paragraph is how the scientific information derived from the prose-writers is subordinated to the poetic intention of building up a sense of wonder at the marvels of nature (cf. 11 *sponte sua;* 19 *matris . . . umbra;* 28-9 *summumque . . . cacumen;* 30 *mirabile dictu;* 34 *prunis lapidosa rubescere corna*) and a feeling of religious awe (15-16, 21).

9 Principio: a favourite way of beginning a didactic passage; cf. Lucr. 1.503; 2.1048; *Geo.* 4.8.

varia est natura: 'there are various natural ways'.

10-13 Virgil here refers to the ancient belief (Varro *RR* 1.40.1; Theophr. *HP* 2.1; 3.1.4) that certain trees could be produced spontaneously (αὐτόμαται) without seeds, or from invisible seeds in the air or the water (a view said to be derived from Anaxagoras). This is in antithesis with *posito de semine* (14). It is noticeable that the examples given here are of trees that grow near to water; seeds floating downstream and producing trees far from the mother tree could easily give rise to this notion of spontaneous generation. For the general idea, cf. the 'spontaneous' generation of cattle (3.274f.) and bees (4.200).

12 siler: a kind of willow or osier; cf. Pliny *NH* 16.77. *salix* (cf. *salicta* in 13) is a commoner type.

14 posito: i.e. by falling naturally into the soil; cf. 403.

15-16 'and the winter oak which is the mightiest of the trees of the groves which spread their leaves in Jupiter's honour'; the *aesculus* is a taller variety of the common oak (*quercus,* 16); the reference is to Jupiter's sacred oak groves at Dodona, regarded as oracular (16); cf. Hom. *Od.*

14.327f. and see notes on 1.8; 148-9.

16 Grais: dative of agent after *habitae.*

17 aliis: 'in the case of others', dative.

18 Parnasia: the laurel, or more correctly the bay, is connected with Mt Parnassus, the mountain of Apollo and the Muses in northern Greece, because the laurel crown was the adornment given by Apollo to poets.

19 parva: 'when small'; notice the personification of the baby tree and its mother (cf. 23; 268).

20 primum: 'from the beginning', as opposed to the gradual discovery by man of other methods (22).

21 fruticumque: the word *frutex* is used of bushy plants as opposed to trees: Columella cites roses and reeds as examples.

nemorumque sacrorum: there is no clear agricultural distinction between this phrase and *silvarum;* Virgil's intention is to reiterate the religious associations of the countryside (cf. 15).

22 'There are other methods which actual experience has discovered for itself, finding a way', as contrasted with the *modi* of Nature (20). The use of *via* is very extraordinary and Ribbeck followed Scaliger's conjecture *sunt aliae quas ipse vias,* but basically Virgil is paraphrasing Lucr. 5.1452-3 *usus et impigrae simul experientia mentis paulatim docuit pedetemptim progredientis. Via* then is something like 'on its course', 'by finding a way': the phrase is a variation for *sunt alii modi quibus usus viam repperit.*

23 plantas: 'shoots', torn off (with a heel) from the parent tree (παρασπάς in Theophr. *HP* 2.1); cf. Pliny *NH* 17.65f.; Varro *RR* 1.40.4.

24-5 stirpes . . . sudes . . . vallos: these are all larger pieces of a tree than *plantae,* hence planted more deeply. *Stirps* means the stock with roots attached.

25 quadrifidasque sudes: 'pieces of stem notched with a cross' at the bottom, to facilitate rooting; cf. Pliny *NH* 17.65f.; Colum. 4.33-4; Varro *RR* 1.40.4.

acuto robore vallos: 'poles with sharpened points', again to facilitate rooting; cf. 1.264.

26-7 'other trees of the woods look for curved branches pressed into the ground for propagation and living offshoots in their own soil'. This refers to layering or pegging down branches into the soil so that they root from a bud while still attached to the mother tree, as with vines, brambles etc.

Cf. Cato *Agr.* 32; 51; 133; Pliny *NH* 17.212.

28-9 These are cuttings: Virgil rhetorically emphasises their independence of the roots of the mother tree by stressing that in some cases they can be taken even from the very top of a tree. Contrast 299-301.

30 caudicibus: 'blocks' or 'chunks' of wood, which in some cases (like olives or myrtles, cf. 63-4) will root themselves when put in the soil; cf. Cato *Agr.* 45; Theophr. *HP* 2.1.4. This seems more remarkable than the other methods described (Servius says *quod sine dubio est mirandum*), and leads Virgil to the final 'miracle' of this passage, the alteration of a tree's nature by grafting.

32 The effect of grafting is more fully described in 78f.; *impune* suggests without damage. On grafting, cf. Varro *RR* 1.40.5f.

33-4 mutatamque ... pirum: 'a pear-tree change its nature and bear the apple that had been grafted on to it, and stony cornels grow red on plum trees'; the cornel was less useful than the plum (cf. *Aen.* 3.649) except perhaps for flavouring (Pliny *NH* 15.105), but Virgil is concerned here to emphasise the miraculous effect of grafting and the colour of the cornel (*rubescere*) gives the image which he wants.

35-46 *Therefore let the farmer set to work to win the rich rewards. Assist, Maecenas, in my task.*

35-46 Virgil renews the invocation of the first eight lines, having separated his appeal to the god Bacchus from this address to his patron, Maecenas. It is presented with an energy and intensity appropriate to the subject of Nature's wonders with which the previous section was concerned.

36 mollite: 'domesticate'; cf. 51; Lucr. 5.1367f.

37-8 Ismara ... Taburnum: Ismara or Ismarus (*Ecl.* 6.30) was a mountain in Thrace, here used as a literary reminiscence of Homer (*Od.* 9.196f) and to generalise the picture of the vine growing everywhere in the Mediterranean area. By contrast Taburnus, famous for olives, was in a part of Italy probably well-known to Virgil, adjacent to Campania.

39f. Maecenas is invoked in all four books, see note on 1.2.

39 una decurre laborem: 'speed with me on the task'; the accusative is cognate, an extension of such usages as *decurrere viam*.

43-4 These phrases are repeated in *Aen.* 6.625-6; they are based on Hom. *Il.* 2.488f.; Enn. *Ann.* 561-2.

44 primi ... oram: 'skirt the edge right

by the shore'. Virgil here modestly limits his poetic hopes.

47-82 *There are many artificial methods of improving the productivity of trees; hard work can domesticate wild trees, and methods like layering, taking suckers and, above all, grafting, will produce fertile crops of fruit.*

47-82 In this passage Virgil elaborates the themes of lines 10-19 and 23-34, separating the two topics with lines summarising the theme of toil and its reward (61-2) which forms so prominent a part of the whole poem. He gives most space to the subject of grafting, ending with a brilliantly evocative picture of the tree marvelling at unfamiliar leaves and fruits not its own.

47 sponte sua: Virgil now elaborates the classification he made at 10f.; lines 47-52 correspond with 10-13; lines 53-56 with 17-19, and lines 57-60 with 14-16.

luminis oras: cf. Enn. *Ann.* 114; Lucr. 1.22; *Aen.* 7.660.

49 quippe ... subest: 'because nature is present in the soil beneath them', so that they flourish 'naturally' (although not fruitful).

49-51 'And yet these too, if any one engrafted them or transplanted them and moved them into well-worked trenches, will surely put off their wild personality'. The object of *inserere* can be either the tree which receives the graft or scion (as here, cf. 69) or the scion put into a tree (cf. 33). *Tamen* contrasts with *infecunda*; for *subigere*, cf. 1.125; Cato *Agr.* 161. For the general sense, cf. Lucr. 5.1367-9; and Shakespeare, *Winter's Tale*, 4.3.92f.

... You see, sweet maid, we marry
A gentler scion to the wildest stock,
And make conceive a bark of baser kind
By bud of nobler race: this is an art
Which does mend nature. ...

52 voces: so Servius and some later MSS; M has *voles*, which has been accepted by modern editors; but the construction of *vocare in* is idiomatic, while *sequentur in* would be strange. The personification of the trees as the object of *vocare* is wholly in keeping with Virgil's method of presentation (cf. *animum* in 51).

artis: i.e. 'they will learn whatever lessons you choose to teach' (Conington).

54 hoc faciat: i.e. the sucker which would otherwise be barren would do the same (i.e. become fertile) if transplanted into more congenial surroundings than the shade of the mother tree.

55 nunc: 'as it is now', before you transplant it.

56 'and as it grows destroy its fruits, and parch its attempts to produce'.

57 iam: equivalent to *praeterea*, 'the next point is'; cf. 1.383. This section corresponds with 14-16, dealing with self-seeded trees like oaks and chestnuts, with the addition (59-60) of apples (or perhaps fruit-trees generally) and vines.

59 sucos ... priores: 'forgetting their old flavours', if left to themselves; for the personification, cf. especially 82. The accusative after *oblita* is not uncommon (cf. *Aen.* 2.148). It has been suggested that *sucos* is governed by *degenerant* (cf. Ov. *Met.* 7.543), but this seems less likely.

60 turpis ... racemos: i.e. the bunches are not worth picking and may as well be left to the birds; for the unsatisfactory practice of growing grapes from seed, cf. Pliny *NH* 17.59.

61 Virgil here summarises the uselessness of leaving it all to nature: *labor* (the key theme of the *Georgics*) is necessary for success. The line is made highly emphatic by the rhythm with the most unusual diaeresis after the second foot (as well as the first and third), the heavy alliterative word *impendendus* and the pause after the trochee in the fifth foot.

omnes: i.e. *arbores* (57).

62 cogendae ... domandae: again an element of personification, cf. *respondent* (64).

mercede: 'cost', the price you pay.

63f. These lines resume in different order the theme of 23f.; for *truncis* cf. 30-31; for *propagine* 26-7; for *solido robore* 25; for *plantis* 23; for *inseritur* 33. The cuttings from tree-tops (28-9) are here omitted.

63 truncis: 'chunks' of wood, 'truncheons', taken from the stock; cf. 30-31.

64 solido ... myrtus: 'Paphian myrtles better from solid wood'; *de robore (respondent)* is a variation on the ablatives used previously (*truncis, propagine*). The town of Paphos in Cyprus was especially connected with Venus, whose sacred tree was the myrtle (1.28).

65 edurae: 'very hardy'; the better MSS have *et durae*, but cf. 4.145.

nascuntur: 'spring from seed', cf. 68. The correct punctuation of this line was given by Phillimore (*CR* 1913, p. 22); previously (and sometimes since) the stop before *nascuntur* was omitted, giving a

statement about propagation from cuttings which could not reasonably be true in the case of ash or oak.

66 The tree which Hercules wore as a crown was the poplar; see note on *Ecl.* 7.61.

67 Chaoniique: Chaonia was the area of Greece in which the sacred oaks of Jupiter were situated; see note on 15-16.

68 abies: fir was commonly used for ship's timbers; cf. *Aen.* 9.85f.

69-82 The last of the methods of propagation (grafting, cf. 32-4) is given much fuller treatment: the instances given of what can be grafted are not in accordance with modern scientific methods.

69 'but the wild arbute is engrafted with the wood of a nut-tree'; for the arbute, see note on 1.148. For the hypermetric elision of *horrida,* see note on 1.295.

71 castaneas fagus: 'the beech bears chestnuts'; this is Scaliger's emendation of the manuscript reading *castaneae fagos (fagus* Priscian). The passage has been much discussed; Servius rightly says that *castaneae fagos* makes no sense, because the chestnut (it is the sweet chestnut) is fertile and the beech is much less so (even allowing that pigs eat beech nuts), and all the other items in this list deal with the engrafting of wood from fertile trees upon unfertile ones. To this it may be added that *fagos* ('beech trees'; *fagum* is the word for beech nut) is not a good parallel with the fruits referred to in *nucis, malos, piri, glandem.* Some modern editors place a stop after *valentis* and run on the words of the next line so that the meaning is 'the beech and the ash grow white with the pale flower of the chestnut and the pear'; but this destroys the balance of the sentence and is very inelegant.

fagus: if this reading is correct the last syllable is lengthened in arsis (see note on *Ecl.* 1.38) or else is a rare fourth declension form of the nominative plural (cf. *Culex* 141).

73 'Nor is the method of engrafting and inserting buds a uniform one': Virgil gives two different methods, 74-7 and 78-80. For the infinitive after *modus,* cf. the use after *tempus* in 1.213.

74 gemmae: 'buds', a synonym of *oculi* (73) and (in this context) of *germen* (76).

75-6 angustus ... sinus: 'a narrow slit is made in the actual knot'; i.e. on the tree which is to receive this kind of graft it is important to select a place where there is a knot and a bud.

77 **docent:** again a personification; cf. 52, 59.

78 **enodes:** 'without knots', in contrast with 76.

80 **plantae:** the same as *germen* (76); this method differs from the previous one in that the receiving tree has no knots and therefore is cut more deeply to receive the graft.

81 **felicibus:** 'fruitful'; cf. 188.

82 This line is a memorable example of Virgil's personification of the trees; cf. 59 and 1.103. Servius calls it *ingens phantasia.*

83-108 *There are many different varieties of trees, especially of vines.*

83-108 This section is largely taken up with a catalogue of wines in which Virgil selects a few: Pliny (*NH* 14.150) says there are 185 varieties, while Columella (3.2) gives a list of 58. Virgil has aimed at enlivening his catalogue with a touch of humour (94), with rhetorical apostrophe (95-6; 101-2), with personification (98) and finally a gesture of despair at the impossible task of enumerating them all (103-8).

83 **genus haud unum:** *i.e.* elms have different varieties, as have willows, cypresses, olives, etc.

84 The rhythm is unusual, with absence of main caesura in third or fourth foot, and a quadrisyllabic ending.

lotoque: the fabulous lotus (Hom. *Od.* 9.84) gave its name to other trees (as here, the *Celtis Australis*) and plants (3.394).

Idaeis: the geographical epithet adds to the pictorial impact; for the association of cypresses with Mt Ida in Crete, cf. Pliny *NH* 16.141.

86 'nor orchades nor radii nor pausia with its bitter berry'; all three of these are types of olive (Cato, *Agr.* 6, gives eight kinds). *Orchades* scans as a dactyl with the final short syllable of the Greek declension (cf. *Mareotides,* 91), there is hiatus at the caesura: see note on *Ecl.* 3.6.

87 The orchards of Alcinous, king of the Phaeacians, were famous from Homer (*Od.* 7.112f.).

surculus: in a general sense, 'plant'.

88 **Crustumiis ... piris:** 'in the case of Crustumerian pears and Syrian pears and the heavy volema'; the volema was a large type of pear. Crustumium was a Sabine town, and Syrian pears were said to be second best to these (Pliny *NH* 15.53).

90 Methymna was a city on the island

of Lesbos famous for its wine (Ov. *AA* 1.57).

91 Thasos is another island in the Aegean; Mareotic wine came from Egypt (Hor. *Odes* 1.37.14).

93 **passo psithia utilior:** 'the psithia more useful for raisin wine'; cf. 4.269; Juv. 14.271.

tenuisque lageos: 'the light lageos', as opposed to 'heavy' wine, *vinum crassum* (Hor. *Sat.* 2.4.52). *Lageos* is a Greek type of wine (here in a Greek nominative form), cf. Pliny *NH* 14.39. Servius says that *tenuis* means *penetrabilis,* an idea conveyed in the next line.

94 Compare Philips, *Cyder* 1.64-6 'Thy press with purest juice Shall flow, which in revolving years may try Thy feeble feet, and bind thy faltering tongue'; and Thomson, *Seasons, Autumn* 535f., including the fine phrase 'pavement faithless to the fuddled foot'.

olim: 'one day'; cf. 190, *Ecl.* 10.34; *Aen.* 1.203.

95 **purpureae preciaeque:** both types are mentioned by Pliny, *NH* 14.29.

96 **Rhaetica:** from northern Italy; Servius says that it was praised by Cato but disliked by Catullus.

Falernis: Falernian wine from Campania was one of the most famous Italian wines; cf. Hor. *Odes* 1.27.10; Pliny *NH* 14.62f.

97 **Amnineae:** a white wine of Campania; cf. Pliny *NH* 14.21.

98-9 'to which Tmolian wine and the Phaenaean king itself rise in respect, and also the lesser Argite wine'. The masculine adjective *Tmolius* is influenced by Greek (the word for wine, οἶνος, is masculine). Tmolus (1.56) was a mountain in Lydia; Phanae a port in Chios famed for its wine which is here called *rex,* the king of wines. *Argitis* was a type of white wine (some types were divided into *maior* and *minor*).

101 **dis ... secundis:** 'acceptable to the gods during the second course'; libations were poured to the gods at the *mensae secundae,* dessert stage of the meal.

102 **Rhodia ... bumaste:** *bumastus* (feminine) was a type of large-size grape from Rhodes.

104 **enim:** 'indeed', an archaic use of the word; cf. 509; *Aen.* 1.19.

refert: 'is it worthwhile', impersonal (like *interest*).

105 **aequoris:** 'plain', 'desert' (cf. 1.50), rather than 'sea'.

108 **Ionii:** the storm is located in the Ionian sea to make the picture more

specific; cf. 84.

109-35 *Just as different trees grow better in different localities, so different countries have their own special products.*

109-35 This brief introductory section to the famous passage in praise of Italy (136f.) is based on Theophrastus (*HP* 4.4.2f.) and Varro (*RR* 1.6f.). Virgil has aimed to convey the variety of nature's gifts, especially by the use of remote geographical names, in order to form an antithesis to the unique characteristics of Italy.

109 This very simple statement serves to introduce the theme of varying conditions for various trees, then the theme of different countries, and finally (136f.) the special virtues of Italy.

113 **Bacchus:** i.e. the vine or the grape, as often (cf. 37; 191).

114 **aspice:** with the personal exhortation (cf. 118 *tibi*) Virgil raises the tone for his geographical excursus about the marvels of distant lands.

115 **Gelonos:** Scythians; cf. 3.461.

116 **divisae . . . patriae:** 'countries are distinguished by their trees'.

116-17 India was the special (though not exclusive) home of ebony: cf. Theophr. *HP* 4.4.6; Pliny *NH* 12.17; and Arabia (*Sabaea*) of incense: cf. 1.57.

118-19 'Why should I tell you of the balsam dripping from its fragrant bark and the berries of the evergreen acanthus?'. In line 119 -*que et* means 'both . . . and'; cf. 436. Both these trees are associated with the East in general, and perhaps Arabia in particular.

120 **molli . . . lana:** i.e. cotton; cf. Pliny *NH* 19.13.

121 The Seres (in the far east) were said to produce their silk from trees, a misconception reiterated by Pliny (*NH* 6.54).

tenuia: the word scans as a dactyl, the *u* being treated as a consonant; cf. 180 and 1.397.

122 'or the groves which India produces, nearer the Ocean'; the line is the object of *referam* (118). Ocean is thought of as encompassing the world (Cat. 64.30), with India near the eastern limit.

123 The unusual rhythm (no main caesura in third or fourth foot) emphasises the strangeness of distant lands.

sinus: here a projecting curve of land;

cf. Tac. *Ann.* 4.5.

123-4 **aera . . . arboris:** 'the air around the treetops', i.e. no arrow can be shot as high as the trees (Pliny *NH* 7.21). Dryden (*Palamon and Arcite*, 3.953-4) has 'So lofty was the pile, a Parthian bow, With vigour drawn, must send the shaft below'.

125 The reference is to the fame of Parthian archers; cf. 4.314.

126 **tristis . . . tardumque:** 'bitter . . . lingering'.

127 **felicis mali:** apparently a type of citron, with healing powers as an antidote to poison.

praesentius: 'more immediate in action'; cf. *Ecl.* 1.41.

128 Stepmothers were proverbially cruel; cf. 3.282; *Ecl.* 3.33.

129 This line occurs in 3.283, and is probably spurious here (it is omitted by the original hand of M).

131 **faciem:** Greek accusative of respect; see note on *Ecl.* 1.54. In the *Georgics*, cf. 3.58; 84; 421; 427; 4.99; 181; 357; 371.

132-3 'were it not that it scatters far and wide a quite different smell, it would be a laurel'. The use of *erat* in the apodosis instead of *esset* gives a rhetorical touch indicating how very nearly it is a laurel; cf. Ov. *Am.* 1.6.34.

134 **ad prima:** 'maxime', Servius.

134-5 'The Persians doctor bad breath and malodorous mouths with it, and use it as medicine for asthmatic old men'; for this use of *fovere*, cf. 4.230. The deponent form of *medicare* is rare, cf. *Aen.* 7.756. Cf. Philips, *Cyder* 2.206-7 'balsamic cups to wheezing lungs medicinal, and short-breath'd ancient sires'.

136-76 *No other land can compare with Italy: it is free of the dangers found elsewhere, it is beautiful and fertile and can be rightly proud of its peoples and heroes.*

136-76 This famous passage in praise of Italy is central to the theme of the *Georgics* and at the same time looks forward to the proud imperial note of the *Aeneid;* cf. especially 6.756f. (see note on 2.174); 8.626f.; and the catalogue of Italians in 7.641f. It was perhaps partly inspired by Varro (*RR* 1.2.3f.), and it has typical features of a rhetorical panegyric (e.g. in the large number of repetitions, and in the interplay between negative and positive, the undesirable things which Italy is free from and the desirable

things which she has); but the details are
Virgil's own. Much of the imagery is
based on the contrast between the
exotic and the familiar, while the landscape
of Italy serves as a context for Italian
religion (146f.) and history (161f.; 167f.).
Compare the imitation by Propertius (3.22)
and for a detailed comparison of the two
passages see G. Williams, *Tradition and
Originality in Roman Poetry*, pp. 417f.;
cf. also Soph. *OC* 668f. and the end of
Pliny's *Natural History*, 37.201f. There is
a most sympathetic analysis by A. G.
McKay, *Studies in Honour of Harold
Hunt*, 1972, pp. 169f.

136 Medorum: picking up the last
sentence of the previous section (134);
ditissima terra is in apposition to *silvae*.
Others punctuate so that *silvae* is genitive
after *ditissima*.

137 Hermus: a river in Lydia; cf.
Aen. 7.721; its tributary Pactolus was
famous in legend as the golden river.

139 Notice this very patterned line
reinforced with marked alliteration to
round off the list of distant and exotic
places: Panchaia was a half-mythical
island near Arabia; cf. 4.379.

140-42 Virgil refers to the mythical
story of Jason's search for the Golden
Fleece. In Colchis he had to yoke the
fire-breathing bulls, sow the dragon's teeth
and kill the armed warriors who sprang
up from the sown teeth (Ap. Rhod.
3.1278f.).

142 seges: the metaphor from bristling
corn is used again in *Aen.* 3.46; 7.526;
12.663.

143 Massicus umor: a Campanian wine;
cf. 3.526; Pliny *NH* 3.60.

144 implevere: the verb, which indicates
abundance, the key-note of this passage,
is emphasised by the unusual trochaic
pause in the second foot. The idea of
abundance is picked up again by *laeta*
at the line-end. Notice the hiatus at the
pause between *oleae* and *armenta*.

145 'From here comes the warhorse
prancing proudly over the plain'; *arduus*
indicates the high neck of the spirited horse.

146 Clitumne: a river in Umbria with
a cult of Jupiter at its source; cf. Prop.
2.19.25; Pliny *Ep.* 8.8; Macaulay,
Horatius 7 '*Unwatched along Clitumnus/
Grazes the milk-white steer*'; Wordsworth,
Prelude 8:

Smooth life had herdsman, and his snow-
white herd

To triumphs and to sacrificial rites
Devoted, on the inviolable stream
Of rich Clitumnus.

149 alienis . . . aestas: 'summer in
months not its own', i.e. extending
beyond the normal summer season.

150 Cf. Varro *RR* 1.7.6 for two crops
a year.

151f. Compare the description of the
Golden Age in *Ecl.* 4.21f.

152 semina: 'generations', 'brood', a
Lucretian expression; cf. Lucr. 3.741f.
aconita: 'deadly nightshade'; cf. *Ecl.*
4.24.

153-4 'nor does the scaly snake coil
itself into a spiral with so mighty a
movement'; cf. 3.416f. The rhythm in
line 153 is imitative of the sense, with the
dislocation between word accent and
ictus in the fifth foot; cf. *Aen.* 5.274
(also of a snake), with my note (Oxford
edition).

156 Italian hill-towns were and are a
feature of the landscape.

157 A famous line where the rhythm,
especially through the sonorous word
subterlabentia, conveys the sense of peace
and idyllic beauty.

158 supra . . . infra: i.e. the Adriatic
and the Tyrrhenian seas; cf. *Aen.* 8.149.

159-60 Lari . . . Benace: Larius is now
called Lake Como and Benacus Lake
Garda; Garda was a large lake from which
the river Mincius flowed (*Aen.* 10.205-6).
This was the area which Virgil knew from
his childhood.

161f. The Lucrine Lake, near Naples,
was in the area of Campania which Virgil
knew well in his later life. Virgil refers
to the military works carried out by
Agrippa in 37 BC when Lake Avernus
was joined by a canal with Lucrinus and a
breakwater built on the coast. In this
highly descriptive passage note the
personification (*indignatum*) and the slow
movement of 162, the *-on-* sounds in
163, the *s*'s in 164.

163-4 'where the Julian wave echoes
from afar where the sea is pushed back,
and the tide of the Tyrrhenian sea is let
in to the Avernian waters'. The wave is
Julian because Octavian Caesar (adopted
son of Julius Caesar) was the organiser of
the work; the complex was called Portus
Iulius. Cf. A. G. McKay, *Vergil's Italy*,
pp. 210f.

165-6 Pliny (*NH* 37.202) refers with
enthusiasm to the production of all sorts
of precious metals in Italy.

167 **genus acre:** cf. *Aen.* 9.603 *durum a stirpe genus.*

Marsos pubemque Sabellam: for the Marsi as great Italian warriors, cf. Hor. *Odes,* 3.5.9; *pubes Sabella* refers to the Sabines, a race associated with the Romans from earliest times: cf. 532; Hor. *Epod.* 2.41-2; *Odes* 3.6.37f.

168 **Ligurem Volscosque:** these were peoples who figured largely in Rome's early history; cf. Livy 2.22f. For *verutos,* 'armed with darts', cf. *Aen.* 7.665.

169 The list of famous Roman families is taken up again more fully in the pageant of Roman heroes at the end of *Aen.* 6 and the pictures on Aeneas' shield at the end of *Aen.* 8. For the Decii, cf. *Aen.* 6. 824; for Camillus, cf. *Aen.* 6.825; *Marii* (Gaius Marius, the conqueror of Jugurtha) and Camilli seem to be generalised plurals.

170 **Scipiadas:** cf. *Aen.* 6.843; Scipio Africanus the elder won the battle of Zama against the Carthaginians, ending the Second Punic War; Scipio the younger (Aemilianus) finally destroyed Carthage in the Third Punic War.

Caesar: Octavian Caesar, at this time waging successful warfare against the Eastern peoples (cf. 4.561; *Aen.* 8.685f.); this is probably one of the latest passages of the *Georgics,* perhaps dating to 30 BC, after the battle of Actium.

172 This is a patterned line to conclude the preliminaries to the great invocation which follows, a famous passage imitated by Thomson, *Liberty* 5.81f., *Seasons, Summer* 1442f.; compare the even more famous passage in Shakespeare, *Richard II,* 2.1.40f. 'This royal throne of kings, this scepter'd isle. . .'.

173 **salve:** the spondaic word following the first foot gives an impressiveness of movement; cf. *Aen.* 5.80, 8.301.

Saturnia tellus: *Saturnia* is one of the most evocative epithets for Italy, recalling the mythical golden age under Saturnus: cf. *Ecl.* 4.6.; *Geo.* 1.125f.; 2.538f.; *Aen.* 6.792f.; 8.319f.; Varro *RR* 3.1.5; Hes. *WD* 111f.

174 **magna virum:** the concept of Italy as mother of heroes is elaborated in *Aen.* 6.784f. *felix prole virum. . . .*

res . . . artis: 'a subject of ancient glory and skill'; P has *artem* which some modern editors follow, 'a subject and a skill of ancient glory'.

175 **fontis:** the imagery of poetic fountains recalls Lucr. 1.927f.

176 Again a patterned line to round

off the section; Hesiod of Ascra (in Boeotia) was Virgil's model for didactic poetry on agriculture (cf. Prop. 2.34.77). He was very greatly admired by the Alexandrian poets (see note on *Ecl.* 6.69-70).

177-225 *The nature of the soil should determine the type of crops grown, whether olives, vines, grass for grazing, or corn.*
177-225 Virgil turns from the highly poetic description of the previous section to a catalogue of technical details concerned with the potentialities of different kinds of soils. It is based on Theophrastus (*CP* 2.4); cf. Cato *Agr.* 6 and Varro *RR* 1.7 and 1.9. The catalogue is enlivened by the use of vivid terminology often amounting to personification (see note on 177), by the mention of specific places in Italy (Tarentum, Mantua, Capua, Vesuvius, Acerrae), by a quick glimpse of sympathy for bird-life (209-10) and, as so often in the *Georgics,* by a reference to religious ritual (192f.).

177 **Nunc . . . ingeniis:** 'Now is the place for speaking of the natural qualities of fields'; the phrase is elaborated in the next line, 'what is each one's nature for crop production' (cf. 9). There is some personification in the word *ingeniis,* as often in this section (179; 189; 215; 218; 223; etc.).

179 **maligni:** 'unfertile'; cf. Pliny *Ep.* 2.17.15.

180 **tenuis . . . argilla:** 'thin clay'; for the scansion of *tenuis,* see note on 121.

181 **Palladia . . . silva:** 'the Palladian growth'; for the connection of Pallas Athene with the olive, see note on 1.12-13.

vivacis: the olive is a long-lived tree; cf. Pliny *NH* 16.241.

182 **oleaster:** the wild olive, growing in profusion (*plurimus*) in this kind of soil; cf. 314; 4.20.

183 **silvestribus:** 'wild', 'uncultivated'; cf. 51.

184 **quae . . . humus:** i.e. *humus quae pinguis est:* cf. the next line *campus qui frequens est.* Notice the assonance of *i* in this line.

185 **frequens . . . ubere:** 'thickly covered with grass and fertile with rich soil'; for the noun *uber,* cf. 275.

188 **felicem:** 'fertile', as often of trees and crops; cf. 81.

editus Austro: 'rises from the south', i.e. has a south-facing slope.

189 Fern (*filix*), growing abundantly

in the rich soil described, would choke
the ploughshare with its abundant roots
and foliage. Notice the personification of
the plough which 'hates' the fern.

190 **olim:** 'one day'; cf. 94.

191 **uvae:** genitive of respect, commonest
with adjectives of fullness and the like,
e.g. 468 *dives opum;* Hor. *CS* 29 *fertilis
frugum.*

192 **laticis:** 'the liquid', i.e. wine; cf.
3; 519.

pateris ... et auro: hendiadys, 'in golden
dishes'; cf. 4.99. Notice again the association
of agriculture and religion.

193-4 'when the stout Etruscan has
blown his ivory pipe at the altars, and we
duly place the smoking entrails in wide
dishes'; for the playing of pipes in religious
ceremonies, cf. Pliny *NH* 16.172; Livy
9.30.5. Catullus (39.11) refers to the
obesity of Etruscans.

195 **studium ... tueri:** for this poetic
use of the infinitive, cf. 1.21; *Aen.* 2.10.

196 The damage done by goats to crops
is mentioned in Varro, *RR* 1.2.18; 2.3.7;
compare lines 378f.

197 **saturi ... Tarenti:** 'seek the distant
parts of rich Tarentum'; *petito* is the
emphatic form of the imperative; cf.
408-10. *longinqua* is used as a noun. For
the richness of the area of Tarentum in
southern Italy, cf. 4.126f.; Hor. *Odes*
2.6.10f.

198-9 The reference is to the land-
confiscations around Mantua; cf. *Ecl.*
9.27-9 where the swans on the river
Mincius (*herboso flumine*) are mentioned.
Notice the slow movement of these two
lines.

200 **derunt:** contracted for *deerunt;*
cf. 233.

202 **exigua ... nocte:** 'in the brief
night' of summer.

205 **aequore:** 'plain', a quite frequent
meaning; cf. 105.

207 'or one from which the angry
ploughman has cleared woodland'; he is
angry because of the waste of good ground.

208 **ignava:** 'untouched'.

209-10 Notice how the focus suddenly
shifts from the agricultural advantages of
clearing woodland to a sympathetic
comment on the disturbance to the bird
life; for the phraseology, cf. Lucr. 1.18, and
for the effect of the pause after *eruit*, see
note on 1.108-9.

211 **enituit:** partly metaphorical —
the soil looks splendid, cf. 1.153; but
partly literal, referring to the shine on

newly-ploughed soil (Pliny *NH* 17.37
post vomerem nitescens).

213 **roremque:** 'and rosemary', cf.
Pliny *NH* 24.101.

214 **tofus scaber:** 'rough volcanic stone'.

215-16 **negant alios ... ferre:** 'say that no
other fields produce'; the unfertile land
is presented as taking a pride in its snakes.

218 **cum vult:** again a personification
of the land.

221 For the elm-tree as a support for
the vine, cf. 1.2.

224 Capua was one of the richest towns
in Campania, no doubt known to Virgil
personally; similarly the area of Mt
Vesuvius south of Naples would be familiar
to him.

225 The river Clanius in Campania was
liable to overflow and flood the town of
Acerrae: cf. Sil. 8.535. There is a curious
story in Aulus Gellius (6.20), echoed by
Servius, that Virgil wrote *Nola* for *ora* and
subsequently changed it because of a dispute
with the people of Nola.

226-58 *How to test for different types
of soils.*

226-58 Servius' comment on this passage
is that the poetry is superb because it
contains so much repetition without
anything superfluous (*tantam habent sine
aliqua perissologia repetitionem*). Modern
opinion is more likely to regard the passage
as one of the less exciting parts of the
poem, where the didactic matter is too
direct and simple to arouse enthusiasm.

227 The word order is *si requires (utrum)
sit rara an supra morem densa.*

229 An explanation of the previous
line — heavy soil for corn and light for
vines. *Lyaeus* is an epithet of Bacchus;
cf. *Aen.* 4.58.

232 **harenas:** the soil is called 'sand' to
indicate that it is friable now it has been
dug; it is to be levelled by stamping.

233 **si derunt:** 'if the soil doesn't fill
the hole'; for the contracted form of
deerunt, cf. 200.

almis: because wine, like corn (cf. *alma
Ceres* 1.7) nourishes (*alere*).

234 **posse negabunt:** 'say that they
cannot'; for the personification, cf. 215.
For the omission of the reflexive subject of
posse, cf. *Ecl.* 3.24.

235 **superabit terra:** 'some soil is over';
for *superare,* 'to be in excess', cf. 1.189.

236 **glaebas ... terga:** 'stubborn soil
and thick clods'; *terga* gives an image of
the ridges on ploughed land; cf. 1.97.

238 **quae perhibetur amara:** 'for which

the term is 'bitter' '; our term would probably be 'salt' (*salsa*).

239 mansuescit: 'lose its contamination', i.e. become less salt.

240 'and does not maintain the stock of the vine or the individual quality of apples', i.e. trees degenerate in salty soil. For the technical use of *nomen*, cf. Cato *Agr.* 25 *ne vinum nomen perdat.*

241-2 spisso . . . prelorum: 'baskets of thick wickerwork and the strainers of the wine-presses', i.e. containers that would let liquid through (244). These would be stored in smoky buildings for seasoning and better preservation; cf. 1.175.

246-7 'and will pucker the wry faces of the tasters with a bitter flavour'; line 247 has vividly-coloured diction accentuated by the alliteration of *t*. *Amaro* is the reading of the best MSS, but many modern editors read *amaror* ('bitterness'; cf. Lucr. 4.224), which Gellius (1.21) reports as having been read by Hyginus, and Servius prefers it. But the phrase reads much more elegantly if *sensu* has a qualifier; cf. Lucr. 2.401 (of wormwood and similar substances) *foedo pertorquent ora sapore.*

249 manibus iactata fatiscit: 'crumbles when handled'.

250 ad digitos . . . habendo: 'grows sticky to the fingers when held'.

258 quis cui color: 'what the colour is of each soil'; the double interrogative ('what . . . to which') is idiomatic in Latin. Servius discusses the alternative readings, *quisquis color* or *quis cuique color. sceleratum . . .*

sceleratum . . . frigus: 'coldness' in soil would presumably be caused by a combination of aspect, drainage, and heavy consistency. *Sceleratum* is a vivid, rather colloquial usage.

257 nocentes: 'poisonous'; cf. *Ecl.* 9.30; *Geo.* 4.47. Compare 113 for the yew's fondness for cold situations.

258 hederae . . . nigrae: 'or black ivy reveals indications of it'; the epithet *nigrae* is used to differentiate it from white ivy (cf. *Ecl.* 7.38).

259-87 *The preparation of a vineyard — the cultivation of the soil, the transplanting of cuttings, their spacing in regular rows.*

259-87 The didactic tone continues in this passage, much of which is based on Theophrastus. It is given poetic impetus by the simile (279f.), by the characteristic personification of the plants (268; 272; 277) and by an insistence on the need for man to work with Nature (263-4; cf. 204).

260 excoquere: 'expose to the sun'; cf. 1.66. The phrase is balanced in 261 (with repetition of *ante*) by reference to the beneficial effect of cold weather also on the up-turned soil, and both ideas are finally elaborated in 262f.

magnos . . . montis: 'to cut through great mountains with trenches', an exaggerated expression reinforced by alliteration. This idea is restated in 264.

265 Literally, 'but if there are any farmers whom no precautions escape'; i.e. farmers who take the utmost pains to prepare in advance.

266 ante: adverbial.

266-7 ubi prima . . . seges: 'where the first crop can be prepared for its trees'; *arboribus* refers to the trees which will support the vines.

267 et: the coordination is a little awkward, the meaning being that the one place and the other should be similar, but there is no need to accept Madvig's conjecture *ei.* Cf. Pliny *NH* 17.79.

quo mox digesta feratur: 'where it is shortly to be put when planted out'; the *prima seges* is a line of cuttings close together, which are later transplanted.

268 The personification here, of the cuttings (*semina;* cf. 302; 317; 354) perhaps not being able to recognise their mother (the earth), is very vivid; cf. 272.

269f. The shoots are marked so that they can be transplanted in the same relationship to the points of the compass as before; cf. Theophr. *HP* 2.5.3. Pliny (*NH* 17.83) denies the necessity for this, on the grounds that Cato did not mention it.

271 quae . . . axi: 'which side backed on to the north'; *axis* means the north pole; cf. 3.351; Lucr. 6.720.

272 adeo . . . multum est: 'so important is habit in the young'; notice the very strong correlation of plants with humans (as in 268).

273-4 The construction is *quaere prius (utrum) melius sit ponere vitem collibus an plano.* This decision is evidently to be based on the general requirements of the whole farm, or perhaps on the type of vine: Virgil goes on to say that if it is decided to plant the vines on level ground, then plant closely; if on hills, plant further apart. Cf. Theophr. *CP* 2.4.7.

275 densa: adverbial; cf. 3.500, and see note on *Ecl.* 3.8.

in denso . . . ubere: 'closely spaced in rich soil'; *densus* is rather curiously transferred from the vines to the soil. For *uber*, cf. 185; 234.

276 **supinos**: 'sloping'; cf. 3.555; Liv. 4.46.5.

277 **indulge**: 'indulge' in the sense of 'give plenty of room to', again a personification.

277-8 **nec setius . . . quadret**: 'and in just the same way, when the trees have been planted, every path must exactly make a right angle with the main way which it intersects'; *nec setius* means no less for the widely spaced trees than would be (more obviously) necessary for those spaced more closely. *Limites* are the main avenues of the field; *via* here refers to the path alongside the row which intersects with the main avenues. For *in unguem* (literally 'to the test of the fingernail', a metaphor from sculpture), cf. Hor. *AP* 294.

279f. The simile is based on a memorable passage in Lucretius (2.323f.); Virgil recalls Lucretius verbally (see note on 281-2), but has changed the image from the actual battle in Lucretius to the moment before battle. There is no need to see a specific reference to the Roman *quincunx* formation, although Varro (*RR* 1.7.2), Pliny (*NH* 17.78) and others recommend it for planting; the comparison is simply with the order and precision of straight lines. Notice how the majority of the descriptive phrases in this simile run on from one line into the next.

279-80 **longa . . . legio**: 'when the long legion has deployed its cohorts', i.e. its subdivisions.

280-81 The marching column (*agmen*) has halted and the battle-formations (*acies*) are then drawn up.

281-2 **late . . . tellus**: 'far and wide the whole land ripples with the flashing bronze'. For *fluctuat*, cf. Sen. *HF* 699 (of a corncrop); Lucretius (2.325) has *fulgor ubi ad caelum se tollit*. For *aere renidenti*, cf. Lucr. 2.325-6 *Totaque circum aere renidescit tellus* and Hom. *Il.* 20.362f. γέλασσε δὲ πᾶσα περὶ χθὼν χαλκοῦ ὑπὸ στεροπῆς.

283 **dubius . . . Mars**: i.e. the battle has not started and so the god of war has not yet decided which side to favour. The personification adds to the visual imagery of the simile as we picture the giant figure of the god towering over the battlefield.

284 **paribus numeris . . . viarum**: 'with matching symmetry of the paths'.

285 **animum . . . inanem**: 'an idle satisfaction'; i.e. it is not only for aesthetic pleasure, but for practical reasons.

288-314 *Vines can be planted in shallow trenches, but their supporting trees should be put in more deeply. Vineyards should not face west; hazels should not be used as supports; cuttings should be taken from low down, with a sharp knife; above all oleasters should not be used as supports, for fear of fire which would destroy the vines.*

288-314 As in the previous section Virgil gives a series of precepts enlivened by poetic description. He dwells much longer on his two descriptive passages than on the half-dozen pieces of practical instruction: the picture of the massive oaktree is superbly presented, and stayed in Virgil's mind for re-use in a crucial moment of *Aeneid* 4 (see note on 291-2); and the forest fire (for which no source is known) is a piece of rhetoric in the high style comparable with the storm description in 1.316f.

288 **fastigia**: 'depth'; the word much more often means 'height'; cf. the two corresponding meanings of *altus* (290).

290 **terrae** = *in terram*, a common poetic use of the dative.

291 **aesculus**: a kind of oak, see note on 15-16.

291-2 **quantum . . . tendit**: this line-and-a-half is repeated in *Aen.* 4.445-6 in a simile about Aeneas. The phrase *immota manet* (294) also occurs there (449) of Aeneas' purpose, immovable like an oak.

295 'outlives and sees many generations of men roll past while it endures'; as Page says, the tree is said to do what it sees done. For this usage of *volvere*, cf. Hor. *Odes* 4.6.40 *volvere menses* (of the moon rolling away the months). For the phrase, cf. Lucr. 1.202 *multaque vivendo vitalia vincere saecla*; Lucr. 3.948 *vivendo vincere saecla.* Notice the strong alliteration of *v* (as in the Lucretian passages), suggesting (as often) strength.

296 **tum**: in the sense of *denique*, marking a further stage in the narrative; cf. 3.357; *Aen.* 1.164.

298 Cf. 188, where a south-facing vineyard is recommended; Pliny (*NH* 17.19) and Columella (3.12.39) mention this Virgilian precept.

299 Servius explains that the roots of hazel are harmful to the vine; cf. Pliny *NH* 17.240.

299-301 'and do not seek the topmost

shoots or take cuttings from the tops of
trees — such is their love of the earth'.
Compare lines 28-9, where it is said that
with certain trees it is possible to take
cuttings from the top, with the implication
that this is not true of most trees. With
tantus amor terrae, cf. *nil radicis egent
aliae* (28).

302 **semina:** the word is used as a
synonym for *plantae* (cf. 268): cuttings
must not be taken with a blunt knife.

neve oleae ... truncos: the meaning of
this phrase (and consequently of 312-14,
where see note) is much disputed, but the
starting point surely must be that Virgil is
talking about vines, so that *insere* should
be taken as equivalent to *intersere* (cf. 299)
and the meaning is 'do not plant wild
trunks of olive among them (the vines)'.
Others render 'do not graft wild trees
with olive', but this has no connection
at all with what has gone before or with
what follows. Theophrastus (*CP* 3.10.6)
tells us that figs and olives are harmful to
vines, and elsewhere (*HP* 5.9.6) says that
these trees burn most easily.

303f. Virgil now enlivens the series of
didactic precepts with a highly rhetorical
account of a forest fire: the connection of
thought is the mention of the wild olive
tree which because of its oily bark (304) is
said to be especially combustible.

307 **victor ... regnat:** notice the
personification in both these words.

308-9 **et ruit ... nubem:** 'and it hurls a
cloud'; for this transitive use of *ruere*,
cf. 1.105. The conflict of ictus and accent
in the fifth foot helps to convey the
violence of the fire.

310 The rhythm is Lucretian (cf.
2.32 *praesertim cum tempestas ...*),
and unusual in Virgil.

311 **incubuit:** 'has swooped down', a
colourful word, a favourite with Virgil:
cf. 377; 3.197; *Aen.* 1.84.

glomeratque ... ventus: 'and the wind
carries and concentrates the fire'. Observe
the rapid dactyls and the alliteration of
-en-.

312 **hoc ubi:** supply, as Servius says,
contigerit.

312-14 The subject of *valent* must be the
vines: once burnt they do not recover when
the blackened wood is cut away. All that is
left of the vineyard is the wild olives (302)
which had been so ill-advisedly planted
among the vines. Some commentators take
oleae as the subject of *valent* (having
interpreted 302 as a warning against

grafting the cultivated olive on to
oleaster); this would fit well with 314, but
see note on 302.

315-45 *Do not plough in winter: spring
or autumn is the best time. Spring is the
season when all things blossom and
flourish.*

315-45 After a brief didactic sentence
or two (315-22) Virgil gives a description
of the glories of spring, one of the famous
poetic passages of this book. In it he often
recalls Lucretius (e.g. the opening
passage of Book 1; 1.250f.; 2.992f.;
5.783f.) and he translates his predecessor's
enthusiastic love of the season of birth
and growth into a memorable paean of
praise for the growing-season from a
farmer's point of view, showing how
Nature is ready to help the farmer's efforts.
One of the most famous poems on spring
and love is the *Pervigilium Veneris*, written
some centuries later:

*cras amet qui numquam amavit quique
    amavit cras amet:*
*ver novum, ver iam canorum, ver renatus
    orbis est;*
*vere concordant amores, vere nubunt
    alites,*
*et nemus comam resolvit de maritis
    imbribus. ...*

315-16 **nec ... persuadeat ... movere:**
for the poetic infinitive after *persuadere*,
see note on *Ecl.* 1.55.

315 **tam prudens ... auctor:** 'any
so-called expert'.

317-18 'and when you put in the
cuttings it does not allow the frozen root
to take in the soil'; *concretam* is quite
naturally transferred from the soil which is
frozen to the root which equally would
be frozen up. Some editors read *concretum*
with M, taking it as a noun — 'the frozen
state of the soil'. *Adfigere* is used
reflexively (= *adfigere se*); this is better
than supplying *semen* from *semine* as the
subject of the infinitive, with *radicem* as the
object. *Semen* is used here of the vine-
cutting; cf. 268; 302. Note that Virgil
has retained *iacere* in this context even
though *semen* does not have its usual
meaning of seed.

319-20 'The best time for planting
vineyards is when in the rosy spring that
white bird has arrived which long snakes
dread', i.e. the stork; cf. Philips, *Cyder*
1.375-6 'when the stork, sworn foe of
snakes, returns'; Pliny *NH* 10.62; Juv.
14.74.

321   **sub**: 'just before'; cf. 1.445.

rapidus Sol: the monosyllabic ending, with the juxtaposition of -s and s- gives an archaic lilt to the line; see note on 1.181.

322   **nondum . . . equis**: 'has not yet reached winter as he drives through the sky'; the sun has a chariot drawn by horses (cf. *Aen*. 5.739) which moves both through the days and through the seasons.

323f.   Virgil introduces this idyllic poetic description with a favourite device of diction, three parallel clauses introduced with repetition (*ver . . . ver . . . vere*); cf. 368-9. Cf. Spenser, *FQ* 4.10.45 'Then doth the daedale earth . . .'.

324   The personification of Mother Earth (*tument, genitalia semina*) is taken up and elaborated in 326f. and 330f. Cf. the famous passage at the beginning of Lucretius 1; and for *genitalia semina*, cf. Lucr. 1.58 *genitalia corpora* ('creative bodies').

325   The fertilisation of Mother Earth by rain from heaven is a concept often found in ancient literature, cf. *Ecl*. 7.60; Lucr. 1.250f.; 2.992f.

326-7   'and in his mightiness nourishes all newborn things as he unites with her mighty frame'; cf. *Aen*. 6.727. The repetition of *magnus* and the alliteration of *m* conveys the impressiveness of the powers of nature.

328   The pattern of *a* and *v* sounds helps to draw attention to this descriptive line, for which cf. Lucr. 2.344f.

329   **Venerem**: 'love'; cf. 3.97; Lucr. 5.737. *Certis diebus* refers to the in-season period of the females.

330-31   **parturit . . . sinus**: 'the nourishing field brings forth increase and under the warm breezes of the west wind the lands open their bosoms'; the metaphors from childbirth are very evident (cf. Pliny *NH* 16.94). For *parturit*, cf. *Ecl*. 3.56; for *sinus*, cf. Ov. *Her*. 1.45. For *tepentibus* (M), PR have *trementibus*.

332   **germina**: the best MSS read *gramina*, but Servius cites Celsus as attesting *germina*, and it is clearly *le mot juste*.

336f.   For the idea of perpetual spring when the world was born, cf. Lucr. 5.780f.

340   **lucem . . . hausere**: 'breathed the light of day', an extended use of *haurire* (= drink in).

340-41   **virumque terrea progenies**: 'an earth-born race of men', with reference to the story of Deucalion and Pyrrha populating the world after the flood with stones from which humans sprang up;

cf. 1.62f.; Ov. *Met*. 1.313f. Most MSS have *ferrea*, but Lactantius (*Inst*. 2.10.16) reads *terrea* and an explanation in Servius points to it; it is clearly the right reading. Cf. 1.63; Lucr. 5.925f. (*humanum genus*) *tellus quod dura creasset*; 5.1411 *silvestre genus . . . terrigenarum*.

342   Ovid relates how stars first appeared in the sky, popping out all over the heavens (*Met*. 1.71f.).

343   **hunc . . . laborem**: 'the trials they have to endure', i.e. extremes of heat and cold.

344-5   **frigusque caloremque inter**: the preposition is postponed; -*que . . . -que* means 'both . . . and'. The second -*que* is elided hypermetrically; cf. 443 and see note on 1.295.

345   **exciperet**: 'take over, embrace'; cf. Lucr. 5.829.

346-70   *You must attend to providing manure and drainage for the vine-shoots; see that they are hoed and properly supported; prune them when they are ready, but not before.*

346-70   Much of this passage, concerned with precepts, is based on Theophrastus (e.g. *CP* 3.7.3); it is enlivened by personification (350; 362-3; 369), and closes with the military metaphor of struggle which figures so frequently in the *Georgics* (note on 369-70).

346   **premes**: 'plant', with the idea of firming-in; cf. 4.131.

348   Virgil here prescribes the use of stones or shells for drainage: *bibulum* does not necessarily mean that the individual stones are porous, only that a mass of stones is porous.

squalentis: 'jagged'. Virgil is fond of this word; cf. 4.13; 4.91.

349-50   **tenuisque subibit halitus**: 'a thin passage of air will enter'.

350   **animos tollent sata**: 'the crops will be cheered', a very marked personification.

iamque reperti: 'nowadays people have been known to . . .'.

351f.   The reference is to covering the young shoots with stones or pots to protect them against heavy rain or extreme drought.

353   'this is a protection when the dog-star of summer cracks the gaping earth with drought'; cf. Cat. 68.62 *Aestifer* is a rare poetic word, used by Lucretius (1.663; 5.613). *Canis* is the dog-star (Sirius) associated with the 'dog-days' of July; cf. 1.218.

354   **seminibus**: 'cuttings'; cf. 268.

355 capita: 'stems'; cf. Cato *Agr.*
33.3 *circum capita addito stercus.* The soil
is drawn up to the plants to help to
stabilise them.

355-7 Hoeing, or alternatively
ploughing, between the rows has the
effect of aerating the soil by 'working'
it (*exercere*) and of keeping down weeds.

358-60 These canes and poles, and
stakes and pronged props, are to act as
supports to lead the vines to the trees up
which they finally climb (367); cf. Varro
RR 1.8.2. Servius suggests that these were
peeled and trimmed to prevent contamination of the vines by disease.

361 tabulata: literally 'stories', i.e. the
lower, middle, and upper branches of the
elm, especially those stretching out more or
less horizontally. The elm would be
pruned so that its branches would produce
an appropriate climbing-frame for the
vines.

362-3 Notice once more the personification
of the young plants (*adolescit . . . teneris*);
as Wilkinson says, 'It might almost be
Quintilian speaking'.

364 laxis . . . habenis: 'at full gallop',
a metaphor from horseriding; cf. Lucr.
5.787; *Aen.* 6.1.

per purum: 'through the air'; cf. Hor.
Odes 1. 34.7.

365-6 ipsa . . . legendae: 'the vine itself
must not yet be touched by the blade of a
sickle, but you must pick off the leaves
with your fingers and thin them out'. *Inter*
may be taken adverbially, or as the prefix
separated from the compound verb
interlegere by tmesis. For the subject-
matter, cf. Cato *Agr.* 33. Some MSS read
acies, 'the blade of the sickle must not be
employed', but this gives a much weakened
force to *ipsa.*

368 exierint: 'they have got away',
i.e. established themselves and shot up from
their roots, cf. 81.

comas . . . bracchia: for this
personification, cf. *Aen.* 12.209. It is
anticipated by *laetus* (363) and continues
with *reformidant* (369) and *compesce* (370).

369-70 dura exerce imperia: 'apply stern
control'; the military metaphor (cf.
1.99; 104-5) is emphatic and a rounding-off
effect is given by the triple structure (with
repetition of *tum*) of the final sentence in
the paragraph. Cowper (*Task* 3.413) has
'discipline the shoots'.

371-96 *It is necessary to guard the
vines against cattle and goats; goats have a*
particularly poisonous bite, and that is
*why goats are sacrificed at the festivals
to Bacchus.*

371-96 In this brief section about the
dangers to vines from cattle and goats
Virgil takes the opportunity to introduce
a description of religious ritual in honour
of Bacchus. We may compare the account
of the festival of Ceres (1.338f.); it is a
feature of the *Georgics* that wherever
possible Virgil links rural activities with
the worship of rural gods. The part played
by the goat in Bacchus' festival enables
the poet to allude to the far-distant
origins of two of the great literary genres,
tragedy and comedy (see notes on 381;
382; 385f.).

373-5 'because in addition to the cruel
winters and the power of the sun, wild
oxen and persistent goats perpetually
threaten it'; *cui* refers to the vine foliage
(*frons,* 372); for *uri* cf. 3.532; for
inludere ('enjoy themselves on it'), cf.
1.181.

376-8 nec tantum . . . quantum: 'nor
does (cold or heat harm) as much as
(animals)'; this is an elaboration of 373
(cold and heat) and 374-5 (animals).

378 The poisonous bites refer more
particularly to goats than to the other
animals mentioned in 374-5; cf. Varro
RR 1.2.18f., where he says that goats are
sacrificed to Bacchus in vengeance for their
poisonous effects on vines, and Ov. *Fast.*
1.353f.; Hor. *Odes* 3.8.7; Dryden *Pal. and
Arc.* 2.60 'Nor goats with venomed teeth
thy tendrils bite'.

379 admorso: 'gnawed'; the MSS vary
here, and some editors read *admorsu*
('by their bite').

380 non aliam ob culpam: the mention of
goats gives Virgil an opportunity to refer
to aspects of rural religion (festivals of
the countryside such as the Paganalia and
Compitalia; see note on 371-96).

381 veteres . . . ludi: 'the traditional
performance goes on the stage'; the
origins of tragedy in Greece (beginning
from a 'goat-song', τράγος, ὠδή) are here
suggested. Cf. Hor. *AP* 220. '

382 pagos et compita circum: 'around
the villages and crossroads'; there is here
a reference to comedy and its supposed
derivation from κώμη, the Greek word for
a village; cf. Hor. *Epist.* 1.1.49.

383 Thesidae: the Athenians, descendants
of Theseus.

384 unctos . . . utres: i.e. goatskins.
385f. The reference here seems to be

to the Fescennine verses (cf. Hor. *Epist.* 2.1.145; Livy 7.2), and perhaps to the Liberalia (a festival in honour of Bacchus, cf. Ov. *Fast.* 3.713f). The point of *Troia gens missa* (the theme of the *Aeneid*) is that the previous festival (380-84) was derived from Greece; this one however is more indigenous (*Ausonii* is a poetic word for Italians, frequently used in the *Aeneid*).

387 The masks (made of bark) were said by Horace (*AP* 278-9) to originate from Aeschylus.

389 oscilla: 'little faces', i.e. effigies; *mollia* probably means 'made of soft material', but may have an undertone of 'genial'.

390 hinc: because of the festivals, because we show proper religious deference.

392 caput egit honestum: 'shows his venerable face'. The word *honestus* basically means 'worthy of honour'.

393-6 Notice the series of short clauses with main verbs, often used by Virgil to describe the stages of action in a religious ritual (e.g. *Aen.* 5.101-3).

394 lancesque et liba: 'bowls and cakes', ritual items at sacrifices.

396 colurnis: Servius says that hazel was used because it, like the goat, was harmful to the vine (299). The section is rounded off with a golden line.

397-419 *The farmer must constantly hoe and prune his vines; the work is never finished.*

397-419 After the digression on religious ceremonies in honour of Bacchus, Virgil gives a few last precepts on the culture of the vine, stressing the need for constant work (400) and the advantage of not taking on more than can be coped with (412-13). The moment of completion is described (416-17), but immediately modified by a warning that more hoeing is still desirable and the weather may still pose problems.

397 alter: besides the establishment of a new vineyard, with which Virgil has been mostly concerned, there is the other task of attending to established vineyards by hoeing and pruning.

398 cui numquam exhausti satis est: 'on which the effort expended is never enough'; *exhausti* is used as a noun ('enough of toil achieved'; Servius says *finitionis*); cf. 3.348.

400 The absence of main caesura in third or fourth foot helps to convey the unceasing nature of the toil; this is reinforced by the

repetition of *omne* from 398 in the same position of the line. *Aeternum* is adverbial accusative; cf. *Aen.* 6.401.

401-2 Cf. Thomson, *Seasons, Autumn* 1233-4: 'their annual toil begins again the never-ceasing round'; Cowper, *Task* 3.624f. 'reiterated as the wheel of time runs round'.

402 'and the year revolves again upon itself in the same tracks'; the alliteration of *s* and *v* emphasises this line, as does the unusual rhythm (with barely a trace of caesura in the third foot and none in the fourth).

403-5 ac iam olim . . . iam tum: the tautology here puts tremendous emphasis on the need for immediate action; *olim* (like *dudum* in this sense) suggests that the time is almost gone past, however prompt the farmer is.

404 'and the cold north wind shakes their glory from the woods'; the foliage is the 'glory' of the woods — for this use of *honos*, cf. Hor. *Odes* 1.17.16; *Epod.* 11.6.

406 The curved tooth of Saturnus is the sickle; cf. Ov. *Ibis* 216; Juv. 13.39 *Relictam* means neglected.

408-10 The series of imperatives in the emphatic form (*fodito* rather than *fode*) continues the strong didactic tone.

409 vallos: Varro (*RR* 1.8.6) recommends that the vine-poles should be taken in and stored during the winter.

410-12 bis . . . bis . . . uterque: the two tasks (pruning and clearing rank undergrowth) have each to be undertaken twice a year.

411 segetem: the grape crop.

412-13 laudato . . . colito: these two phrases are adapted from Hesiod, *WD* 643, 'praise a small ship, but put your wares in a large one'. Servius comments that Cato advised his son to have a small farm.

413 rusci: a kind of broom; its shoots, like reeds and the osiers of the wild willow, could be used for tying up the vines (416 *iam vinctae vites*). There is some doubt about the spelling of the word — most MSS have *rusti,* but the scholiasts support *rusci.*

416 falcem . . . reponunt: 'the bushes have done with the sickle', an unusual expression.

417 canit effectos . . . antes: 'proclaims in song that the rows are finished': *antes* is a very rare word indeed, perhaps a military term.

418 Virgil returns to the theme of 399-400 — *aeternum frangenda bidentibus.*

419 Iuppiter: in the sense of 'weather';

cf. 325; 1.418; *Aen.* 9.670 *Iuppiter horridus Austris.*

420-57 *Olives need no special attention once they are established; fruit-trees too look after themselves. Various trees naturally provide products useful to man — wood for night-lights, pasture for cattle, timber for ships and wagons, and so on. Even the vine cannot compare with these — in fact Bacchus has on occasion caused drunken violence, as with the Centaurs and Lapiths.*

420-57 The very brief account of the olive (420-25) contrasts most sharply with the full attention which has been given to the vine throughout the book, and this is the more surprising in view of the proclamation in lines 2-3 that the subject of the book is vines, saplings and olives. The reason is that in this last passage before the peroration of the book (458f.) Virgil wishes to leave behind his series of precepts about the work which the farmer must do and to give a picture of Nature's unaided contributions to human welfare. The great theme of the whole work is the balance between the bounty of Nature and the toil of man; when Nature offers so much, surely we should be ready to work with her when necessary (433 *et dubitant homines serere atque impendere curam?*).

422 **aurasque tulerunt:** 'and endured the breezes', i.e. became sufficiently established not to be blown over (cf. 360).

423 **satis:** probably here 'sufficiently' rather than 'to the crops' as in 436.

424 **cum vomere:** 'with the plough's assistance', a repetition of *dente . . . unco.*

425 **hoc:** 'by this means', i.e. by ploughing.

placitam Paci: the olive was always associated with peace, being the symbol of a truce; cf. *Aen.* 11.101.

nutritor: imperative of the very rare deponent form of *nutrire.*

429 **nec minus interea:** 'and meanwhile just as much', i.e. all the other trees too grow naturally, like olives and fruit-trees.

430 **aviaria:** 'the homes of the birds', i.e. the woods and forests (cf. 209; Lucr. 1.18); there is no reference here to man-made aviaries.

431 **cytisi:** a leguminous plant with various species, some like clover; cf. *Ecl.* 1.78; 10.30; *Geo.* 3.394; but here clearly a sort of bush (allied to broom). Martyn (*ad loc.*) has an interesting botanical note; see also J. Sargeaunt, *Trees, Shrubs and Plants of Virgil,* p. 40.

432 An elaboration of the previous phrase; wood suitable for burning and providing light is available through Nature's gifts (cf. *Aen.* 7.13).

433 This sudden rhetorical question emphasises that if Nature provides so much free, should we not be all the more anxious to do our part in crop production? See note on 420-57.

434 **maiora:** 'larger themes' than willow and humble broom which he now mentions as being of use to the farmer.

435 **aut illae:** 'even they either . . .'.

436 **saepemque satis:** 'both fences for the crops'; *-que . . . et* is a less common form for *et . . . et* or *-que . . . -que;* cf. 119.

437f. From the generalised picture of Nature's bounty Virgil suddenly specifies particular places which it is a joy to see; cf. 37f; 486f. Cytorus was in Asia Minor (cf. Cat. 4.13 *Cytore buxifer*), Narycium in the Locrian area of Greece (*Aen.* 3.399), but the reference here may be to Locri in southern Italy. Pliny (*NH* 14.127) refers to this area as producing pitch (from pitch-pines, *piceae*).

437 **undantem:** 'shimmering with'; cf. 1.472. *fluctuare* is used in this way; cf. 281.

439 **obnoxia:** 'indebted', *debitricia* (Servius).

440 **steriles:** i.e. trees on the cold Caucasus mountains do not yield fruit, but they provide timber for man's use in all kinds of activities.

441 Virgil here uses metrical devices for descriptive purposes, heavy elisions in the first half of the line and strong alliteration in the second half; for *frangunturque feruntque* 'break and blast', cf. Ennius' line-ending (*Ann.* 405) *frangitque quatitque.*

442 **dant . . . fetus:** 'offer their various products'; cf. Spenser, *FQ* 1.1.8f.

443 Pine was a wood very frequently used in shipbuilding; cf. Theophr. *HP* 5.7; Cat. 64.1.

cupressosque: hypermetric elision, see note on 344.

444 **trivere:** 'men have shaped', (*tornavere*, Servius); the subject is indefinite.

tympana: 'drums', i.e. solid wheels, as opposed to *rotae* with spokes (*radii*), cf. Lucr. 4.905.

445 **agricolae:** probably genitive dependent on *plaustris;* if it were nominative, an awkward switch to an indefinite subject for *posuere* would be required.

446 Cf. 434; the osiers are useful for fences or basketmaking and the like; the leaves of the elm could be used as fodder (Cato *Agr.* 6.3; Varro *RR* 1.24.3).

447-8 'but the myrtle and the cornel valuable in war are fertile in strong branches'; these were used for spear-shafts; cf. *Aen.* 3.23; 9.698. 12.267.

448 Bows are given the epithet 'Iturean' from an area of Asia Minor famous for archery; cf. Luc. 7.230. Servius identifies the Itureans with the Parthians.

451 **undam ... innatat alnus:** 'the alder-tree floats on the wave'; for boats of alder, cf. 1.136; the transitive use of *innatare* is very rare (cf. *innare* 3.142; *natare* 3.260).

452 **Pado:** again the specific place-name; cf. 437f. The construction is dative of place to which (= *in Padum*), rather than ablative of route.

453 'both in hollow bark and in the trunk of a rotted evergreen oak'; the mention of bees looks forward to the fourth book.

454f. The final lines before the peroration of the book (458f.) are playful; after having described the cultivation of the vine during the greater part of this book Virgil ends with a criticism of the excesses to which Bacchus may lead.

455f. The reference is to the famous battle between the Centaurs and the Lapiths (cf. 3.115) when wine had flowed too freely at a wedding feast (Ov. *Met.* 12.210f; Spenser, *FQ* 4.1.23); scenes from this story are depicted on the metopes of the Parthenon. Rhoetus, Pholus and Hylaeus were Centaurs (cf. *Aen.* 8.294) who came to an unhappy end.

458-74 *Farmers are happy beyond all other people, because they do not need luxury but enjoy the peace and rich satisfaction of country scenery and country virtues.*

458-74 Virgil begins his peroration with a contrast between the luxury and corruption of city life and the gentle peace of the countryside. The description of city life is handled in satirical vein, and taken up again in the final section of the book (see note on 475-542); likewise the happiness of the farmer is reasserted in 513f. The ending of this book has always been famous; it is closely imitated by Thomson, *Seasons, Autumn* 1235-1351 and many others (Philips, Somerville, Akenside, Cowper; see note on 458-9 and Wilkinson, pp. 296f.). A full analysis of it is given by

Klingner, *Virgil,* pp. 265f. It may be inspired by the rhetorical schools (Quintilian, 2.4.24, says that the contrast between town and country is a stock theme; cf. Hor. *Epod.* 2), by passages in Cato (*Agr. init*), Varro (*RR* 2 init., 3.2.3f.) and Lucretius (2.20-36), and perhaps by Hesiod (*WD* 582f.); but it reflects a specially Virgilian note, an optimistic note which contrasts with the ending of the first book and is deliberately intended to portray the happiness of a life whose difficulties and toil have been stressed throughout the poem.

458-9 'Happy farmers, all too happy if they realised their blessings'; the accusative of exclamation introduces with a note of immediacy the long encomium of rural life; the emphasis on *bona* is increased by the conflict of accent and ictus in the fifth foot. These phrases are imitated by Milton, *PL* 7.631-2 'thrice happy if they know Their happiness'; Dryden, *Medal* 123 'Too happy England, if our good we knew'; Herrick, *The Country Life* 70-71 'O happy life! if that their good The husbandmen but understood'.

458 **norint:** contracted for *noverint,* future perfect.

460 **iustissima tellus:** this is a summary of the great theme of the *Georgics;* the earth is fair to those who work it, repaying their efforts.

461f. The account of city life, which occupies the next six lines, is in a satirical vein, with frequent use of pejorative words (*superbis, vomit, inhiant, corrumpitur*). It is based on the famous passage in Lucr. 2.24-36, in which Lucretius contrasts the peace of Epicureanism with the wild rush of materialist living; cf. also Hor. *Epod.* 2.

461-2 Notice the great build-up of noun phrases each with its adjective — accusative, ablative of description, nominative, nominative, ablative, genitive qualified by adverb, ablative of separation, verb, ablative, and finally accusative again: the impact of the contemptuous rhetoric is very strong indeed.

462 The clients call on the rich man in the morning to pay their respects (*salutare*), a custom pilloried by Juvenal (cf. 3.243f.; 5.19f.) and Martial (4.8.1). *Totis vomit aedibus* means 'disgorges from every cranny of the house'.

463 **nec ... inhiant:** 'nor do they gape at ...'; the rich man, on the other hand,

cannot take his eyes off his splendid decorations. Cf. Hor. *Sat.* 1.1.71.

464 **inlusasque auro:** 'tricked out with gold'. Most MSS have *inclusas;* Servius knew both readings and rightly preferred the vivid *inlusas,* a usage unparalleled in this meaning (except for late imitations), but wholly appropriate in the context of derision.

Ephyreiaque aera: 'bronze from Corinth'; Corinth was said to have its other name Ephyra from the sea-nymph Ephyre (4.343).

465 **Assyrio . . . veneno:** the term Assyrian is used loosely to cover Tyrian, the most famous of the purple dyes; cf. 506; 3.17 *Venenum* is not necessarily a derogatory word for dye (cf. Hor. *Epist.* 2.1.207), but in this context may well imply some contempt.

466 The idea is that the purity of olive oil is corrupted by the addition of scent (cf. *Ecl.* 2.49) for luxurious uses.

467 The use of *at* to introduce the main clause is idiomatic and emphatic; cf. Cat. 30.11 *si tu oblitus es, at di meminerunt.* This emphasis is reinforced by its repetition and by the piled-up list of subjects involving the long postponement of the verb *non absunt.* For praise of the simple life in comparison with that of kings, cf. Shakespeare, 3 *Henry VI* 2.5.41f. 'Ah! what a life were this! . . .'

nescia fallere vita: 'a life that knows nothing of deceit'; both in the immediate sense that you are not tricked by Nature (as you may well be tricked in city life) and in the wide sense that the life is richly satisfying in a total way. For the infinitive with *nescia* (poetic in this sense), cf. 4.470 and Hor. *Odes* 1.6.6 *cedere nescius.*

468 **dives opum:** the use of this Greek genitive of respect is much extended in Latin by the poets; cf. 191; *Aen.* 1.14.

468-9 **latis . . . lacus:** 'peace in broad acres, caves and living lakes'; *vivi* referes to natural lakes as opposed to artificial fountains and pools in the city.

469 **frigida Tempe:** 'cold valleys'; the Greek beauty spot at Tempe (cf. 4.317) is sometimes used by the Romans as a word for any valley; cf. Ov. *Fast.* 4.477.

472-4 After the description of country and animals Virgil concludes the section with man himself and his gods.

472 This line is almost exactly repeated at *Aen.* 9.607 in Numanus' fine speech about native Italian qualities.

473 **sacra . . . patres:** 'there is worship of the gods, and fathers of families are held in reverence'; Roman insistence on the importance of family obligations (especially in their early days and in rural life) is frequently attested. Cf. Varro *RR* 3.1.5 for the belief that piety was especially characteristic of country folk.

473-4 Cf. *Ecl.* 4.6 (with note) and Aratus, *Phaen.* 105f. (especially 127) where Justice (*Dike*) after dwelling with men of the Golden Age, is forced to depart from the ensuing Silver Age because of man's depravity; Cat. 64.398f., where all the gods leave the earth because men care no longer for Justice; Juv. 6. 19f., where Astraea (Justice) and Pudicitia withdraw from the wicked world; Ov. *Met.* 1.150 *ultima caelestum terras Astraea reliquit.* In Hesiod (*WD* 200) it is Aidos and Nemesis who are destined to quit the world when men become totally corrupt.

475-542 *The poet proclaims that above all he would wish to write poetry about natural science, but failing that will be content with writing about the people of the countryside and their religion. Such people are not disturbed by ambition for power or greed; they work their fields and reap their rich rewards. This was the life of the Romans of old and of the Golden Age when strife and battles were unknown.*

475-542 This continuation of the peroration begun at 458 (see note on 458-74) takes the theme of the farmer's happiness further, and rejects not only luxury but the whole political and military scene with which the *Aeneid* is so much concerned. It has very much in common with the elegiac writers (Tib. 1.1.1-6; 75-78; Prop. 3.5 3-6; 3.12.1-6), and with the idyllic world of the *Eclogues.* It presents an attitude to life which contrasts with the description of Jupiter's regime for mortals (1.129f.), where the emphasis is on toil, and its intention is to present the bright and idyllic side of the farmer's life. It also contrasts sharply with the patriotic notes of the *Aeneid* (cf. especially 495f., 498 *non res Romanae . . .*), and yet at the end it returns (532f.) to the Roman virtues which made Virgil's country great (cf. Hor. *Odes* 3.6.37f.; 3.24; 4.5.29f.).

475 **me vero primum:** the final peroration begins with a personal statement by the poet: above all (*primum*) Virgil says he would wish to understand the

science of Nature, but failing that (*sin
. . .*, 483) he will be satisfied with a
countryman's love of her marvels.

476 **ingenti . . . amore:** compare 3.285,
a similar statement about intensely-felt
love for the subject, and in general cf.
Lucr. 1.922f. . . . *et simul incussit suavem
mi in pectus amorem musarum . . . .*

477f. The subject-matter is that with
which Aratus and Lucretius dealt, and
the phraseology is often Lucretian (e.g.
478 and Lucr. 5.751; 479 and Lucr.
6.577f.; 482 and Lucr. 5.699). Compare
also Silenus' song in *Ecl.* 6.31f., the
minstrel's song in *Aen.* 1.740f., Prop.
3.5.23f.; Hor. *Epist.* 1.12.16f.; Ov. *Met.*
15.69f.

478 **defectus . . . labores:** both words
refer to eclipses; cf. *Aen.* 1.742; Milton,
PL 2.665 'the labouring moon'.

479-80 Virgil is here referring to
exceptionally high tides, perhaps tidal waves;
compare the simile in *Aen.* 11.624f.

480 **obicibus:** the first syllable is long
because the word is pronounced *objicibus;*
cf. 4.422.

481-2 These lines describing the
shortness of winter days and the length
of the nights are used again in *Aen.*
1.745-6.

484 'the cold blood around my heart
stands in my way', i.e. if it is intellectually
too difficult; we would refer to the brain
rather than the heart in this context.
Servius tells us that the physicists said
cold blood was a sign of foolishness, and
warm blood of cleverness; a fragment of
Empedocles (*Frag.* 105) says that the
blood round the heart is the seat of
thought.

485-6 'let the countryside and the
flowing streams in the valleys be my
pleasure, let me love the rivers and the
woods though fame be lost'; there is
extreme emphasis on the last word in the
sentence *inglorius,* coming as it does
after the syntax is complete and at a
bucolic diaeresis. Cf. *Aen.* 12.397.

486 **o ubi:** the hiatus and the fifth-
foot conflict of ictus and accent give a
sonorous effect at the beginning of the
new sentence.

487-8 **Spercheosque . . . Taygeta:**
Virgil now makes specific his idyllic
picture (cf. 437f.), choosing places with
rich literary associations in Greek literature;
Spercheos is a river near Mt Pindus in
Thessaly (cf. Hom. *Il.* 16.174), and
Taygeta (sometimes Taygetus) a famous

mountain-range near Sparta (*Lacaenis*), cf.
3.44. *Bacchata* is used transitively,
'revelled over'; cf. *Aen.* 3.125. *virginibus*
is dative of agent. The word *Taygeta*
scans as a long and three shorts.

488-9 'Oh that someone would set
me in the cool vales of Haemus'; Haemus
is a mountain range in northern Greece,
cf. 1.492.

490f. These three lines unmistakably
refer to Lucretius, author of *De rerum
natura* (cf. *rerum . . . causas*) whose
Epicurean doctrine denied the existence
of the after-life (*strepitumque Acherontis
avari;* cf. Lucr. 3.37f.), and insisted that
there was therefore no need for men to
fear what might happen after death.
The passage is imitated by Arnold,
Memorial Verses (of Goethe's death):

And he was happy, if to know
Causes of things, and far below
His feet to see the lurid flow
Of terror, and insane distress,
And headlong fate, be happiness.

493f. **et ille:** the antithesis here to *felix
qui potuit* clearly refers to Virgil himself
and those who think like him: *deos . . .
agrestis* once again reminds us of the
insistence on religion in the *Georgics.*

494 **Panaque . . . senem:** 'both Pan
and old Silvanus'; *-que . . . -que* is 'both
. . . and'; *Pana* is Greek accusative. For
Pan, cf. 1.17; for Silvanus, cf. 1.20.

495f. Virgil now uses various devices
of diction and metre to emphasise the
carefree happiness of the farmer; the
accusative *illum* filling the first foot, the
marked alliteration of *p* and *f* (495-6)
and *r* (498), the repetition of *ille* (498)
after the unusual pause in the fifth foot.
The subject-matter is closely imitated by
Thomson, *Seasons, Autumn* 1299f.

495 **populi fasces:** 'the authority
conferred by the people'; the *fasces* were the
rods symbolising office carried by the
consul's lictors. The phrase is used by
Lucretius (3.996) in a passage attacking
worldly ambition.

496 **infidos . . . fratres:** Virgil here
refers to the personal ambition which
can break even family obligations; cf.
Lucr. 3.72f. Others take him to refer
more specifically to civil war, or dynastic
rivalry in general or in particular (as
between Phraates and Tiridates in Parthia
about this time; cf. Hor. *Odes* 1.26), but
the more personal interpretation suits the
context better.

497 The Dacians (Rumanians) attacking from the Hister (Danube) were troublesome to Rome throughout the period when the *Georgics* were being written; the culmination was their support for Antony before and at the battle of Actium in 31 BC (cf. Hor. *Odes* 3.6.14f.).

498-9 These are the two extremes offered by city life (pity for the poor, envy for the rich); the countryman avoids both extremes (cf. Tib. 1.1.78). This detachment from the mundane world has much in common (paradoxically) both with Epicureanism and with Stoicism, but here is specifically concerned with the thought that in the country there are no poor and no rich.

501-2 The reference to iron laws, the mad forum (cf. Prop. 4.1.134), the public bureaucracy, is very contemptuous; see note on 475-542. For these lines and those which follow, cf. Hor. *Epod.* 2.6f.

503 **sollicitant:** a pejorative word suggesting interference with nature; cf. Hor. *Odes* 1.3.21f. Greed, violence and political ambition were aspects of contemporary life which the elegists constantly attacked.

505 **petit excidiis urbem:** 'aims to destroy a city'; literally, 'seeks a city with destruction'. The man described is reckless of the suffering he causes to humble families (*miserosque penatis*) as long as he can satisfy his ambition. Some have sought contemporary allusions in this line and those that follow (to Caesar, Crassus etc.) but Virgil is deliberately most unspecific.

506 **Sarrano:** from Tyre (Sarra); cf. 465; Juv. 10.38.

507 The miser who broods over his gold and gives none to others is allocated a place in Tartarus in *Aen.* 6.610, where the same verb *incubare* is used.

508 The would-be politician listening to speeches from the *rostra* is satirised by the unfavourable words *stupet attonitus:* he is intoxicated by the prospect of swaying a great audience.

508-10 'Another is entranced as the applause both of people and senators, redoubling as it does along the rows of the theatre, takes hold of him'; the satire is pointed by the unfavourable words (*hiantem, corripuit*) and the emphatic alliteration of *p.* It is possible that there is an allusion to Pompey's theatre and the pleasure he and others took in receiving

plaudits there (cf. Lucan 1.133); at all events it certainly refers to the politician appearing to the people in a theatre (cf. Hor. *Odes* 1.20.3; 2.17.26).

509 **enim:** an archaic use of the word, intensifying the word it qualifies; cf. 104.

510 **gaudent . . . fratrum:** cf. 496 and Cat. 64.399.

512 Cf. Hor. *Odes* 2.16.18-19 *quid terras alio calentes sole mutamus?*

513 **agricola:** the antithesis with 503-12, describing various types of wicked ambition, is not pointed by a word like *sed* or *tamen* but merely by the expectation of a contrast aroused by the previous section. This line has a slow and serene spondaic movement; cf. 1.494.

514-15 Again at a moment of high tension Virgil uses his favourite tricolon with repetition (*hinc . . . hinc . . . hinc*), cf. 323f.

515 **meritos:** 'loyal'; the note of sympathy with the animals who serve their master is very forceful here; cf. 3.525.

518 **horrea vincat:** 'defeats the barns', i.e. produces so much that they cannot cope; cf. 1.49.

519 **venit hiemps:** 'now winter has come'; the perfect tense brings immediacy to the following descriptive phrases.

Sicyonia baca: the olives of Sicyon near Corinth were well known; cf. Ov. *Pont.* 4.15.10.

522 The description of late autumn's fruits is rounded with a golden line.

523 As Virgil passes from the produce of the fields to the farmer's domestic happiness he clearly recalls the famous passage in Lucr. 3.894f.

526 Again the sentence ends with a patterned line, very close to a golden line.

528 'where there is a fire in the middle and his friends crown the bowl'; *cratera* is Greek accusative. The phrase 'crown the bowl' is imitated from the Greek (e.g. Hom. *Od.* 1.148) where it means 'fill to the brim'; it seems that Virgil has altered the meaning so that it literally means 'crown with a garland'; cf. *Aen.* 1.724; 3.525.

529 **Lenaee:** Bacchus; cf. line 4.

531 Again a golden line (cf. 522; 526) to round off the section.

532-3 The Sabines (see note on 167) take the thoughts back to the days of Romulus and Remus (533) and Romulus' successor, the Sabine Numa Pompilius; the reference to Etruria suggests the

Tarquin dynasty.

534 **rerum . . . Roma:** 'Rome became the most beautiful city in the world', literally 'the most beautiful of things' — *rerum* is partitive genitive.

535 'and as a single city surrounded her seven hills with a wall'; the same line occurs (with the change of tense to *circumdabit*) in Anchises' prophecy in *Aen.* 6.783.

536 **Dictaei regis:** Jupiter, said to have been brought up on Mt Dicte in Crete (cf. 4.152), succeeded his father Saturn and abolished the golden age; cf. 1.125f. and note on 1.118-46.

537 This line is based on Aratus, *Phaen.* 130f., esp. 132 (of the men of the bronze age) 'who first ate the oxen of the plough'; cf. Ov. *Met.* 15.111f., especially 120f. and 138-9 (a passionate attack on the eating of meat); Varro *RR* 2.5.4 (where he says that the Romans of old

imposed the death penalty for killing oxen).

538 Cf. Varro *RR* 3.1.5 *qui eam (terram) colerent, piam et utilem agere vitam credebant et eos solos reliquos esse ex stirpe Saturni regis.*

539 **necdum . . . necdum:** the repetition, especially with the pause at the end of the fifth foot, and echoing *ante . . . ante* in 536, puts great emphasis on the happy days of old.

539-40 Compare Tib. 1.3.47-8.

540 The final line before the personal statement of the last two lines is again a golden line (cf. 522; 526; 531).

541-2 Books 1 and 3 end with narrative, Books 2 and 4 with a personal statement by the poet; for the imagery of the poetic 'team of horses', see note on 3.17-18 and cf. Spenser, *FQ* 4.5.46.

541 **immensum spatiis . . . aequor:** 'a plain enormous in expanse'.

GEORGICS 3

The third book is about farm animals; its subject-matter is often based very closely on prose sources such as Aristotle and Varro, but its treatment is far removed from the method of a didactic handbook. After a prologue in honour of Octavian, the first half (1-283) is concerned with horses and cattle; Virgil's aim is to present these animals in their full vigour and dignity, interweaving the two subjects as his poetic requirements suggest to him. The individuality and the independence of the horse (as racehorse or warhorse) are constantly stressed, and the draught oxen are seen as strong and indispensable helpmates of the farmer, as they toil with the plough. Above all these animals are constantly described in human terms (see the notes at the beginning of individual sections.)

The second half deals with sheep and goats in a totally different way, underlining their dependence on human care. There is a brief account of dogs, but none at all of any other animals such as pigs, mules, asses. The didactic material is varied by vivid descriptive passages, as for example the pastoral picture of summertime (322-38), the problems of the farmer in the far south (339-48) or far north (349-83), the menace of snakes (414-39). A long section on diseases is concluded by the account of a disastrous plague (closely modelled on Lucretius' description of the plague at Athens), so that the book ends (like Book 1, but unlike Books 2 and 4) with a feeling of horror and pessimism, a sense of the puniness of men and animals in the face of the inexplicable calamities of nature. The mood of sorrow at suffering which is so marked a feature of the *Aeneid* is here expressed very strongly, particularly in the picture of the death of the faithful ox (515f.).

For further discussion, see Otis pp. 169f.; Wilkinson pp. 92f.; 252f.; T.F. Royds, *The Beasts, Birds and Bees of Virgil,* pp. 1-29.

1-48 *Virgil proclaims his intention to seek immortal glory for his home town Mantua by avoiding the trite paths of poetry and instead one day undertaking to celebrate Caesar's victories in song. Till then he will continue his poem of the countryside.*

1-48 The beginning of the third book resembles the beginning of the first in its extensive prologue in praise of the achievements of Octavian; but it differs in its emphasis. The prologue of the first book spoke of Octavian's future deification; this one speaks of his mortal triumphs, and of the part which Virgil himself will play in celebrating them. The imagery of the temple of song owes much to Pindar, as Wilkinson has shown (pp. 166f.), and in its extended and vividly pictorial symbolism is one of the most memorable passages of Latin literature. It clearly is an allegorical promise of the poem which finally turned out to be the *Aeneid.* In the end of course the *Aeneid* was something much larger than the promise *dicere pugnas Caesaris* (46-7), and it may well be that Virgil originally planned an epic of a more directly historical and panegyric kind; if so he was wise to modify his plan. But the phraseology which he uses here is wide and vague, and there are no adequate grounds for thinking that he refers here to an abandoned project. The battles of Octavian Caesar came explicitly into the *Aeneid* on occasion (especially in their depiction on the shield of Aeneas, 8.675f., which shows considerable similarities with this passage); and the achievements of the emperor, the hopes placed in him and the problems awaiting him are frequently implicit in the legend of Rome's first founder.

There are clear indications (referred to in the notes which follow) of the historical background of the times: the triple triumph of Octavian in 29 BC and the building of the temple of Apollo on the Palatine (dedicated in 28 BC) are behind many of the references. This has led many (such as D.L. Drew, *CQ* 1924, pp. 194f.) to attempt a precise dating of the passage and precise identification of the references; Virgil's method, however, is too wide-ranging to admit this kind of interpretation. His imagery varies from triumphal procession to celebration of religious rites and of games and again to poetic celebration; his references to the triple triumph and the temple of Apollo are in terms sufficiently unspecific as to be capable of

having been written in anticipation, and in any case these two great events of the post-Actium years are treated by means of imaginative symbolism and not historical reporting. We can say no more historically than that these things had happened or were in the air at the time when the passage was written; but we can also say that we have here a poetic expression in the most vivid terms of their importance in the Roman world as symbols of peace and religious thanksgiving.

For fuller discussion (with bibliography) see Wilkinson pp. 165f. and Appendix 3.

1 Te quoque, magna Pales: Pales was an old Italian deity (generally female, but Servius quotes Varro for the use of the masculine gender) who presided over shepherds and pasturage (cf. 294; *Ecl.* 5.35; Ov. *Fast.* 4.722); for her festival *Parilia,* cf. Ov. *Fast.* 4.721f. The force of *quoque* is that just as Ceres and others were invoked at the beginning of *Georgics* Book 1 and Bacchus at the beginning of Book 2 so now in a book about the care of animals the goddess of pasturage is invoked.

2 pastor ab Amphryso: i.e. Apollo, who was compelled, as a punishment for killing the Cyclopes, to serve Admetus as a mortal shepherd in Thessaly, near the river Amphrysus: hence his name Apollo Nomios, Apollo of the pastures. Compare *Aen.* 6.398; Eur. *Alc.* 1f.; Tib. 2.3.11f.; Ov. *AA* 2.239-40. Apollo is linked with Pales in *Ecl.* 5.35.

Lycaei: the mountain home in Arcadia of the shepherds' god Pan; cf. 1.16; *Ecl.* 10.15; 26.

3f. Virgil gives a selection of well-worn mythical themes, many of which were doubtless the subject of epyllia in his time. The transition of thought from the two previous lines is abrupt: I shall now sing of shepherds and after that (when the *Georgics* are finished) not of trite mythological themes but of Caesar Augustus.

3 tenuissent: 'could have held', had they not become so hackneyed.

4 Eurysthea: Greek accusative. Eurystheus was a Greek king who at Juno's instigation imposed upon Hercules his twelve labours; cf. *Aen.* 8.292; Theocr. 25.204f.

5 inlaudati ... Busiridis: Busiris was an Egyptian king who made human sacrifices of strangers (cf. Ov. *Trist.* 3.11.39); he was killed by Hercules. Aulus Gellius (2.6) discusses the epithet *illaudatus* (= *illaudabilis*, cf. 17) comparing *inamabilis* of the Styx in *Aen.* 6.438; it is a somewhat strange litotes for 'detestable'.

6 cui: = *a quo*, dative of agent.

Hylas: the story of Hylas, beloved of Hercules but snatched from him by the nymphs, is told in Ap. Rh. 1.1207f. and Theocr. 13; cf. *Ecl.* 6.43-4.

Latonia Delos: the island of Delos was the legendary birthplace of Apollo and Diana — their mother was Latona; cf. Callim. *Hymn.* 4; *Aen.* 3.75-6.

7 Hippodame: Servius tells the story of how Oenomaus, King of Elis, refused his daughter Hippodame (Hippodamia) to all her suitors unless the suitor could defeat his wind-swift horses in a chariot race, the penalty for failure being death. Pelops with his winged horses (*acer equis,* 8) succeeded when Hippodame bribed Oenomaus' charioteer.

umeroque ... eburno: this refers to the story of how Tantalus killed his son Pelops and served up his flesh at a banquet for the gods in order to test their omniscience: all except Ceres refrained from eating the human meat. Pelops was given an ivory shoulder to replace the part Ceres had eaten. Compare Pind. *Ol.* 1.27; Ov. *Met.* 6.401f.

9 victorque ... ora: 'and in triumph fly from place to place on the lips of men'; a very apparent reminiscence (retaining the alliteration) of Ennius' self-written epitaph: *Nemo me lacrimis decoret nec funera fletu faxit. Cur? Volito vivus per ora virum;* compare also *Aen.* 12.235 *vivusque per ora feretur.*

10 primus: for the claim to be the first to achieve a particular kind of poetry, cf. Lucr. 4.1f.; Prop. 3.1.3f.; Hor. *Odes* 3.30.13-14. Page quotes Milton, *PL* 1.16 'things unattempted yet in prose or rhyme'.

modo vita supersit: 'if only life lasts long enough'. This use of *superesse* is common; cf. the discussion in Aul. Gell. 1.22.

11 Aonio ... vertice: the mountain of Aonia is Helicon in Boeotia, mountain of the Muses; cf. *Ecl.* 6.65. Some have thought that there is also an association with Hesiod, from Ascra in Boeotia; cf. *Geo.* 2.176; but this seems inappropriate in a context of epic poetry. For the thought, compare Lucr. 1.117f. (of Ennius) *qui primus amoeno detulit ex Helicone perenni fronde coronam.*

deducam: the imagery is that of a

conquering general (*victor,* 9) returning (*rediens*) in triumph with his captives in procession (*deducere;* cf. Hor. *Odes* 1.37.31). The phraseology anticipates the more specific references to Augustus' triple triumph in 29 BC; see note on 27.

12 Idumaeas ... palmas: again a reference to a triumphal procession with the general bearing the victor's palm: Idumaea was in Palestine in an area famous for palm-trees; cf. Mart. 10.50.1.

Mantua: Virgil's birthplace; cf. *Ecl.* 9.27; *Geo.* 2.198.

13 templum de marmore: the metaphor of the triumphant returning general is continued, as he dedicates his votive temple. For the allegorical significance of Virgil's temple of song, see note on 1-48. Compare Propertius' description (2.31) of the marble temple to Apollo on the Palatine, dedicated in 28 BC, and see Camps' notes for further references.

15 Mincius: the Mincio, on which Mantua stands, runs out into the south-east corner of Lake Garda; cf. *Ecl.* 7.13; *Geo.* 2.198-9; *Aen.* 10.206; and Milton, *Lycidas* 86 'Smooth-sliding Mincius, crown'd with vocal reeds'.

16 Caesar (i.e. Augustus) is to be the god to whom this temple of song will be dedicated; his statue is visualised in the centre — *nam semper ei sacratus numini locus est, cuius simulacrum in medio collocatur* (Servius).

17-18 The imagery of the triumphal procession now begins to shade into a picture of the festive games held to commemorate a victory (like Augustus' great Actian games in 28 BC). Both a triumphing general and the president of the games would wear purple. The ambiguity continues as Virgil pictures himself driving a hundred chariots; in one sense this suggests presiding over chariot-races, but in another, as Wilkinson points out, it symbolises his verses: Wilkinson compares *Geo.* 2.541-2; Pind. *Ol.* 6.22f.; and Thomas Gray, *The Progress of Poesy:*

Behold, where Dryden's less presumptuous car
Wide o'er the fields of glory bear
Two coursers of ethereal race,
With necks in thunder clothed, and loud-resounding pace.

19f. The description of the games continues: all the Greek athletes will come from Olympia (on the river Alpheus) and Nemea (another famous centre of Greek games). Molorchus was a shepherd who entertained Hercules on the occasion when he killed the Nemean lion.

20 **crudo ... caestu:** this refers to the Roman type of boxing, with the heavily reinforced glove of raw hide (*crudus*); see my note on *Aen.* 5.364 (Oxford edition). Augustus was said to have been particularly interested in boxing (Suet. *Aug.* 45).

21 **caput ... olivae:** cf. *Aen.* 5.774, almost the same line. *Caput* is retained accusative, see note on *Ecl.* 1.54; *tonsae* means 'trimmed' to a uniform length, or possibly simply 'cut'.

22-3 ' **iam nunc ... iuvat:** 'already I feel the joy' (Wilkinson); Virgil foresees the occasion with eager anticipation. Cf. Hor. *Odes* 2.1.17.

24f. 'or how the scene disappears as the setting revolves, and how the Britons depicted on the tapestry raise the purple curtains'. The construction after *videre* changes from direct object (*iuvencos*) to an object clause introduced by *ut*; cf. 1.252-4. Stage performances were often a feature of Roman games, as at the dedication of the temple to Divus Julius in 29 BC. Servius explains that *versis ... frontibus* refers to the *scaena versilis* when the stage was turned right round to produce a change of scene, and *discedat* to the *scaena ductilis*, when the front was drawn apart in two sections from the middle to reveal the scene behind; but it seems more likely that the whole phrase refers to the *scaena versilis*.

25 **tollant aulaea;** an indication of the end of the performance, as the curtain was pulled up from the floor to cut off the stage from sight; cf. Ov. *Met.* 3.111.

Britanni: '*hoc secundum historiam est locutus*' (Servius). Octavian was said to have planned an expedition against Britain in 34 BC (and again in 27 BC), and the poets frequently introduce Britain (like Parthia, cf. 31) as an area at the edge of the world which Rome had conquered or would conquer; cf. 1.30; Hor. *Odes* 3.5.3-4.

26 **in foribus:** i.e. on the doorways of the temple (16); the architectural metaphor continues as Virgil visualises his epic poem in terms of a vast religious building. For an ecphrasis describing pictures on the temple doors, cf. *Aen.* 6.20f.; there were pictures on the doors of Apollo's Palatine temple (Prop. 2.31.12f.).

elephanto: a quadrisyllabic ending is rare, but occurs occasionally, especially with Greek words; cf. line 60.

27 **Gangaridum:** 'sons of the Ganges'; for the archaic form of the genitive (for *Gangaridarum*), cf. *Aen.* 1.565; 3.21. The reference is to the Eastern peoples who fought at Actium against Octavian on the side of Antony and Cleopatra; cf. 2.171-2.

Quirini: often applied to Romulus, but here with a more general application to the god Quirinus representing the whole Roman people. There may be a hint that the god Quirinus is manifested on this occasion in Octavian: cf. the proposal mentioned in Suet. *Aug.* 7 that the title of Romulus should be conferred on him.

29 **Nilum:** as a symbol of Egypt, defeated at Actium, cf. *Aen.* 6.800; 8.711-13.

navali ... columnas: 'columns rising high with the bronze of ships', i.e. made from the captured bronze beaks of enemy ships. Servius says that these columns were later transferred by Domitian to the Capitol, and survived there in his time; cf. Dio 51.19.

30 **Niphaten:** a mountain or river in Armenia, cf. Hor. *Odes* 2.9.20; Octavian was in Syria in 30 BC and concerned himself with the affairs of Armenia.

31 The favourite manoeuvre of the Parthian cavalry (to ride off as if in flight and suddenly to turn and shoot) is often referred to in Latin literature; cf. Hor. *Odes* 1.19.11-12; 2.13.17; and compare Dryden, *Love Triumphant* 2.1 'Oh let us gain a Parthian victory! Our only way to conquer is to fly'.

32 'and two trophies forcibly seized from far-sundered peoples': Servius suggests that the reference is to the Britons in the west and the Gangaridae in the east, but it seems more likely that the reference is to the Morini in the west (a Belgic tribe, cf. *Aen.* 8.727) and either the Dalmatians in the north-east or the Bastarnae on the Black Sea; the Morini and the Dalmatians figured in the triple triumph of 29 BC, and the Bastarnae were defeated in the same year.

33 This line (cf. Prop. 3.9.53) elaborates the previous line. *Triumphatas* is here used transitively, 'triumphed over'; cf. *Aen.* 6.836.

34 These are marble statues of ancestors (marble from Paros; cf. *Aen.* 1.593). For *spirantia*, cf. *Aen.* 6.847; Prop. 2.31.8. Compare Pope, *Temple of Fame* 73-4, 'Heroes in animated marble frown, And legislators seem to think in stone'.

35-6 Assaracus was the great-grandfather of Aeneas, Tros the father of Assaracus and grandson of Dardanus, son of Jupiter.

36 **Cynthius**: Apollo, from Mt Cynthus in Delos, his birthplace, cf. *Ecl.* 6.3. He and Neptune built the walls of Troy; he was the patron deity of Augustus; cf. *Aen.* 8.704.

37 **Invidia**: 'envy', 'malicious hatred'. Virgil has outlined a happy state of triumph and success both for Octavian as the emperor who ended civil discord and for himself as chosen poet of Rome's new greatness — now he hopes that the malice of those jealous of such prosperity may be brought to naught. For the idea, cf. Hor. *Odes* 3.24.30f.; for the use of *invidia*, cf. *Ecl.* 7.26. The personification is rather like that of *Furor impius* in *Aen.* 1.294f.

37f. The imagery of the underworld — the avenging Furies (*Aen.* 6.280), the river Cocytus (6.297), the wheel on which Ixion was tortured (6.616-17), the rock which Sisyphus had to push to the top of a mountain (6.616) — conveys very vividly the idea that malicious opponents of Rome's happy state will be consigned to oblivion and punishment. Compare Hor. *Odes* 3.4.65f. The snakes by which Ixion was lashed to his wheel are not mentioned elsewhere; the meaning of *non exsuperabile* ('unconquerable') seems to be that Sisyphus could not get the better of the rock by pushing it successfully to the top of the mountain.

40 **interea**: until the time comes for Virgil to write his epic in honour of Octavian he will continue with his *Georgics*.

41 **intactos**: i.e. the theme has not been handled before; cf. Lucr. 1.927 *integros . . . fontes*.

Maecenas: each book of the *Georgics* is dedicated to Maecenas, the most famous patron of letters of the time; see note on 1.2.

haud mollia iussa: a much discussed phrase, taken by some to refer to the insistence of Maecenas that Virgil should write the *Georgics* (and thus suggesting that Virgil was writing under some compulsion); but it is more likely that Virgil refers conventionally to the difficulty of the task which Maecenas suggested, rather than to the severity of Maecenas' insistence.

42-3 **en age . . . moras**: 'come now, away with lazy delay'; the poet urges himself on to his task.

43 **Cithaeron**: a mountain in Boeotia, mentioned in *Aen.* 4.303 as especially associated with Bacchic rites; it is also connected with the Muses. Here the particular association is with animals and

hunting (*ingenti clamore*), part of the subject-matter of Book 3, as the following references to dogs and horses indicate.

44 **Taygetique canes**: Taygetus was a mountain range near Sparta (2.488); Spartan dogs were famous (345; 405). Cf. Shakespeare, *A Midsummer Night's Dream* 4.1.125 'My hounds are bred out of the Spartan kind'.

Epidaurus: a town in the Argolid, famous for its horses; cf. 121; Hor. *Odes* 1.7.9.

45 'the sound is magnified and echoed with the applause of the groves'; the groves are personified as hearing and applauding the noise of the hunt.

46 **mox tamen**: i.e. after completing the *Georgics* Virgil will return to the task he has been outlining in the prelude to this book.

accingar dicere: the infinitive after *accingi* (on the analogy of *parabor*) is found also in Tac. *Ann.* 15.51. The metaphor is military to match the military subject-matter.

48 'as Caesar is distant from the remote birth of Tithonus'; Tithonus was a brother of Priam, and is chosen not only as a distant figure, but also as long-lived (he was the husband of Aurora and received the gift of immortal life). Virgil's prophecy, in fact, has been much more than fulfilled.

Notice how the word *Caesar* takes great emphasis as it ends the paragraph; cf. Hor. *Odes* 1.2.52.

49-71 *In the rearing of horses and cattle it is vital to select the right breeding-stock. The cows should be spirited and physically powerful, and it is most important to continue systematically to replace the stock, for age and diseases take their toll just as inevitably as they do with men.*

49-71 Virgil now turns directly to his didactic subject and deals with the breeding of horses and cattle. Throughout the first half of this book he interweaves his two subjects, horses and cattle, in order to avoid excessively organised and schematic categorisation and in order to convey the similarity of these two classes of animals; they each offer their powerful physical strength for man's use, and form a part of the total cosmos with man. This aspect of the oneness of Nature's creatures is strongly stressed in this first section; in line 60 the mating of cattle is like a human marriage; in lines 66f. cattle are specifically equated with mortals in their loss of vigour, their ageing and their death.

Virgil closely follows Varro (*RR* 2.5) in many parts of this section (cf. also Colum. 6.1f;; 6.20f.); but he elevates his material into poetry by his sophisticated diction, by the metrical movement, and in particular by the identification of the beasts with the world of man.

49 Olympiacae: the reference to chariot victories in the Olympic games (one of the reasons for breeding horses) picks up the imagery of the previous section (17f.); cf. Hor. *Odes* 1.1.3-6.

miratus: 'passionately anxious for'; cf. Hor. *Epist.* 1.6.18.

palmae: the palm as a prize for victory dates in Greece from about 400 BC, and in the Roman world from 293 BC (Livy 10.47.3 *palmaeque tum primum translato e Graeco more victoribus datae*).

51 corpora . . . legat: 'let him select with particular care mothers with the right qualities of physique'. Compare Varro *RR* 2.5.7f. and Colum. 6.1, where detailed descriptions are given.

51-2 The construction is *optima forma est torvae bovis cui* . . . 'the best physique is that of a proud-eyed cow whose head is ugly, whose neck is very large . . .'. For the connotation of *torvus,* cf. 59 *et faciem tauro propior.*

52 turpe: 'ugly' in the sense of abnormally large, cf. 4.395 *turpes phocas.* Varro recommends a cow *latis frontibus, cervicibus crassis,* and Columella *fronte lata, cervice longa et torosa.*

53 'and whose dewlaps hang from its chin to its legs'; the preposition *tenus* follows its noun and sometimes takes the genitive (cf. *Aen.* 10.210), sometimes the ablative.

55 et camuris . . . aures: 'and hairy ears under horns that curve inwards'. Varro has *pilosis auribus;* for the meaning of the rare word *camur,* cf. Macr. *Sat.* 6.4.23 *in se redeuntibus.*

56 nec mihi displiceat: an example of Virgil's technique of adding didactic force by speaking in the first person. *Nec displiceat* is an instance of litotes: Virgil means that the kind of cow he goes on to describe is much to be sought after.

maculis insignis et albo: probably 'marked with white spots', hendiadys (cf. 2.192 *pateris . . . et auro*), rather than 'notable for its white colour and its spots'.

57 iuga detrectans: 'or one that refuses the yoke'; the use of the participle among

the adjectives *insignis, aspera, propior* gives a slight grammatical variation to the sentence. The next two phrases elaborate this description of a spirited cow, with some of the qualities of a bull.

58 faciem: accusative of respcet; cf. 84 and 2.131.

60 Virgil now elevates the description from the technical to the poetic by setting up a similarity between animals and humans (*Lucinam, hymenaeos*). Lucina was goddess of childbirth; cf. 4.340. By *iustos* Virgil means 'appropriate' — earlier or later would be wrong.

pati hymenaeos: for the hiatus and the polysyllabic ending, see note on *Ecl.* 2.24; cf. line 26.

62 cetera: i.e. *aetas.*

habilis: 'suitable'; cf. 2.92.

64 primus: again the immediate and urgent didactic note; cf. 2.408.

65 suffice: 'provide'; cf. line 301; 2.191; 424.

66-8 These sorrowful reflections on the fortunes of all living things, destined to old age and illness and death, very closely link the animal world (of which Virgil has been speaking) with the human world. *Miseris mortalibus* (cf. *Aen.* 2.268; 11.182) has a Homeric ring (δειλοῖοι βροτοῖσιν) which strengthens the sense of antiquity in these almost proverbial phrases.

69 'There will always be those whose bodies you would prefer to be replaced', i.e. the old and weak cows will need replacing for breeding purposes. *Corpora* draws attention to the physical aspect of the subject; cf. 51.

70 enim: 'indeed', an archaic usage; cf. 2.509.

70-71 'in case you may later miss what you have lost take steps in advance and every year choose new stock for the herd'; cf. Varro *RR* 2.5.17.

72-94 The qualities of a thoroughbred stallion; his spirited splendour recalls the horses of myth and legend.

72-94 After his description of the ideal breeding-cow Virgil switches to horses and describes the thoroughbred stallion. This variation is characteristic of his whole treatment of cattle, and his poetic intention is to avoid the danger of organised cataloguing: Servius calls it *exquisita varietas.* The aim is to produce a series of vivid and varied pictures of different aspects of the animal world; as the cow was described in muted and slow-moving phrases, with reflections on the transience of the prime of life, so now by contrast the horse is vital, energetic, proudly brave. Seneca (*Ep. Mor.* 95.68) quotes this passage as a description that might be applied to a *vir fortis*, like Cato. The essential oneness of the animal world and the human world is thus again stressed.

Much of the material for the passage is taken quite closely from Varro *RR* 2.7.5. (cf. also Colum. 6.29). But the effect is totally different from the prose technical treatise. It uses the factual information to build up a series of images designed to move the reader to admiration. Instruction is wholly subordinated to an attempt to capture the essence of the spirited horse, just as the details of sowing corn are less important to Virgil than the picture of the ripe ears rustling in a light breeze. This is the reason why he ends this description with famous horses from Homer and Greek mythology; Achilles and Saturnus are vital to reinforce and conclude the intense visual imagery. For a detailed analysis of the contrast between Virgil and Varro, see Wilkinson, pp. 187-9.

72 **dilectus**: i.e. the choice of stock for breeding, as important for horses as for cattle.

73 **tu modo**; again the direct didactic touch; cf. 64.

quos . . . gentis: 'for those which you will decide to raise for the future benefit of the herd'; supply *eis* as the antecedent to *quos. Summittere* (cf. 159; perhaps *Ecl.* 1.45) is a technical term in Varro and Columella for rearing.

74 **iam inde a teneris**: 'right from their early days'; cf. *Aen.* 6.385.

75 **pecoris generosi pullus**: 'the foal out of a thoroughbred stable': i.e. if you have bred wisely, the foal will immediately (*continuo*) show signs of high quality, and will in turn be suitable as a stud-horse.

76 **ingreditur**: the last syllable is lengthened in arsis, see note on *Ecl.* 1.38. Servius has a good gloss on this phrase: *cum exultatione quadam incedit.*

mollia crura reponit: 'places its steps delicately'; *reponit* answers *altius ingreditur* — the horse lifts its legs high and 'replaces' them elegantly, delicately, because they are *mollia*, 'lissom'. The phrase is used by Ennius, *Ann.* 556, of cranes — *perque fabam repunt et mollia crura reponunt*; cf. Pliny *NH* 8.166 *quibus non vulgaris in cursu gradus, sed mollis alterno crurum explicatu glomeratio.*

The Greek word is ὑγρός (Xen. *Eq.* 1.6), conveying a fluent and supple movement like flowing water.

79 **ardua cervix**: reminiscent of the Greek epithet ὑψαύχην (Plat. *Phaedr.* 253d); cf. Xen. *Eq.* 11.7 (of a spirited horse) ὅταν καλῶς μετεωρίξῃ ἑαυτῷ.

80 *argutumque caput*: 'an alert head', i.e. quick-moving, appearing to be light, as opposed to the cow's heavy head, *turpe caput* (52). For *argutus*, cf. Ov. *Am.* 3.3.9 (of sparkling eyes). The epithet is highly poetical, and a good example of the difference between Virgil and Varro in approach can be seen by Varro's factual *caput non magnum* and Virgil's suggestive and indefinite *argutum caput* (other renderings of the adjective are 'finely-tapering', Day Lewis; and 'clean-cut', Page).

81 **luxuriatque . . . pectus**: 'its proud chest ripples with muscles': for *toros*, cf. *Aen.* 12.7 (of a lion) *excutiens cervice toros*. Many of Virgil's points are taken up in Shakespeare's catalogue of points (*Venus and Adonis*, 294f.):

Round-hoof'd, short-jointed, fetlocks
  shag and long,
Broad breast, full eye, small head and
  nostril wide,
High crest, short ears, straight legs and
  passing strong,
Thin mane, thick tail, broad buttock,
  tender hide:
Look, what a horse should have he did not
  lack,
Save a proud rider on so proud a back.

81-3 'The good horses are the chestnuts and the greys, the worst colour is that of the whites and duns'. This parenthetical comment on the best colours (not mentioned by Varro) interrupts the flow of the description of the spirited horse; when Seneca quotes this passage (*Ep. Mor.* 95.68) he omits this sentence. *Spadix* is reddish-brown (bay); the word *glaucus* is difficult: Aulus Gellius (2.26) regards it in this passage as a Greek equivalent for *caeruleus*, and some commentators have thought that here it refers to the colour of the eyes. However, this seems to upset the balance of the sentence, and it is better to take it as a rather strange word for silvery-grey, perhaps like a blue roan. *Gilvus* is a very rare word indeed which Servius says means 'honey-coloured'. Servius suggests a reading (adopted by Sabbadini and Richter; the latter has a full discussion in his note *ad loc.*) *albis e gilvo*, i.e. *albogilvis* ('whitish-fawn'), but this seems unlikely.

83f. For the pride of the war-horse, cf. Aesch. *Sept.* 393f.; Ap. Rh. 3.1258f.; and Job 39:20-22 '. . . the glory of his nostrils is terrible. He paweth in the valley, and rejoiceth in his strength: he goeth on to meet the armed men. He mocketh at fear, and is not affrighted: neither turneth he back from the sword.'

84 **micat auribus et tremit artus:** 'his ears prick up and his limbs quiver'; Virgil varies from the ablative of respect (*auribus*) to the accusative of respect (*artus;* cf. 58 and Lucr. 3.489). Cf. Shakespeare, *Venus and Adonis* 271f. 'His ears up-prick'd . . . His nostrils drink the air, and forth again, As from a furnace vapours doth he send'. The rhythm of the second half of the line is imitative of the sense with its dactyls and clash of ictus and accent in the fifth foot.

85 'and in his nostrils rolls the breath of pent-up fire' (Wilkinson). *Premens* (M has *fremens,* possibly rightly) seems to refer to the idea of restraining the breath in brief snorts. Compare Lucr. 5.1076 *et fremitum patulis sub naribus edit ad arma.* For breathing fire, cf. *Geo.* 2.140; *Aen.* 7.281; Lucr. 5.29; for *volvit,* Page quotes Byron, *The Destruction of Sennacherib:*

And there lay the steed with his nostrils all wide,
But through them there rolled not the breath of his pride.

86 **dextro . . . armo:** i.e. when he tosses his flowing mane it falls to the right; cf. Varro *in dexteriorem partem cervicis;* Columella *per dextram partem profusa;* Prop. 4.4.38; Ov. *Met.* 2.674.

87 'Through his hind-quarters his spine runs doubly wide'. This strange phraseology is found in Xen. *Eq.* 1.11 (διπλοῦς); Varro *spina maxime duplici;* Columella *spina duplici.* Servius was worried about it and said, *aut revera duplex aut lata, ut duplicem gemmis auroque coronam..* It seems likely that the reference is to the double ridge of muscle protecting the spine.

88 **et solido . . . cornu:** the dactylic movement conveys prancing or galloping; cf. Enn. *Ann.* 439; *Aen.* 8.596. Compare Homer's κρατερώνυχες ἵπποι (e.g. *Il.* 5.329); Isaiah 5:28 '. . . their horses' hoofs shall be counted like flint'; Shakespeare, *Venus and Adonis* 267-8 'The bearing earth with his hard hoof he wounds, Whose hollow womb resounds like heaven's thunder'.

89f. The extended imagery of famous horses reinforces the impact of this highly descriptive and visual account of a spirited horse. The intention has been to use the traditional technical 'points' of a good horse in order to produce the kind of picture which a painter might put on canvas. Conington strangely says, 'These mythological allusions are obviously intended to ennoble the subject; but they tend to injure its genuine character'. On the contrary, Virgil's passage does not aim at any 'genuine character': it aims to universalise in a poetic way the concept of a proud stallion. Compare the fine lines of Pope (*Windsor Forest,* 151-4):

The impatient courser pants in every vein,
And pawing seems to beat the distant
    plain:
Hills, vales and floods appear already
    crossed,
And ere he starts, a thousand steps are
    lost.

89-90 Cyllarus was a horse given by Neptune to Juno who gave it to the twins Castor and Pollux to tame; cf. Stat. *Th.* 6.327f. Amyclae, near Sparta (cf. 345), was the birthplace of Castor and Pollux (Stat. *Th.* 7.413).

91 The reference is to the twin horses of the chariot of Mars (Hom. *Il.* 15.119), and Xanthus and Balius the famous windswift horses of Achilles (Hom. *Il.* 16.148); *currus* is used by a frequent metonymy for *equi qui currum trahebant;* cf. 1.514.

biiuges: here and in *Aen.* 12.355 Virgil has the third-declension form; elsewhere he uses *biiugus.*

Achilli: for this fifth-declension form, cf. *Aen.* 1.30; 2.7 (*Ulixi*).

92f. Servius tells the story of how Ops, the wife of Saturnus, caught him with his mistress Philyra, whereupon he turned himself into a horse and became in due course father of the Centaur Chiron, who was always associated with Mt Pelion in Thessaly. Compare Ap. Rh. 2.1231f, where the speed of Saturnus' departure (*iubam effundit, pernix, fugiens*) is also emphasised. Virgil's passage ends magnificently with the supernatural image of the king of heaven transfigured into a neighing horse, galloping over the mountains with its mane streaming out.

95-122 *A young horse must be chosen for stud purposes, endowed with that enthusiasm and desire for victory which we see exemplified in chariot races.*

95-122 In this paragraph Virgil presents another visual image of a strikingly vivid kind; the warhorse was pictured with all his splendour in 83f., and now the horses in a chariot-race are portrayed in their proud passion for victory. The picture is based quite closely on Hom. *Il.* 23.362f., and phrases from it are used again in the extended simile in *Aen.* 5.144f. The relationship of the horse with the human world is very close in the description of the chariot-race, where the horse's enthusiasm and love of glory matches that of the rider. The mythological references to Ericthonius and the Lapiths serve to give an air of antiquity and tradition to this cameo of a mettlesome horse.

95 **Hunc quoque:** i.e. even such a top-class thoroughbred as the one described in the previous passage.

gravis: 'enfeebled by'; cf. Livy 21.48.4 *gravis vulnere.*

96 **abde domo:** 'keep him away in his stable', i.e. retire him from stud; this is in contrast with 64 *solve mares.*

nec . . . senectae: 'and do not be indulgent to horrid old age'. Servius suggests the possibility of taking the negative with *turpis* (cf. Hor. *Odes* 1.31.19) — 'be indulgent to his old age which is nothing to be ashamed of'; but this is most unlikely. *Turpis* is common enough of something unpleasant which involves no moral failing; cf. 299; *Aen.* 5.358.

97 **in Venerem:** 'for mating'; this use of the goddess for her attribute is very common; cf. 64; 137.

98 **proelia:** metaphorical for the battles of love (cf. *Aen.* 11.736, Prop. 2.12.16) as the context shows, rather than literal.

99-100 'like a mighty fire sometimes in the stubble which loses its strength and flares up uselessly' i.e. runs out of fuel, the stubble being all consumed. For *quondam* in similes, cf. 4.261; *Aen.* 2.416. Notice how the rhythm of *incassum furit* echoes that of *ingratum trahit.*

101 **prolemque parentum:** 'the stock of their parents', i.e. their pedigree; cf. Varro *RR* 2.7.6 *de stirpe magni interest qua sint;* Hor. *Odes* 4.4.29f.

103 **nonne vides:** a vivid way of introducing the striking visual image which follows; cf. 250; 1.56.

104 This line occurs again in *Aen.* 5.145 in a simile; compare also line 103 with *Aen.* 5.144. *Corripuere* means 'speed over'; cf. *Aen.* 5.316; 6.634. *Carcer* is the technical

term for the starting-pens on a race course; cf. 1.512.

105-6 **exsultantiaque . . . pulsans:** 'and the throb of nervous excitement clutches at their leaping hearts'; cf. Hom. *Il.* 23.370-71. *Pavor* is the feeling akin to trembling felt by a keyed-up athlete; *haurire* literally is 'to drain of blood'. The phrase is used again in *Aen.* 5.137-8.

106 **verbere torto:** 'with the lash of their whips'; cf. *Aen.* 7.378; *Geo.* 1.309; Hom. *Il.* 23.362-3.

107 **et proni dant lora:** 'and leaning forward give the horses free rein': cf. *Aen.* 5.147. The pause after the third-foot trochee gives an unusual rhythm, appropriate to express energy and effort.

volat . . . axis: 'the hot wheels fly fiercely onwards'; for *fervidus,* cf. Hor. *Odes* 1.1.4-5. *Axis* is a common metonymy for the chariot-wheels or the chariot itself; cf. *Aen.* 12.379.

108 **iamque . . . sublime:** 'and at one moment they are near the ground, at another bounding high. . .'. *Sublime* is adverbial; cf. *Aen.* 10.664. The passage is modelled on Hom. *Il.* 23.368-9; there as here the reference is to the effect on the charioteers of the bouncing of the chariots.

111 **umescunt . . . sequentum:** 'they are soaked by the foam and breath of the pursuing horses'; again the image is based on Homer's description of the chariot-race (*Il.* 23.380-81).

113f. As the previous paragraph about the warhorse had ended with mythology (89f.), so now Virgil brings a mood of antiquity to the end of his description of the prize-winning racehorse.

113 **Ericthonius:** an ancient Athenian king, inventor of the four-horse chariot.

115 **Pelethronii Lapithae:** Pelethronium was a town or district in Thessaly, traditional home of the Lapiths (cf. 2.457). They were always associated with the Centaurs of this same area, whom they defeated in a famous victory —their connection with horsetaming here may be associated with that legend. They are contrasted with Ericthonius, first to yoke horses in a four-horse chariot, as being first to ride on horseback and to control the horse with a bridle. For Thessalian horses, cf. Varro *RR* 2.7.6.

gyrosque dedere: 'introduced wheeling', i.e. by means of bridles were able to make horses wheel round when they wished. Conington and others take the word *gyrus* to mean 'the ring for breaking horses in', but cf. 191;

Tib. 3.7.94.

117 'to prance over the ground and to pick up the legs high in proud movements'; the horseman is said to do what the horse does; cf. Hor. *Epod.* 16.12 *eques sonante verberabit ungula. Glomerare* is a favourite word with Virgil, meaning 'to collect in a circle'; cf. 4.79; *Aen.* 1.500; 2.315; 4.155. Pliny (*NH* 8.166) uses *glomeratio* of the high action (*haute école*) of a horse.

118 **uterque labor:** i.e. of producing a good chariot-horse or a good warhorse. Notice the lengthened last syllable of *labor;* see note on *Ecl.* 1.38.

120 **ille:** 'another (older) horse', referring back to the beginning of the section (95-6); in spite of the veteran horse's great accomplishments, the younger is to be preferred.

121 **Epirum:** Epirus in northern Greece was famous for horses; cf. 1.59.

Mycenas: in the Argolid in southern Greece; cf. line 44.

122 **Neptunique:** in legend Neptune (Poseidon) produced the first horse from the ground with a blow of his trident (1.12-14).

123-56 *Rules for the care of stud-horses and mares and of pregnant cattle.*

123-56 In this section Virgil's technique of treating horses and cattle together is especially marked as he switches the imagery from one to the other and sometimes speaks ambiguously in a way that could be applied to both. Lines 123-37 refer to both, but horses especially, except for 133-4. Lines 138-40 refer to cows, 141-2 to horses, 143-5 to both, and 146-56 to cows, leading into the next paragraph (157-78) which is specifically about cows. The poetic intention of this method of treatment is partly to give opportunity for a series of varied images, and partly to suggest the unity of the world of the domestic animals and the world of men.

The personification of horses and cattle, already a marked feature of this book (see notes on 72-94, 95-122) continues in this section: in line 125 the stud-horse is called not *admissarius* (the technical word), but *dux et maritus;* in 128 the offspring are called *nati* rather than *pulli;* the imagery of 135-7 is like that used by Lucretius of humans; the frequent use of *mater* and *pater* strengthens the identification of the animal world with the human world.

123 **His ... tempus:** 'When they have taken thought for all this, they take action as the time approaches ...'; i.e. just before

the stallion is to be mated. *His animadversis* refers to the advice of the previous paragraph about choosing a stallion of appropriate youth and mettle and good pedigree.

124 **denso ... pingui:** 'to fatten with firm layers of flesh'; on *denso* Servius says *'non laxo ... id est, viribus pleno'. Pingue* is used as a noun; cf. Lucr. 1.257. Advice is given on feeding up the male before mating by Varro (2.5.12, of bulls) and Columella (6.24.2 of bulls; 6.27.9 of horses).

125 **quem:** understand *eum* as the antecedent.

dixere maritum: 'they have appointed as husband', i.e. stud-horse. The phraseology is ornate and personifies the horse.

127 **blando ... superesse labori:** 'suffice for the work of love'; cf. Colum. 6.27.8 *ut Veneri supersit.*

128 'and in case feeble offspring should reflect the emaciation of their sires'; for *referre,* cf. Lucr. 4.1219.

129 'But they deliberately starve the herds and make them thin'; *ipsa armenta* refers to the female animals; cf. Varro *RR* 2.5.12.

131 **frondesque ... et:** for *-que ... et* ('both ... and'), a rarer version of *-que ... que,* cf. 223.

132 **cursu quatiunt:** 'exercise them by making them run'.

135-7 Servius points out how agricultural metaphors are applied to the act of mating: *bene rem turpem, aperte a Lucretio tractatam* (e.g. 4.1107f.,1272-3), *vitavit translationibus.*

138-9 **Rursus ... incipit:** 'In turn your care for the fathers begins to diminish and that for the mothers to take its place'; i.e. after mating the pregnant mother needs the special attention which previously was divided between the males and females. Cf. Varro *RR* 2.5.14; 2.7.10.

139 **exactis ... mensibus:** 'as the months go by', during their pregnancy.

140 **non:** for *ne;* cf. *nec* for *neve* in 96; *Ecl.* 10.5; *Geo.* 1.456.

140-42 The first line clearly refers to cows and the next two evidently to mares.

141-2 **acri ... fuga:** 'to rush over the meadows at headlong speed'; for *carpere* in this sense, cf. 191; 347.

143-4 **secundum flumina:** 'along the rivers'; this is a normal prose use of *secundum.* These lines (143-5), which are based on Varro *RR* 2.5.11, are made pastoral and idyllic, reminiscent of the scenery of the *Eclogues;* cf. also *Geo.* 2.195f.

145 **procubet:** 'must extend around';
cf. Claud. 1.120, the only other instance of
the word. The jussive subjunctives in this
line vary the construction from *pascunt*
(143), where some inferior MSS have changed
to *pascant.*

146f. The description of the gadfly (*asilus,
oestrus*) is relevant to cows rather than to
horses, as *mugitibus* (150) and *iuvencae*
(153) makes clear. Cf. Varro *RR* 2.5.14
(where he calls the gadfly *tabanus*), and
Sen. *Ep. Mor.* 58.2. For its use in a simile,
cf. Hom *Od.* 22.299f.; Ap. Rh. 1.1265f.;
3.275f.; and compare Shakespeare, *Antony
and Cleopatra* 3.8.24 'the breese (i.e. gadfly)
upon her, like a cow in June'; *Troilus and
Cressida* 1.3.48-9 'The herd hath more
annoyance by the breese Than by the tiger'.

146-7 Silarus is a river and Alburnus a
mountain in Lucania; *circa* governs *lucos*
and *Alburnum.* Notice the interlaced order
of *plurimus* and how *volitans* acts as a
noun: 'there is multitude of flying
creatures — the Romans call them gadflies
...'.

147 **asilo:** the dative (attracted to *cui*) is
the normal Latin construction; cf. 4.271.

148 **oestrum ... vocantes:** 'the Greeks
call it *oestrus* in their idiom'; *vertere*
generally means 'translate', but here simply
'have their own word for'.

149 **acerba sonans:** 'with a strident
buzz', *acerba* is adverbial; cf. *Aen.* 12.398
acerba fremens.

150 The trochaic pause in the third foot
adds to the emphasis on *furit*, personifying
the heavens which feel the same mad panic
as the cows; cf. Aesch. *Sept.* 155.

151 **Tanagri:** Tanager is a river of
Lucania; it is dry because the scene of the
gadflies is set in summer (154).

152f. A mythological touch is used to
end the description, as in 89f. and 113f.

153 Juno expressed (*exercuit*) her anger
against Io, daughter of Inachus the Argive
king, by turning her into a cow (*iuvencae*)
and planning torture for her (*pestem
meditata*) by means of the gadfly; for the
well-known story, cf. Aesch. *Prom.* 567f.;
674f.; Ov. *Met.* 1.588f.

155 For the hiatus after *pecori*, see note
on *Ecl.* 3.6. For the dative after *arcebis*, cf.
Ecl. 7.47.

156 **sole recens orto:** 'fresh from the
sunrise', i.e. immediately after sunrise;
cf. *Aen.* 6.450.

157-78 *The proper care of the calves,
according to the use required of them.*

157-78 The passage is based on Varro *RR*
1.20 and 2.5, and is again notable for the
use of human terms; cf. especially 163-4
(with note) and 178 *in dulcis ... natos.*
This is a quiet section, directly didactic,
contrasting with the previous passage
where the image of the gadfly was
developed by means of mythological
allusion, and with the following section
where the horse is treated in epic fashion.

158 For the branding of cattle with an
identifying mark, cf. 1.263; Colum.
7.9.12. The subject of *inurunt* is general:
cf. 123; 212.

159 **et quos:** there is an ellipse here;
supply *et designant eos (quos)* from the
previous line.

pecori ... summittere habendo: 'to use
as breeding cows for the continuation of
the herd'; *pecori ... habendo* is dative of
purpose; cf. 1.3.

160-61 **scindere ... invertere:** there is a
change of construction, as *quos* (object of
servare) now becomes the subject (*quos
malint scindere ... et invertere*).

161 **horrentem:** used here of uncultivated ground, cf. Cic. *ND* 2.19. Some
commentators take it proleptically, 'to
make it ridged' (cf. the use of *horrescere*
applied to the sea, note on 199).

162 **cetera ... armenta:** referring to
what follows, i.e. those not selected as
draught-oxen (163f.).

163-4 'but those which you propose to
train for activity and employment in the
fields you must encourage when they are
still calves'. The language here (*studium,
formabis, hortare, faciles animi iuvenum*)
is that which would be used of young children.

165 **mobilis:** 'flexible', 'pliant'; cf.
mobile ingenium (e.g. Sall. *Jug.* 46.3).

166 **circlos:** 'nooses', 'halters', a
syncope for *circulos* not found elsewhere;
cf. *vincla, saecla.*

167 **dehinc:** the word scans sometimes
as an iambus (as here; cf. *Aen.* 5.722),
sometimes as a single syllable (*Aen.* 1.131).

168-9 **ipsis ... pares:** 'join them in pairs
by linking them with these same halters',
i.e. without using a yoke; for *aptos* (=
aptatos); cf. *Aen.* 4.482.

170 'And they must often drag empty
wagons'; *illis* is dative of the agent, and
rotae metonymy for *plaustra* (cf. 107).
Varro (*RR* 1.20.3) has *ut inania primum
ducant plaustra.*

171 i.e. because they are not pulling a
heavy weight their feet will not sink deeply

into the dust.

172 **post:** adverbial. The rest of the phrase is a close translation of Homer *Il.* 5.838-9 μέγα δ᾽ ἔβραχε φήγινος ἄξων/ βριθοσύνη ('the oaken axle groaned loudly with the weight').

173 'and let the pole of brass pull the twin wheels'; the wooden pole had reinforcements of brass or iron.

175 **vescas:** 'siccas et teneras' (Servius). The point is the inadequacy of willow-leaves, grass, and sedge for diet when the animal is young and being broken in; it must have corn too; cf. Varro *RR* 2.5.17; 2.7.11.

176f. Cows that have recently calved (*fetae*) are not to be milked (which our forefathers did), but to use their milk for their young; cf. Varro *RR* 2.2.17. The Romans used cow's milk much less than we do.

179-208 *The training of a racehorse or a charger destined to outstrip the winds in the pride of his gallop.*

179-208 The diction and tone of this passage is highly ornate and elevated as Virgil uses material from Varro (*RR* 2.7.11f.) to draw his own picture of the spirited horse which is trained for the racecourse or the battlefield. Cf. Job 39: 23-5 'The quiver rattleth against him, the glittering spear and the shield. He swalloweth the ground with fierceness and rage; neither believeth he that it is the sound of the trumpet. He saith among the trumpets, Ha, ha; and he smelleth the battle afar off, the thunder of the captains, and the shouting.' Compare too Shakespeare, *Henry V*, 3.7.29f. '. . . his neigh is like the bidding of a monarch, and his countenance enforces homage'. The famous picture by Jacques David of Napoleon on his charger gives a wonderful impression of the almost supernatural splendour of the warhorse. For a good discussion of the poetic impact of this passage, with its full-scale epic simile, see Richter on 196f.

179 **turmas:** 'cavalry squadrons'.

180-81 These are references to the Olympic games; for the river Alpheus see note on 19f.; Pisa was a city on the river, close to the site of Olympia.

180 **praelabi:** infinitive after *studium (est)*, parallel to *ad bella*; cf. 1.21.

182 **animos atque arma:** 'the bravery and the weapons', i.e. to become accustomed both to the excitement of battle and to the weapons of war. Day Lewis has 'pride and panoply'.

183-4 **tractuque . . . sonantis:** 'to accept the noise of the chariot-wheels as they squeal under the strain, and to hear the clanking of the bridles in their stables'; for the last phrase, cf. Varro *RR* 2.7.12.

186 **plausae . . . cervicis:** 'its neck being patted'; cf. *Aen.* 12.85-6; Pope, *Essay on Man*, 3.35-6 'The bounding steed you pompously bestride Shares with his lord the pleasure and the pride'.

188 **inque vicem:** 'between times', 'now and then', i.e. he is to learn to wear a halter by gradual stages.

det . . . capistris: 'let him submit his mouth to the soft halter', made all of leather as opposed to the iron of the bridle and bit.

189 **invalidus:** the last syllable is lengthened in arsis; cf. 76.

inscius aevi: 'ignorant of life'; the genitive is objective (cf. *Aen.* 8.627), but also very similar to the genitive of respect as in *aevi maturus, Aen.* 5.73.

190 **accesserit:** some of the major MSS have *acceperit* (cf. *Ecl.* 8.39). but the omission of the object *eum* would be harsh in the context.

191 **carpere . . . gyrum:** 'to speed round in circles'; cf. 115. *Carpere* is in the same sense as *carpere viam, carpere iter;* cf. 142. It is possible, but not necessary, that *gyrus* here may be used in the sense of a circular ring constructed for the purpose.

191-2 **gradibusque sonare compositis:** 'to gallop with rhythmic sound'.

192 **sinuetque . . . crurum:** 'and to pick up his front and hind legs in great curving movements', a most highly ornate expression (cf. 117), similar to that used of the sea-serpent in *Aen.* 2.208 *sinuatque immensa volumine terga.* Heyne says *alte tollat, iactet, crura alternis; at quam ornate!*

193 **sitque laboranti similis:** i.e. although he is only practising, let him go hard; for the phrase, cf. *Aen.* 5.254.

194 **provocet:** this is the reading of P; the other main MSS have *tum vocet* which is accepted by most modern editors, but the repetition of *tum* in this position is stylistically un-Virgilian, and *provocare* has more force than *vocare.*

195 The image is recalled in the description of Camilla, *Aen.* 7.807-11; cf. Shakespeare, *Henry V*, 3.7.13f.; 'He bounds from the earth as if his entrails were hairs: *le cheval volant*, the Pegasus, *qui a les narines de feu!* When I bestride him,

I soar, I am a hawk: he trots the air; the earth sings when he touches it. . .'.

196f. The extended simile picks up the phrase in 193-4 (challenging the winds) and develops and elaborates it so that the attention in the end is concentrated for a moment on the wind and its effect rather than on the horse with which the point of likeness began.

196 **Hyperboreis:** the word is applied in an unspecific way to the far distant north; cf. 381; 4.517; Hor. *Odes* 2.20.16.

196-7 **densus . . . incubuit:** 'swoops down in all its might'; cf. *Aen.* 1.84.

197-8 'and spreads far and wide the cold of Scythia and the dry clouds'; Servius rightly says for *arida* 'sine pluviis'. The north wind was often associated with cold clear weather; cf. 1.460.

198 **campique natantes:** the context shows that this phrase means 'the sea' (Lucr. 6.1142) rather than 'lakes' (Lucr. 6.267): Virgil describes land (*segetes*), sea *(campique natantes)*, land (*silvae*), sea (*fluctus*), land (*arva*), sea (*aequora*).

199 **lenibus:** the winds are 'gentle' at first, as the storm begins; cf. Cat. 64.272 (*undae*) *tarde primum clementi flamine pulsae.*

horrescunt: words connected with *horror* are fairly often used of the ruffled surface of the sea; cf. *Aen.* 5.11; Cat. 64.270.

200 **urgent:** a very unusual intransitive usage, equivalent to *urgent se.*

201 **ille:** i.e. Aquilo; after the changes of subject in the simile Virgil returns to the original subject.

202 **hic:** 'such a horse'; some of the major MSS have *hinc,* which most modern editors read, but a reiteration of the subject of the narrative is needed after the long simile.

202-3 **ad Elei . . . spatia:** *metae* are the turning-points for the chariot-race; cf. *Aen.* 5.129. Elis is the name of the district in which Olympia is situated (cf. 1.59), and *Eleus* its adjective. Notice the interwoven order 'at the turning-points and long laps of the stadium at Elis'. For *spatia,* cf. 1.513.

204 **Belgica . . . esseda:** Belgian war-chariots were well-known in the Roman world after the campaigns of Julius Caesar. The context makes it likely that Virgil is speaking of chariots for war, though it is known that this particular type was in civilian use in Rome in Virgil's time.

205f. If you feed the horses on mash before they are broken in, they will be too

high-spirited to tame; so do this only (*tum demum*) after they are broken in (*iam domitis*). *Farrago* (Varro *RR* 1.31.5) is a mixture of green crops such as barley, vetch and legumes.

206 **sinito:** the emphatic form of the imperative; cf. 2.197.

domandum: the gerund is used as a noun; cf. 215.

207-8 **negabunt . . . pati:** 'will refuse to endure'; cf. *Aen.* 4.428.

208 **verbera lenta:** the lash of the whip or the reins, which are flexible (*lentus*).

lupatis: bits furnished with metal points (like wolves' teeth); cf. Hor. *Odes* 1.8.6.

209-41 *The compulsion exercised on cattle and horses by sexual desire. Description of a fight between rival bulls.*

209-41 This is a highly poetical description of one special aspect of the power of Venus in the animal world — the rivalry of two bulls for a heifer. It takes one or two small factual details from Varro (*RR* 2.1.18; 2.5.12) and Aristotle (*HA* 6.18; 21), and it draws some inspiration (as the next section does far more fully) from the beginning of Lucretius' *De Rerum Natura:* but essentially it is Virgil's own creation, and one of the finest passages he ever wrote. Its impact is due partly to his amazing control of heightened diction as he describes with full power the fight, the defeat, the return for vengeance, rounding off the last picture with a great epic simile based on Homer; but mainly it is the culmination of the theme which has been running throughout this book, namely the similarity of the animal world and the human world. The heifer's attractions (217) are described in the terms of love elegy, and the bulls are personified to the point of heroic splendour (225; 228; 236). For further discussion of this point, see Otis pp. 174-6.

209 **industria:** 'care', taken by humans; the action that most of all builds up their strength is to keep them away from the opposite sex; cf. Varro *RR* 2.1.18; 2.5.12.

211 **cui:** = *alicui.*

212 **relegant:** again the general third person; cf. 158.

214 **satura:** 'well-stocked'.

216 Cf. Thomson, *The Seasons, Spring* 792-4 'Through all his lusty veins The bull, deep-scorched, the raging passion feels. Of pasture sick, and negligent of food . . .'.

217 **dulcibus illa quidem inlecebris:** 'possessing sweet enchantment as she

does'; for the reinforcement of the subject by *illa*, cf. Page's note *ad loc.* and 362; 501; 4.257.

218 **decernere:** 'to do battle'; cf. 20. Compare Ap. Rh. 2.88-9.

219 'Upon the heights of Sila is grazing a beautiful heifer'; the sudden switch in the narrative from the general to the particular is strangely effective here, making this one of the most memorable lines in the poem. Most MSS have *silva,* but the proper name *Sila* adds greatly to the particularising effect aimed at. Sila is a mountain in Lucania; cf. *Aen.* 12. 715; a passage about bulls very similar to this one. The impact of the line depends very much on its simplicity, with the assonance of final *-a* and the uncontrived order with juxtaposition of adjective, noun, adjective, noun. For a similar effect in descriptive passages, cf. *Aen.* 6. 268-70; 638-9.

220 *illi* are the *amantes* of 218. Notice the strong conflict of ictus and accent to convey **struggle**; cf. *Aen.* 12.720 (the same subject) *illi inter sese multa vi vulnera miscent,* and *Aen.* 8.452 (the Cyclopes at work in their smithy) *illi inter sese multa vi bracchia tollunt.*

221 **lavit:** archaic for *lavat;* cf. 359.

ater: there is very strong emphasis on the single spondaic word filling the fourth foot and giving coincidence of ictus and accent after the previous strong conflict.

222 **versaque . . . cornua:** 'and their horns take the impact as they face their battling adversary'; cf. *Aen.* 12.721 *cornuaque obnixi infigunt;* Stat. *Th.* 4.399. *Urgentur* is literally 'are pressed against hard'.

223 **silvaeque . . . et:** for *-que . . . et* ('both . . . and'), cf. 131.

longus Olympus: 'the heavens afar'.

224 **una stabulare:** 'share the same stable'; *stabulare* is intransitive; cf. *Aen.* 6.286. Compare Shakespeare, *Antony and Cleopatra* 5.1 39-40 (Octavian to Antony) . . . 'we could not stall together In the whole world'.

225f. Lucan (2.601f.) and Statius (*Th.* 2.323f.) both use this image as a simile for a defeated hero's departure from the battlefield. The semi-personification of the bulls in Virgil's description is very noticeable; see note on 209-41.

227 **amores:** object of *gemens* and antecedent of *quos.*

229 As in 220, the slow spondees and the clash of accent and ictus convey effort and toil.

230 **pernox:** 'all night', an adjective used adverbially; cf. *Aen.* 8.465 *Aeneas se matutinus agebat* and line 260. The word *pernox* is not common, but cf. Livy 21.49.9; Ov. *Met.* 7.268. The MSS have *pernix,* but the scholiast on Juvenal 8.10 and Servius *auctus* on this passage knew the reading *pernox. Pernix* (swift) makes hardly any sense in the context; efforts to get the sense of 'restless' or 'persistent' out of it are vain.

instrato: this must mean 'uncovered', (cf. *intectus*) though there is no other instance of such a meaning. Normally the word would mean 'covered with' (Lucr. 5.987 *instrata cubilia fronde*), but the suggestion that it might go with *frondibus* is quite impossible because of the run of line 231 where *et* must link *frondibus* and *carice* as objects of *pastus.*

231 **carice . . . acuta:** 'prickly rushes'.

232 **irasci in cornua:** 'to put his fury into his horns'; this phrase (cf. Eur. *Bacch.* 743) and the next two lines are repeated in *Aen.* 12.104-6 where Turnus arming for war is compared with a bull rehearsing for the battle.

233 **obnixus:** 'butting'; cf. 222.

236 **signa movet:** 'advances to battle', a very strong personification of the bull as the general of an army bent on battle. Compare the bees in 4.108.

oblitum: 'who has forgotten him'; cf. 245; Servius says, *iam securum ex ante acta victoria.*

237f. The full-scale simile rounds off this high-flown epic description; cf. Hom. *Il.* 4.422f. and *Aen.* 7.528f. where the beginning of the battle between Italians and Trojans is illustrated by a simile of the same subject-matter which begins with an almost exact repetition of 237. The point of comparison is the onward movement with ever-increasing impetus, but as in the previous simile (196f.) Virgil develops the imagery beyond the point of comparison

238 **longius . . . trahit:** 'rolls its billow from afar and out of the deep'.

239 **immane:** adverbial, 'terribly'; cf. *Aen.* 12.535.

239-40 **ipso monte:** the actual cliff itself, standing above the rocks.

240 The rhythm reflects the violent movement, with a trochaic pause in the third foot and elision over the main fourth-foot caesura.

242-83 *All of earth's creatures are servants to the power of love: lions, bears, horses, wild boars, human beings. But*

an epic touch as Virgil urges the farmers not to shirk the task.

289f. The phrases which follow very strongly recall Lucretius; cf. Lucr. 1.136-7 *nec me animi fallit Graiorum obscura reperta difficile illustrare Latinis versibus esse*, 5. 97-9, and 1. 921-30 (see note on 291).

289 animi: genitive of respect (not locative); cf. 4.491 and my note on *Aen.* 5.202 (Oxford edition).

289-90 verbis ... quam sit: 'how great a task it is to master this in words'; cf. *vincere verbis* (Lucr. 5.735), i.e. to overcome the problem of finding the right words.

290 angustis ... rebus: cf. 4.6 (of the bees) and Pliny *NH* 19.59 *Vergilio quoque confesso quam sit difficile verborum honorem tam parvis perhibere.*

291-3 Cf. Lucr. 1. 926f. *avia Pieridum peragro loca nullius ante trita solo. iuvat integros accedere fontes* ....

291 Parnasi: the mountain of Apollo and the Muses, near Delphi; cf. 2.18.

ardua: 'steeps', the neuter plural of the adjective is used as a noun; cf. 315.

dulcis: there is strong stress on the adjective at the line-ending, emphasised by the alliteration of *d;* see note on 285.

292-3 qua ... clivo: 'where no path trodden by anyone before winds down with gentle slope to Castalia'; cf. Lucr. 1.926 (quoted above) and Hor. *Epist.* 1.19.21. *Castaliam* is accusative of motion (= *ad Castaliam*). Castalia was the spring on Parnassus (291); cf. Hor. *Odes* 3.4.61.

294 veneranda Pales: see note on line 1.

295-321 *The care of sheep and goats in winter. Sheep are especially valuable for their fleeces, but goats also have much to offer: they are more fertile, they supply milk in abundance and their hair too has its uses.*

295-321 This passage is closely based on Varro *RR* 2.2.7-8 and 2.3. 6-7, and it is presented in strong didactic tones (*incipiens ... edico,* 295; *post ... iubeo,* 300; *hae ... tuendae,* 305; *omni studio ... avertes* 318-20; *feres ... nec .. . claudes,* 320-21). On Virgil's general treatment of the subject of sheep and goats see note on 284-94.

295-6 stabulis edico ... carpere ovis: 'I prescribe that the sheep should feed in comfortable pens'. For *edico* with the infinitive, cf. *Aen.* 11. 463.

297 duram: notice the emphasis on the adjective separated by a whole line from its noun — because the ground is hard the sheep need straw and ferns. This aspect of animal husbandry was strongly stressed in antiquity; cf. Cato *Agr.* 5.7; Varro *RR* 2.2.7-8; Colum. 7.3.8.

298 sternere: supply *te*; the construction after *edico* is varied — *edico ovis carpere et te sternere.*

299 scabiem: see note on 441.

turpisque podagras: 'foul foot-rot'; *turpis* refers to the ugly effect of disease on the body and its movement. On this disease, cf. Pliny *NH* 26.100.

300 digressus: i.e. he now turns from the winter care of sheep to that of goats; the word suggests that we are moving from one place to another on the farm.

301 arbuta: see note on 1.148.

sufficere: 'supply', transitive; cf. 2.436. For the feeding of goats, cf. Varro *RR* 2.3.7; Colum. 7.6.

303-4 'at the time when cold Aquarius sets and brings its rain at the year's end': the constellation Aquarius (the watercarrier) sets in February; cf. Hor. *Sat.* 1.1.36. The farmer's year begins with the spring in February (Varro *RR* 1.28.1).

303 olim: as correlative to *cum,* an archaic use equivalent to *illo tempore quo.*

305 hae ... tuendae: i.e. the goats are worth as much care as the sheep, though the sheep might seem more valuable because of their better fleeces. Some MSS (perhaps rightly) have *haec ... tuendae,* in which case *haec* would be an archaic form of the feminine plural. M has *haec ... tuenda* and Servius comments on the use of the neuter, but this seems very unlikely.

306-7 'although Milesian fleeces dyed with Tyrian purple are sold at a great price'. The splendour of Milesian fleeces was proverbial; cf. 4. 334; Cic. *Verr.* 2.1.86. For *mutare* ('sell'), cf. Hor. *Sat.* 1.4.29; for the retained accusative *rubores,* see note on *Ecl.* 1.54.

308 hinc: i.e. from goats, picking up *hae* in 305.

309-10 'the more the pails foam when their udders have been emptied, the more the joyful streams will flow when their teats are again milked'. To *magis* in line 310 supply *tam;* cf. *Aen.* 7. 787-8.

311 nec minus interea: 'and moreover it is also the case that ...'; two features in which goats surpass sheep have been given (number of offspring, milk) and now it is pointed out that though the fleeces of sheep are admittedly very valuable yet goat's hair has some uses.

311-12   **barbas ... hirci:** 'men clip the beards and hoary chins of the Cinyphian goat ...' The phrase conveys a half-humorous personification: *incana* would suggest old age in humans (cf. *Aen.* 6.809), but not necessarily in goats. The geographical epithet *Cinyphius* refers to the river Cinyps in Libya.

313   The reference is to ropes and cloth made of goat's hair and used for various military and nautical purposes; cf. Varro *RR* 2.11.11.

miseris: a subjective addition typical of Virgil, emphasising the hard lot of the sailor; Servius' comment is *qui frequenter patiuntur pericula.*

314   **pascuntur ... silvas:** for the deponent form with the accusative ('feed on'), cf. 458; 4.181.

Lycaei: the mountain Lycaeus in Arcadia is used to illustrate specifically the height and inaccessibility of the goat's pasturage.

318f.   Because the goats ask so little, we should all the more give what they do ask: supply *eo magis* in the main clause to balance *quo minor.*

322-38   *The care of sheep and goats in the summer.*

322-38   This is one of the most highly coloured passages in the book, standing in strong contrast to the previous didactic and factual section. Its tone is pastoral and idyllic, and in its sunny atmosphere of calm beauty it may be compared with the 'praises of Italy' in 2.136f. It owes a debt to Theocritus, especially *Idyll* 7, and it contains phrases reminiscent of Virgil's own pastoral *Eclogues*. It is based factually on Varro *RR* 2.2.10-11, but its method is poetic rather than didactic: it aims to convey by descriptive and musical verse the deep love which Virgil felt for the summery loveliness of his own countryside. Wilkinson (pp. 11-12) sets it side by side with its source in Varro and finds an effect like a painting by Brueghel.

323   **utrumque gregem:** i.e. both sheep and goats.

mittet: most MSS (and Servius) have *mittes,* but this would go badly with *carpamus* (325).

324   **Luciferi:** Venus, the morning star; cf. *Ecl.* 8.17.

325   **carpamus:** 'let us graze'; the

shepherds are identified with their flocks: Servius says *carpere cogamus animalia.* The interpretation preferred by some – 'hasten to the countryside'; cf. *carpere iter* – is very unlikely indeed.

mane: this word is more normal in an adverbial sense, but for its use as a noun, cf. Hor. *Sat.* 1.3.17-18 *vigilabat ad ipsum mane.*

326   Compare *Ecl.* 8.15, an almost identical line.

327   **sitim ... collegerit:** 'has brought the parching heat', when the dew has all evaporated in mid-morning; cf. Hor. *Odes* 4.12.13.

328   This line especially is in the pastoral mode, cf. Theocr. 7. 139f., 16. 94f.; *Ecl.* 2.13; 5.77. *Rumpent arbusta* means that their song breaks through the shrubs, comes bursting out from the shrubs in which they are hidden.

329-30   'I shall order the flocks at the wells or at the deep marshes to drink the water which runs in its oak troughs': *ilignis* is an alternative form for *iligneis,* the adjective of *ilex.* Some MSS read *iubeto,* but this is impossible in sense with *dare* and *pascere* (335).

332   **sicubi:** 'if somewhere', 'wherever'.

332-4   The description of shade is in the high ornate style; the specification of the oak tree is given mythological content by the reference to Jupiter which recalls his famous oak grove at Dodona (cf. 2.15-16) and the grove with its sacred shade brings to mind Diana, guardian goddess of the groves.

334   **accubet:** 'reclines'; the image seems to be of the bed of shadows on which the grove itself sleeps.

335   **dare ... pascere:** dependent on *iubebo* (329); after the siesta the flocks are again fed and watered.

tenuis: 'clear', not stagnant and cloudy.

336   **Vesper:** Venus as the evening star.

337   **reficit:** 'revives', from the heat; *recreat* (Servius).

338   The final line of this pastoral description of summer is especially reminiscent of the phraseology and atmosphere of the *Eclogues.* For *alcyon,* the kingfisher, cf. Theocr. 7.57 and see note on 1:399. *Acalanthis* ('gold-finch' or perhaps 'warbler') occurs only here; the commoner form is *acanthis* (cf. Theocr. 7.141). It is connected with the Greek word ἄκανθα ('thorn-bush'); the Latin equivalent is *carduelis,* 'thistle-bird'.

alcyonen ... acalanthida: very striking

instances of a cognate accusative after
the intransitive verb *resonant* ('give out
the sound of'); cf. *Aen.* 1. 328 *nec vox
hominem sonat; Ecl.* 1.5. *formosam
resonare doces Amaryllida silvas.*

339-48 *The task of nomadic shepherds
in the parched deserts of Libya is very
different from the conditions in Italy.*

339-48 The connection of this episode
(and the next) with the immediate context
is not close, as Virgil suggests with his
opening rhetorical question; but its
poetic intention is clear, namely to make
a contrast between the favoured climate
of Italy and the extremes on both sides,
heat in Libya and cold in Scythia. The
theme of geographical variations in the
farmer's conditions in different parts of
the world is a constantly recurring one
in the *Georgics* and is due not only to
Virgil's love of exotic description but
also to his desire to set Italian agriculture
in a world context, showing the advantages
of Italy (cf. especially 2.136f.).

340 'and their settlements inhabited by
sparse buildings'; *mapalia* is a Carthaginian
word (a variant of *magalia*; *Aen.* 1.421; 4.259).

343 hospitiis: 'places of habitation,
shelters'.

344 The rhythm of the first half of
the line is most unusual, with no break till
the diaeresis after the second foot; the
effect is stressed by the strong alliteration
of *a* (armentarius *A*fer agit). *Armentarius*
is a somewhat uncommon word for
herdsman; cf. Lucr. 6.1252; Varro *RR*
2.5.18.

tectumque laremque: 'both his house and
his home ...'. The piling up of -*que*
in this line and the next conveys the
completeness of his self-sufficiency on his
long trek.

345 Amyclaeumque canem: dogs from
Sparta (cf. 89) were famous; cf. 44; 405;
Hor. *Epod.* 6.5.5. The epithet, like *Cressam*,
is 'ornate', i.e. of literary interest rather
than of specific reference to the context.

Cressamque pharetram: Cretan archers
were famous; cf. *Ecl.* 10.59; *Aen.* 4.70;
5.306.

346f. The comparison is with Roman
soldiers on a forced march, fully equipped
(*iniusto sub fasce*, 'bearing a terrible
burden').

347 carpit: 'eats up'; cf. 142; *Aen.* 6.629.
hosti: dative after *stat* in the sense of
obstat.

348 ante exspectatum: the participle

acts as a noun; cf. 2.398. Wilkinson
(p. 198) draws attention to the sudden
switch to staccato, 'suggesting the brisk
drill of the disciplined guardsman'.

349-83 *In Scythia and the far north the
bitter cold involves a totally different way
of life, a much harsher one where men are
more cruel.*

349-83 The description of the frozen lands
of the north balances the previous section on
Libya's heat, but is much longer and
more elaborately written. It gives Virgil the
opportunity to display his rhetorical and descriptive skill to the full, and it also serves to set
the tone for the long description of disease
and death with which this book ends. It
indicates aspects of Nature's harshness
which contrast very strongly with the
idyllic description of the farmer's life at the
end of Book 2 (see Otis, pp. 176f.).
The subject-matter may be compared with
Herodotus 4.28f.; for other sources, see
Richter *ad loc.*

349 At non: 'but it is not so ...'; the
abrupt phrase sets up the contrast between
the desert lands and the frozen north,
and the terseness continues in what follows.

Maeotia: the sea of Azov in southern
Russia; cf. *Aen.* 6.799.

351 'and where Rhodope which stretches
out towards the heart of the (north) pole
comes back south again'; Rhodope was a
mountain range in Thrace (cf. 462) which
ran in a great arc north and then south. For
axis in this sense, cf. 2.271.

353 The spondaic line helps to reflect
the dull deadness of the frozen land.

354 informis: not so much 'ugly' as
'shapeless', because covered in snow; cf. Hor.
Odes 2.10.15.

355 septemque ... ulnas: 'and rises up
to a height of seven cubits', i.e. the snow is
piled three or four metres deep.

356 Cauri: North-West Winds; cf. 278.
Observe the alliteration of *s* for the whistling
of the wind.

357 tum: 'furthermore'; the word
indicates an additional point in the
narrative; cf. 2.296.

358 nec cum ... nec cum: the repetition
with the pause after the fifth foot and the
unusual line-ending point the fact that
neither in the morning *nor* in the evening
does the sun break through the mist.
Cf. Hom. *Od.* 11.15f., of the land of the
Cimmerians.

360 concrescunt ... crustae: 'chunks of
ice form'; cf. Lucr. 6.626.

361 tergo ... orbis: 'supports on its

surface iron-shod wheels'; cf. Ov. *Trist.*
3.10.31f. Much of this passage is imitated by
Thomson, *Seasons, Winter,* 228f.; 723f.

363   **aeraque dissiliunt vulgo:** 'bronze vessels
frequently split open', because the water
in them is frozen and expands.

364   The absence of main caesura in the
third or fourth foot helps to convey the
hacking of frozen wine. *Umida* means
'normally liquid'. Servius is firm that wine
does not freeze, and suggests that *umida*
means 'mixed with water'; but cf. Ov. *Trist.*
3.10.23f. Martyn quotes a Captain Monck
who related of Greenland in 1620 'that no
wine or brandy was strong enough to be
proof against the cold, but froze to the
bottom, and that the vessels split in
pieces, so that they cut the frozen liquor
with hatchets, and melted it at the fire
before they could drink it'.

365   **vertere:** supply *se.* The sudden
change of tense invites us to visualise
what *has* happened.

366   As so often in Virgil, a highly
descriptive passage is rounded off with a
golden line.

   horrida: 'bristling', sharp and pointed, the
basic meaning of the word; cf. 4.407; *Aen.*
3.23 (of myrtle branches); *Aen.* 4.251 *glacie
riget horrida barba.*

367   **non setius:** 'without let-up', *non
segnius quam incohaverat* (Servius).

368   **stant:** paradoxically the dead oxen
stand upright, frozen in the snow.

369-70   **confertoque . . . mole nova:** 'and
in dense throng stags are frozen stiff in the
fresh-piled snow'; again the sentence has
a paradoxical turn in that one would expect
after *conferto agmine cervi* a verb expressing
speed. This whole passage is imitated by
Thomson, *Seasons, Winter,* 820f.

372   **puniceaeve . . . formidine pennae:**
'with the frightening device of the purple
feather'; *formido* is a technical term for a
device used in hunting, made of bright
feathers attached to a rope; cf. *Aen.*
12.750.

373   **trudentis:** 'as they strain against'.

375   **caedunt.** the spondaic word filling
the first foot, followed by three more
spondaic feet, gives an air of finality to this
parody of a hunt: see note on 317.

376f.   For references to cave-dwellers,
Conington cites Aesch. *PV* 452f.; Tac. *Germ.*
16; Mela 2.1.10.

377   **totasque:** hypermetric elision, see note
on 1.295.

379   **ducunt:** 'consume'; cf. *Aen.* 6.539.

380   **vitea:** 'of the vine', a very rare word;

they substitute for wine a drink made of
fermented corn or sour apples.

381   **Hyperboreo . . . trioni:** 'beneath the
Hyperborean Northlands'; the word *septentrio*
(here separated into its two parts by tmesis)
is derived from the seven stars of Ursa Major (the
Plough with its oxen), cf. *Aen.* 1.744. For
Hyperboreus (beyond the North Wind), cf. 196

382   **effrena:** 'wild', a poetic form of
effrenatus, a favourite word of Cicero's.

   Riphaeo: a range of mountains in Scythia; cf
1.240.

383   **velatur corpora:** 'cover their bodies',
retained accusative; see note on *Ecl.* 1.54.

384-403   *How to get the best wool, fit for
Pan when he wooed the Moon; how to get
the best goat's milk.*

384-403   These two brief didactic
sections on sheep's wool and goats milk
balance symmetrically (ten lines each);
the next brief section on dogs (404-13) is
also the same length. The account of
snowy-white wool is given a haunting
touch of mythology at its end (391-3); the
paragraph on goat's milk (the goat was the
main source of milk in the ancient world,
see Wilkinson pp. 257-8) is also concluded
with a lively picture, that of the farmer
selling his produce on a journey to town.

384-5   The instruction is to avoid for
pasturage both rough undergrowth (which
would tear the wool) and also over-lush
meadows; cf. Colum. 7.2.3.

385   **lappaeque:** *-que* is lengthened in
arsis, see note on 1.153, the same phrase.

387   **illum:** supply *arietem;* the Latin
idiom takes the antecedent noun into the
subordinate clause, cf. 4.33f.

388   'if he only has a black tongue
beneath his moist palate'; cf. Arist. *HA*
6.19; Varro *RR* 2.2.4; Colum. 7.3.1.
Tantum means, 'if the black tongue is his
only fault'. Modern knowledge supports
this statement.

389   **reice:** the word scans as a dactyl;
cf. the poetic lengthening of the first
syllable of *religio* (1.270), *reliquiae.*

391-3   The myth of Pan and the moon
is said by Macrobius (*Sat.* 5.22.9f.) to
have been taken from Nicander; Servius
is of the view that Virgil has transferred to
Pan the story of Endymion.

391   **si credere dignum est:** cf. *Aen.*
6.173.

394   **lactis:** Virgil is talking about
goat's milk, the type normally used by
the Romans; see note on 176f.

   cytisum: see note on 2.431.

   lotosque: apparently a type of plant

allied to the tree mentioned in 2.84.

396 The salt makes them thirsty, and thus increases the milk yield.

398 excretos: 'separated', from *excernere* rather than 'grown' from *excrescere* (as Servius says).

399 'and fix to the ends of their noses iron muzzles'; another golden line.

401 premunt: 'make into cheese'; cf. Varro *RR* 2.11.4.

402 calathis: 'bowls', 'churns', for milk or curds.

404-13 *The farmer needs good dogs to guard his property and to hunt wild animals.*

404-13 This brief section (equal in length to each of the two preceding passages) is the only notice which Virgil gives to dogs. It is based on Varro *RR* 2.9.1f. (see also Hes. *WD* 604 and Colum. 7.12) and it is designed to universalise this aspect of farming (notice the Greek names *Spartae* and *Molossum,* the specific mention of Spaniards, 408, and the reference to wild asses, 409, not found in Italy).

404 nec . . . fuerit: 'let it not be'; *nec* is poetic for *neve.*

405 For Spartan dogs see note on 44; for Molossians (from Epirus), cf. Hor. *Epod.* 6.5; Lucr. 5.1063; Varro *RR* 2.9.5.

406 sero: 'whey'.

408 impacatos . . . Hiberos: 'the unpacified Spaniards'; Servius sweepingly says, *feri enim Hispani omnes acerrimi abactores sunt,* but the reference is rather to the constant troubles with Spain in Virgil's time; cf. also Varro *RR* 1.16.2.

409f. Apart from being watchdogs, the dogs will be used in the chase (*cursu*), whether for wild asses, hares, deer, boars or stags.

411 volutabris: 'from their pools', where they wallow (*volutare*); the word is very rare.

414-39 *It is also necessary to keep snakes away from your flocks and herds; there are many dangerous types, especially the Calabrian snake.*

414-39 This is a highly ornate passage in which Virgil uses his descriptive power to create a frightening picture of dangerous snakes. It is a theme which he elaborates in rhetorical style elsewhere; cf. 2.153f; *Aen.* 2.203f.; 5.84f.; 273f. The subject-matter is partly based on Nicander's *Theriaca* (see notes on 415, 425) but Virgil makes it his own by the personal

tone of the last five lines and by his extraordinary command of diction and metre.

415 'and to drive off the dangerous watersnakes with the smell of resin'. Cedar smoke is mentioned as prophylactic against snakes in Nicander, *Ther.* 51f.; Pliny *NH* 24.19; Colum. 7.4.6.

416 immotis: 'neglected', not treated or checked for pests.

aut mala tactu: the conflict of ictus and accent in the fifth foot puts powerful emphasis on to *mala.*

420 fovit humum: 'hugs the ground'; cf. 4.43.

cape saxa: notice the sudden impetus, conveyed by the dactylic movement and the repetition, to reinforce the personal exhortation to the shepherd.

421 Cf. *Aen.* 2.381 (of a snake) *attollentem iras et caerula colla tumentem; colla* is accusative of respect (cf. 427).

422 deice: the dactylic first foot followed by a pause is often used by Virgil to express powerful action; cf. 1.333; 3.516. The rest of the line is dactylic; cf. 420.

iamque . . . alte: the snake is now visualised in a wounded condition hiding its head deep in the undergrowth.

423-4 'while its spirals in the middle and the march of its tail at the end are without strength, and its last coil drags its slow revolution'; compare the snake simile in *Aen.* 5.275f.

425f. The description of this water-snake from Calabria (in southern Italy) is imitated from Nicander (*Ther.* 359f.).

426 Cf. the simile in *Aen.* 2.474, almost the same line; lines 437 and 439 are also repeated in that passage.

427 longam maculosus . . . alvum: 'spotted all along its great belly'; *alvum* is accusative of respect, cf. 421.

430 hic: 'here', in the marshes, as opposed to his movements in summer (432f.).

430-31 piscibus . . . explet: 'immoderate-ly fills his black maw with fish and croaking frogs'; for *improbus* see note on 1.119; observe the alliteration of *q* and *c* for the croaking of the frogs.

434 asperque . . . aestu: 'both fierce from thirst and terrified by the heat'; these phrases give the picture first from the point of view of those menaced by the snake and then from the snake's point of view.

437 These phrases are repeated in *Aen.* 2.473.

438 catulos: normally used of lions, puppies, etc., here of baby snakes.

439 Cf. *Aen.* 2.475, the same line.

440-69 *The causes and treatment of diseases, especially scab.*

440-69 Virgil has here probably based his account on Varro (*RR* 2.1.21f.; 2.11.6f.); cf. also Cato *Agr.* 96 and Colum. 7.5.5f. There is a mixture of prophylactic and remedial measures. The paragraph serves as an introduction to the vivid account of the Norican plague with which the book ends.

441 scabies: this is a skin disease, scab or scabies; it is in fact due to a parasite, not to the causes which Virgil gives (441-4).

442 ad vivum persedit: 'has penetrated into the quick', i.e. deeply within the animal's flesh.

443-4 After they have been sheared the sheep are thought to be vulnerable to the penetration of their own sweat if it is not washed away, and to scratches caused by brambles.

447 The trochaic caesura in the third foot with no main caesura in the fourth conveys an idea of movement appropriate to the picture of the ram floating downstream (cf. 1.514).

448 amurca: the dregs of olive oil, cf. 1.194; Cato *Agr.* 96; Colum. 7.5.7. For the general treatment, cf. Varro *RR* 2.11. 6-7.

449 For the idea that flecks of silver were curative, cf. Pliny *NH* 33.105f.

vivaque: i.e. fresh sulphur as opposed to a preparation made by heating it.

sulpura: the final syllable is elided hypermetrically; see note on 1.295.

450 The pines from Mt Ida were famous; the reference is to the use of pitch (cf. 4.41). 'Wax rich with oil' means that the wax is softened and made pliable.

451 Scilla is a type of bulb (Varro *RR* 2.7.8); hellebore a plant frequently used as a medicine (Hor. *Epist.* 2.2.137); bitumen a pitch-like substance (*Ecl.* 8.82).

452 fortuna laborum: 'happy remedy for suffering'.

454 os: we speak of festering places as coming to a 'head'; for the following phrases, cf. Lucr. 4.1068.

456 abnegat: 'refuses to'; cf. *Aen.* 2.637.

459-60 avertere et . . . ferire: 'to dispel and to cut', i.e. to dispel by cutting. For the letting of blood from the foot to diminish fever, cf. Colum. 7.5.10.

461-3 These are northern tribes (*fugit*

refers to their nomadic habits) who drink milk mixed with horses' blood which they procure from the foot: the point of this reference is to show that blood may be safely taken from the feet of the animals.

464-5 quam . . . videris: 'if you see one . . .'; the antecedent is *eius*, understood with *culpam* (468).

466 extremamque sequi: 'following last'; *extremam* is in agreement with the subject (*quam*).

467 serae . . . nocti: 'departing alone from the late night'; cf. *Ecl.* 8.88.

468 culpam . . . compesce: i.e. kill the animal which otherwise would spread its disease (*culpa*) through the whole flock.

469 The section is rounded with a golden line.

470-566 *Disease may strike whole flocks, as in the plague at Noricum. On that occasion vast numbers of animals died in spite of all efforts; plough-oxen dropped in their tracks; wolves, fish, birds and all nature's creatures were stricken by the deadly disease.*

470-566 The book ends with an intense and tragic account of suffering and death, a lurid description of disaster in the animal world. It presents Nature in hostile mood, in stark contrast with the optimism of the ending of Book 2 and with the happy picture of Stoic providence which has generally dominated the *Georgics*. In a way it balances the political pessimism at the end of Book 1, but it is more terrible because not explicable in terms of man's folly.

No specific historical sources can be identified for this plague, but the literary source is very patent throughout — Lucretius' description of the plague at Athens (6.1138f.), itself to be compared with the account in Thucydides (2.49f.). Instances where Virgil has followed Lucretius particularly closely are cited in the note on 502. Virgil has produced a rhetorical elaboration of death and disaster on the most powerful scale, comparable in its effect with the memorable and moving pictures in Thucydides and Lucretius; compare also Ov. *Met.* 7.523f.

Perhaps the most memorable section of all is that of the death of the faithful draught-ox (515f.); it is in some ways inspired by Lucretius' description of the cow which has lost its calf (2.352f.), but it has about it a special pathos which is characteristically Virgilian.

For fuller discussion of this section see

Richter's note on 478f.; Wilkinson, pp. 206-8; and W. Liebeschütz, *GR* 1965, pp. 64f.

470-71 The manifold diseases of flocks and herds are compared in intensity with winter storms; cf. *Aen.* 1.85.

472 **tota aestiva repente**: 'whole summer flocks all of a sudden'; *aestiva* is used of summer camps, and hence, by a military metaphor, of summer flocks. *Repente* has tremendous stress, as adverbs are rare at line-endings.

473 The rhyme of *-em* and alliteration of *-que* emphasise this elaboration of *aestiva*.

474-7 'Then a man would realise this fact if he saw the lofty Alps and the Norican forts on their hillocks and the fields of Iapydian Timavus even now so long afterwards and the deserted kingdoms of the shepherds and the groves empty far and wide'. Virgil here introduces his extended account of a particular plague which wiped out flocks and herds over a wide area of northern Italy and beyond; Noricum is between the Alps and the Danube; Timavus (*Ecl.* 8.6, *Aen.* 1.244) is a river at the head of the Adriatic where the Iapydes lived.

478-9 'Here it was that once because of a plague in the sky a pitiful time struck the world and blazed white with the whole heat of autumn'; for this plague see note on 470-566; for *morbo caeli*, cf. *Ecl.* 7.57; and for the phraseology generally, cf. *Aen.* 3.137f.

482-3 **sed ubi . . . artus**: 'but when the parching thirst driven through all the veins had contracted the wretched limbs'; for *adduxerat*, cf. Ov. *Met.* 3.397; for the general sense, cf. Lucr. 6.1145f.

484-5 **omniaque . . . trahebat**: 'and drew into itself all the bones which had one after the other collapsed because of the disease'; the image, a very exaggerated one, is of the watery fluid so possessing the whole body (after the departure of the raging fever described in the previous lines) that even the bones dissolved.

486 **in honore deum medio**: 'in the middle of a sacrifice to the gods'; for this use of *honos*, cf. *Aen.* 3.406.

488 Notice the alliteration in this highly pictorial line, and the alternation of the slow spondaic beginning (the attendants are confused and uncertain) and the rapid dactyls of the onset of death.

490 **inde**: = *ab ea hostia*, the antecedent to *si quam* in the previous line.

491 The seer cannot give a reply because the victim is so emaciated that the normal consultation of the entrails is impossible; cf. Ov. *Met.* 7.600f.

493 **summaque**: 'only the surface'.

494 **laetis**: emphatic, although the grass is luxuriant for cropping; cf. *plena* (495), *blandis* (496), *victor*(499).

497 **faucibus . . . obesis**: 'torments them in their swollen throats', cf. Lucr. 6.1147f.

498 **studiorum**: many commentators take this with *infelix* (cf. 1.277), but the rhythm and sense favour taking it with *immemor*.

499 **fontisque avertitur**: 'rejects water'; the passive form *avertitur* takes a direct object on the analogy of the Greek middle; cf. Stat. *Th.* 6.192 and *praevertitur* in *Aen.* 1.317, and compare the deponent word *aversari*.

500 **crebra**: adverbial; cf. 149.

500-501 **incertus . . . frigidus**: 'the sweat comes there intermittently, cold sweat it is, presaging their death', cf. Lucr. 6.1187; the unusual pause after the fifth foot adds emphasis both to *frigidus* and *aret*.

502 **ad tactum . . . resistit**: 'is tough and unyielding to the touch when you put your hand on it'; cf. Lucr. 6.1195. There are other reminiscences of Lucretius' account of the plague in the following lines (505 = Lucr. 6.1180; 505-6 = Lucr. 6.1186; 507 = Lucr. 6.1160; 511 = Lucr. 6.1229).

504 **crudescere**: 'grow fiercer'; cf. *Aen.* 7.788; 11.833.

509-10 The forcible administration of wine (*latices Lenaei*, cf. 2.4) corresponds with our use of brandy; cf. Colum. 6.30.1.

511-12 **furiisque refecti ardebant**: 'and though revived they became burning hot and maddened'.

513 'May the gods give happier fortune to the righteous and such madness to our enemies'; supply the verb *dent*. The line is based on Nicander *Ther.* 186.

514 The passage is rounded with a golden line.

515f. In this memorable passage of deeply moving pathos Virgil switches from the general picture of the victims with which he has been concerned to a specific and vivid cameo (*ecce autem . . .*) of the faithful bull, suddenly smitten with the deadly disease. It is probably inspired by Lucr. 2.352f. (the cow pining for its lost calf), but Virgil has adapted the idea

to his own purposes; see further, note on
470-566.

516 **concidit:** the run-on verb adds
dramatic emphasis; cf. 422.

517-18 'sadly the ploughman goes as he
unyokes the bullock who laments his
brother's death'; alliteration of *t* and *m*
and spondaic rhythm contribute to the
descriptive impact of the scene.

520f. The description (with continued
strong alliteration of *m*) switches back to
the dying bull: cf. Lucr. 2.361f. *nec tenerae
salices atque herbae rore vigentes fluminaque illa queunt summis labentia ripis
oblectare animum subitamque avertere
curam.*

521-2 **non qui . . . amnis:** the antecedent *amnis* is postponed till the end of its
long antecedent clause.

522 The unusual trochaic pause in the
fifth foot marks the strong contrast
between all the pleasing things in life
just described and the cold fact of death.

524 **fluit devexo pondere:** 'droops under
its nodding weight'; for *fluit,* cf. *Aen.*
11.828 (of Camilla falling in death).

525f. Conington quotes Scaliger: 'I
would sooner have planned and achieved
these lines than have Croesus or Cyrus
himself as my servant'.

525-6 'Of what avail his toil and service?
Of what avail to have worked the heavy
lands with the plough?' The double
rhetorical question powerfully conveys the
idea of devoted service by the farm animals;
cf. 2.515 *meritosque iuvencos;* Varro *RR*
2.5.4 (of the ox) *hic socius hominum in
rustico opere; Anth. Pal.* 6.228 (of
Alcon's old ox) 'he honoured it for its
service' − αἰδεσθεὶς ἔργων.

526-30 The contrast between riotous
living and the simple country life is
reminiscent of the end of Book 2; cf.
especially 461f.; 503f.

526-7 **Massica . . . munera:** for Massic
(Campanian) wine, cf. 2.143.

527 **repostae:** 'renewed'; cf. 4.378. The
form is contracted for *repositae;* cf. *Aen.*
1.26.

529 **exercita cursu:** 'rapid in their
course'; cf. Lucr. 2.97.

531f. The meaning is that never before
had it been impossible to find appropriate
cows for the sacrifice to Juno (*quaesitas*
means 'sought and not found'), so that
wild cattle (for *uri,* cf. 2.374) which did
not match each other had to be used as
offerings (*donaria* means the place where
the offerings were made; cf. Ov. *Fast.*

3.335). In the well-known Greek festival to
Juno at Argos the carriage was drawn by
oxen which would be well-matched and
unblemished.

534f. In the absence of the cattle the
farm-workers have to perform all the tasks.

536 **contenta:** 'straining'; cf. *Aen.* 5.513.

537f. For the reversal of what is normal
in the animal world, cf. *Ecl.* 5.60f.; 8.27f.;
52f.

537 **insidias explorat:** 'looks for a place
to plunder from'; cf. *Aen.* 9.59f.

538 **nec . . . obambulat:** 'and does not
prowl by night after the flocks', a
splendidly vivid phrase made more striking
by the rhythm where the absence of main
caesura in the third or fourth foot and the
trochaic lilt help to convey sliding
movement. For *nocturnus* used adverbially
in this way, cf. *matutinus* in *Aen.* 8.485.

acrior: i.e. disease, worse than hunger.

541-3 The cumulatory effect of the
disaster is expressed in this sentence by means
of the series of phrases preceding the
subject *fluctus;* the simile *ceu naufraga
corpora* has metrical emphasis through the
relatively unusual feature of the fourth
foot and the fifth foot, each consisting of a
single dactylic word in agreement.

543 **insolitae . . . phocae:** 'seals take
refuge in rivers where they are never
normally found'; cf. Hor. *Odes* 1.2,7f.;
Ov. *Met.* 1.300. The alliteration of *f* and *ph*
is unusually violent.

544-5 **interit et . . . et:** the verb is given
emphasis by its position at the beginning of
the sentence and the line; *intereunt* is to be
supplied with *hydri.*

545 The image of the water-snakes
with scales standing on end is elaborated
to the point of grotesqueness.

547 Compare *Aen.* 5.517, the bird shot
in the archery contest.

548 **nec . . . refert:** 'it does not matter',
i.e. it is no help.

549 **artes:** medical skills, methods of
treatment.

550 Chiron the Centaur, son of Saturnus
and Phillyra, was famous for his medical
skill; Melampus, son of Amythaon, for his
power of religious expiation. Both of these
magistri have given up (*cessere*), i.e. when
invoked cannot assist.

551-2 'Pale Tisiphone rages and sent
from the Stygian darkness to the light
drives before her Diseases and Panic';
Tisiphone is one of the three Furies (cf.
Aen. 6.571, where she is the guardian of
Tartarus, the lowest part of the underworld);

Stygius (from the river Styx) is used of the underworld generally. The personification of *Morbi* and *Metus* is reminiscent of the greatly elaborated list of shapes at the entrance to the underworld in *Aen.* 6.273f., especially 275-6.

556   catervatim dat stragem: 'she deals destruction group by group'. *Catervatim* is used by Lucretius in his description of the plague (6.1144); the meaning is that it is not merely individuals but whole communities that die.

559f. These normal methods of disposing of dead bodies were useless because of contamination, and mass burial had to be used instead. *Coriis* refers to the use (in

normal circumstances) of the hide of dead animals, after which the flesh would be either boiled or roasted.

562   telas: i.e. if the wool were spun. The passage describes various stages: (i) the fleece cannot be sheared, (ii) if it is sheared, it cannot be woven, (iii) if it is woven into clothes, it cannot be worn.

563   temptarat: contracted for *temptaverat*, frequentative use of the pluperfect — 'if ever anyone tried . . .'.

565-6 'and the victim did not linger long, but the accursed fever consumed his infected limbs'; for *sacer ignis*, cf. Lucr. 6.660; 1167; Colum. 7.5.16. The book ends abruptly, on a stark note of pessimism.

GEORGICS 4

The fourth book is about beekeeping; the first half is concerned directly with bees, and the second half is a mythological story about how Aristaeus replaced his lost bees, containing within it the story of Orpheus and Eurydice. The connection between the two parts is discussed in the notes on 281-314 and 315-424; the literary qualities of the second half, always regarded as one of the greatest passages in Latin poetry, are discussed on 315-424 and 425-558.

The sources of Virgil's information about bees cannot be determined with accuracy: we know that he took material from Aristotle (*HA* 5.21-2; 9.40; *Gen. An.* 3.10) and Varro (*RR* 3.16), and he may have used the *Melissurgica* of Nicander (a work now lost). But what is very evident, especially if we contrast Book 4 with Columella's treatment in his Book 9, is that Virgil is using his own practical experience and knowledge of bee-lore in addition to literary sources. There is a vigour and directness about his writing which brings the didactic material to life, and an imaginative sympathy with the bees which is characteristic of the spirit of the rest of the *Georgics*.

Two themes in particular are used to ennoble 'the humble subject' (line 6); the first is the constant personification of the bees as social creatures similar on their tiny scale to the great world of man. Suggestions of this are in Virgil's sources (Aristotle calls the bees πολιτικαί, and Varro uses personification and military imagery), but Virgil has developed this aspect to a far greater extent, particularly emphasising the selfless work involved in the organisation of the bees (see the notes on 8-50; 51-115; 149-227; 228-80).

Secondly Virgil relates the marvels of the bees' activities to the omnipresence of God in all the works of Nature; in a memorable passage (219-27) he tells how it is thought that the bees too have a share in the divine spirit which prevades the world. A hint of this is found in Aristotle (*Gen. An.* 3.10) and it is taken up by Seneca (*De Clem.* 1. 19.4) and Pliny (*NH* 11.12). The association of bees with the supernatural world went far back in ancient tradition and folklore (see D. E. W. Wormell in *Vergiliana*, ed. H. Bardon and R. Verdière, pp. 429f. and H. M. Ransome, *The Sacred Bee*, London, 1937), and Virgil has built on these beliefs

in order to illustrate once more the pantheistic view of the whole world and
its creatures which dominates the *Georgics*.

For further information about the bees in Virgil and other ancient sources
see Wilkinson pp. 260-69 (with full references); H. M. Fraser, *Beekeeping in
Antiquity* (London, 1931); R. Billiard, *L'Agriculture dans l'antiquité d'après
les Géorgiques de Virgile* (Paris, 1928); T. F. Royds, *The Beasts, Birds and Bees
of Virgil*, (Oxford, 1918); B. G. Whitfield, *Virgil and the Bees (GR* 1956, pp. 99f.).

1-7 *My subject now is bees: Maecenas,
look with favour on this section too. I have
to tell of tiny creatures, but the importance
of the theme is large.*

1-7 The brief statement of the theme of
the book is parallel with that at the beginning
of Book 2. Its tone contrasts entirely with
the gloom of the end of Book 3 as Virgil
speaks now in happy and optimistic terms
of the wonderful world of the bees. He
makes it evident that his subject is one of
strange fascination, and he equates the
behaviour of the bees with human society
(notes on 3-5 and 149-227), a theme which
recurs throughout the whole of the book.
Compare Shakespeare, *Henry V.* 1.2.187f
'... for so work the honey-bees,/
Creatures that by a rule in nature teach/
The act of order to a peopled kingdom.'

1 **Protinus:** 'next in order', cf. *Aen.*
3.291.

aerii ... dona: 'the heavenly gifts of
honey sent from the air'; the adjectives
link the ideas of honey-dew descending
from the sky (Arist. *HA* 5.22) and of the
bees' share in the divine world above; cf.
219-21.

2 **Maecenas:** all four books of the *Georgics*
are dedicated to Maecenas; see note on 1.2.

3-5 'I will tell you of the marvellous
sights of this tiny world, and the great-
hearted generals, and the way of life and
ideals of their whole race in order, and
their peoples and their battles'. Here
Virgil begins the personification of the
world of the bees which continues
throughout his description; instances will
constantly be commented on in the notes
which follow. For *levium ... rerum*, cf. 6;
for *magnanimos*, an epic word, cf. 83;
for *proelia*, cf. 67f.

6 Compare Cowper's imitation (*Task*
1.6) 'The theme though humble yet
august and proud The occasion'; and
Pope, *Rape of the Lock*, 1.5-6 'Slight is
the subject, but not so the praise, If she
inspire and he approve my lays'.

7 **laeva:** 'unfavourable', as Gellius says
(5.12); Virgil hopes to be able to overcome

the difficulties which his subject is bound
to offer (cf. 2.483-4). Some commentators
have followed Servius in his explanation of
laeva as *prospera*, because omens on the
left can be favourable (e.g. *Aen.* 2,693;
9.631), but this is impossible in the context,
especially with *sinunt.*

8-50 *The choice of a site for the hives;
the proper method of their construction.*

8-50 Virgil goes straight away into
didactic precepts partly based on Aristotle
(*HA* 9.40) and Varro (*RR* 3.16.12f.).
But he makes his theme appropriate for
poetry by means of occasional mythological
imagery (15; 29), by brilliantly descriptive
lines (11-12; 17; 18-20; 30-32; 49-50),
and above all by beginning his personification of the tiny world of the bees, making
it seem parallel with the world of human
society (8; 20; 43; 45). This aspect is
increasingly developed as the book proceeds;
see note on 1-7. Much of Virgil's material
is reproduced in Colum. 9.5 and Pliny
NH 11.11f.

8 **sedes ... statioque:** a continuation of
the military metaphor of *magnanimosque
duces* (4).

10 **petulci:** 'mischievous'; cf. Lucr.
2.367-8 *haedi ... agnique petulci.*

11 **insultent:** 'may trample on', final
subjunctive parallel to *sit* in the previous
neque clause.

13 **absint:** the single spondee in the
first foot carries an emphasis appropriate to
the didactic passage; compare *adsint* (19).

picti ... lacerti: 'lizards with brightly-
coloured scaly backs'; *terga* is retained
accusative or accusative of respect; cf.
15 and note on *Ecl.* 1.54.

14 **meropes:** 'bee-eaters'; cf. Pliny
NH 10.99.

15 'and Procne, her breast stained by
bloody hands'; the reference is to the
story of how Procne murdered her son and
was turned into a swallow, bearing the
sign of murder on her breast: cf. *Ecl.*
6.78f.; Ov. *Met.* 6.424f.

16-17 'and carry off in their beaks the
bees themselves in flight as tasty morsels

for their cruel nestlings': *nidis*, literally nests, is used for the birds in the nests; cf. *Aen.* 5.214; 12.475.

20 vestibulum: the 'porch' of the hive again personifies the bees; cf. *iuventus* (22).

21 reges: it was commonly believed in the ancient world that the leader of the bees was male (Arist. *HA* 5.21; 9.40; Varro *RR* 3.16.8. Ov. *Fast.* 3.556) though there are some isolated passages to the contrary (Xen. *Oec.* 7.17f.); for a collection of these passages see T. Hudson-Williams, *CR* 1935, pp. 2-4. The truth about the queen bee was first discovered by means of the microscope by the Dutch naturalist Jan Swammerdam in the seventeenth century.

22 vere suo: 'in the spring they love'; the spring is their own special time.

23 calori: 'from the heat'; for the dative; cf. 3.467.

25 'into the midst of the water, whether it is standing stagnant or flowing'; cf. 18-19.

26 'throw willow trunks across and big rocks', as bridges (27); *grandia* is from the bee's point of view (Varro has *lapilli*). *Conice* is a dactyl, with the first syllable lengthened before the consonant *i* which is pronounced but not spelled in compounds of *iacere* (cf. 46).

28-9 'if perchance a violent east wind has besprinkled the slow ones or dipped them into the water'. For Neptunus as god of fresh water, cf. Cat. 31.3.

30-32 All these plants are particularly fragrant, thyme being especially picked out as 'strongly aromatic'; cf. Varro *RR* 3.16.10, 13f.

33 ipsa: the noun *alvaria* with which *ipsa* agrees is taken into the second subordinate clause.

cavatis: 'hollowed', i.e. curved strips of bark; cf. 2.387; 453.

36 cogit . . . remittit: 'solidifies . . . melts'; the extremes (*vis*) of temperature must be avoided (by having narrow entrances) because of their adverse effect on the texture of the honey.

37-8 neque . . . nequiquam: 'and that is why . . .'.

38-9 tenuia . . . spiramenta: 'tiny cracks'; for the scansion of *tenuia* as a dactyl (the *u* being treated as a consonant), cf. 1.397.

39-41 'and they fill up the edges with pigment from petals and they preserve the glue which they have collected for this very purpose, glue that is more sticky than mistletoe or the pitch of Phrygian Ida'.

Fucus is not used elsewhere in this sense, and Madvig's conjecture *suco* has something to be said for it, but *fucus* seems to be Virgil's word for what Varro (*RR* 3.16.23) calls *propolis* ('bee-glue'). *Fucoque et floribus* is a hendiadys; for the idea, cf. Pliny *NH* 11.14 *cera ex floribus. Gluten* (a neuter word; cf. 160) has the same meaning (*propolis*), and defines the previous clause in a different way. The reference to Phrygian Ida concerns the pitch-pines for which Mt Ida near Troy was famous (cf. 3.450).

43 fovere larem: 'they keep their house snug'; for *fovere*, cf. 3.420; *Aen.* 9.57. *larem* is another marked personification; cf. *cubilia* (45); *tectis* (47).

45-6 'But you must still smear the chinks in their bedrooms with smooth mud, working it snugly around, and throw on a few leaves'. *tamen* means that, although the bees take all these precautions against cold and intruders, you must still help them.

47 taxum: yew is a very poisonous tree; cf. *Ecl.* 9.30; *Geo.* 2.257.

48 cancros: the strong smell of roasted crabs (used as fertiliser) would scare the bees away; cf. Pliny *NH* 11.62; Colum. 9.5.6.

49-50 'or a place where rocky caves resound when struck, and the reverberating sound of the voice echoes back'; cf. Varro *RR* 3.16.12; Colum. 9.5.6. *Offendere* here has its primary sense of 'strike': the sound of the voice is struck by the rock and rebounds. For *imago*, cf. Lucr. 4.571.

51-115 *Once spring comes, the bees must be attracted to settle in the place which you have prepared. If they fight they can be controlled easily. The best 'king' must be chosen, and if the bees exhibit swarming-fever you must remove the kings' wings.*

51-115 This section contains a series of precepts based particularly on Aristotle and Varro (see note on 8-50), and presented in high epic diction. The personification of the bees continues, and the battle of the rival 'kings' is described in military and heroic terms. Here Virgil has subordinated didactic correctness to poetic imagination: 'kings' in fact fight each other in this way only within the hive, and the poet has conflated details from swarming and from attacks by a rival hive in order to produce a superb battle-scene which elevates the tiny creatures to human dimensions. We may compare the treatment of the battle of the bulls in 3.219f. Some have seen political allegory in the rival kings (88f.), relating them to Antony and Octavian, but this is very unlikely; see also note on 149-227.

51-7 Notice the build-up of words suggesting light and joy: *aureus, aestiva luce, reclusit, purpureos, leves, dulcedine laetae, fovent.* Compare Milton's bee simile in *PL* 1.768f.

                                    As bees
In spring-time, when the Sun with Taurus rides,
Pour forth their populous youth about the hive
In clusters: they among fresh dews and flowers
Fly to and fro, or on the smoothed plank
The suburb of their straw-built citadel,
New rubb'd with balm, expatiate and confer
Their State affairs.

52 **reclusit:** 'unveiled', removed the clouds; cf. 1.217.

55 **leves:** the position of the adjective at the end of its sentence enhances the pictorial image; cf. Lucr. 3.11.

nescio qua . . . laetae: the same phrase is used (1.412) of rooks in sunny weather.

56-7 **progeniem . . . fingunt:** 'they care for their offspring in the nests; then they skilfully fashion fresh wax and make sticky honey'; the reference is first to bee-bread (the pollen which feeds the young) then to the wax of the honeycombs and then to the honey itself; cf. Varro *RR* 3.16. 23f.

58 **hinc:** 'then', indicating the next stage in the narrative. Some MSS read *hic,* but the three-fold repetition of *hinc* is very much in Virgil's manner.

caveis: 'from their hives'; the word is used several times in this sense by Columella.

61 **contemplator:** 'just watch'; the rare pause after the second foot trochee adds further stress to the emphatic form of the imperative (cf. 1.187).

62 **tecta:** 'coverts', not 'hives' as in 38 and 187.

iussos: 'prescribed' in the treatises (cf. Varro *RR* 3.16.10), and defined in the next line.

63 'crushed balm and the humble herb honeywort'; the branches of trees in the chosen area are to be treated to make them more attractive. Cf. Varro *RR* 3.16; and Milton, *PL* 1.773f., quoted in note on 51-7.

64 The mock-epic picture of the clashing cymbals of the Great Mother (Cybele) refers to the legend of how the bees looked after Jupiter in Crete, while the clashing cymbals of the Curetes drowned his infant cries, which would have betrayed his presence to his father Saturnus; cf. 149f., where the legend is dealt with more fully; and Lucr. 2.600f. The Curetes of Crete were closely linked with the cult of Cybele in Phrygia; see my note on *Aen.* 3.111 (Oxford edition). Notice the powerful alliteration of *t* and *c* in this line, imitating the noise of cymbals. The idea that musical noise influences bees is found in Aristotle (*HA* 9.40) and Varro (*RR* 3.16.30); cf. also Pliny *NH* 11.68; Colum. 9.8.10; and the old belief that the sound of church bells caused bees to swarm.

67f. The subordinate clause *sin . . . exierint* is by-passed by the parenthesis which follows and is left without a main clause; the description in the parenthesis is so vivid and extensive that a grammatical return to the subordinate clause would seem artificial. In effect lines 86-7 serve as the main clause.

68 **regibus:** the battle between the contending queens (see note on 21) is presented throughout in human terms; see note on 51-115.

71 Here the noise of the bees is compared with the resonant blare of a war trumpet; cf. Varro *RR* 3.16.9 *duces conficiunt quaedam ad vocem ut imitatione tubae.*

et vox: the double monosyllable at the line ending gives an impressive effect; see note on 1.181.

72 Notice the alliteration of *t,* used to reflect the harsh notes of the trumpet; cf. Ennius *Ann.* 140 *at tuba terribili sonitu taratantara dixit.* For *fractos,* cf. *Aen.* 3.556 with my note (Oxford edition).

74 **spiculaque exacuunt rostris:** 'they sharpen their stings on their beaks' a vivid but inaccurate description of the familiar sight of bees stroking their bodies and faces with their legs to clean them. Virgil's incorrect explanation of this is influenced by the military presentation of the whole passage.

75 **praetoria:** cf. Shakespeare, *Henry V.* 1.2.195f. (of bees) 'Which pillage they with merry march bring home/To the tent-royal of their emperor'.

77 **nactae:** supply *sunt;* cf. 3.235.

78-9 The military imagery here becomes

very explicit, with the alliteration of *m* in line 79 increasing the idea of vast effort; cf. Caes. *BC* 2.14.1; Sall. *Jug.* 53.2.

81 tantum ... glandis: 'so many acorns'; for the use of the partitive genitive after a neuter adjective, cf. 1.478. The singular *glandis* is collective; Huxley compares Hor. *Odes* 1.5.1 *multa ... in rosa.*

82-3 The emphasis of metre and diction here is very considerable as Virgil turns to the 'kings' themselves: the first foot filled by a spondaic word gives emphasis, and the juxtaposition of adjective and noun (*medias acies, insignibus alis, ingentis animos, angusto in pectore*) is sufficiently unusual in the hexameter to command attention; cf. *Aen.* 6. 269-70; 638-9.

83 This is perhaps the most memorable line of all in the personification of the bees: cf. the imitation in Milton *PL* 7.486 (of the emmet) 'in small room large heart enclosed', and Shakespeare, *Henry V*, 2.Chorus 16 'O England! model to thy inward greatness, Like little body with a mighty heart'.

84-5 'until the fierce victor has forced either this side or that to turn their backs and retreat in flight'; the metre at the end of 84 is unusual with the conflict of word-accent in the fifth foot and the double monosyllabic ending; cf. *Aen.* 10.9.

86-7 'These passions and these epic conflicts are controlled and vanish if you throw a little dust'; these lines are very calm and serene after the excitement of the activity described in the previous lines. For the subject-matter, cf. Varro *RR* 3.16.30 (where throwing dust is recommended for swarming); Pliny *NH* 11.58.

89-90 'put to death the one who is seen to be inferior, so that he does not cause waste and loss', i.e. by splitting the harmony and wasting the honeymaking efforts; cf. Varro *RR* 3.16.18.

90 melior ... sine regnet: 'let the better one rule'; for *sine* with the jussive subjunctive in parataxis, cf. *Ecl.* 9.43.

91 alter: i.e. the better one; cf. Arist. *HA* 5.21; Varro *RR* 3.16.18f.

auro squalentibus: 'stiff with gold', i.e. well-covered with gold; cf. *Aen.* 10.314; 12.87.

92 melior: the final syllable is lengthened in arsis; see note on *Ecl.* 1.38.

93 rutilis clarus squamis: a variation on line 91.

93-4 'the other one is shaggy-looking and idle, and ingloriously drags along a broad belly'; Columella (9.10) calls the better sort light and unhairy, and the worse sort shaggy; cf. also Varro *RR* 3.16.19; Pliny *NH* 11.59 *deterrimae ... pilosae.*

95 plebis: the personification is very obvious here.

96 turpes horrent: 'are ugly and squalid'; cf. *horridus* in 93, and Plin. *NH* 11.59 *horridae aspectu.*

96-8 'like a parched traveller when he comes out of clouds of dust and spits out soil from his dry mouth'. Columella (9.10) quotes this passage and explains it as meaning that the inferior bee is like dirty spittle (*sordido sputo similis*), but this seems a ludicrous misinterpretation: the comparison is between the bee and the traveller, and the picture of the traveller is elaborated further to show his rough and dishevelled condition. Both the bee and the traveller are *horridi*, 'scruffy'; it is the antithesis of the bright and shining bee in the next phrase.

99 'their oily bodies gleaming with gold and symmetrical markings'; for *gutta*, cf. Ov. *Met.* 4.578. *Corpora* is accusative of respect; cf. 181 and see note on 2.131. *Lita* is from *linere*, to anoint or cover with oil.

101 nec tantum ... quantum: 'and not only sweet, but also ...'.

102 Mixing of wine (Bacchus) with honey to make *mulsum* was common in the Roman world; cf. Hor. *Sat.* 2.4.24.

104 frigida: predicative, 'leave their homes cold'.

108 iter: cognate accusative with *ire;* cf. 2.39; *Aen.* 6.122.

castris ... signa: for the human military metaphor, cf. 75; 3.236.

110-11 'and as protection against thieves and birds let the guardianship of Priapus of the Hellespont defend them with his willow bill-hook'. Priapus was the rural divinity who protected gardens; cf. *Ecl.* 7.33; Hor. *Sat.* 1.8, 1-7; Tib. 1.1.18; 1.4.8; Ov. *Fast.* 6.333. He was said to have come from Lampsacus on the Hellespont.

112-13 ipse ... cui talia curae: i.e. the man who is proposing to keep bees must personally see that everything is properly prepared.

112 tinosque: 'laurustine' an evergreen shrub; some MSS have *pinosque* (there is the same variation in 141).

113 tecta ... circum: the preposition is postponed.

115 **inriget:** 'let him provide as irrigation'; transitive; cf. *Aen.* 1.691-2.

116-48 *If I had the space I would sing of gardens like the one at Tarentum which the old Corycian gardener tended; as it is I must leave this topic to others.*

116-48 This is one of the most famous passages in the *Georgics,* and Virgil's *praeteritio* (mentioning the subject but not treating it fully) was taken up later by Columella; the tenth book of his prose treatise is written in verse on the subject of gardens. Virgil's source is Varro *RR* 3.16.10, where there is a mention of two soldiers who had a small garden for their bees; notice the way in which Virgil links his account with the main subject of this book in 139-41. The passage with its note of pride in the working of the land may be compared with the praises of Italy in 2.136f., and the theme of the reward which hard work brings to the gardener is characteristic of the whole of the *Georgics.* The passage is made particularly striking by the personal note (125 *namque . . . memini*) and the contrast of small means (128-9) with deep contentment (132-3).

117 **vela traham:** for the naval metaphor of the poet's journey, cf. 2.41; compare the metaphor from horse-riding at the end of Book 2. The present subjunctive is used instead of the imperfect to express a present unfulfilled condition; cf. Tib. 1.4.63.

118 **et:** 'both', picked up by *-que* (*biferique*).

119 **biferique . . . Paesti:** Paestum in southern Italy was proverbial for its twice-flowering roses; cf. Ov. *Met.* 15.708; Prop. 4.5.61.

120-21 'and how endive rejoices in the rills which it drinks, and the green banks delight in their parsley'; the idea of the joy of Nature (cf. *laetus* in 1.1) is explicit here.

122 **cresceret in ventrem:** 'swells out into a round', i.e. becomes rotund from its pencil-like beginning; cf. Prop. 4.2.43.
sera: adverbial accusative; cf. 2.275.

124 **hederas . . . myrtos:** cf. *Ecl.* 3.39; *Geo.* 2.112.

125 **Oebaliae . . . arcis:** 'the citadel of Tarantum'; Oebalus was a legendary king of Sparta, mother city of Tarentum.

126 **Galaesus:** a river near Tarentum; cf. Hor. *Odes* 2.6.10f.; Prop. 2.34.67.

127 **Corycium:** a Cilician, perhaps settled in southern Italy by Pompey after his campaigns (so Servius); Cilicians were famed for their horticulture (Mart. 8.14.1).

relicti: 'left over', i.e. the best land was already allocated. Others render 'inherited' (cf. Varro *RR* 3.16.10), but this has less point in the context.

129 **seges:** 'plot of land'; the word is here used in a very wide sense (cf. 1.47; 2.267); some critics have approved Salmasius' conjecture of *Cereri* for *pecori,* but there is not sufficient reason to change.

130-32 'But he, planting a few cabbages among the scrub and white lilies round about, and verbena and slender poppy, equalled the wealth of kings in his proud imagination'. For *premere,* cf. 2.346; for *vescus,* cf. 3.175. Notice the remarkable serenity of this picture of the old gardener.

134 **primus . . . carpere:** supply *erat* rather than taking *carpere* as historic infinitive; cf. 140.

137 'he was already picking the flowers of the soft hyacinth'; *coma* (used metaphorically) means the growth, often the foliage but here the flower; cf. 122. Notice the Greek-type line-ending, a quadrisyllable with the last syllable of *tondebat* lengthened in arsis; cf. *Ecl.* 6.53.

139 **apibus fetis:** 'bees that had brought forth their young'; contrast 199.

140-41 **spumantia . . . favis:** 'to compact his foaming honey when he had pressed out the combs'; he squeezed the honey out of the combs so that it could congeal as pure honey; cf. 101.

141 **tinus:** see note on 112 (here, as there, some MSS have *pinus:* pines are mentioned as useful in this connexion by Colum. 9.4.2., but the less common word is probably to be preferred).

142-3 'and all the fruit with which the fertile tree had bedecked itself when it first flowered it retained in the autumn, fully ripened'; for the metaphor of *induere,* cf. 1.188.

144 'He also transplanted elms into rows when it was late'; i.e. this gardener had fingers sufficiently green to achieve success when it might seem too late for transplanting (cf. *iam, iamque* in 145-6). For *versus* in this sense, cf. *Aen.* 5.119.

145 **eduramque:** 'very hardy', an extremely rare word; cf. 2.65, and *edurare* in Colum. 11.1.7.

147-8 See note on 116-48; Columella at the beginning of his Book 10 uses Virgil's phrases . . . *spatiis exclusus iniquis . . . Vergilius nobis post se memoranda reliquit.*

149-227 *The social organisation of the bees, how they apportion the various tasks among themselves. They reproduce without sexual coition; they sacrifice their individuality for the common good of their tribe and show great devotion to their 'king'. Indeed they have their own share in the divine spirit which permeates all creation.*

149-227 In this section Virgil gives an elaborate and sympathetic picture of the complex organisation of the society of the bees. It is again based on material found in Aristotle (especially *HA* 9.40) and Varro (*RR* 3.16.4f.) and it develops the human parallels found in these sources: cf. especially Varro *RR* 3.16.6 *haec ut hominum civitates, quod hic est et rex et imperium et societas*; 3.16.9 *omnes ut in exercitu vivunt*. It is now known that much of this information about the specialised activities of bees is incorrect (see Wilkinson, pp. 264f.), but Virgil reflects the ideas that were believed in the ancient world, and uses them to build up the picture of a marvellously intricate organisation of these tiny creatures. He stresses very strongly the qualities of industry and self-sacrifice which ensure the survival of the species, writing in such a way as to suggest that the world of the bees has lessons to teach human society; in particular he emphasises the importance to the bees of their leader, using phraseology appropriate to human society. Varying degrees of political allegory have been read into this passage (cf. note on 51-115), but as always Virgil is extremely careful to avoid specific allegory; see on this subject, Wilkinson pp. 176f., especially 178f.

149 Iuppiter ipse: Virgil here links the mythology of how the bees nurtured Jupiter in Crete with the pantheistic idea of how the bees share in the divine mind (219f.).

150-52 'as a reward because they nurtured the king of heaven in a cave on Mt Dicte, following the melodious sounds of the Curetes and the clashing bronze'; see note on 64, and cf. 2.536, Callim. *Hymn.* 1.49f. The antecedent *mercedem*, in apposition to *naturas*, is taken into the relative clause.

153 The single spondee (*solae*) in the first foot gives metrical emphasis to reinforce the thought. Huxley points out that other insects like wasps, ants, hornets have this 'social' habit; cf. Pliny *NH* 11.108.

153-4 consortia ... urbis: 'the communal dwellings of a city'; the presentation of the society of the bees in human terms is at its most marked here and in the phrases which follow.

156 This phrase is reminiscent of the proverbial activity of ants; cf. 1.186.

157 in medium: 'for the common store'; cf. 1.127.

158 victu invigilant: 'toil for food'; *victu* is dative. Cf. 198; *Aen.* 9.605.

159 saepta domorum: 'the enclosure of their home'; for the neuter of an adjective followed by the partitive genitive, cf. 81; *Aen.* 11.882 and see note on 1.478. For this phrase, cf. Lucr. 1.489.

160 narcissi lacrimam: 'the teardrops of the narcissus', a vivid phrase describing the exudation of the flower; cf. Milton *Lycidas* 150 'And Daffadillies fill their cups with tears'. Servius sees a reference to the myth about the youth Narcissus who wept as he pined for his own reflection in the river, but Aristotle (*HA* 9.40) uses the word δάκρυον ('tear') of the secretion of trees and flowers.

gluten: cf. 40.

161 prima ... fundamina: in apposition to the previous line.

162-3 aliae ... fetus: 'others lead forth the next generation, the hope of the race as they grow up'. This phrase and the next two are repeated with small changes in *Aen.* 1.431f.; cf. Milton *PL* 1.770 'pour forth their populous youth about the hive'. Lines 167-9 are repeated exactly in *Aen.* 1.434-6.

165-8 Notice the military phraseology of this sentence: *ad portas, custodia, sorti, inque vicem, speculantur, agmine facto, arcent.*

165 cecidit ... sorti: 'fell by lot'; *sorti* is probably an archaic form of the ablative rather than predicative dative; cf. *Aen.* 9.271. Drawing of lots was one of the methods used in the Roman world for assigning guard-duties.

168 ignavum fucos pecus: 'the drones, a lazy tribe'; the word order with *ignavum ... pecus* in apposition to *fucos* is very striking; cf. 246.

170f. The point of comparison in this simile is the sharing of the work (*munere quamque suo*, 178); but much of its impact arises from the magnificent mock-heroic comparison of the little bees with the mighty Cyclopes (as Virgil himself indicates in 176). The picture of the Cyclopes

is a splendid piece of rhetorical grandilo-
quence, and the elevation of the bees to
this level has a most attractive humorous
impact. Lines 171-5 are almost exactly
repeated in *Aen.* 8.449-453, the description
of the Cyclopes making new armour for
Aeneas; they are imitated by Spenser *FQ*
2.7.36.

170-72 'Just like the Cyclopes when
they speedily make their thunderbolts from
molten lumps of metal; some suck in and
blow out the air with their leather
bellows . . .'.

173   **impositis incudibus:** 'under the
anvils placed on its floor'.

Aetna: the Cyclopes had by Virgil's
time long been localised in the area of
Mt Etna; cf. Eur. *Cycl.* 20f.; *Geo.*
1.471-2; *Aen.* 3.569.

174-5   These lines metrically portray
the rhythm of the work: 174 is spondaic
with total clash of accent and ictus,
conveying toil and effort, while 175 (with
its absence of main caesura in third or
fourth foot) has an unusual degree of
coincidence of accent and ictus, suggesting
that the next stage of the work is easier.

177-8   **Cecropias . . . suo:** 'an innate
love of possession inspires the Athenian
bees, each in his own task'; Cecrops was a
legendary king of Athens, and the bees
of Mt Hymettus, near Athens, were
proverbial; cf. 270; Ov. *Trist.* 5.4.30.

178   **grandaevis . . . curae:** 'the older
ones look after their settlements'; the
personification in human terms continues.

179   **daedala . . . tecta:** 'making their
intricate houses'; *daedala* is a favourite
adjective with Lucretius; for *tecta,* cf.187.

181   **crura:** accusative of respect; cf. 99.

183   **ferrugineos hyacinthos:** for the
quadrisyllabic ending with a Greek word,
cf. 137.

184   **labor omnibus unus:** the theme of
labor, so prominent a theme of the whole
work, is here shown to be essential for
the life of the bees too.

186   **decedere:** for the poetic infinitive
after *admonuit,* cf. *Aen.* 9.109, and
compare *Geo.* 1.457.

188   **oras:** 'the edges' of the hives;
cf. 39.

189   **siletur:** 'silence reigns', impersonal
passive; the word is emphasised by the
unusual pause in the fifth foot which
precedes it.

190   **sopor suus:** 'each one's slumber',
the slumber which each has earned by its
activity.

191   **stabulis:** this word used of their
hives equates the bees with domestic
animals (cf. 14), a variation of their
equation with humans (*tecta,* 187;
thalamis, 189; *moenibus urbis,* 193).

193   **aquantur:** 'they get water', a
military term like *excursus* in the next
line.

194-6   **lapillos . . . tollunt:** this erroneous
idea of honey-bees carrying little stones
as ballast is found in Arist. *HA* 9.40;
Pliny *NH* 11.24.

197f.   The suggestion that bees reproduce
without sexual activity is referred to in Arist.
HA 5.21, Pliny *NH* 11.46. Parthenogenesis
is indeed known in certain groups of
insects, but in the case of bees sexual
intercourse takes place in flight.

200-202   'but by themselves they pluck
their young from the leaves and the
pleasant grasses with their mouths, by
themselves they produce their king and
their little citizens and refashion their
courts and their kingdoms of wax'. The
personification in human terms here is
very strong indeed (*Quirites, aulas, regna*);
for *cerea regna,* cf. *Aen.* 12.589 *cerea
castra.*

203-5   As these lines appear to
interrupt the train of thought, various
scholars have suggested transposition (after
196, or after 183); but the connection is
the idea of the subordination of the
individual to the group to ensure the
group's survival.

203   **cotibus:** 'hard rocks' (cf. *Ecl.* 8.43)
which their wings brush against as they
fly around (*errando*) in search of honey.

204   **ultroque . . . dedere:** 'and voluntarily
sacrifice their lives under their burden',
i.e. the weight of the pollen which they
are carrying causes them to dash their
wings against rocks, but this does not
diminish their desire to collect the largest
possible amount. The past tense (like
attrivere; cf. *rupere* 213) is a gnomic
aorist.

207   **plus septima . . . aestas:** 'more than
the seventh summer'; the omission of *quam*
in this idiom is normal in prose.

209   This line most grandiloquently
continues the imagery of the bees as
being like a human family or society.
Cf. Enn. *Ann.* 500 *moribus antiquis res
stat Romana virisque.*

210-11   The peoples of the East were
ruled by autocratic monarchs to whom
extreme reverence was shown by their
subjects. Hydaspes was a river in India,

which Virgil here thinks of as part of
the Persian Empire.

213 **amisso:** supply *rege* from the
previous line.

214 **cratis:** 'the structure'; Virgil uses
the word which literally means 'wicker-work'
as a metaphor for the appearance of the
honeycomb.

217 Aristotle (*HA* 9.40) refers to
carrying the queen when she cannot fly,
but Virgil relates the idea to triumphal
military acclaim.

218 The section ends with another
military personification of the bees; cf.
Aen. 11.647.

219-21 'Because of these signs and
following these indications some people
have said that bees have a share in the
divine mind and drink ethereal draughts';
cf. *Aen.* 6.724f.; 747. This passage
reflects very clearly the pantheistic
notion of the *Georgics,* the idea that God
is present in every living creature; it is a
concept of Stoicism deriving from
Pythagoreanism to which Virgil has
given his own special meaning. On this
see Richter *ad loc.*

222 **terrasque:** the -*que* is lengthened
in arsis; see note on *Ecl.* 4.51, where the
same line occurs.

223 Cf. *Aen.* 6.728 *inde hominum
pecudumque genus vitaeque volantum.*

224 **quemque:** in apposition to the
previous line, 'all at their birth derive
their subtle breath of life'.

225-7 'And indeed all things then
return thither (i.e. to God) and when
dissolved go back there, and there is no
place for death, but living they ascend
to the rank of a star and enter the heavens
on high'. The concept of the return of
the soul after death to the universal
spirit which is God was a Stoic belief.

227 **sideris:** 'so as to rank as a star',
rather than 'into the number of the stars',
which would make the singular *sideris*
a very unusual instance of singular for
plural.

228-80 *The gathering of honey; the
defences against pests; the treatment of
diseases.*

228-80 This is a didactic passage (cf.
Arist. *HA* 8.27; 9.40; Varro *RR* 3.16)
given poetic life by the continued
personification of the bees (cf. especially
239-40; 251-2), by passages of mythology
(232f.; 246f.), and by powerful descriptive
imagery (237-8; 249-50; 260-63; 273-5).

228 **augustam:** R has *angustam*, but the

mock-heroic exaggeration is in keeping
with the whole tone of this book.

229 **relines:** 'open up' a very rare word
(cf. Ter. *Heaut.* 460) literally meaning
'unseal' from the wax (cf. 39).

229-30 **prius . . . fove:** 'first sprinkle
and protect your face with handfuls of
water', in order to prevent sparks burning
or bees settling on the face (cf. Servius
ad loc. and see F. R. Dale, *CR* 1955,
pp. 14-15). Others render 'first purify
your breath', comparing 2.135 and
Colum. 9.14.3 where much is said about
the need for personal cleanliness in
handling the hives; others again read *ore
fave* with MP and see a religious reference —
'observe a sacred silence'. For *haustu
aquarum,* cf. Ov. *Fast.* 2.294 *palmis hausta
duabus aqua;* for *fovere,* cf. *Aen.* 10.838;
12.420.

230 **fumosque . . . sequacis:** 'penetrating
smoke'; cf. the simile in *Aen.* 12.587f.

231 'Twice a year people collect the
heavy produce, there are two seasons for
harvesting it'; the second half of the line
is a variation on the first. *Fetus* means the
honey produced; this usage is common of
the produce of plants; cf. 1.55; 82; 2.442.

232-5 These are the two seasons: the
rising and the setting of the Pleiades,
i.e. May and November; cf. 1.138.

232-3 **Taygete . . . Pleas:** the words are
in apposition, Taygete (which scans as
four syllables) being one of the seven
Pleiades, daughters of Atlas and Pleione;
cf. 1.221.

232 **simul:** 'as soon as', equivalent to
simul ac; cf. *Ecl.* 4.26.

honestum: 'comely', a playful touch
linking the constellation with its mythology,
the star with the maiden; cf. 2.392.

233 **et Oceani . . . amnis:** 'and has
rejected the streams of Ocean and pushed
them away with her foot'; a highly
coloured phrase indicating the rising of
the constellation from the streams of
Ocean below the horizon.

234-5 'or when she has fled from the
constellation of the watery fish and sadly
departed from the sky into the waves of
winter'; i.e. at her setting in November
when the winter comes on.

236f. The narrative resumes from 230,
after the parenthetical sentence about
seasons for collecting honey, by describing
the anger of the bees when their honey
is taken (cf. *Aen.* 12.590). Some scholars
have wished to transpose 236-8 so as to
follow 230.

238 **animasque . . . ponunt:** 'sacrifice their lives by stinging'; a well-known fact about bees, due to the difficulty of withdrawing the sting; cf. Plat. *Phaed.* 91c, where Socrates says he may leave his sting behind like a bee.

239-40 **parcesque . . . fractas:** 'and you want to spare them from what lies ahead, and you pity their broken spirit and their shattered world . . .'; the phrases are epic in dignity.

241 **at:** for this use of *at* after a subordinate clause, cf. 208.

suffire . . . inanis: 'to fumigate with thyme and cut back their empty combs'; cf. Lucr. 4.1175. The object, as Servius notes, is to discourage the pests mentioned in the next lines; cf. Varro *RR* 3.16.17.

242 **ignotus:** 'unnoticed', *ex improviso veniens* (Servius).

243 **stelio:** 'newt'; this seems to be the correct spelling (some MSS have *stellio* or *stello*); the *i* is treated as a consonant; see note on 1.482 and cf. 297.

et lucifugis . . . blattis: 'and bedchambers packed with light-hating woodlice'; the construction here is rather loose with *adederunt* to be supplied. The sense is that the woodlice have invaded the combs and are consuming them.

244 **immunis:** 'that makes no contribution'; cf. Hor. *Odes* 4.12.23. Again the verb to be supplied is *adedit* (242).

245 The phraseology is military, personifying the hornet as a mighty warrior, too strong for the bees.

246 **dirum . . . genus:** 'grubs, a fearful pest'; for the word order, cf. 168.

246-7 The spider is hateful to Minerva because the maiden Arachne challenged her to a spinning competition and for her arrogance was changed into a spider; cf. Ov. *Met.* 6.1f.

247 **cassis:** properly 'hunting-nets', here applied metaphorically to the spider's web.

249-50 'will set about restoring the wreckage of their ruined race and will fill up the combs and construct their storehouses from flowers'; the infinitive with *incumbere* is rare; cf. 84; 264; Tac. *Hist.* 2.10. Both *fori* and *horrea* refer to the honeycombs, which the bees will renew after disaster by gathering more wax. Aristotle (*HA* 9.40) speaks of the energetic reaction of bees to adversity; cf. Colum. 9.15.3.

251f. The conditional clause is left

without a main clause as Virgil rushes to a description of the diseases which can strike the bees. The idea that they suffer like us (*apibus quoque nostros . . .*, notice the unusual rhythm) is developed in the very human description of illness and death (254f.).

256 **tristia funera ducunt:** the metrical effect (each foot consisting of a single word) is emphatic; cf. *Aen.* 5. 840 with my note (Oxford edition).

257 **illae:** for this use of *ille* to emphasise the subject, see note on 3.217.

pedibus conexae: 'with their legs intertwined'; cf. *Aen.* 7.66; i.e. in a cluster. Cf. Varro *RR* 3.16.30 *ut uvae aliae ex aliis pendent conglobatae.*

259 **contracto frigore:** 'with the chill they have caught', rather than 'shrivelled by the cold', taking *contracto* as transferred for *contractae.*

260 **tractimque susurrant:** 'they heave long sighs'; for *tractim,* cf. Lucr. 3.530; Servius says *sine intermissione.* This is an invention of Virgil's, designed to reinforce the sense of tragedy.

261-3 The three clauses introduced by *ut* give a series of rapid comparisons: their buzz is like winds in the woods, like the ebb of big waves on shingle, like fire in a furnace; cf. Hom. *Il.* 14.394f.; Lucr. 6.142f. The feature in common is the loud low pitch.

261 **quondam:** 'sometimes'; cf. 3.99.

262 Page quotes Tennyson 'I heard the shingle grinding in the surge'. Notice the dactylic movement and the alliteration of *s.*

264 **galbaneos:** cf. 3.415.

suadebo incendere: poetic infinitive; cf. 249; 2.315; *Ecl.* 1.55.

265 **mellaque . . . canalibus:** 'to bring in honey in the stalks of reeds' — to feed the bees and to try to persuade them to resume their activities, the point elaborated in the next line.

266 **hortantem . . . vocantem:** understand *te,* subject of *incendere.*

267 **tunsum gallae . . . saporem:** 'the extracted flavour of gall', i.e. essence of crushed gall. The potions which follow are (i) extract of gall mixed with roses or must, (ii) grapes mixed with thyme and centaury.

269 **defruta:** the 'must' of wine, concentrated by being boiled; cf. 1.295.

psithia . . . racemos: 'dried bunches of grapes from a psythian vine'. For psythian vines, used especially for making raisins, cf. 2.93.

270 **Cecropium:** see note on 177-8.
centaurea: a type of herb (cf. Lucr. 4.125) so called from the myth that Chiron the Centaur discovered its medical value. For the spondaic ending, cf. 3.276.
271 **amello:** Virgil makes an etymological connection between the name of this herb (*Aster amellus*) and the river Mella (278). The dative is normal in Latin in this construction (*cui nunc cognomen Iulo additur, Aen.* 1.267-8).
273 'for it produces a great bushy growth from a single clump', i.e. from one root.
277 **tonsis:** 'cropped' by pasturing animals.
278 The river Mella, which Virgil associates with *amellus,* was near his native Mantua.

281-314 *If you lose your bees they can be renewed by killing a calf and treating its carcase so that bees are born from it.*
281-314 This is a transitional passage leading in to the epyllion about Aristaeus and Orpheus which concludes Book 4. The relevance of this mythological story to the rest of the poem is discussed in the note on 315-424. The idea that bees could be spontaneously generated from the rotting carcase of a calf can be called by its Greek name bugonia: it may be compared with the Biblical story (Judges 14:14f.) illustrated on modern golden syrup tins, of honey from a lion's carcase. It is without any scientific truth, but was widely believed in ancient times: it is said to have originated in Egypt, where the bee was a royal emblem, and Greek authors refer to it (Philetas, Nicander and others, but significantly not Aristotle). Varro (*RR* 2.5.5; 3.16.4) speaks of it; cf. Ov. *Fast.* 1.363f.; *Met.* 15. 364f.; Pliny *NH* 11.70; Colum. 9.14.6. The fullest account is in Florentinus (*Geop.* 15.2). It is thought that the idea may have originated from the fact that bees sometimes settle on dried-up carcases, or that the drone-fly (somewhat similar in appearance to the bee) does breed in rotting flesh. See further Wilkinson, pp. 268f.; A. E. Shipley, *J. Phil.* 1918, pp. 97f.; H. M. Ransome, *The Sacred Bee,* pp. 112f.
There is nothing surprising about Virgil's location of the practice of bugonia in Egypt (cf. Antigonus Carystius, *Mir.* 19), but that he should devote such a long passage (287-314) to the Egyptian connection seems striking, since the

rest of his story describes the legendary origins of the bugonia in Thessaly. Perhaps he saw an opportunity to introduce a few lines in praise of his friend Gallus, prefect of Egypt; if so the praises were deleted when Gallus fell into disgrace, but the Egyptian introduction to them remained. This may be the cause of Servius' statement (almost certainly false, see note on 315-424) that the 'praises of Gallus' constituted the original ending of the poem and were subsequently replaced by the Aristaeus story.
283-4 **et ... quoque modo:** 'both ... and how', the second clause is really epexegetic of the first, as it defines the noun *inventa.*
283 **Arcadii ... magistri:** Aristaeus, as described in 317f.; he was said to have once been a king of Arcadia before moving to Ceos (1.14).
285 **insincerus:** 'rotting', a very rare word; for the idea, cf. Varro *RR* 2.5.5 *ex hoc putrefacto nasci ... apes;* Ov. *Met.* 15.365f. This idea perhaps derives from the fact that bees often choose to settle in hollow trees or dried-up carcases; see note on 281-314.
287 Canopus is a town of Egypt, called Pellaean from Alexander the Great who was born at Pella in Macedonia and who conquered Egypt: it is a frequent epithet of Egypt in Lucan. For the relevance of Egypt to the bugonia see note on 281-314.
289 **circum ... vehitur sua rura:** 'sails around its territory'; *circum* is separated from *vehitur* by tmesis.
290 'and where the neighbouring territory of the quiver-bearing Persian touches it'; the fame of the Persians (Parthians) as archers is frequently referred to; cf. 314; *Aen.* 12.856f. The geography of the East presented here exaggerates the extent of Egypt.
291-3 The order of lines varies in the MSS and it seems that 291 had dropped out in the archetype, been inserted in the margin and then included at different points by subsequent scribes (or possibly Virgil wrote 291 and 292 as alternatives).
293 The origin of the Nile was a mystery to the ancients; for the idea that it rose in the far south-east, cf. Lucan 10.292f.
294 **iacit:** 'casts', 'puts', a curious use of the word, said (by Servius) to be used for *ponere* on the analogy of *iacere fundamenta = ponere fundamenta.*
295 **ipsos ... usus:** 'confined for this

very purpose'.

296-7 hunc . . . artis: 'people shut it in both with the tiling of a small roof and with close walls'.

297 parietibus: scanned as four syllables with consonantal *i;* cf. *ariete, abiete* and line 243.

301 multa . . . obstruitur: the unusual rhythm reflects the idea of struggle. *Multa* is adverbial.

perempto: 'when it has been killed', dative.

306 rubeant quam: for the conjunction following its verb, cf. 314.

309 modis . . . miris: a Lucretian phrase used elsewhere by Virgil; cf. 1.477.

310 trunca pedum: genitive of respect (or perhaps separation) in imitation of Greek; cf. Lucr. 5. 840 *orba pedum.*

311 miscentur: 'swarm'.

314 'whenever the light-armed Parthians first engage in battle'; i.e. the arrows come thickest at the beginning. For the Parthians cf. 290.

315-424 *The method of getting a new swarm of bees from the carcase of a bull was discovered by Aristaeus. When he had lost his bees he went to his mother Cyrene who told him to consult Proteus, the old god of the sea.*

315-424 From this point onwards Virgil concludes his *Georgics* with the mythological story of Aristaeus and his lost bees, including the inserted story of Orpheus and Eurydice. There was a tradition, reported by Servius on *Ecl.* 10.1 and *Geo.* 4.1 (but found nowhere else), that the fourth *Georgic* originally ended with praises of Gallus, but that when Gallus fell into disgrace after his prefecture of Egypt Virgil altered the ending. On the whole this is an unlikely story (cf. W. B. Anderson, *CQ* 1933, pp. 36f.; 73f.), and it is more useful to consider what Virgil aimed at in the ending as we have it.

The presentation of the myth, with its 'digression' about Orpheus and Eurydice, is very much in the style of the epyllion, a type popular with the Alexandrian Greeks and represented in Latin by Catullus 64. It is constructed so that the Aristaeus framework is in an objective Homeric style (see Otis, pp. 190f.) and the Orpheus-Eurydice insert is subjective and highly emotional; its moral impact (as Otis points out) is that Aristaeus learns to do the correct thing

and is successful while Orpheus' visit to the underworld ends in disaster because of his failure to observe the conditions required. For this contrast as it compares with Catullus 64, see also Klingner, *Virgils Georgica,* pp. 234f. But perhaps more important is Virgil's wish to conclude the *Georgics* with narrative about people; so far the poem has been almost without characters, and here Virgil tries his hand at the kind of writing which was to lead him (with many differences, of course) to the legendary narrative of the *Aeneid.*

Much of the treatment is original with Virgil; he has made the Aristaeus episode into a typically Alexandrian αἴτιον, that is to say an aetiological explanation of an existing practice. There is no evidence to suggest that Aristaeus was linked with the bugonia (the birth of bees from the carcase of a bull) before Virgil, or that Proteus played any part in such a story; as far as we know the Orpheus-Eurydice legend had not previously been linked with Aristaeus; and again the normal version of the Orpheus-Eurydice story was that Orpheus was successful in his quest. That Eurydice was running from Aristaeus when bitten by a snake seems to have been a Virgilian invention to link the two stories. In the end what he has produced is an exceptionally moving piece of writing about Orpheus and Eurydice, set in a narrative framework about Aristaeus of strange and other-worldly description so that at the end of his didactic poem we look beyond the bees to the universal symbolism of myth.

On the whole subject see Otis, pp. 190f. and Appendix vii, and Wilkinson pp. 108f.; 213f.; and Appendix iv.

315 extudit: 'forged'; cf. 328; 1.133.

316 'From what source did this new human practice take its beginnings?'

317 Aristaeus, a mythical hero of various aspects of pastoral life, was invoked in 1.14 as *cultor nemorum;* he was the son of Apollo and the water-nymph Cyrene. Cf. Ov. *Fast.* 1.363f., and see also note on 315-424.

Peneia Tempe: Tempe (Greek neuter plural) was a famous valley in northern Greece (cf. 2.469); the river *Pēnēŭs* flowed through it. The river god Peneus was the father of the nymph Cyrene; cf. 355. According to another version she was the daughter of Hypseus, king of the Lapiths, cf. Pind. *Pyth.* 9.13f.

319 extremi . . . amnis: 'of the river's

end'; the source as well as the mouth can be regarded as one of the 'ends' of the river. (Servius says *summi, unde nascitur*). Aristaeus goes to the source of the Peneus to make his plea.

321 The rhythm is highly emphatic, wholly spondaic with the relatively unusual pause after the first spondaic foot; cf. *Aen.* 8.71. The plea is based on Achilles' plea to his mother Thetis, the sea-nymph (cf. Hom. *Il.* 1.349f). For the phrase *gurgitis ... ima,* cf. 385 and note on 159.

323 **Thymbraeus:** Thymbra was a town in the Troad where Apollo had a famous temple; cf. *Aen.* 3.85.

324-5 **aut quo ... amor:** 'or where has your love for me gone?'; cf. *Aen.* 2.595 *quonam nostri tibi cura recessit?*

325 As son of a god he could expect deification; cf. *Aen.* 1.250; as it is he finds even human life intolerable.

326 **honorem:** 'glory', i.e. successful farming (such as he alludes to in 329-31), but particularly bee-keeping, which has now met with disaster.

327-8 'which my careful management of crops and cattle barely achieved for me as I tried every resource'; for *extuderat,* cf. 315.

328 **te matre:** 'although you (a goddess) are my mother'.

329 **ipsa manu:** these words emphasise the sarcasm of the passage.

330 The elisions of *inimicum ignem atque* help to convey his indignation, as does the personified use of the verb in *interfice messis.*

333 **thalamo ... alti:** 'down in the bower of the deep river'; for the word order, cf. 419; 3.276.

334f. Virgil now slows the narrative with a long descriptive passage (of some sixteen lines) in which he deploys his expertise with Greek words to produce a highly pictorial tableau. It is based on Hom. *Il.* 18.35f., where Thetis hears Achilles' cries and summons her nymphs (see note on 321); it also is reminiscent of Poseidon's underworld domain in Hom. *Il.* 13.21f.

334 **eam circum:** the dissyllabic preposition is postponed, as often in verse; cf. 430.

Milesia: the beauty of fleeces from Miletus was proverbial; cf. 3.306.

335 **carpebant:** 'were spinning'; cf. 1.390; Cat. 64.310.

hyali ... colore: 'dyed with the deep colour of green glass'; for *saturo,* cf. Sen.

NQ 1.5.12.

336 Homer's list of Nereids in *Il.* 18.39f. gives Virgil his model here (cf. also Hes. *Theog.* 240f.), though his names are different. He uses a Greek rhythm (lengthening of the *-que* of *Drumoque,* absence of main caesura in third or fourth foot, polysyllabic ending); compare 339; 343.

337 **caesariem ... nitidam:** 'their shining hair outspread'; for the retained accusative, cf. *Aen.* 10.838 and see note on *Ecl.* 1.54.

338 This line occurs at *Aen.* 5.826, and is certainly spurious here, being omitted by all the best MSS.

339 There is hiatus after *Cydippe* and no main caesura in third or fourth foot.

340 **Lucinae:** the goddess of childbirth; cf. 3.60.

341 **Oceanitides:** the word is given its Greek scansion with a short final syllable.

343 Again this line has a Greek rhythm (cf. 336; 339); there is hiatus after *Ephyre,* no main caesura in third or fourth foot, and a polysyllabic ending.

344 Arethusa was originally a huntress (like Clio and Beroe; cf. 341) before becoming a sea-nymph; see note on *Ecl.* 10.1, and cf. Ov. *Met.* 5.572f.

345-6 Clymene's song (it was normal to sing while weaving; cf. Theocr. *Id.* 24.76f) is the well-known one about how Mars seduced Vulcan's wife Venus; *curam ... inanem* seems to refer to Vulcan's vain efforts to prevent this. The equally well-known sequel (that Mars was caught in Vulcan's net; cf. Hom. *Od.* 8.266f.), is not referred to here.

347 **aque Chao:** 'starting from the flood', as we would say. Chaos was the original state of the world before the gods organised it. *Densos* means 'frequent' — *crebros* (Servius).

348-9 **fusis ... devolvunt:** 'unwind the soft threads from the shuttles'; cf. *Ciris* 446.

349 Cyrene had heard him the first time (333), but the nymphs had not.

352 Cf. *Aen.* 1.127 (of Neptune) *prospiciens summa placidum caput extulit unda.*

354 **tibi:** ethic dative, 'I tell you'.

355 **Penei:** a dissyllable by synizesis; cf. 1.279.

357 **percussa ... mentem:** accusative of respect; cf. 371 and see note on 2.131.

360 **qua ... inferret:** 'in order that the youth could enter that way', final subjunctive.

361-2 The image is highly colourful, giving a supernatural touch as the great wave embraces Aristaeus and takes him below the waters; it is based on Hom. *Od.* 11. 243-4: 'a shining wave encompassed him, like a mountain, curving over him'. Cf. also Ov. *Met.* 15.509.

364 This descriptive line is emphasised by the alliteration of *l* and *s* and the assonance of the long vowels (especially *u*).

367 **diversa locis:** 'in their different places'; cf. Ov. *Met.* 1.40. Virgil pictures a great underground source from which all the rivers flow in their different directions up to the world above; cf. *Aen.* 6.658f.; Plat. *Phaed.* 112a.
Phasis was a river in Colchis, Lycus a river in Asia Minor.

368 **Enipeus:** a river in Thessaly which flowed into the river Peneus.

369 **Aniena fluenta:** the Anio, a famous river near Rome; notice the dactylic movement.

370 **saxosusque sonans:** 'roaring over its rocks'; this use of an adjective (in an adverbial sense) with the participle is characteristic of Virgil, see note on 1.163. Notice the imitative alliteration of *s.* The Hypanis was in Scythia, and the Caicus (as Virgil says) in Mysia, in Asia Minor.

371-2 'and Eridanus, bull-faced, his two horns gilded'. *cornua* is accusative of respect; cf. 357. River-gods were often depicted with bulls' faces; cf. *Aen.* 8.77; 727. *Auratus* derives from the Roman practice of gilding the horns of sacrificial bulls; cf. 1.217. Huxley quotes Pope, *Windsor Forest* (of the River Thames), 'His shining horns diffused a golden gleam'.

372 **Eridanus:** the Po; cf. 1.482.

373 **purpureum:** the Greek word for 'purple' is a frequent epithet of the sea in Homer, e.g. *Il.* 16.391.

374-5 'when he had arrived beneath the hanging pumice roof of her abode'; the meaning is that the ceiling was formed of pumice 'hanging' above the room; *pendere* is often used of the high parts of buildings 'suspended' by their supports, e.g. Lucr. 6.195. *Perventum est* is impersonal passive; notice the pattern of alliteration (*p, t*).

375 **fletus cognovit inanis:** 'learned that her son's lamentations were needless', because she could easily remedy the problem. This seems better than 'learned of the hopeless lamentations of her son',

taking *inanis* as a stock epithet of lamentation, 'which serves no purpose'.

376f. These preparations for a banquet are repeated in *Aen.* 1. 701f.

378 **plena reponunt:** 'refill'.

379 **Panchaeis:** i.e. fragrant with incense from Arabia; cf. 2.139.

adolescunt: 'burn'; cf. *adolere*, a technical term in sacrifices, as in *Aen.* 1.704.

380 **Maeonii . . . Bacchi:** Lydian wine; cf. 2.98.

382 **Oceanumque patrem rerum:** 'both Oceanus, father of the world'; cf. Hom. *Il.* 14.246.

383 The reference is to Dryads and Nereids; *servant* means 'watch over'.

384 **Vestam:** 'the hearth'; cf. Bacchus (wine) in 380.

385 **ad summum tecti:** 'to the height of the roof', a variation for *ad summum tectum;* cf. 321-2.

subiecta: i.e. the flame which was below the nectar poured on it now shoots upwards; cf. Ov. *Her.* 13.113.

387-90 **Est . . . hic:** this figure (setting a scene and then subsequently locating the action in it) is called ecphrasis; cf. 418-23 and Austin's note on *Aen.* 4.480f. For the story about Proteus, cf. Hom. *Od.* 4.351f.; Ov. *Met.* 8.731f.; Spenser *FQ* 1.2.10 (of Archimago) 'For by his mighty science he could take As many forms and shapes in seeming wise As ever Proteus to himself could make'.

387 **Carpathio:** the Carpathian sea, around the island Carpathos, is between Crete and Rhodes.

388-9 I.e. he drives a chariot pulled by sea-horses; his steeds could be called fishes or two-footed horses.

389 **iuncto:** 'yoked'.

metitur: 'traverses'; cf. Hom. *Od.* 3.179; *Aen.* 7.160.

390-91 **Emathiae . . . Pallenen:** Pallene was a town in Macedonia (Emathia; cf. 1.492); according to one version of the legend this was Proteus' original homeland. According to another he moved there from Egypt.

392 **Nereus:** a major deity of the ocean, father of the Nereids; cf. *Ecl.* 6.35.

393 **trahantur:** 'are destined', a metaphor from drawing out the threads of Fate.

394-5 'whose vast herds and ugly seals Proteus looks after beneath the sea'; Proteus acts as a kind of head herdsman of Neptune's fishy flock; cf. Hom. *Od.*

4.385-6; Spenser *FQ* 3.8.30 'Proteus is
shepherd of the seas of yore, And hath the
charge of Neptune's mighty herd'.

397 eventusque secundet: 'prosper the
outcome'.

399-400 vim ... inanes: 'capture him
and impose fierce violence and fetters
upon him; his fruitless stratagems will be
finally shattered against these'. For *tende*,
cf. *contende* in 412, and *vincula intendere*
in *Aen.* 2.237; *circum haec* suggests the
encompassing barrier which he will not
be able to break.

401 medios ... aestus: 'its midday heat';
the time when Proteus takes his afternoon
siésta.

406 eludent: 'will confuse you', will
try to deceive you into giving up hope of
holding him captive. The lines which follow
are based on Hom. *Od.* 4.456f. Cf. also
Hor. *Sat.* 2.3.71f.; Ov. *Met.* 8.730f.

407 horridus: 'bristling', the basic
meaning of the word; see note on 3.366,
and cf. Lucr. 5.25 *horrens Arcadius sus.*

atra: 'grim'; Servius says *saeva.*

409-10 The diction is highly fantastic —
it is hard to visualise how one would tighten
fetters (412) around flames or water.

412 tam tu: some MSS read *tanto*, but
cf. Lucr. 5. 452f.; *Aen.* 7.787f.

413-14 i.e. until he returns to his
original shape, as he was when you saw
him at the beginning of his sleep; cf. Hom.
Od. 4.421; Ov. *Met.* 11.252f.

415 Cf. Milton, *PL* 9.851-2 (of the
apple of the tree of knowledge) 'A bough
of fairest fruit that downie smiled, New
gathered, and ambrosial smell diffused'.
As Conington points out, in Homer (*Od.*
4.445f.) Menelaus has ambrosia to overcome the smell of the seals; the purpose
of the ambrosia in Virgil's passage is to
invigorate Aristaeus.

416 perduxit: 'drenched', a rare
meaning; cf. Pers. 2.56.

417 dulcis ... aura: 'a sweet fragrance',
cf. 3.251. Notice the emphasis on *dulcis*
as a spondee filling the first foot; this
verse is a golden line.

418 habilis: 'invigorating', making him
'suitable' for the task.

est specus ingens: notice the heavy stop
after the fourth foot, and the conflict of
accent and ictus in the fifth, introducing
the ecphrasis (see note on 387) with
power and emphasis.

419 For the word order, cf. 333.

419-20 quo ... reductos: 'where many a
wave is driven by the wind and parts into

receding ripples'; the second phrase is
repeated in *Aen.* 1.161.

421 deprensis: 'caught by a storm';
cf. Lucr. 6.429; Hor. *Odes* 2.16.2.

olim: 'at times'; cf. 433; *Aen.* 5.125.

422 obice: the word is pronounced
objice, and scans as a dactyl, cf. 26; 2.480.

423 aversum a lumine: 'turned away
from the light', hidden in the shadows.

424 nebulis ... resistit: 'stood back,
hidden in mist'.

425-558 *Aristaeus finds Proteus, and
forces an answer from him. Proteus tells
the story of how Eurydice died from a
snake-bite while running away from
Aristaeus, and how Orpheus was allowed to
go down to the underworld to bring her
back provided that he did not look back.
He forgot this condition, and Eurydice
was lost for ever: Orpheus lamented her
fate so unremittingly that he was finally
torn to pieces by the women of Thrace.
Cyrene tells her son that he must therefore
placate the spirits of Orpheus and Eurydice;
he does so and his bees are renewed from
the carcases of sacrificed cattle.*

425-558 The story of Orpheus and
Eurydice, inset into the narrative about
Aristaeus and his bees, is one of the most
famous and moving passages in Latin
poetry. It is superbly analysed by Otis,
pp. 197f.; cf. also Wilkinson pp. 108f.;
213f. Its haunting pathos in a setting in
the world of ghosts shows Virgil at his
most typical, using all his skill in
manipulating the language of the hexameter
so that the sound of the rhythm reflects
the mood and tone of the passage. It is
told in the style of the epyllion, with
elliptical narrative, sensitive empathy, and
concentration on the emotional reaction
of the characters. Here are the liquid notes
of sorrow and pathos which form so
striking a part of the *Aeneid;* here they are
presented by themselves in Hellenistic manner,
but in the *Aeneid* they are set in tension
with the hard requirements of the Roman
mission.

For the contrast between the Aristaeus
framework and the Orpheus centrepiece,
see note on 315-424.

425-7 'Now the consuming Dog Star,
parching the thirsty Indians, was burning
in the sky and the fiery sun had completed
half its course'. For *rapidus*, cf. 1.92.
Probably the first clause refers to the time
of year, and the second to the time of day,
though some argue that both clauses refer
to the time of year (after the summer

solstice). Sirius, the dog star, was always associated with the hottest weather; cf. 2.353 *canis aestifer; Aen.* 3.141; 10. 273. Richter's suggestion, that Sirius here means the sun, seems unlikely and is unparalleled in Latin. The Indians are mentioned as people who experience heat at its fiercest. The midday heat was the right time to approach Proteus; cf. 401. *Haurire* means basically 'to drain', hence 'to consume'; cf. Stat. *Th.* 1.369.

427-8 'the rays of the sun were heating and boiling the hollow rivers, their channels dried up, right down to the mud'.

429-30 cum ... ibat: 'when Proteus began to move ...'; inverted *cum* is not common with the imperfect, but cf. *Aen.* 5. 270-72.

430 eum ... circum: cf. 334; 478. This whole passage is based on Hom. *Od.* 4.403f.; 448f.

431 amarum: 'briny'; cf. Lucr. 4.438 *rorem salis.*

432 Observe the spondaic movement and the very strong alliteration of *s.*

433f. The simile is based on Hom. *Od.* 4. 411f.

433 olim: 'at times'; cf. 421.

435 lupos acuunt: 'whet the wolves' appetites'.

437 cuius ... facultas: 'the chance of catching him'.

440 occupat: 'caught him'; notice how the rhythm of a run-on dactyl reinforces the sense of drama. This line is a very close adaptation of Hom. *Od.* 4.455.

445 nam quis: Servius is probably right in regarding this as equivalent to *quisnam;* cf. Plaut. *Amph.* 660.

confidentissime: Huxley well remarks on the 'humorous use of this remarkable polysyllable to "cut Aristaeus down to size"'.

447 neque ... quicquam: 'nor is it possible to deceive you in anything'; *quicquam* is adverbial. *Est* in the sense of 'it is possible' is a Grecism. This line is based on Hom. *Od.* 4.465.

448 sed ... velle: 'but you must stop wanting (to deceive me)'. The rather elliptical thought is: 'I know I cannot deceive you; you for your part must not want to deceive me'. The rhythm is very unusual here with a diaeresis after the second foot and a heavy pause after the trochee in the third foot.

449 lassis ... rebus: 'to seek an oracular reply for my sad situation'; *quaesitum* is the supine. For *lassis ...*

rebus, cf. *Aen.* 3.145; 11.335 *fessis rebus.*

450 Again the sense pause (after the trochee in the second foot) is unusual: there is a staccato effect about this interchange of conversation.

vi ... multa: 'under the strong constraint of force'.

452 'and grumbling bitterly thus opened his lips and expounded the fates': literally 'for the fates' *(fatis canendis)* which speak through him; cf. *Aen.* 2.246.

453 'It is not the case that no divinity's anger harasses you'; the heavy double negative represents the oracular style; cf. *Aen.* 11.725. Notice the lengthening of the final syllable of *nullius* at the caesura; see note on *Ecl.* 1.38.

454 magna ... commissa: again the oracular style is echoed with the emphatic short sentence and the pause after the trochee in the third foot.

455 haudquaquam ob meritum: 'which you have not deserved'; although responsible for Eurydice's death you did not do it deliberately. Others take the phrase with Orpheus, 'pitiable for no deserved reason', but this is harsh. P reads *ad meritum,* which would mean 'not as great as you deserve'.

ni fata resistant: 'did not fate forbid it', i.e. the consultation with Proteus means that Orpheus' hostility is fated to be turned aside (cf. *fatis,* 452).

457 dum ... fugeret: 'while seeking to avoid you', the subjunctive indicates purpose (cf. *Aen.* 10.800). The story that Aristaeus was responsible for Eurydice's death is not found elsewhere.

460 aequalis: 'of her playmates'; in Ov. *Met.* 10.9 they are Naiads.

460-61 supremos ... montis: 'the tops of the mountains' *(summos,* Servius); cf. Lucr. 1.274. Some MSS have *supremo,* which would refer to the last call on the dead, but a corruption to the nearer word is probably the reason for this reading.

461-3 For the attribution of human qualities to inanimate objects (pathetic fallacy), see note on *Ecl.* 1. 38-9; cf. *Aen.* 7.759f.

461 Rhodopeiae: the final diphthong is shortened in hiatus; see note on 1. 280-83. Rhodope, like Pangaea in the next line, was a mountain in Thrace; cf. 1. 332; 3.351; 462.

462 Rhesi Mavortia tellus: Rhesus was a famous Thracian leader who took part in the Trojan war (cf. *Aen.* 1.469). Thrace is often called martial (cf. *Aen.* 3.13;

Hor. *Odes* 2.16.5); in Homer, Ares, god of
war, lived there.

463 There is hiatus after *Getae,* no
strong caesura in third or fourth foot
and a polysyllabic ending (cf. 343) with a
spondaic fifth foot (Ōrīthyīā); cf. 270.
The Getae (3.462) were a northern people,
here associated with Thrace; the Hebrus
was a river of Thrace (*Ecl.* 10.65) and
Orithyia (daughter of Erectheus, king
of Athens, hence *Actias* from *Acte,* Attica)
was the wife of the North Wind.

464 cava . . . testudine: 'on his hollow
tortoise-shell lyre'; cf. Hor. *Epod.* 14.11.

465-6 The slow spondaic movement
and assonance of long *e* with alliteration
of *t* and *d* in 466 is very marked indeed;
the repetition and the direct address to
Eurydice by the poet also heightens the
pathos. Cf. *Aen.* 7.759-60.

467 Taenarias . . . fauces: one of the
fabled entrances to the underworld was
at Taenarum, in the extreme south of
Greece.

468 The patterned line is made
additionally impressive by its slow
movement.

470 corda: referring to Dis, poetic
plural.

471 Erebi: the underworld; cf. *Aen.*
4.26.

472 ibant: 'were moving towards him'.
Notice how the long *i* picks up the long
i's in the second half of the previous line.
simulacraque luce carentum:
a phrase from Lucr. 4.35; cf. 255.

473-4 This simile is given a different
turn in *Aen.* 6.311f., where the ghosts
are compared first with leaves and then
with birds flying in to land from the ocean
in winter. Here the point is that the birds
flock from the open sky into the trees
for shelter.

475-7 These three lines are repeated in
Aen. 6.306-8; they are based on Hom.
Od. 11.38f.

476 magnanimum: this is the only
adjective with which Virgil employs this
archaic genitive plural form; cf. *Aen.*
3.704.

479 Cocyti: a river of the underworld,
the river of lamentation; cf. 3.38.

479-80 tardaque . . . coercet: repeated
(with a small variation) in *Aen.* 6. 438-9.

480 Styx: cf. 1.243. This phrase is a
variation on the previous one (as in *Aen.*
6. 438-9); Styx is the *palus inamabilis.*

481 domus: plural, 'the dwelling-
places', defined by *intima Leti Tartara.*

481-2 intima Leti Tartara: a strange
phrase, 'innermost Tartarus, abode of
Death'. *Tartarus* or *Tartara* specifically
means the deepest pit of hell (as here),
but is sometimes used generally for the
underworld; *Letum* is personified also in
Aen. 6.277. For the phrase, cf. Lucr. 3.42
Tartara Leti.

482-3 'and the Eumenides with black
snakes entwined in their hair': Eumenides
was the Greek name for the Furies
(1.278); *angues* is a retained accusative
(see note on *Ecl.* 1. 54) after *implexae*
used in a reflexive sense. Some MSS have
innexae (cf. *Aen.* 6.281) and some
impexae; Servius' authority supports
implexae, which he glosses as *involutae,
implicitae.* For snakes in the Furies'
hair, cf. Cat. 64. 193f.; *Aen.* 7.329;
12.847f.; Hor. *Odes* 2.13.35f.

483 tenuitque . . . ora: 'became silent';
cf. *Aen.* 2.1. Compare Hor. *Odes* 2.13.
33f., where he says that enchanted by the
songs of Sappho and Alcaeus in the underworld Cerberus lets his ears droop and
the snakes in the Furies' hair stop writhing;
cf. also *Odes* 3.11.15f. (Mercury's power
of song stills Cerberus and relieves Ixion
of his pain.)

484 'and the circle of Ixion's wheel was
halted by the wind', i.e. by the wind
stopping; cf. *Ecl.* 2.26. For Ixion, cf.
3.38; *Aen.* 6.601; Ov. *Met.* 10.42.
Pope imitates this passage in *Ode on St
Cecilia's Day* 63-70 'But hark! he strikes
the golden lyre: and see! the tortured
ghosts respire, see shady forms advance!
Thy stone, O Sisyphus, stands still, Ixion
rests upon his wheel, and the pale spectres
dance! The Furies sink upon their iron
beds, and snakes uncurl'd hang listening
round their heads'.

485-6 Otis draws attention to the
dactylic movement indicating the
'triumphal advance towards the world of
life'.

486 redditaque: Milton, *L'Allegro* 150
speaks of Orpheus' 'half regained Eurydice'.

487 namque . . . legem: 'for Proserpina
had imposed this condition'; Proserpina
as queen of the underworld (cf. 1.39)
had made the agreement with Orpheus
along with her husband Pluto (492).
Notice the elliptical way of alluding to
this part of the well-known story, i.e.
that Orpheus was not to look back. The
whole story is told by Ovid, *Met.* 10.1f.;
cf. especially 10.51.

488 The dramatic moment is reflected

by the diction and order of words, with inverted *cum,* one of the strongest ways of emphasising action, and *subita* and *incautum* preceding their nouns.

489   The line elaborates 470; notice how it is emphasised by the repetition and the alliteration of *-sc-.*

491   **victusque animi:** 'defeated in will', Greek genitive of respect, see note on 1.277, and cf. 3.289.

respexit: tremendous emphasis is put on the word which tells the whole story by the unusual very heavy pause after the fifth foot.

492   **effusus labor:** the conflict of accent and ictus helps to convey the sense of disaster. Compare 495 *quis tantus furor,* and 497 *iamque vale. feror* . . . .

493   **stagnis . . . Avernis:** *Avernus* is here an adjective (cf. 2.164; *Aen.* 6.118). Some MSS have *stagnis . . . Averni,* and one *stagni est . . . Averni.*

495   **furor:** a key-word in the *Aeneid* for wild and irrational behaviour.

496   The absence of strong caesura in the third and fourth feet gives a lilting soporific effect; cf. *Aen.* 2.9 *suadentque cadentia sidera somnos, Aen.* 5. 856.

498   Eurydice's last words are made memorable by the apposition of *heu non tua* (contrast 490) to the subject, and the very powerful alliteration of *t.*

500   **tenuis:** with *auras;* cf. *Aen.* 2.791, rather than with *fumus.*

diversa: 'away from him'; cf. *Aen.* 5.166.

501   **prensantem . . . volentem:** the assonance concentrates the attention on Orpheus' futile actions; cf. *Aen.* 2.790-91 (Aeneas and Creusa) and *Aen.* 4.390-91 (Aeneas and Dido).

502   **portitor Orci:** the ferryman Charon; cf. *Aen.* 6. 298. Orcus is the underworld; cf. 1.277.

505   **qua:** unlike most modern editors I have accepted the reading of some inferior MSS in preference to *quae* (MR), because the balance of the line requires it, and the theme and variation (*quo fletu, qua voce, manis, numina*) is very much in Virgil's manner. The awkward absence of balance in the generally accepted reading may be paralleled by Lucan 1.649-50, and Val. Fl. 1.848-9, but is not Virgilian.

506   **nabat:** 'was voyaging'; *nare* sometimes has a very general meaning (cf. 59; Cat. 66.46). It is strange that Heyne and Ribbeck regarded this line as unworthy of Virgil: as it suddenly shifts

our attention from Orpheus to Eurydice it has a sad finality about it.

508   **Strymonis:** Strymon was a river in Thrace; cf. 1.120.

509   **flesse sibi:** so R; M and others have *flevisse.* The more difficult reading is here preferable; *sibi* will mean 'to himself', with no other audience. Some MSS have *antris* for R's *astris,* but *astris* gives the more vivid picture.

509-10   **haec evolvisse . . . quercus:** 'sang of these events beneath the cold stars, charming tigers and moving oak-trees with his song'; Orpheus' ability to enchant animals and inanimate objects with his songs is frequently referred to; cf. Ov. *Met.* 10.143f.; Hor. *Odes* 1.12.6f. For *evolvere* cf. *Aen.* 9.528.

511   **philomela:** the nightingale', the Greek word means 'song-lover'; the story of the maiden Philomela who was changed into a nightingale is told in Ov. *Met.* 6.424f. Compare also *Ecl.* 6.79, and Thomson, *Seasons, Spring* 717f. '. . . she sings her sorrows through the night . . . till, wide around, the woods sigh to her song, and with her wail resound'. Virgil's simile is based on two Homeric passages (*Od.* 16.216f.; 19.518f.) and is characteristically given greater pathos especially by the reference to the suffering caused by man (*durus arator*).

513   **detraxit:** again the unusual pause after a trochee in the fifth foot (cf. 491) compels the attention.

514   **noctem:** *= per noctem.*

515   **integrat:** 'renews'; cf. Lucr. 2.1146. *Redintegrare* is commoner in this sense.

516   **nulla Venus:** 'no love', a very clear example of the use of the goddess for her attribute (cf. Ceres, Bacchus, Vulcanus, etc.).

517-18   Tanais was a major river (the Don) to the north of Greece with its source in the Riphaei mountains (cf. 1.240; 3.382).

519-20   **inrita . . . dona:** the concession made to him which had turned out fruitless.

520   **Ciconum:** a people of Thrace; cf. Hom. *Od.* 9.39.

quo munere: 'spurned because of this devotion', a curious use of *munus* which in this context means the devotion or tribute he paid to Eurydice by rejecting all other women.

522   **discerptum:** the story recalls the legend of Pentheus (told in Euripides'

Bacchae and Ov. *Met.* 3.511f.) who was torn to pieces by Bacchantes.

523-5 'Even then, when Oeagrian Hebrus carried away his head torn from his snow-white neck, and whirled it round in the midst of the eddies . . .' Hebrus was a river of Thrace; cf. 463. Oeagrus was a king of Thrace, father of Orpheus. Milton, *Lycidas* 61-2 has (of Orpheus) 'His gory visage down the stream was sent, down the swift Hebrus to the Lesbian shore'.

525   **vox ipsa:** 'his disembodied voice'.

525-7 **Eurydicen:** the emotional repetition is very much in the style beloved by the Alexandrians. It is imitated by Pope, *Ode on St Cecilia's Day*, 113-17 'Yet e'en in death Eurydice he sung, Eurydice still trembled on his tongue, Eurydice the woods, Eurydice the floods, Eurydice the rocks and hollow mountains rung'. In Ovid (*Met.* 11.61f.) the story has a happy ending as Orpheus is reunited with Eurydice in what Martyn calls 'the happy mansions of the other world' — *Eurydicenque suam iam tuto respicit Orpheus.*

529   **spumantem . . . torsit:** 'he made the foaming water whirl around beneath its surface'; i.e. his rapid disappearance causes an underwater eddy.

530   **at non Cyrene:** i.e. she did not disappear suddenly, but stayed to interpret the story to her son. Servius says *deest territa est quod ex sequentibus datur intellegi,* but this seems less likely.

532   **morbi:** the disease which carried off Aristaeus' bees.

533   The reference is to the nymphs (Dryads, 460) with whom Eurydice was dancing when she received the fatal snake-bite.

535   **facilis . . . Napaeas:** 'the wood-nymphs who can easily be appeased': *facilis (exorabiles,* Servius; cf. *Ecl.* 3.9) is explained in the next line; *Napaeae* is a Greek word meaning 'daughters of the grove'.

539   **Lycaei:** a mountain in Arcadia; cf. 1.16 and 4.283 where Aristaeus is called *Arcadius magister.*

540   **intacta:** i.e. by the yoke.

541   **dearum:** the Nymphs.

544   The reference may be to the sacrifice, performed nine days after a funeral, called *Novendiale;* cf. *Aen.* 5.64.

545   'You will send poppies of Lethe as funeral offerings to Orpheus'; poppies were always associated with sleep and forgetfulness (Lethe is the river of forget-

fulness in the underworld); cf. 1.78; *Aen.* 4.486. *Orphei* is Greek dative, scanning as two syllables; cf. *Pelei* (Cat. 64.382).

546-7 Some editors follow Bentley in reversing the order of these lines, but the point is that the sacrifice of a calf is to follow the revisiting of the grove as a thank-offering for success.

549   **excitat:** 'sets going', probably with the idea of lighting the sacrificial fires; cf. *Aen.* 8.543.

550-51 The Homeric type of repetition (from 538 and 540) — followed in the next two lines by the repetition of phrases from 544-6 — conveys a sense of speed and fulfilment appropriate for the ending of the story — 'and it was so . . .'.

555-8 'that in every part of the carcases throughout all the putrid flesh of the cattle bees were buzzing, swarming out of the decomposed sides — great clouds of them made a trail and met together on a treetop, hanging their clusters from the bent branches'. The final part of the story is highly pictorial (cf. *Aen.* 7.64f.), particularly the metaphor of the bees as a cluster of grapes (cf. Hom. *Il.* 2.89 and Juv. 13.68f.).

559-66 So ends the poem I have written, while Augustus was safeguarding the boundaries of the Roman Empire. I wrote my poem at Naples, I who in my earlier days was the author of the Eclogues.

559-66 An epilogue like this, of a biographical kind, is sometimes called a sphragis ('seal'), because the poet as it were sets his personal imprint on the poem. It was a technique used by the Greeks, particularly the Alexandrians (e.g. Theocr. *Epigr.* 27); cf. also Prop. 1.22; Hor. *Odes* 3.30; *Epist.* 1.20.20f.; Ov. *Met.* 15.871-9. The reference to Augustus rounds the poem off as it had begun (1.24f.) by paying tribute to the emperor: it also enables us to date this passage to 30 BC (cf. Dio 51.18).

559-60 In this biographical *envoi* to his work Virgil first summarises the subject-matter of Books 1, 3 and 2 of the *Georgics.*

560   The reference is to Augustus' Eastern campaigns; cf. 1.509; 2.171; and *Aen.* 8. 724f. where again the river Euphrates is mentioned in a list of conquests in the far east.

561-2   **victorque . . . iura:** this is the concept of the Roman mission which the *Aeneid* presents: after warfare the

conquered peoples are ready (*volentis*)
to accept Rome's government (*iura*). For
dare iura, cf. *Aen.* 1.293; Hor. *Odes* 3.
3.44.

   562 **viamque . . . Olympo:** for the future
deification of Augustus, cf. 1.24f.;
503; 3.12f.; *Aen.* 1.286f. *Olympo* is poetic
dative of place to which; cf. *Ecl.* 8.101.

   564 **Parthenope:** i.e. Naples, so called
after one of the Sirens who were located

near Capreae, just off Naples; cf. *Aen.*
5. 864-5.

   ignobilis oti: 'of ignoble ease', as
opposed to the glorious exploits of
Augustus. Cf. 2.486.

   565-6 The reference is to the *Eclogues;*
for *ludere* of pastoral poetry, cf. *Ecl.* 1.10.
Line 566 quotes the first line of the first
*Eclogue: Tityre, tu patulae recubans sub
tegmine fagi.*

INDEX TO THE NOTES

Reference is given to the main note or
notes on each subject, where further
references will often be found. There are
separate sub-headings under 'metre' and
'prosody'.

   A full index of proper names is to be
found in Mynors's Oxford Text, and
there is a complete word-index of Virgil's
works by M.N. Wetmore (New Haven, 1930).

diminutives, *Ecl.* 2.50, 4.18, 9.3.
Dodona, *Geo.* 1. 148-9, 2.15-16.

elegy, *Ecl.* 2. intro, 10. intro, 46f., 50-51, 69.
Elis, *Geo.* 3. 202-3.
enim (archaic), *Geo.* 2.104.
Eratosthenes, *Geo.* 1.233.
Eudoxus, *Ecl.* 3.40.
Euphorion, *Ecl.* 6. intro, 7.25, 10.50-51.
exempla, Ecl. 2.63-4, 3.80-83.

Fauni, *Geo.* 1.10.
felix, Geo. 2.81.
fovere, Geo. 4.43, 4.229-30.
frondator, Ecl. 1.56.

Galatea, *Ecl.* 1.30.
Gallus, *Ecl.* 6. intro, 10. intro, *Geo.* 4. 315-424.
genitive
  objective, *Ecl.* 1.65, *Geo.* 3.189.
  partitive, *Geo.* 4.81, 159.
  respect, *Geo.* 1.277, 2.191, 3.289, 4.310.
  (in *-um*), *Geo.* 3.27, 4.476.
  (form *dies*), *Geo.* 1.208.
  (form *Ulixi*), *Ecl.* 8.70.
glaucus, Geo. 3.81-3.
glomerare, Geo. 3.117.
Golden Age, *Ecl.* 4. intro, 4.6, *Geo.* 1.118-46.
gracilis, Ecl. 10.71.
gravis, Ecl. 1.49.

hendiadys, *Geo.* 2.192.
Hesiod, *Ecl.* 4. intro, 6.69-70, *Geo.* 1.259-310, 2.176 *et passim.*
hordea, Geo. 1.210.
horrere, Geo. 1.151, 3.161.
horridus, Geo. 3.366.
Hybla, *Ecl.* 1.53-5.
Hylas, *Ecl.* 6.43f.

Iacchus, *Geo.* 1.166.
ille, Geo. 3.217.
imperative, *Geo.* 1.187, 2.408-10.
impius, Geo. 1.468.
improbus, Ecl. 8.49, *Geo.* 1.119, 3.430-31.
incondita, Ecl. 2.4.
incrementum, Ecl. 4.49.
incumbere, Geo. 2.311.
indicative, *Ecl.* 5.6-7, *Geo.* 1.56-7.
Indigetes, Geo. 1.498.
indignus, Ecl. 8.18.
infelix, Geo. 1.154.
infinitive
  (epexegetic), *Ecl.* 5.1-2, 10.32, *Geo.* 1.284.
  (historic), *Geo.* 1.200.
  (after noun), *Geo.* 1.21, 2.73.

infinitive *(continued)*
  (after *admonere*), *Geo.* 4.186.
  (after *monere*), *Ecl.* 9.14.
  (after *nescius*), *Geo.* 2.467.
  (after *orare*), *Ecl.* 2.43.
  (after *permittere*), *Ecl.* 1.9.
  (after *suadere*), *Ecl.* 1.55.
  (archaic form in *-ier*), *Geo.* 1.454.
inserere, Geo. 2.49-51.
intonsus, Ecl. 5.63.
iam, Geo. 2.57.
iamdudum, Geo. 1.213.

Jupiter, *Ecl.* 7.60.

labor, Geo. 1.118-46, 145-6, 199f.
laetus, Geo. 1.1.
laevus, Geo. 4.7.
Laomedon, *Geo.* 1.502.
laurel, *Ecl.* 2.54, 7.62.
Lenaeus, *Geo.* 2.4.
Liber, *Geo.* 1.7.
Lucretius, *Ecl.* 6. 31-40, *Geo.* 2.490f., 3.502 *et passim.*
ludere, Ecl. 1.10, 6.1-8.
Lycoris, 10.2.

Maecenas, *Geo.* 1.2, 2.39f., 3.41, 4.2.
magic, *Ecl.* 8.69, 73-4, 97-9.
Mantua, *Ecl.* 1.20, 47-8, 9.28, *Geo.* 2.198-9.
meditari, Ecl. 1.2.
Meleager, *Ecl.* 2.1, 2.45f.
Meliboeus, *Ecl.* 1.1.
Menalcas, *Ecl.* 2.15, 9. intro.
metre *(see also prosody)*
  accent and ictus, *Geo.* 3.220, 4,174-5 *et passim.*
  caesura, *Ecl.* 1.70, *Geo.* 1.513-4, 4.336 *et passim.*
  diaeresis, *Ecl.* 1.7, 2.53, 6.55f., *Geo.* 2.61, 3.344.
  elision, *Ecl.* 3.37.
  elision, hypermetric, *Geo.* 1.295.
  golden line, *Ecl.* 1.2, *Geo.* 2.540 *et passim.*
  hiatus, *Ecl.* 2.24, 2.53, *Geo.* 1.4, 437 *et passim.*
  hiatus with shortening, *Ecl.* 2.65, *Geo.* 1.280-83.
  lengthening in arsis, *Ecl.* 1.38, *Geo.* 1.153 *et passim.*
  monosyllabic ending, *Geo.* 1.181.
  polysyllabic ending, *Ecl.* 2.24, *Geo.* 3.26.
  spondaic fifth foot, *Ecl.* 4.49.
Mincius, *Ecl.* 7.12.
myrtle, *Ecl.* 2.54, *Geo.* 1.28.

Naides, *Ecl.* 10.10.

CPSIA information can be obtained
at www.ICGtesting.com
Printed in the USA
LVHW011640070722
722963LV00009B/442

9 781853 995088